The
Honky
Tonk
on
the
Left

*Progressive Thought in Country Music*

# The Honky Tonk on the Left

Edited by
Mark
Allan
Jackson

UNIVERSITY OF MASSACHUSETTS PRESS
*Amherst and Boston*

ISBN 978-1-62534-338-3 (paper); 337-6 (hardcover)


Designed by Sally Nichols

Set in Arno Pro

Printed and bound by Maple Press, Inc.

Cover design by Tom Eykemans


Library of Congress Cataloging-in-Publication Data

Names: Jackson, Mark Allan.
Title: The honky tonk on the left : progressive thought in country music /
edited by Mark Allan Jackson.
Description: Amherst : University of Massachusetts Press, [2018] | Series:
American Popular Music. | Includes bibliographical references and index. |
Identifiers: LCCN 2017050250 (print) | LCCN 2017054484 (ebook) | ISBN
9781613765760 (e-book) | ISBN 9781613765777 (e-book) | ISBN 9781625343376 (hardcover) | ISBN
9781625343383 (pbk.)
Subjects: LCSH: Country music—Political aspects. | Progressivism (United
States politics) | Country music—History and criticism.
Classification: LCC ML3918.C68 (ebook) | LCC ML3918.C68 H66 2018 (print) | DDC
781.642/1599—dc23
LC record available at https://lccn.loc.gov/2017050250


British Library Cataloguing-in-Publication Data

A catalog record for this book is available from the British Library.

# Contents

The
Honky
Tonk
on
the
Left

# Richard Nixon, Johnny Cash, and the Political Soul of Country Music

MARK ALLAN JACKSON

ON THE evening of March 16, 1974, President Richard Nixon strolled onto the stage of the newly minted Grand Ole Opry, waving to the 5,000-strong audience as he hugged his wife, Pat, and smiled broadly. His appearance was part of the dedication ceremony for the new facility, as the venerable country music program moved from the confines of the old Ryman Auditorium in decaying downtown Nashville to its bright, new suburban home in Opryland USA, a music-themed amusement park.

During his time in the Opry's spotlight, Nixon joked with the crowd, had master of ceremonies Roy Acuff school him on the Yo-Yo, and even banged out a couple of tunes on an upright piano, most notably "God Bless America."

He also managed to fit in a brief speech wherein he extolled the values of country music as he saw it, lauding it "as native as anything American we could find" and adding that "it comes from the heart of America." Then Nixon hit the particulars of the music that made it so essential to him: "It talks about family, it talks about religion, the faith in God that is so important to our country and particularly to our family life. And as we know, country music radiates a love of this Nation, patriotism."

Once on these themes, the president shifted into a broader political point: "Country music, therefore, has those combinations which are so essential to America's character at a time that America needs character, because . . . the peace of the world for generations, maybe centuries to come, will depend not just on America's military might, which is the greatest in the world, or our wealth, which is the greatest in the world, but it is going to depend on our character, our belief in ourselves, our love of our country, our willingness to not only wear the flag but to stand up for the flag. And country music does that."[1] Here Nixon presented country music as having the exact values and attitudes that the president had been lauding throughout the 1960s and early 1970s, such as in his historic November 3, 1969, "Silent Majority" speech. For Nixon saw the country music audience as part of his core constituency: those who did not join in the mass demonstrations against the Vietnam War that made the nightly news, who did not stand as members of the counterculture protesting against racism and sexism. Instead, as he saw it, they adhered to the Bible and the flag—and kept their mouths shut, except to sing along with the latest country hit.

Nixon had been cultivating a political relationship with country music and its audience for many years prior to his appearance on the Opry stage. For example, bluegrass legends Lester Flatt and Earl Scruggs, in their last-ever joint public appearance, performed on the Tennessee float in the 1969 inaugural parade for Nixon. The president had also brought several country music stars to the White House, including such luminaries as Glen Campbell, Merle Haggard, and Johnny Cash. In an even more expansive move, Nixon had proclaimed October "Country Music Month." All these efforts were a part of a long-term plan to connect with certain voters rather than to express an actual love of the music itself. In a 1971 op-ed in the pages of the *Washington Post*, Kevin P. Phillips (the much touted architect of Nixon's Southern strategy of coded racism and white working-class pandering) had urged the president to use this music to connect with "forgotten whites" whose tastes were the antithesis of the counterculture: "More and more people are evidently finding the 'straight' songs and lyrics of country music preferable to the tribal war dances, adolescent grunts and marijuana hymns that have taken over so many pop stations."[2]

Here Phillips broadly references the growing renaissance of country music, for by the early 1970s, it again enjoyed the popularity it had once held from the late 1930s to the mid-1950s. By the time of Nixon's visit to the Opry, this music again stood as a major force in popular culture on a nationwide scale through radio play but also other media, such as television, movies, and records. But the rewards of mainstream fame still did not remove the perceived conservative taint from country music, leaving it mired in the stereotypes that Nixon referenced in his comments from the Opry stage. For if the Civil Rights Movement and counterculture as a whole had a soundtrack, one filled with gospel staples like "We Shall Overcome," folk-styled tunes such as "Blowin' in the Wind," or rock anthems on the order of "Eve of Destruction," then the forces that resisted this push for change in racial restrictions, economic inequality, foreign entanglements, or gender norms listened to country music—at least in Nixon's view.

Others during this same time period also shared the president's perspective—although they were often more fearful than accepting of country music, and their comments still gave credence to the argument that country music was fundamentally conservative. In the late 1960s and early 1970s, a number of liberal commentators, voicing their views in a range of periodicals, attacked this music as purely restrictive and destructive.[3] None was so damning as Florence King in her essay "Red Necks, White Socks, and Blue Ribbon Fear," which appeared in *Harper's*. There, King claimed, "Many of today's country music songs are hymns to the fear of change that is dividing America along strict political, social, and sexual lines, and encouraging all working people to emulate and identify with the very worst sort of Southern reactionaries," then added, "There is now a calculated psychology to country music, a 'message' that promotes alienation and a spirit of testy readiness that is disturbing to hear." Just for good measure, the author also made connections between some members of the country music audience and mass murderer Richard Speck and between the country hit "Red Necks, White Socks, and Blue Ribbon Beer" and the Nazi Party anthem "Horst Wessel."[4]

We can see that many public persons in this time period made the argument that country music only voiced an essentially conservative perspective on family, faith, patriotism, and many other issues. But although this position broadly manifested itself during the late 1960s, it had been a part of the public discourse on country music from its beginnings, and it has now continued even into the present. For the political Right, the mass media Left, and some knowledgeable music critics have focused heavily on this conservative image. Politicians from various parties have often done so in an attempt to co-opt white, working-class voters for their own electoral gains. Yet media critics have frequently posited those same citizens, especially in the South, as extremists. Too often, commentators on both the right and the left have not accurately represented the entirety of political/social attitudes found in this music culture and expressed in the songs that fall into the broad canon of country. For throughout its existence, country music has expressed a pronounced progressive view-point, one that counters (at least in part) the conservative stereotype of this quintessential American musical genre.

Even in some of the earlier mentioned examples of country performers associated with the Nixon presidency, we can find progressive standouts in terms of their actions, attitudes, or songs. Earl Scruggs—near the end of the same year that he attended Nixon's inauguration and in the very same city—appeared at the Moratorium to End the War in Vietnam, where he performed his hit "Foggy Mountain Breakdown." Of the conflict, the South's reaction to it, and the protest itself, he said, "I think the people in the South is just as concerned as the people that's walking the streets here today," and added, "I'm sincere with bringing our boys back home. I'm disgusted and in sorrow about the boys we've lost over there. And if I could see a good reason to continue, I wouldn't be here."[5] Certainly, this appearance at a massive leftist protest and his comments set Scruggs in opposition to both Nixon's Vietnam strategy and the popular image of the country star as flag-waving jingoist.

Even those specifically invited to the White House could and did present progressive credentials at times. Glen Campbell, not particularly known as a politically charged artist at the time, recorded "Universal Soldier," penned by Native-American activist and folksinger Buffy Sainte-Marie. The lyrics lay out the exploits of all soldiers, past and present, as they kill for God and country. But in the last verse, the collective guilt for these bloody actions does not remain theirs alone, for the song also turns to the listener and the singer, suggesting that everyone has a hand in the creation of war:

> They come from . . . you and me
> And brother, can't you see?
> This is not the way to put an end to war.[6]

This song, protesting against all wars, helped set Campbell on his extensive solo career when it went to number 45 on the U.S. charts in 1965. Occurring at the beginning of an era of protest against the growing conflict in Vietnam, Campbell's decision to record the song and its popularity set the performer and some of his fans as questioning not just the morality of all wars but also the one in which America was currently engaged.

Another White House visitor, Merle Haggard, also commented on the Vietnam War, but his "Fighting Side of Me" and "Okie from Muskogee" did not contain the questioning element of Campbell's selection. Instead, Haggard firmly denounced those who criticized America's involvement in Vietnam, although decades later he called the latter song "a really good snapshot of how dumb we were in the past."[7] However, even if Haggard can be seen as a supporter of the war then, he can be considered a progressive voice when it comes to race relations. On the 1967 album *Branded Man,* he included "Go Home," which was written by his mentor Tommy Collins. The song tells of an interracial love affair between a dark-skinned Mexican woman and a white American man, although his friends do not approve and break up the relationship. Certainly, the lyrics side with the couple, not the prejudice. Even more striking, in 1969, Haggard himself wrote and then later recorded "Irma Jackson," which again offers a tale of interracial romance (this time between white and black lovers) broken by racial animus. Here, the narrator denounces "a world that draws a line" between people based solely on color.[8] Both of these songs appeared in the era of *Loving v. Virginia* (1967), the Supreme Court decision that overturned several states' laws against miscegenation. Thus, Haggard repeatedly took an explicit progressive stand at a time when the issue of interracial relationships remained contentious, especially in the South.[9]

But of all the country music performers whom Nixon picked for a White House visit, none had more experience taking on controversial subjects than Johnny Cash. Well before he ever met the president, Cash had championed Native-American rights and prison reform, issues on which he commented both in song and through his own political activism. Thus, Cash had quite visibly been against law-and-order policies and racialized restrictions, setting him in opposition to some of Nixon's key positions well before his visit, although he did offer some support for Nixon's Vietnam policies for a time. But when Cash performed for the president on April 17, 1970, it came with a bit of a dustup. Nixon's staff had earlier contacted the country star, requesting that he perform Merle Haggard's "Okie from Muskogee," Guy Drake's "Welfare Cadilac" (*sic*), and Cash's own "A Boy Named Sue." However, Cash refused to perform either of the first two, offering various excuses over time but suggesting that he did not agree with their conservative point of view.[10] Instead, he chose to offer Nixon "What Is Truth?" This song runs through several examples of young people being dismissed, always by an older generation that seems uninterested in their music, their uncertainty about the war, or their views in general. Music critic Ralph Gleason, writing in *Rolling Stone,* called the song "a Country & Western 'Times They Are a-Changin.'"[11] Certainly, Cash was not alone in having the attitude expressed in the song, for it hit number three on the country charts.

Yet even with these countering examples firmly established in the public sphere, as scholar Bill Malone has stressed, in the public mind, "in the late sixties and early seventies, for the first time in its history, country music began to be identified with a specific political position, gaining a reputation for being a jingoistic and nativistic music."[12] Yet it would be more accurate to state that country had never been identified before this time as a conservative Republican expression. For early on in its life, country music became part of America's political backdrop. It lent its earthy authenticity to a number of operatives who ran for office pre-1970, men such as Tom Watson, Bob and Alf Taylor, W. Lee "Pappy" O'Daniel, Jimmie Davis, Eugene Talmadge, Glen Taylor, Roy Acuff, Orville Faubus, and George Wallace, just to name a few examples. In fact, many of the politicians who had drawn on country music before the beginning of the 1970s were conservative Democrats, although there are a few populists, progressives, and even Republicans among them. Thus, country music could long be seen as often having a particular political voice, if only through association, and its supposedly conservative stance has always been a part of the public narrative about it.

During the early years of country music, media commentators often debased the music, its performers, and its fans. Most of this criticism manifested itself in a condescending attitude, often based on stereotypes of "hillbillies," that at times suggested rather than outright denounced the music as being conservative.[13] Part of such negativity stems from the connection between country music and Southern culture as a whole, especially its working-class elements. As Malone has noted, "To many people hillbilly music was just one more example, along with Ku Kluxism, Prohibition, sharecropping, racial violence, and religious bigotry, of the South's retarded and degenerate culture."[14] Thus the prejudices and assumptions about the South—rural, ignorant, unsophisticated, religious, patriarchal, racist, patriotic, homophobic—drifted onto the public image of this artistic expression early in its life. A prime example of these kinds of views found its way onto on the front page of *Variety* in 1926. Critic Abel Green first focused more on the fans than the performers by defining the group: "The 'hill-billy' is a North Carolina or Tennessee and adjacent mountaineer type of illiterate white whose creed and allegiance are to the Bible . . . and the phonograph." He went on to add, "The mountaineer is of 'poor white trash' genera. The great majority, probably 95 per cent, can neither read nor write English. Theirs is a community all unto themselves. Illiterate and ignorant, with the intelligence of morons." Then the music itself got its lashing as he described it as "the singing, nasal-twanging vocalizing of a Vernon Dalhart or a Carson Robinson . . . reciting the banal lyrics of a 'Prisoners Song' or 'The Death of Floyd Collins.'"[15] These kinds of demeaning comments and negative projections of poor Southern whites lingered throughout the early decades of commercial country music, along with a broader but still negative presentation of the people who made it and listened to it, often with rather conservative overtones concerning their political and social beliefs.[16] Thus, the supposedly white, homogeneous, right-wing nature of country music has long dominated the public discussion of it, excluding most of the performers, songs, and actions that do not fit this simplistic dynamic.

But during this same time period, country music offered up numerous progressive comments, often tied directly with social and economic issues of the day. For example, early country star Fiddlin' John Carson recorded a number of songs commenting on the plight of the farmer, such as the populist tune "The Farmer Is the Man Who Feeds Them All," which places the blame for economic hardships on merchants, lawyers, judges, and even preachers. In 1929, Blind Alfred Reed created a song in a similar vein, "How Can a Poor Man Stand Such Times and Live." But although the lyrics also denounced merchants and preachers, along with the police and doctors, this song moved beyond farmers and embraced the entirety of the working class as unjustly abused victims in the beginning year of the Great Depression. Reed also penned the religious song "There'll Be No Distinction," which illustrated an egalitarian afterlife and included the lines, "We will all sit together in the same kind of shoes, / The white folks and the colored and the gentile and Jew."[17] Even country legends recorded progressive comments in this era. Gene Autry celebrated the actions and lamented the passing of an iconic labor radical in "The Death of Mother Jones," while the Carter Family decried the domestic restriction of women in "Single Girl, Married Girl." Thus, we find numerous instances where country performers took bold stands on labor injustice, religious tolerance, and other issues. Many more examples from the early decades of commercial country music could be offered up as evidence of a progressive vein in country music, even as this reality was not reflected in public commentary about this music in these decades. However, the majority of any media coverage of country music, from the 1920s to the 1950s, focused much more on this genre as an entertainment, not as a vehicle for political expression of any stripe.

Yet in the late 1960s and early 1970s, a particular shaping of the public perception of country music took place. But what factors came together to create this shift? There can be no doubt that the music, whether in its early years or later during the Nixon era, contained some conservative political and social expression. But this kind of commentary that some country songs or performers espoused in the past had often jibed with the majority position of the nation, state, or region in the moment when it appeared. For example, when Carson Robinson sang "We're Gonna Have to Slap the Dirty Little Jap" in 1941, it echoed the sentiments of a country reeling from the attack on Pearl Harbor. As country music scholar Jeffrey J. Lange argues about this time period, as "jukeboxes across the nation reverberated with the sounds of country music, thousands upon thousands of Americans grew increasingly attracted to the genre's earthy and patriotic lyricism."[18] But when many Americans encountered Haggard's "The Fightin' Side of Me" in 1969, the response to this pro-Vietnam song was different because this war was growing increasingly unpopular, especially with left-leaning and even many mainstream Democratic voters, along with some members of the party's leadership.[19] However, many Republican voters—along with some of their white, working-class, Southern Democrat counterparts—were more likely to be pro-Vietnam in the early years of the war, thus setting up an opportunity for Nixon to pick up the mantle of patriotic country music fan and wear it as a visible sign of his down-to-earth, conservative persona.

Several country performers did offer up explicit and even dynamic songs expressing support for the war. Thus, the linkage between the Vietnam War, some of country music's response to it, and Nixon's embrace of both might be considered one of the primary reasons that this genre was first unfairly set as exclusively and explicitly representing a conservative viewpoint. We can see how this kind of narrative played out in the media of the era by the way a writer in the *Nation* bluntly stated, "The ideology for [country] war songs seems to be keep silent and see what ... President [Nixon] will do."[20] But this kind of thinking was also shared, in part, by scholars, as one argued, "No country songs about the war in Vietnam ... failed to support unquestioningly the policies of our government there. The men who died were heroes and their cause is never disputed."[21] But these comments and others like them ignore the fact that country music also expressed ambivalence or outright resistance to the war, such as in Loretta Lynn's "Dear Uncle Sam," Johnny Cash's "Singin' in Vietnam Talkin' Blues," or Arlene Harden's "Congratulations, You Sure Made a Man Out of Him."[22] Still, the patriotic songs of the 1960s and early 1970s, along with other anti-counterculture commentary and the genre's working-class image, certainly contributed to cementing the idea in the public mind that country music was mainly a vehicle for conservative expression.

Since that time period, the political Right has often gathered country music to its bosom, trying to draw on its working-class energy for cultural marketing purposes, and many candidates have endeavored to use this music to help them play the role of the patriotic common man struggling against the elites. In particular, it has become the norm for Republicans seeking the presidency to put on this guise, for Ronald Reagan, George H. W. Bush, George W. Bush, and even Donald Trump have all used country music as an essential part of some of their public programs, either before, during, or after their elections. But during this same period, many Democratic politicians have moved further and further away from country music, perhaps suggesting that it no longer expresses their values or fits with their tastes. For example, in releasing his listening choices, either on his iPod or on Spotify, President Obama has revealed a rather eclectic range of musical tastes—but not even one country song.[23] This individual reality may well reflect an ideological split in how this genre is perceived politically, no matter its more complex truth. As music critic Chris Willman argues, "Certainly there are a good chunk of Democrats, even self-professed liberal/progressive wing nuts, in the industry and the audience. But the stereotype that country music has become the house genre of the GOP isn't easily or persuasively disproven."[24] In fact, some liberal media commentators have continued only to project the conservative stereotype onto this music, perhaps due to their own prejudices based on how particular politicians have embraced it or their limited knowledge of what many country music performers have recorded or have publically stated.

One recent episode well sets how this configuration manifests itself. As part of his campaign for president, conservative Republican senator Ted Cruz announced his allegiance to country music on CBS *This Morning*, "My music tastes changed on 9–11 . . . I didn't like how rock music responded. And country music collectively, the way they responded, it resonated with me . . . I had an emotional reaction that says, 'These are my people.'"[25] A day later, on MSNBC's *Now with Alex Wagner*, liberal African-American commentator Jamilah Lemieux quipped in response to Cruz's admission, "Nothing says, 'let's go kill some Muslims,' like country music."[26] Both Cruz and Lemieux came to a rather similar conclusion about country music but from very different positions; they believe that the music and its listeners are ultimately conservative: one with the hope of luring this group to his voter base and the other with the belief that this group is basically jingoist and racist. But both casually ignore the reality that many country performers—Merle Haggard, Rosanne Cash, Kris Kristofferson, the Dixie Chicks, Rodney Crowell, and Steve Earle just to name a few—in the aftermath of 9/11 either rejected Bush, his wars, or religious and racial prejudice.

However, not only politicians and media pundits have been presenting country music as being primarily conservative in the post-9/11 era but also knowledgeable music commentators have played a part in reinforcing this perception. For example, in 2003, during the brouhaha over Dixie Chicks lead singer Natalie Maines's comment that the group was ashamed that President Bush was from their home state of Texas, legendary music critic Chet Flippo argued, "Country fans are largely conservative and patriotic—as is well-known." He went on to note, "What do you expect country fans to say when a country star dumps on the president? That tells me that none of them—Chicks, PR, label, management—knows anything about the country music audience." Finally, Flippo surmised, "What the audience will not tolerate is an artist turning on that audience. And Maines' attack on Bush was in effect a direct attack on the country music audience. And its values. And its patriotism."[27] Once again, the claim that the entirety of the country music audience, and hence the music itself, was essentially conservative and restrictive floated out from one of the people who spoke from supposed knowledge of the form. Certainly, some radio stations and even a contingency of the Dixie Chicks' fans rejected Maines's comment, her politics, and her subsequent progressive activism; but that same year the band managed to book a mostly sold-out, record-breaking tour and afterward crafted a Grammy-winning, double-platinum album, strongly suggesting that many in the country music community remained committed to the group.

Despite the potential backlash, country music has continued to contain provocative comments on a variety of public issues in the contemporary era, and these kinds of left-leaning views proclaimed by country performers and supported by some of their fans are not isolated examples, for this music has always contained a progressive element and not just at the margins—from its first commercial moments up to the most current releases. However, very few country performers—of the past or present—can be seen as formulating a unified political philosophy through their music. As a result, they and their genre can contain a wide spectrum of reactions to or comments on political or social issues. Sociologist George H. Lewis noted this range when he states that in country music, "there are expressions of social conservatism, yet also an economic position that can be, in many ways, interpreted as liberal. There are strong expressions of patriotism as an unquestioning acceptance of the political order and, at the same time, a respect for personal autonomy and freedom. There is the importance of work and the rejection of it as alienating, dull and demeaning.

And there is the glorification of illicit sex, yet the yearning for a stable, loving marriage."[28] But despite this reality, as a whole, country music does not stand primarily as political music, coming from the right or the left.

Instead, country music, like many pop culture forms, primarily focuses on romantic relationships. In fact, most scholars who have looked at the form in longitudinal studies have found that the vast majority of songs discuss love, not politics, although country music historian Robert Cornfield suggests that economic and social discontent may be metaphorically sublimated in these works.[29] But undeniably, only a small percentage of country songs are explicitly political.[30] In fact, Robert W. Van Sickel, after completing a statistical study of country music lyrics from 1960 to 2000, concluded, "Commercial country music is perhaps best seen as antipolitical, rather than reliably populist or conservative."[31] Certainly, some portion of country songs have been subtly or expressly political, crafted to appeal either to the Left or the Right. However, the majority of country music more accurately reflects the varied attitudes of the songwriter/performer in response to a particular moment, an idea, or an emotion—and driven by the need to make sense of a complex world, whether it involves romance or politics.

As a result, it does not surprise when we consider the whole of the genre that many voices across the political spectrum can be heard commenting on a variety of public issues. Even individual performers can express conservative and progressive stances on different issues in the same moment in time or even on the same issue at different points in their careers. These varied political positions suggest that country performers are just ordinary people, not slavering political zealots. As historian Robert McElvaine notes, "Most 'ordinary' people are never ideological in a way that would suit an ideologue. This does not mean, of course, that their thoughts and actions are not based upon a set of underlying assumptions and values but only that they are not conscious adherents of a systematic approach to the world."[32] Country performers express themselves as we all do from time to time, offering their reaction to important economic and social events. They do not work out of a desire to set public policy. Instead, they sometimes craft politically varied artistic responses to the issues important to our nation. Their assumptions and values fall along a range of possibilities, from the extreme right to the extreme left and all points in between. Thus, it is a great injustice that their work often has been unfairly tainted as only or as primarily expressing right-wing positions. For country music has never been a conservative monolith, although some public figures have posited it as such for their own use and abuse—and often out of their own ignorance of or prejudice against the music, its performers, and its fans.

Over the years, some media critics and academics have taken up the issue of country music's political soul, and a number of them have even focused on the progressive side of the spectrum. One of first people who took on these issues directly was *Rolling Stone* writer John Grissim in his book *Country Music: White Man's Blues*, which appeared in 1970. In it, he explored a number of trends in country, including both the conservative elements in the music along with its progressive tendencies (although he argued that the former typically won out). At one point, he notes, "Country music has been hailed as America's great gift to people the world over. It has also been called shit-kicker music and variously described as simplistic, unsophisticated, right wing, boring, bedrock Baptist, redneck, ignorant and underneath it all probably racist. It is the only native American music that has been simultaneously damned as a fossilized art form and praised as the wellspring of modern folk music and rock."[33] In a similar vein, *Entertainment Weekly* writer Chris Willman argued this yin-yang view of country music in *Rednecks & Bluenecks: The Politics of Country Music*, which was published in 2005. But he, too, concluded that country music, "though hardly unilateral as a genre, typically gravitates more toward expressing the fears, beliefs, and hopes of conservatives, who occupy a majority of the artist roster as well as the fan base at this point in the music's evolution."[34] Thus, even in some important popular-press releases, the scale has dipped toward the conservative side in terms of weighing the music politically.

Scholarly explorations of country music have sometimes had more success in emphasizing the more liberal side of the music, such as in Pamela Fox and Barbara Ching's *Old Roots, New Routes: The Cultural Politics of Alt. Country Music* and Travis P. Stimeling's *Cosmic Cowboys and New Hicks: The Countercultural Sounds of Austin's Progressive Country Music Scene.* However, both these studies focus on specific subtypes rather than a broad review of the genre of country across several historical periods. Those that do offer a wider range of the music often include the argument that both conservative and liberal comments can be found, such as in Diane Pecknold's edited collection *Hidden in the Mix: The African American Presence in Country Music* or Mary Bufwack and Robert Oermann's *Finding Her Voice: Women in Country Music, 1800–2000*. Sometimes this split has been presented as expressing a populist tendency in country music, which involves both progressive responses to some social and economic realities and right-wing extremism concerning patriotism, religion, or other issues.[35] These comments do not mean to suggest any flaws in these previous offerings, for they have laid the groundwork for this collection, which wishes to engage in a long-standing discussion of the political soul of country music. But even some of the best of these efforts that discuss both right and left presences in country music create a limited counterweight to the conservative narrative that has been pushed for decades by some politicians and media voices.

With this collection, the emphasis is to firmly focus solely on the more liberal side of the commentary found in country music. These positions might be variously embraced by terming them "tolerant" or "broad minded" or dismissed as "bleeding heart" or even "radical." However, the views discussed here will be broadly grouped under the designation "progressive." In general, progressives believe in the politics of remedy; they advocate for correction of social injustice, push for fair change. They demand, explicitly or implicitly, a progression from present wrong to future equality. In part, country music has always had a progressive vein due to its realist foundations. No less an authority than legendary A&R man Art Satherley noted this tendency: "Whereas the sophisticated city person likes these humbug, boy-girl love songs, with everything pretty-pretty, the mountaineer is a realist. His songs deal with loneliness, misery, death, murder."[36] Before you can wish to change the world for the better, you have to recognize the reality of its problems, and country music—right from its folk roots—has always taken notice of gritty realities involving economic or social wrongs. As a result, the writers in this book discuss how the performers who expressed these varied progressive positions were and are a product of their time and place, which is reflected in both their work and the analysis of it found in this collection. Some of the performers discussed here have also expressed opinions that could easily be seen as conservative. Still, this reality does not in any way diminish their progressive stances. Instead, as already noted, it should suggest that these artists are not sectarians. Like many Americans, they can hold simultaneous views that run the gamut of political thought. So rather than offer one particular or restrictive meaning for the term "progressive" as it is used throughout this collection, each essay will set its own definition, explicitly or implicitly.

This collection makes other arguments through the communal efforts of the contributors. First, country music's progressive stance has occurred across historical periods, not just during specific eras. Thus, the chapters are presented chronologically, which will show how progressive thought has informed the genre from its commercial beginnings to its latest incarnations. Second, these left-leaning positions have also been expressed in a variety of forms of country music. So many types are considered here (either briefly or in depth), including pop country, outlaw, old time, alt-county, hick-hop, and country soul. Third, country music offers progressive comments on a variety of issues, concerning not only class but also gender, sexuality, religion, and race—a range well represented in this collection. Fourth, country music presents its leftist stance through song lyrics but also through other means, so some contributors discuss performance styles, costuming, and political activism. Fifth, both country music stars and little-known performers and have expressed progressive positions. Thus, figures such as Loretta Lynn and Garth Brooks are discussed alongside Glen Taylor and Steve Young. Sixth, these leftist expressions and attitudes expressed by performers have been welcomed by the country music audience as is strongly suggested by chart success, album sales, and their general popularity—a point noted in many of the essays. Finally, the mainstream country music industry, especially that represented by the Nashville establishment, does not always accept, accommodate, or promote these progressive efforts. But country music is not located in or controlled by any one place, for it has found a home in Chicago and Memphis, New York and Bakersfield, Atlanta and Austin, and a wide range of other locales throughout the nation during various eras. Many of the contributors both note and comment on these realities. In achieving all these goals, the contributors draw on a variety of analytical approaches taken from the fields of history, communication studies, musicology, folklore, sociology, cultural studies, music history, and gender studies—thus providing a rather broad-reaching view of how country music has presented progressive thought through lyrical content and the actions, attitudes, and images generated by performers and the industry itself.

The early period of country music, roughly from the early 1920s to the mid-1950s, contains many examples of progressive commentary and action from a variety of performers, especially that centered on economic issues and government policies. Musicologist Gregory Reish discusses how several musicians, such as Fiddlin' John Carson and the bluesy Allen Brothers, authored paeans to President Franklin Roosevelt and his populist economic policies during the 1930s. In his analysis, Reish argues that these performers chose to do so for a variety of reasons. Some took up these subjects due to their desire to gain audience approval by tying themselves to a popular president, and others did so out of a shared belief in the necessity of public programs meant to help America's underclass. This insightful discussion reveals a multiplicity of motivations for taking on these topical subjects in the 1930s but also contends that the music is more reflective of Americans' reactions to Roosevelt's public policies rather than a call for direct political action.

In looking at the career of Senator Glen H. Taylor, historian Peter La Chapelle argues that the politician drew upon his folksy demeanor and singing cowboy persona to gain political office. But his motives for doing so stemmed from a progressive drive fashioned in part due to the hardscrabble life of his youth and the influence of industrialist King Camp Gillette's utopian philosophy. As La Chapelle notes, Taylor eventually came to office as a liberal Democrat, one who was often at odds with his own party over its explicit support for conflict abroad and implicit support of racism at home, a reality that pushed him to be on the ticket of the Progressive Party's ill-fated presidential campaign in 1948. As a whole, La Chapelle offers a fascinating political biography of this under-discussed country musician and public figure.

In the final analysis centered on this early period, Stephanie Vander Wel explores how Webb Pierce played against the typical masculine notions of the cowboy through his elaborate costumes, emotional stage presence, and feminized vocal style. Although not always noted as the honky-tonk star that he was, Pierce dominated the charts in the 1950s, even as his public persona and his performances clashed with traditional projections of postwar masculinity in America. As Vander Wel argues, these manifestations may well be the reason that Pierce has not been the focus of much critical discussion of the honky-tonk era.

As discussed earlier, perhaps the most politicized era in country music was the middle period, ranging mainly from the 1960s to the early 1980s, when performers were often faced with the social upheavals brought about by such realities as the Civil Rights Movement, the Vietnam War, and Second-Wave Feminism. During this period, as I argue in my essay, Loretta Lynn was one such artist who did present a number of progressive stances in her songs and public comments, although her most lasting action in this arena concerns her work that argues for gender equality. Although her songs are largely set within the domestic sphere, this move personalizes the issues raised while also setting each narrative as an example for the situations faced by many working-class women. For Lynn herself experienced some of the gender and class restrictions of the era, even as she gained superstar status in country music. But her knowledge of the difficulties within marriage, with reproductive decisions, and with other women's issues allowed her to tap into the real-life problems that drove the women's rights movement of the 1960s and 1970s.

Some African-American performers took up the issue of race within country music in the 1970s and beyond, either directly through their lyrics or by their appropriation of what is often seen as a white music culture. In particular, historian Charles Hughes traces how O. B. McClinton, the self-described "Chocolate Cowboy," worked to establish himself as an authentic, traditional country musician. But at the same time, he challenged the genre by explicitly discussing the color line in such songs as "Black Speck" while also drawing on diverse musical influences, including soul and R&B, thus expanding the realm of country music. But even with a number of chart successes as a result of these strategies, as Hughes explores in depth, McClinton sometimes found himself alienated and racially coded by those individuals who helped him produce this work and even by the country music industry itself.

During this same era, the subgenre "outlaw country" came into vogue. Steve Young was at the vanguard of this anti–Nashville Sound movement. Folklorist Ted Olson interviewed this artist at length, and this conversation revealed how Young saw himself as a radical in terms of his approach to country music aesthetics and his sympathy for under-represented groups. These political positions, at least in part, stemmed from his sometimes difficult upbringing in rural Georgia and his family's own recognition of the economic and racial injustices around them. In adulthood, Young began incorporating these strongly held beliefs into his lyrics, whose honesty helped cement his reputation as a great songwriter. However, his unconventional and uncompromising approach to country music did not find ready acceptance by the Nashville establishment.

In looking at David Allan Coe and a number of other performers who are often linked to the outlaw country genre, Nadine Hubbs also finds a number of progressive positons taken up in the 1970s. In particular, she explores Coe's "Fuck Aneta Bryant," which exhibits a progressive attitude built around the hillbilly humanist ethos that allows listeners to implicitly hear an anti-discriminatory message on homosexuality. But Hubbs also discusses work by Merle Haggard, Johnny Cash, and others—setting them as a kind of working-class agents of protest, an argument that disrupts the all-too-common, middle-class-inspired, and dismissive stereotype of country music as the vehicle for conservative commentary.

The later stage of country, basically running from the middle 1980s to the present, also contains numerous examples of progressive commentary on such issues as the economic consequences of increasing white poverty and the creation of changing racial identity within what is still often considered a whites-only cultural expression.

Commenting on one of the biggest stars of this period, Stephanie Shonekan explores how Garth Brooks has navigated between a traditional country audience and a broader listenership by taking on controversial issues, such as when he condemns racism and homophobia in "We Shall Be Free," thus setting him as an artist willing to upset the assumed status quo of country. Shonekan argues that Brooks was able to navigate these different fan bases and these topics by judicially shifting between conservative themes and more progressive representations in both his lyrics and his public persona, making for a rather nuanced reading of this country music star, his songs, and even his motives behind these kinds of positionings.

During this period, other country performers also worked to address the contentious issue of race through a variety of means. Stephen A. King and P. Renee Foster discuss how various African-American musicians in the contemporary era who have taken up the country mantel, such as Darius Rucker and Rissi Palmer, have responded to racist reactions to their foray into this supposedly whites-only genre. Many of these performers have had to establish themselves as being legitimate or authentic within country music, just as Charley Pride did before them. But even as white fans have often accepted such performers due to their obvious talents, the industry itself has been rather resistant to these musicians having a starring role in country. Yet King and Foster also contend that some hopeful signs concerning African-American participation have and continue to exist in country music culture as a whole in the modern era.

Tressie McMillan Cottom also explores race in country music, but she focuses on how the genre has been collaborating with hip-hop to make a hybrid style, often termed "hick-hop," one that when studied reveals the successes and failures of country's new racial politics. For she argues that the declining economic fortunes of the white working class in rural and suburban environments have pushed this group into a status somewhat analogous to the situation faced by many African Americans, thus setting up a dynamic for cultural crossover and acceptance unlike country music has experienced before. For some of the past resentments and prejudices against African Americans and their culture have been overcome in the contemporary era, allowing for explicit crossover between genres. However, this dualistic creation, when examined by Cottom, also exposes some rifts between these groups, suggesting a sometimes precarious melding of two often racialized forms of popular music, one black and urban, the other white and rural.

Coming out of the alt-country or Americana camp of country music, Uncle Tupelo (and the bands that emerged out of this group), according to musicologist Travis Stimeling, comment through their lyrics on the changing American industrial landscape and white working-class attitudes toward labor, management, and working conditions, resulting in a progressive political stance on these issues. For the founders of this band, Jeff Tweedy and Jay Farrar, witnessed firsthand the decimation brought on by the deindustrialization of the Midwest, presenting them much fodder for rather explicit political commentary that Stimeling argues mainstream country music was rather loath to engage in during the 1990s but that these alt-country stars fully embraced.

A surprising performer to also be considered alt-country is Johnny Cash in his later years, for the country music establishment did not embrace him or his work in this era. Perhaps this slight resulted from the songs themselves, for many from the *American Recordings* series were covers from other genres such as punk or metal. Yet Cash's performance of this material draws on classic country tropes, many of the same ones that brought the star to fame in the 1950s and 1960s. Jonathan Silverman argues that a close look at the songs on these albums reveals a type of political viewpoint if not a specific ideology, whether explicitly through the content of the lyrics themselves or implicitly through a process that involves a rejection of established standards within country music. In his essay, Silverman skillfully leads readers through a history of Cash's past political engagement, both its successes and failures, and then presents these final recordings as having just as much social and economic commentary as ever was expressed by this country music legend.

For too long, the conservative end of country music's political spectrum has gotten the lion's share of the ink, leaving the progressive spirit in country underrepresented in general or ignored completely in some cases. But past emphasis on only certain songs, their performers, or their politics has spotlighted the reactionary image of this music, a focus generated by those who often had a knee-jerk, uninformed response to this genre, one that prefit their ideological agendas, whether they positively embraced it as a right-wing political tool or rejected it as a cultural throwback. As a result of these kinds of representations, country too often appears in broad public discussion as a simple, conservative idea of what it is politically and socially rather than the much more complex, nuanced truth of this music. This collection as a whole works to show that the people who perform and listen to country music do not fit easy stereotypes concerning any cultural/political issues. As a whole, the essays collected here present a broad range of the kinds of progressive thought that has been encoded in country music throughout its complex history in the lyrics, musical influences, costumes, attitudes, and marketing from and of a variety of performers. We hope that these explorations will challenge the traditional narrative of this music as a primarily conservative form and that the volume coming from the progressive end is turned up a bit, resulting in a more complete and more accurate understanding of one of America's most prized musical expressions.

## NOTES

1. Richard Nixon, "Remarks at the Grand Ole Opry House, Nashville, Tennessee," March 16, 1974, *American Presidency Project,* www.presidency.ucsb.edu/ws/?pid=4389.

2. Kevin P. Phillips, "Revolutionary Music," *Washington Post,* May 6, 1971, A19.

3. For example, see the following: Mike Reagen, "The Pious Rhetoric of Country Music," *Music Journal* 27, no. 1 (January 1969): 50, 67–70; Paul Dickson, "Singing to Silent America," *Nation,* February 23, 1970, 211–13; and Richard Goldstein, "My Country Music Problem—and Yours," *Mademoiselle,* June 1973,115, 185.

4. Florence King, "Red Necks, White Socks, and Blue Ribbon Fear," *Harper's,* July 1974, 30–31, 34.

5. Earl Scruggs, "Excerpt from His Moratorium Appearance," in *Earl Scruggs: His Family and Friends,* Columbia Records, 1971, Side 2, Track 8.

6. Glen Campbell, "Universal Soldier," Capitol, 1965, Side A.

7. Haggard quoted in Peter Cooper, "Merle Haggard: As He Is," *American Songwriter,* May/June 2010, 63.

8. Merle Haggard, "Irma Jackson," in *Let Me Tell You about a Song,* Capital, 1972, Side 2, Track 3.

9. Certainly, Haggard has been a complex and controversial figure in country music, with him both supporting and denouncing conservative political positions, including on race, during his long career. For although he engaged (as noted) in two songs that can be read as anti-racist, he also wrote "I'm a White Boy," which can be interpreted as containing white supremacist sentiments, although Haggard biographer David Cantwell argues that the song merely works to overcome negative representations of poor whites by celebrating the group. See David Cantwell, *Merle Haggard: The Running Kind* (Austin: University of Texas Press, 2013), 196.

10. Johnny Cash, *Cash: The Autobiography* (New York: HarperPaperbacks, 1997), 286.

11. Ralph Gleason, "Johnny Cash Meets Dick Nixon," *Rolling Stone,* April 30, 1970, 47.

12. Bill Malone, *Don't Get Above Your Raisin': Country Music and the Southern Working Class* (Urbana: University of Illinois Press, 2003), 239.

13. See Charles K. Wolfe, "Nashville and Country Music, 1926–1930: Notes on Early Nashville Media and Its Response to Old-Time Music," *Journal of Country Music* 4, no. 1 (Spring1973): 12; Charles K. Wolfe, *A Good-Natured Riot: The Birth of the Grand Ole Opry* (Nashville: Country Music Foundation Press and Vanderbilt University Press, 1999), 38–39; and Richard A. Peterson, *Creating Country Music: Fabricating Authenticity* (Chicago: University of Chicago Press, 1997), 6–8.

14. Bill Malone, *Country Music U.S.A.,* 3rd ed. (Austin: University of Texas Press, 1985), 42.

15. Abel Green, "Hill-Billy Music," *Variety,* December 29, 1926, 1, 22.

16. Jeffrey J. Lange, *Smile When You Call Me a Hillbilly: Country Music's Struggle for Respectability, 1939–1954* (Athens: University of Georgia Press, 2004), 64.

17. Blind Alfred Reed, "There'll Be No Distinction," RCA Victor, 1929, Side A.

18. Lange, *Smile When You Call Me a Hillbilly*, 87.

19. Jens Lund, "Fundamentalism, Racism, and Political Reaction in Country Music," in *The Sounds of Social Change*, ed. Serge Denisoff and Richard Petersen (Chicago: Rand McNally College Publications, 1972), 88–90.

20. Dickson, "Singing to Silent America," 212.

21. Katie Letcher Lyle, "Southern Country Music: A Brief Eulogy," in *The American South: Portrait of a Culture*, ed. Louis D. Rubin Jr. (Baton Rouge: Louisiana State University Press, 1980), 157.

22. For a further discussion of this issue, see Melton McLaurin, "Country Music and the Vietnam War," *Perspectives on the American South: An Annual Review of Society, Politics, and Culture* 3 (1985): 145–61.

23. Jan Wenner, "A Conversation with Baraka Obama," *Rolling Stone*, July 10, 2008, 72–73; Gardiner Harris, "The President's Revealing Disclosure, in Rhythm and Prose," *New York Times*, August 15, 2016, A11.

24. Chris Willman, *Rednecks & Bluenecks: The Politics of Country Music* (New York: New Press, 2005), 7.

25. Ted Cruz, *CBS This Morning*, CBS, March 24, 2015.

26. Jamilah Lemieux, *Now with Alex Wagner*, MSNBC, March 25, 2015.

27. Chet Flippo, "Nashville Skyline: Shut Up and Sing?," March 20, 2003, para. 4, www.cmt.com/news/1470672/nashville-skyline-shut-up-and-sing/.

28. George H. Lewis, "Duellin' Values: Tension, Conflict and Contradiction in Country Music," *Journal of Popular Culture* 24, no. 4 (Spring 1991): 105.

29. See Paul DiMaggio, Richard A. Peterson, and Jack Esco Jr., "Country Music: Ballad of the Silent Majority," in *The Sounds of Social Change*, ed. R. Serge Denisoff and Richard A. Peterson (Chicago: Rand McNally College Publishing, 1972), 41; Jimmie N. Rogers, *The Country Music Message Revised* (Fayetteville: University of Arkansas Press, 1989), ix; and Robert Confield with Marshall Fallwell, *Just Country: Country People, Stories, Music* (New York: McGraw-Hill, 1976), 27.

30. DiMaggio, Peterson, and Esco, "Country Music," 44, and Robert W. Van Sickel, "A World without Citizenship: On (the Absence of) Politics and Ideology in Country Music Lyric, 1960–2000," *Popular Music and Society* 28, no. 3 (July 2005): 318.

31. Van Sickel, "A World without Citizenship," 329.

32. Robert S. McElvaine, introduction to *Down and Out in the Great Depression: Letters from the "Forgotten Man,"* ed. Robert S. McElvaine (Chapel Hill: University of North Carolina Press, 1983), 16.

33. John Grissim, *Country Music: White Man's Blues* (New York: Paperback Library, 1970), 13.

34. Willman, *Rednecks & Bluenecks*, 3.

35. For example, see Jock Mackay, "Populist Ideology and Country Music," in *All That Glitters: Country Music in America*, ed. George H. Lewis (Bowling Green: Bowling Green State University Press, 1993), 285–303, and Jimmie N. Rogers and Stephen A. Smith, "Popular Populism: Political Messages in Country Music Lyrics," in *Mass Politics:*

*The Politics of Popular Culture*, ed. Daniel M. Shea (New York: Worth Publishers, 1999), 111–21.

36. Quoted in Maurice Zolotow, "Hillbilly Boom: Uncle Art Satherley Seeks Out Country Music in the Bayous, Canebrakes, and Hills," *Saturday Evening Post*, February 12, 1944, 38.

CHAPTER ONE

# The
# NRA
# Blues

*Commercial*
*Country Music*
*and the*
*New Deal*

## GREGORY N. REISH

ON NOVEMBER 3, 1936, President Franklin D. Roosevelt secured his second term with the largest electoral college landslide in the history of the United States. Roosevelt anticipated an easy victory over his Republican opponent, Kansas governor Alf Landon, and expected to win 360 of the available 531 votes in the Electoral College. In fact, Roosevelt earned 61 percent of the popular vote and came away with every state except Maine and Vermont, an unprecedented 523 votes (98 percent) in the Electoral College.[1] FDR's reelection seemed to offer resounding support of his New Deal, the assortment of laws and executive orders enacted during his first term and designed to bring the nation's economy back from the depths of depression while restoring the people's confidence in the country's financial institutions and federal government. Although not all of the New Deal programs were successful, the widespread positive effects of Roosevelt's initiatives and their broad endorsement by the American middle and lower classes were confirmed by his sweeping victory in 1936.

Just weeks after FDR's reelection, on Saturday, November 28, West Virginian country recording artist Bill Cox and his musical partner, Cliff

Hobbs, entered the New York studio of the American Record Corporation to record Cox's two brand new compositions in honor of FDR's decisive victory, the only sides that Cox cut that day. "Franklin Roosevelt's Back Again" and "The Democratic Donkey (Is in His Stall Again)" directly reflect the outcome of the 1936 election, converting the nation's collective enthusiasm for the efforts and successes of Roosevelt's first term into cheerful, humorous, and slightly ambivalent musical-poetic expressions in the Southern, white, working-class vernacular. Cox's two songs of November 1936 stand out because of their promptness and direct tone but were not, in fact, the only positive responses to FDR and his New Deal policies in early commercial country music. Cox himself had already penned and recorded a paean for FDR's National Recovery Administration (NRA) in 1933; in the same year, the Light Crust Doughboys and Lee "Pappy" O'Daniel recorded a rousing anthem, "On to Victory, Mr. Roosevelt," in support of the newly elected president's policy war on the Great Depression. An original member of the Doughboys who spun off his own influential Western swing band, Milton Brown wrote and routinely sang on his radio shows "Fall in Line with the N.R.A." In 1934 Fiddlin' John Carson, known in the latter part of his career for his support of social conservatives, transformed one of his early hits about struggling farmers to cast Roosevelt as their champion. That same year, the Allen Brothers from neighboring Tennessee held up Roosevelt as the divinely guided savior of the struggling working class in "New Deal Blues." When the U.S. Supreme Court declared the National Recovery Administration unconstitutional in 1935, singing miner George Davis wrote his mournful "Death of the Blue Eagle" in reference to the NRA's well-known emblem.

Such support for progressive politics seems to run contrary to twenty-first-century perceptions of country music's political ethos as staunchly and unapologetically conservative. Peter La Chapelle has drawn attention to this incongruity, noting that despite the strongly right-wing messages and associations of country music in the late twentieth and early twenty-first centuries, "much of the genre's history has been connected with politicians and political causes of a liberal or left-of-center nature," and "this is especially true of the musician activists and musicians-turned-politicians of the 1930s and 1940s."[2] La Chapelle correctly identifies the period of commercial country music's early history, which actually began in the 1920s and lasted through end of the Second World War (roughly to the end

of Roosevelt's life and presidency), as a time when its explicit politic sentiments aligned with progressive politics. But to attribute the phenomenon
especially to political activism and the intertwining of a few individuals'
musical and political careers is somewhat misleading, as La Chappelle
draws general inferences from a handful of isolated and atypical instances
and broadens his definition of country music to include Woody Guthrie
to bolster the discussion. But unlike much of the era's folk music and in
sharp contrast to blues and other African-American commercial genres,
mainstream commercial country music of the prewar era was more often
topical than activist, reflective rather than instigative, typically capturing
and commenting on the prevailing moods of its consumers *after* relevant
events and often reassuring listeners rather than provoking them. Country
songs showing support for New Deal policies may have been sincere, left-
leaning expressions of sympathy with the struggles and hopes of working-
class listeners but were generally not calls to political action. They were
responses to changes already under way or, in some cases, already complete. Moreover, most progressive political songs in 1930s commercial
country music fell squarely into the long-standing traditions, rooted in
Anglo-Celtic folk balladry and nourished by the sentimental parlor song
industry of the nineteenth century, of composing topical songs that reflect
the general mood of the populace.

The various manifestations of support for progressive politics and
New Deal policies in early commercial country music also form part of a
broader process of country music's struggle to establish its collective identity as a cultural and commercial presence. Like other categories of so-
called American roots music, country in this era was a genre in formation.
The folk music of working-class whites in the South and the Midwest,
which manifested in other parts of the United States and Canada as well,
was becoming professionalized and commercialized, reshaped by the
mass-mediated forces of the radio and recording industries even as it continued to absorb and mingle with other musical traditions. The process
of commercialization in early country music expanded its popular appeal
across the country into both urban areas and more socioeconomic classes.
Country music transcended the mostly rural, Southern, Anglo-Celtic mi-
lieu that formed one essential part of its musical and cultural background.
Many country music consumers were migrating northward and westward

into cities and moving from agrarian livelihoods into steel factories, textile mills, and oil refineries. The music they listened to embraced a correspondingly wide range of topics and attitudes reflecting the nation's current affairs, changing demographics, and dynamic economy.

This growth of commercial country reflects the populism of Roosevelt's presidency, cutting across geographic and class divisions. Tellingly, Roosevelt's 1936 reelection was supported by nearly all the country's forty-eight states, in both rural and urban areas, confirming what biographer Conrad Black characterizes as FDR's "long-sought coalition of big-city working-class people and rural progressives."[3] Such a coalition of common Americans, united by their victimization at the hands of greedy industrialists and complicit Republican legislators, had been a cornerstone of FDR's initial presidential candidacy. In his speech accepting his first nomination at the Democratic National Convention in Chicago on July 2, 1932, the very moment that gave rise to the phrase "New Deal," Roosevelt argued passionately for the unity of the American populace in facing the unprecedented economic challenges presented by years of failed Republican policy, corporate excess, and the stock market crash of 1929. Converting these challenges into "human terms," he had identified three interrelated and overlapping groups of Americans affected by these events: those dependent on agriculture, those in industry, and those making modest investments in the modern economy. "On the farms, in the large metropolitan areas, in the smaller cities and in the villages," he reassured the Democratic Party delegates, "millions of our citizens cherish the hope that their old standards of living and of thought have not gone forever."

Just as Roosevelt reached out to a broad swath of America, so did country music. The primary means of country music's expansion, of course, were commercial recordings and radio, the latter being the same medium that Roosevelt used to bring his messages directly to the American people. The sharp decline in record sales brought on by the Great Depression in the early 1930s was at least partially offset by the continued growth in country music's radio presence, from the local stations where many musicians got their start and earned their living, to the syndicated, clear-channel, and Mexican-border broadcasts that made national stars out of Roy Acuff, Gene Autry, the Carter Family, and many others.[4] As Richard Peterson pointed out, country radio remained an effective means of reaching and advertising to working-class Americans during the Depression and "had almost magical power for rural people growing up in the 1930s, drawing families together and at the same time opening isolated communities to the larger world beyond the county and even the state."[5] Also, country music on the radio served similar social functions for families that had migrated away from their familiar communities and agrarian lifestyle into cities and urban industries, providing a nostalgic gathering space for those forced into radically new surroundings and circumstances by the nation's shifting economic climate. Left-wing messages in support of New Deal initiatives appeared in other mass media of the era as well, often involving country music. In the era's Hollywood films, pro-Roosevelt notions were sometimes embedded as underlying plot narratives, dramatic morals, and other thinly veiled elements in an otherwise depoliticized entertainment. In a recent article, country music historian Don Cusic examines the economic motivations of many Hollywood studio heads during Roosevelt's first term and illuminates the progressive ideals embedded in singing cowboy movies by Gene Autry and Roy Rogers.[6]

The mass-mediated populism that supported the flourishing of the commercial country music industry ran parallel to the public relations strategies of FDR and his administration during the First New Deal. Just two days after the inauguration on March 4, 1933, President Roosevelt took to the airwaves in his first "fireside chat." Using the still young technology (radios had been on the consumer market for less than fifteen years), the new president addressed the American people directly in their homes about the nature of the banking crisis and how he intended to begin resolving it. One measure of FDR's success in this endeavor is the volume, variety, and approbation of the letters he received in response to his broadcasts. In their study of these letters, Lawrence Levine and Cornella Levine emphasize the "wide spectrum of the American people" who wrote to express their confidence in FDR's leadership, their renewed hope, and their appreciation for his addressing them on their own terms.[7] For example, responding to President Roosevelt's first radio chat, Mrs. Paul Russell of Haskell, Oklahoma, wrote on March 15, 1933, "[Your address] said more than Mr. Hoover did in four years, and although you have culture, aristocratic breeding and wealth you have one priceless gift, that of reaching out to the 'common people' with a deep sympathy and understanding, that goes into their hearts and you can talk their language and when you talked banking you talked banking so all could understand."[8] President Roosevelt seized upon the contemporary, democratizing medium of radio to bring his message to ordinary Americans of all stripes, across the country, and in all walks of life, just as country musicians and their promoters were doing with their still young genre.

Roosevelt, of course, was seeking grassroots support for the aggressive policies and programs he began pushing through the legislative process immediately at the start of his first term. During the first one hundred days of his presidency, beginning on March 4, 1933, Roosevelt launched a series of programs designed to relieve crises of hunger and housing, improve unemployment, restart economic growth, regulate industry, and repeal Prohibition. Known collectively as the "First New Deal," these programs were largely but not entirely successful. The Economy Act of 1933 faced fierce opposition in Congress but eventually managed to cut government spending by some $500 million. The Emergency Banking Relief Act passed much more easily into law the same year, successfully reopening banks with oversight by the U.S. Treasury, while the Glass-Steagall Act put various bank regulations into place and established the Federal Deposit Insurance Corporation. More controversial was the June 1933 National Industrial Recovery Act, which created the National Recovery Administration and was designed to establish codes of fair competition in industries ranging from coal production to motion pictures. The NRA oversaw the adoption of commodity price controls, collective bargaining guarantees, and minimum wages—all with the legal enforcement of Roosevelt's own executive power. An enormously popular program for the tangible improvements it made in the lives of workers in textile, mining, and other industries, the NRA faced strong opposition from industry leaders and was bogged down by bureaucratic top-heaviness, byzantine requirements, and an overly ambitious scope. The program improved working conditions for the lower classes but did not stem unemployment nearly as much as predicted and, in some industries, stifled commerce. In May 1935, the United States Supreme Court struck down most of the National Industrial Recovery Act as unconstitutional. Although assessments of its economic success or failure vary widely and depend on the specific industry at hand, little doubt exists that the NRA brought tangible

relief to the economic hardships of millions of factory and industry workers. Over the course of its short life, the agency's emblem—a blue eagle—
became a symbol of hope for much of the working class. The promises,
successes, and ultimate demise of the National Recovery Administration
were the subjects of several commercial country songs that flourished in
the era.

One of the first country performers to express musical praise for
this particular New Deal initiative was Milton Brown, the Texas-born
bandleader known as the "Father of Western Swing." As his career grew
in the early 1930s, Brown wrote and routinely sang on his radio shows an
original composition titled "Fall in Line with the N.R.A." Brown's song
strikes a reassuring tone that surely resonated with his audience members,
pointing out immediately in its opening lines that Roosevelt had turned
the country "into a land of smiles" that "put depression on the run" with
"the blue eagle on display." The song's final verse extends the benefits of
the NRA to an unrealistically broad range of working-class and white-
collar occupations, making reference to those who work in gas stations,
drug stores, cafés, clothing manufacturers, banks, electronic shops, and
even "the peanut stand on the corner." Roosevelt's New Deal agency becomes unlimited in its reach and universal in its applicability, a cure-all
that will make *every* American's life a better one. Noteworthy here is the
implied passivity of Brown's grand vision. All Americans will reap the benefits of Roosevelt's program, and all they have to do is "fall in line."

Milton Brown's reasons for choosing not to record "Fall in Line with
the N.R.A." are not known. Perhaps he initially attributed the song's popularity to its timeliness and thought it best to reserve for live performance.
Perhaps executives at his record labels (Bluebird, then Decca beginning
in 1935) feared politicizing an otherwise fun artist playing carefree dance
music. In any case, the song was undoubtedly popular in his concert and
radio repertoire. Brown's biographer, Cary Ginell, reports that "Fall in Line
with the N.R.A." was so loved by fans of Brown's radio show on KTAT in
Fort Worth that the show's sponsor, a local funeral home, included the lyrics on one of its promotional flyers. Even after the demise of the New Deal
agency, the song remained popular enough for Brown to continue performing it; his brother Roy Lee Brown kept "Fall in Line with the N.R.A."
in the Brownies' repertoire for decades after he took over leadership of

the band. Ginell also suggests that Milton Brown's motivation for writing and featuring the song was not simply to please his audience by including uplifting, topical subject matter. Brown's inspiration was sincerely political, according to Ginell, who cites the shared governance, agreeable working conditions, and communal finances of Brown's "commonwealth band that was actually a microcosm of Roosevelt's plan."[9] Although plausible, it seems presumptive to draw conclusions about Brown's personal stance on matters of national politics from the manner in which he organized his swing band. It is clear, however, that Brown successfully tapped into his audience's collective hopes for FDR's relief administration and packaged its universal message in a lighthearted country song.

Milton Brown may have picked up on the power of such songs from his early work (along with fellow Western swing pioneer Bob Wills) as a member of the Light Crust Doughboys in Saginaw, Texas. Formed in 1931, the Doughboys were the marketing brainchild of W. Lee "Pappy" O'Daniel, then president of Burrus Mill and Elevator Company, who created the band to help market his light crust flour during the popular local radio broadcasts that he hosted. O'Daniel wrote and sang much of the group's material, and although his songwriting ability and originality have been criticized, he showed an undeniable aptitude for writing topical songs that reflect current events and the prevailing moods and concerns of his customers.[10] At their second recording session, which took place on October 10, 1933, in Chicago and by which time Brown had already left the band, O'Daniel and his Light Crust Doughboys recorded "On to Victory Mr. Roosevelt" in support of FDR's recently launched policy war on the country's economic hardships. The song exudes a cheerful and reassuring mood, which is particularly cogent when paired with the record's flip side, an account of the stock market crash entitled "In the Fall of '29." Although "On to Victory Mr. Roosevelt" makes no specific allusion to the National Recovery Administration or any other New Deal initiative, references to economic hard times appear in the middle of the song's three verses, and support for Roosevelt's relief and reform are expressed in a general way. Listeners are urged to "tear down the fence between supply and demand," and O'Daniel affirms the necessity of putting people back to work. He also captures something of the swallowed pride surely felt by many of his Depression-era listeners who were reluctantly coming to rely on the support of the New Deal, but the song also confirms that "when they say that they will pay they will not go and bust."

"On to Victory Mr. Roosevelt" has particular interest in any discussion of the political realities of early country music in that its author later turned his business leadership, marketing acumen, and radio popularity into a political career. A probusiness Democrat, O'Daniel ascended to the governorship of Texas in 1938 and to the United States Senate in 1941. But he proved to be fiercely anti-Roosevelt during the 1944 presidential election owing to the administration's more progressive policies, especially those centering on racial issues. Although this shift may certainly have been a genuine change in O'Daniel's political outlook, it may also suggest that his ostensible support for FDR in his songs of the early 1930s was not necessarily a sincere expression of political sentiment but an entertainer's shrewd ability to reflect his audience's collective mood.

La Chappelle cites Fiddlin' John Carson as a "similarly complicated" example, another early country songwriter and radio and recording star whose political alignments seem to have shifted from New Deal progressivism to hard-line conservatism.[11] Well known to students of country music history as an immensely popular local entertainer in the Atlanta area, a hillbilly radio pioneer, and arguably the first significant country recording artist, Carson had already built a catalog of topical material such as "The Grave of Little Mary Phagan" and "My Ford Sedan," alongside a wide assortment of hoedowns, play-party songs, and folk ballads, before the onset of the Great Depression. He also crafted songs about the pre-Depression economic struggles of the working class well before the start of Roosevelt's presidency. The most famous of his early socially conscious songs are "The Farmer Is the Man That Feed Them All" (recorded November 1923); "There's a Hard Time Coming" (recorded June 1925); and "The Honest Farmer" (recorded June 1925). This last piece remains one of Carson's best known, kept alive in the twenty-first century in the repertory of the Dry Branch Fire Squad's politically outspoken front man Ron Thomason. It tells the poignant story of a hardworking farmer whose sweat and toil receive scant reward when he takes his cotton to market and whose struggles are now amplified by the boll weevil blight that drastically affected the Southern cotton industry starting in the 1910s. The song draws a parallel between the natural parasite (the boll weevil) that consumes the farmer's cotton and the economic parasite (the nameless merchant) who takes the farmer's corn. Carson rerecorded "The Honest Farmer" in February 1934 for a different record label, having moved to Bluebird from Okeh. The remake was probably designed to take advantage of that decade's improved (electrical) recording technology, a common practice among successful artists in that era. More important, Carson rewrote the song's chorus entirely, shifting its subject matter away from the boll weevil and toward the practical solutions of the New Deal. Roosevelt is praised as an honest and big-hearted person, doing everything that he can as president to help struggling farmers. Although Bluebird released Carson's remake under the same title, "The Honest Farmer," Peter La Chappelle, Bill Malone, and others have cited this song's title as "Hurrah for Roosevelt."[12] The error is not only factually incorrect but also robs the refashioned song of its broader meaning by failing to connect it explicitly with its original from nine years earlier. Carson's 1934 version of "The Honest Farmer" is more than a simple celebration of Roosevelt and the New Deal, generated by a shortcut recycling of older material. By modifying a pre-Depression song that originally addressed a natural blight, Carson acknowledges the ongoing struggles of the Southern farming industry before and during the Depression, likening natural to man-made agricultural disasters and amplifying the positive effects of FDR's New Deal relief efforts that were then under way.

Carson reinforced his solidarity with rural audiences in his musical response to one of the main planks in the political platform of Georgia governor Eugene Talmadge. Elected to the state's executive office in 1933, Talmadge quickly established an unusually inexpensive three-dollar automobile registration fee as a simple measure to endear him with struggling farmers who needed their trucks on the road.[13] Although the policy ultimately proved much more controversial than Talmadge had anticipated, it succeeded in making him a champion of the farming community. Fiddlin' John Carson celebrated the governor's effort in "Georgia's Three-Dollar Tag," recorded at the same session in February 1934 as his explicitly pro-Roosevelt remake of "The Honest Farmer." Carson had campaigned for Talmadge in 1932, at which time the two men struck up an immediate and lasting friendship. The governor rewarded Carson with jobs as a state game warden and "elevator commissioner" (part-time elevator operator in the state capitol building).[14] Carson remained a fervent supporter of Talmadge, even when his positions became increasingly racist and anti-progressive, especially toward the policies of the Roosevelt administration.

Other country performers had a less complicated relationship with Roosevelt and his political efforts. A commercial country duo from Monteagle, Tennessee, the Allen Brothers routinely included political commentary and satire in their songs of the 1930s. Their recording career began with Columbia in 1927 and consisted mainly of blues and hokum repertory, leading Columbia to release "Chattanooga Blues" and "Laughin' and Cryin' Blues" in its 1400 race series, normally reserved for African-American artists and marketed to the African-American consumer market.[15] After the Allens filed and then dropped a $250,000 suit against Columbia for damage to their reputations, they signed with Ralph Peer and Victor Records in 1928. By 1930, with the onset of the Great Depression, the Allens began to incorporate political material into their songwriting, particularly through references to the struggles and frustrations of the working class. "I've Got the Chain Store Blues," "The Enforcement Blues," and "Price of Cotton Blues," recorded at their earliest Victor sessions in the autumn of 1930, responded to changes in the economy that were being felt in ordinary Americans' everyday lives with a keen sense of biting satire. In his pioneering study of the Allen Brothers, folklorist Donald Lee Nelson points to the "anti-Republican sentiment, 'I voted for Hoover, even shined his shoes'" in their 1932 recording, "Allen's Lying Blues."[16]

The Allen Brothers issued a direct response to FDR's economic policy efforts in October 1934 during one of their last recording sessions, seeking to capture and articulate the general sentiments of their listeners, just as did some other country artists of the time. In "New Deal Blues," the Allen Brothers used a conventional twelve-bar blues form—three-line stanzas in AAB form with a characteristically epigrammatic problem-solution poetic structure—to offer a simplistic contrast between the dark days of economic struggle with the tangible relief offered by New Deal initiatives: the "bad" Depression "had me worried all the time," but now "I got money in my pockets; I'll leave the Depression all behind." In the subsequent verse, the singer appreciates that he is "working every day" and doesn't have to "work so long" because he "belong[s] to the N.R.A."

Ultimately, the singer's appreciation extends beyond the human figure of President Roosevelt, casting his efforts as the intervention of a benevolent Christian god even as he echoes the words of FDR's first nomination acceptance speech of 1932: "My meals are regular, I don't have to beg and steal [2x] / And I'm thankful to the Lord for sending us a brand New Deal." Ascribing government relief from the NRA and other New Deal programs to divine munificence was, for many proud Americans, a way to rationalize and justify their reliance on government aid. With characteristic perspicacity, Roosevelt himself reinforced this notion. He likened the evils of the Depression to those created by corrupt authoritarians in both the Old and the New Testaments and prayed for "divine guidance" as the ultimate source of his leadership.[17] Historian Ronald Isetti has demonstrated that "Roosevelt employed biblical rhetoric, especially the theme of driving out the moneychangers, as a means of defending, maintaining, and advancing a regulatory Progressive state based on political liberalism and Christian humanitarianism."[18] The Allen Brothers sensed this feeling among their listeners and thus reinforced it in their song, reflecting the religiosity of Roosevelt's benevolent message. With their own recording career drawing to an end at the time of this recording thanks to weak sales, the Allens sympathized with their audience members' hardships and gave them a voice, through country music, to express gratitude for their economic salvation.

One of the most compelling commentaries about the National Recovery Administration was Bill Cox's "N.R.A. Blues," recorded and released in August 1933. It is the first of several songs in Cox's output that reveal his willingness to adapt topical songwriting, responding to the prevailing news and themes of the day, to the national politics that FDR himself was bringing directly into common Americans' homes. Cox had recently discovered the power of topical songwriting in a fledgling career that began in his native Charleston, West Virginia. Known also as the "Dixie Songbird" and under a variety of pseudonyms, including Luke Baldwin, Jim Morgan, Charley Blake, and Clyde Ashley, Bill Cox began singing and playing around Charleston in the late 1920s, while working at the city's Ruffner Hotel.[19] In 1928, he made his debut on Charleston's WOBU radio, and in July of the next year, three months before the stock market crash, Cox first recorded, for Starr-Gennett's Champion and Supertone labels. His style and repertoire early on were those of a typical hillbilly entertainer in that era, unashamedly indebted to stars like Harry McClintock, Vernon Dalhart, and especially Jimmie Rodgers. Cox's earliest catalog includes response songs and covers such as "In the Big Rock Candy Mountains No. 2" and "My Rough and Rowdy Ways," along with an assortment of blues, gospel, novelty, and Tin Pan Alley songs delivered in the easygoing, yodel-filled manner associated with Rodgers's enormous influence.[20] Cox's first recorded original composition was topical, if not political. "The Death of Frank Bowen" (recorded October 1929) recounts the story of a local murder in strophic ballad verse replete with lyrical clichés of the genre and a final verse warning all people to "prepare to meet thy God" and "repent from every sin." Such topical material, responding to events in the recent past, articulating his audience's collective emotional response, would come to be one of the hallmarks of Cox's career.

By the time Cox signed with the American Record Corporation in 1933 (for releases on subsidiary store labels such as Banner, Conqueror, and Oriole), he had increasingly distinguished himself from the era's most popular cowboy and hillbilly entertainers, forging his identity through clever, often humorous songwriting on a variety of topics that included social commentary and increasingly political subject matter. "Cause All My Good Times Are Taken Away" (recorded April 1930) and "The Bootlegger's Plea" (recorded November 1930) comment on Prohibition from the first-person perspective of otherwise good men turned criminal in the context of an unjust law. His first overtly political commentary in song and his first compositional references to the onset of the Great Depression appear in the witty future fantasy "In 1992," which Cox recorded in Richmond, Indiana, in August 1931. In the song, Cox imagines the wondrous technological advances of the late twentieth century and all the ways they will make everyone's lives easier. Some of the song's predictions about the era are impressive in their prognostication: travel will be fast and easy, crops will be bigger and more plentiful, and farmers will be relieved of their most arduous manual labor. These and other more "ridiculous" dreams of a worry-free future are offset, however, by Cox's direct references to the real issues of his day, warning that "we'll still be cryin' for farm relief" and "we'll still be making home brew in 1992." Cox demonstrated similar foresight about what seemed at the time a fantastically comic future in his song "When the Women Get in Power" (a reworking of George Reneau's "Women's Suffrage," recorded in 1925).

Thus, when he recorded and released "N.R.A. Blues" in August 1933, less than two months after FDR established the agency for which the song is named, Cox was applying a similarly topical approach to what was certainly the biggest story of the day for his listeners' own lives and for the nation as a whole. Without promoting activism or advocating a specific political agenda, "N.R.A. Blues" captures and conveys the uplifting mood of the time through a simple and direct lyrical tone, expressing both the optimism surely felt by millions of working-class Americans when FDR's sweeping changes were set in motion and the collective hope that the NRA would solve the country's most urgent economic problems. At the same time, Cox tempers this hopefulness with a degree of trepidation, a complex response that may have been intended to reflect workers' mixed feelings about the new president's aggressive actions. The verses enumerate unfair labor conditions (the singer works "like a mule" in "the old sweat shop") and wealth inequality (the rich live on "easy street" while the poor "can't get enough to eat"), themes fairly common in working-class country songs before the New Deal, particularly those associated with the factory work of Southern textile mills.[21] Such lyrical references belong to the tradition of Dave McCarn's "Cotton Mill Colic" (recorded 1930) and the Dixon Brothers' "Weave Room Blues" (recorded 1932). But unlike these and other commercial country songs that describe unfair pay and working conditions in the era before Roosevelt's inauguration, Cox's "N.R.A. Blues" includes a changing chorus that conveys the hope offered by the First New Deal, specifically the National Recovery Administration. The "big boss" may not like it, but working under its reforms assures "short hours" and the "same pay." While still not a call to action, Cox broadens the emotional message of the hillbilly factory song to include a measured dose of New Deal optimism. The previously desperate and mournful nature of the genre is fundamentally altered by the real relief that FDR's initiatives provided.

Significantly, "N.R.A. Blues" also includes a short blues refrain that recurs following each iteration of the chorus: "I've got the blues, I've got them N.R.A. blues / Lord I got them N.R.A. blues." Although customized to fit the specific New Deal content of this song, refrains of this type were stock musical and structural devices, common in Jimmie Rodgers's songs and employed also by Dorsey Dixon in "Weave Room Blues." In Dixon's song, the refrain makes poetic sense; the singer has "them awful weave room blues" precisely because of the deplorable labor and economic conditions described in painful detail through the verses. Exactly why Cox's protagonist should have the "N.R.A. blues" remains unclear, given that the NRA offered much-needed hope and empowerment, which Cox articulates elsewhere in the song. Perhaps Cox—already prone to wield songwriting clichés rather freely—may simply have fallen back on this ubiquitous structural device without much regard for its effect on the song's otherwise uplifting message. By contrast, including the refrain may have been a calculated, if not especially elegant, effort to counterbalance the optimism of the verses with a degree of cynicism that many of Cox's listeners likely felt.

The two songs Cox wrote and recorded in November 1936, "Franklin Roosevelt's Back Again" and "The Democratic Donkey," reflect the nation's continued commitment to FDR and his New Deal policies, revealing a somewhat more self-assured composer. Cox reportedly wrote "Franklin Roosevelt's Back Again," an unusually rapid example of a topical response song, in his New York hotel room within days of FDR's stunning reelection and just before the recording session on November 28, 1936. The uplifting and victorious song celebrates not just FDR's decisive win but also the social freedoms and positive nationwide morale regained during Roosevelt's first term. Chief among these freedoms, not surprisingly, is the repeal of Prohibition that began with Roosevelt's signing of the Cullen-Harrison Act in March 1933 (allowing the sale of beer and wine with an alcohol content of 3.2%) and was completed with the ratification of the Twenty-First Amendment in December of that same year. The importance of Prohibition's repeal—both to Cox and presumably to his listeners—is confirmed in the first iteration of the song's chorus. Here the singer proclaims that "since Roosevelt's been elected, moonshine liquor's been corrected" and rejoices in the reestablished legality of wine, whiskey, beer, and gin. The celebratory nature of the first chorus continues into the ensuing verse, where the social freedoms ensured by Roosevelt's electoral victory broaden to include laughing, joking, dancing, and smoking. Of course, these activities had not been prohibited by law; the song suggests, rather, that under Roosevelt's leadership Americans have regained the happiness and stability that foster such revelry. Only in its last verse does the song allude to the relief generated by Roosevelt's economic policies, assuring that with FDR in charge, "we're all workin' and gettin' our pay."

This last verse also points directly to the song that inspired Cox's "Franklin Roosevelt's Back Again." Bob Miller's "The Good Old Times Are Coming Back Again" is not a country song but a popular tune with a comforting message that Miller and his pop orchestra recorded for the American Record Corporation (also Cox's label) in 1932, arguably the worst year of the Great Depression and obviously before FDR's programs began providing relief. As in Cox's reworking, Miller's song cites the breadline as a prevalent sign of hardship, accompanied here by vague, repeated reassurances that such hardships will one day come to an end and the "good old sun will shine." While the similarities of melody and lyrical structure between Miller's original and Cox's rewrite make the debt unmistakable, Cox's addition of a chorus focused primarily on the figure of Roosevelt enhances the song's musical variety just as it provides a more explicit source of comfort than Miller was able to offer four years earlier. In 1932, Miller's tone could be hopeful and wish filled but remains necessarily vague. By 1936, circumstances were measurably better for most working-class Americans. There were real reasons to celebrate, and Roosevelt was the man they thanked overwhelmingly at the polls. As he had done less successfully in 1933 with "N.R.A. Blues," Cox reworked an existing popular song model and gave it specificity by making reference to President Roosevelt.

Bill Cox's "The Democratic Donkey (Is in His Stall Again)," recorded on the same day in November 1936 as "Franklin Roosevelt's Back Again" and issued on the flip side of the same 78 rpm record, offers a more wholly original, clever, and humorous commentary on Roosevelt's reelection. The song is written in the first person, from the perspective of the well-known symbol of the Democratic party. Although he begins by saying that "they turned me out to die," the donkey is resilient. He kicks down the stable, allows Mr. Roosevelt to "mount to the saddle and grab the bridle rein," and rides triumphantly "on to victory!" and "on to Washington." Each verse—as well as the chorus of "Hee Haw, Hallelujah!"—ends with the charmingly simple image of being "back in old Columbie [*sic*] in the same old stall again," the donkey back in his familiar home in the nation's capital and its rider, FDR, back in the White House for another term. The song's fourth verse makes especially ingenious use of not only the familiar political symbols of the donkey and elephant but also the alternative

Democratic rooster and Republican eagle: "The rooster and the eagle fought a duel in the sky / While I was throwing gravel in the big white elephant's eye." It should be noted that Cox's home state of West Virginia is one of several near the Ohio River Valley that have continued to use the rooster as a Democratic symbol. Into the late twentieth century, voting a straight Democratic ticket on election day was commonly referred to as "scratching the rooster."[22]

Cox's penchant for topical and, at times, overtly political songwriting led to a renewal of interest in his work long after his last prewar recording session in September 1940. Cox had returned to his job at the Ruffner Hotel in Charleston and to relative obscurity. Ken Davidson, founder and president of Charleston-based Kanawha Records, located Cox in 1965 living in a poor section of the city and brought him out of retirement to make a new album of his old songs. Cox had little idea that five years earlier, in 1960, a group of folk revivalists known as the New Lost City Ramblers—which included, at that time, its original lineup of Mike Seeger, John Cohen, and Tom Paley—had featured "N.R.A. Blues" and "Franklin Roosevelt's Back Again" on their Folkways album *Songs from the Depression*. They knew little about Cox's background, nor even that he was still alive, but chose to present his New Deal songs as Appalachian counterparts to the politically conscious songwriting of Oklahoman Woody Guthrie.[23] Cox, however, was no activist. Like others active in commercial country music during the Great Depression, he was a popular songwriter whose wide-ranging repertory found a little room for political-topical songs responding to some of the biggest news stories of the day and capturing some of the collective mindset of his listening audience. Cox's New Deal songs echo the prevailing spirit of his time in an honest and often endearing manner but were never intended to inspire political and social action.

The New Lost City Ramblers' zealous and somewhat misguided effort to re-present political songs of the 1930s in the context of the 1960s folk revival and protest movement also led them to George Davis. Known as the "singing miner of Hazard, Kentucky," Davis was a Southern worker who, like Cox, had written and performed songs expressing a progressive political stance beginning during the Depression. Over the course of his career, Davis built a broad repertory that demonstrated his sensitivity to modern

popular styles (including rock and roll in the 1950s) as well as a willingness to address a range of topical subject matter in his songwriting. He
played frequently on the radio in eastern Kentucky and West Virginia, although his recording career was modest, just two commercial sides on the
Rich-R-Tone label, issued in 1949, and a 1967 LP on Folkways produced
by the Ramblers' John Cohen. Whereas Cox's "N.R.A. Blues" celebrates
the promise of FDR's New Deal program around the time of its founding,
Davis's "Death of the Blue Eagle" laments the NRA's demise in 1935. Davis
wrote "Death of the Blue Eagle" shortly after the legal invalidation of the
National Recovery Administration by the Supreme Court. Its title refers,
like a line in Milton Brown's "Fall in Line with the N.R.A.," to the agency's
well-known emblem, which had served as a visual symbol of hope during
Roosevelt's First New Deal and the darkest days of the Depression. The
NRA had had a particularly strong effect on the mining industry and the
United Mine Workers of America (UMWA), in which Davis was actively
involved. The union's own *Journal* referred to the NRA as "the greatest victory for labor that ever was achieved."[24] In West Virginia, the NRA allowed
the UMWA to boost its membership significantly, which in turn gave the
organization increased bargaining powers.[25]

"Death of the Blue Eagle," a simple strophic song with a repetitive melody and occasionally clever rhymes, begins with news of the blue eagle's
demise, which the singer learns about in the newspaper (another topical
response to recent events). He cites "a man in Washington, Roosevelt is
his name," who joins the common workers in mourning the death of their
beloved symbol of hope and reform. In the ensuing verses, Davis turns the
song's narrative directly to the plight of the mining industry, referring by
name to Hugh S. Johnson, the World War I–era army general and member
of FDR's "brain trust," whom Roosevelt appointed chief administrator of
the NRA. The song ends on a confident note as befits the writer's dedication to his labor organization. Davis encourages his fellow members of
the UMWA to stay true to the principles of the organization despite this
seemingly tragic setback. To those uncertain about the future and who
doubted the staying power of the union's efforts, Davis reminds them how
much better things are since the NRA's price and wage controls went into
effect, asking them to think back to the economic situation in 1932, before
the New Deal.

Commercial country music of the era also found room to satirize and poke fun at some of the era's progressive reforms, as in the case of Tennessee fiddler, singer, and bandleader Roy Acuff's "Old Age Pension Check." Although he did not record the song until July of 1939, Acuff seems to have added it to his repertory in the second half of 1935, around the time FDR established his Social Security program as part of the Second New Deal (1935–36).[26] Acuff's satire may also have been directed toward a more aggressive government pension plan for retired workers promoted by California doctor and businessman Charles Townsend beginning in 1933.[27] Acuff later confessed to having purchased the song from a boy in Knoxville whose name he could not recall, pointing out that despite its somewhat controversial reception, the song is clearly comedic and was popular with audiences.[28] Without specifying whether its target is Townsend's plan or FDR's social security, the song satirizes the very notion of a government pension for elderly retirees. An exaggerated fantasy in the vein of Harry McClintock's "Big Rock Candy Mountain," "Old Age Pension Check" describes all the troubles of senescence, from widowed loneliness to the need for cosmetics to the loss of libido, melting away when the "old age pension check comes to their door."

The popularity of Acuff's "Old Age Pension Check" in live performances long before the song was recorded and released underscores that commentaries on the progressive policies of Franklin Roosevelt and other Democratic leaders showed up in other channels of country music's dissemination in the 1930s. Several of the era's progressive political leaders recognized well the power of country music to reach certain vitally important sectors of the electorate, even if the songs used for such ends were not overtly political. Fiddlin' John Carson's support for Herman Talmadge's Georgia gubernatorial campaign has already provided one example. Another is Louisiana governor and U.S. senator Huey Long, a fascinating and controversial figure who combined his own unique brand of big government populism with a shockingly iron rule. Long recognized and capitalized on country music's appeal to bolster his campaigns and promote his policy agenda, with particular sensitivity to different musical tastes in different regions of the state. As historian Kevin Fontenot has observed: "To reinforce his connection with the common folk, Long used music in his campaigns. He regularly used New Orleans jazz bands, but in northern and southwestern Louisiana, his preferred bands were country. Long even went so far as to hire the Leake County Revelers to campaign with him."[29] While little evidence exists of country song content being tailored to deliver specific messages on the campaign trail, the music's ability to resonate with audiences through general mood, humor, and a variety of cultural references approaches the fundamental methodology by which country songwriters engaged with FDR's New Deal programs and policies. References may occasionally be specific—as in the various NRA songs discussed above—but the success of these songs lies, rather, in their ability to reinforce existing sentiments among audiences.

Given the readiness with which such songwriters as Bill Cox and Fiddlin' John Carson were able to capitalize on widespread pro-Roosevelt sentiment during the early and mid-1930s, it is surprising that such songs are so few in number. That they outweigh anti-Roosevelt songs of the period is expected, given the president's enormous popularity across the nation and across various socioeconomic classes. But why are there so few, practically a handful of strong examples among thousands of commercial country recordings during the era? There is no shortage of songs supporting Roosevelt and his New Deal programs in Anglo-Celtic folk music of the 1930s, a group of genres closely related to commercial country. Of course, some of this flourishing was directly nourished by FDR's own initiatives. A major component of his common-man populism was the institutionalization of folklore studies through such programs as the Works Project Administration, the Resettlement Administration, the Federal Music Project, and the Library of Congress's Archive of American Folk-Song. Public historian Benjamin Filene has shown that, unlike previous folklore projects, the missions of these agencies were all-embracing ("Record *everything*," Sidney Robertson recalled being instructed by the Resettlement Administration's director, Charles Seeger). Filene also emphasizes the activism of New Deal folk song collectors and their newfound attention to "living lore," both of which directed their activity to current topical material.[30] Given these methodological shifts, it is not unreasonable to suspect the greater number of pro–New Deal, politically progressive songs collected compared with that of commercial country music may have been partly attributable to the influence of the collectors themselves.

More perplexing, perhaps, is the much greater prevalence of pro–New Deal songs in the commercial genres of 1930s music made by African Americans—particularly blues and religious music—and marketed under the umbrella term "race records." Indeed, Guido van Rijn found enough such material to support an entire monograph, *African-American Blues and Gospel Songs on FDR*.[31] Van Rijn's exhaustive study covers 349 songs related to FDR and his politics out of the roughly 25,000 blues and gospel recordings made before 1945. It's a small percentage, to be sure, but still a significantly higher number than comparable examples from commercial country music made by white artists. The imbalance becomes even more baffling when considering traditional party affiliations of the time: Southern whites generally supported Democrats, and African Americans aligned with Republicans (although, it should be noted, that black voters shifted to FDR in large numbers in the landslide election of 1936). Why, then, do songs celebrating Roosevelt and his New Deal programs show up less often in the commercial music of white, Southern Democrats, many of them living in rural areas that benefited directly from those programs?

The answer, I suspect, is twofold. First, it is irrefutable that the market forces of early country music played a significant role in their relative scarcity in commercial white music. Commercial country music was still in its infancy during the 1930s, and its very existence as a viable industry was threatened by the nation's severe economic downturn. This reality is true of African-American commercial genres, too; but those were not being shaped quite so aggressively to be brought into mainstream popular culture though mass media. The music and entertainment industries were working to make country music pleasing to a wider array of American audiences, themselves shifting economically, geographically, and politically. Commercial country music of the 1930s, despite its left-leaning political tendencies, was still a culturally and economically *conservative* genre, with less tolerance for activism, social provocation, or even passive political expression as it sought broader mainstream acceptance. With the importance of FDR's policies as the biggest news of the day, policies that had a direct and overwhelmingly beneficial effect on the lives of many country music listeners, it is natural that some of these topics would find their way into the repertory, but only to a rather severely limited degree. Second, the early commercial country music industry wielded a unique combination of nostalgia and contemporaneity in its emotional range. Drawing on established and familiar styles along with the centuries-old tradition of using music to comment on current events, early country songwriters discovered the value in responding to political and cultural developments by confirming, rather than challenging, their audience's collective response.

## NOTES

1. Conrad Black, *Franklin Delano Roosevelt: Champion of Freedom* (New York: Public Affairs, 2003), 390.

2. Peter La Chapelle, "Is Country Music Inherently Conservative?," *History News Network*, November 11, 2007, http://historynewsnetwork.org/article/42602. See also Peter La Chapelle, *Proud to Be an Okie: Cultural Politics, Country Music, and Migration to California* (Berkeley: University of California Press, 2007).

3. Black, *Franklin Delano Roosevelt*, 391.

4. See chapters 7 and 8 of Richard Peterson, *Creating Country Music: Fabricating Authenticity* (Chicago: University of Chicago Press, 1997), for discussions of radio barn dances and radio "barnstorming."

5. Ibid., 97.

6. Don Cusic, "Country Music and Progressive Politics: Singing Cowboys, FDR and the New Deal," in *International Country Music Journal, 2016*, ed. Don Cusic (Nashville: Brackish Publishing, 2016), 109–37.

7. Lawrence W. Levine and Cornella R. Levine, *The People and the President: America's Conversation with FDR* (Boston: Beacon Press, 2002), 3.

8. Ibid., 48.

9. Cary Ginell with Roy Lee Brown, *Milton Brown and the Founding of Western Swing* (Urbana: University of Illinois Press, 1994), 91.

10. Roy Lee Brown later accused O'Daniel of routinely writing new words to existing pop melodies, rather than melodies of his own, citing several examples. Ibid., 50–51.

11. La Chapelle, "Is Country Music Inherently Conservative?"

12. Ibid.; Bill C. Malone, *Country Music, U.S.A.*, 2nd ed. (Austin: University Press of Texas, 2002), 135. Patrick Huber has asserted that this is a rewrite of "one of the stanzas" to "The Honest Farmer," when in fact it is a new chorus. *Linthead Stomp: The Creation of Country Music in the Piedmont South* (Chapel Hill: University of North Carolina Press, 2008), 88.

13. Tammy Harden Galloway, "'Tribune of the Masses and a Champion of the People': Eugene Talmadge and the Three-Dollar Tag," *Georgia Historical Quarterly* 79, no. 3 (Fall 1995): 674–75.

14. Gene Wiggins, *Fiddlin' Georgia Crazy: Fiddlin' John Carson, His Real World, and the World of His Songs* (Urbana: University of Illinois Press, 1987), 120–21.

15. Charles Wolfe, "A Lighter Shade of Blue: White Country Blues," in *Nothing but the Blues: The Music and the Musicians,* ed. Lawrence Cohn (New York: Abbeville Press, 1993), 234–36.

16. Donald Lee Nelson, "The Allen Brothers," *John Edwards Memorial Foundation Quarterly* 7, no. 24 (Winter 1971): 149. See also Donald Lee Nelson, "The Great Allen Brothers Search," *John Edwards Memorial Foundation Quarterly* 7, no. 23 (Autumn 1971): 126–29.

17. Roosevelt concluded his Inaugural Address with the following benediction: "While this duty rests upon me I shall do my utmost to speak their purpose and to do their will, seeking Divine guidance to help us each and every one to give light to them that sit in darkness and to guide our feet into the way of peace." Franklin D. Roosevelt, "Inaugural Address," January 20, 1937, *American Presidency Project,* http://www.presidency.ucsb.edu/ws/?pid=15349.

18. Ronald Isetti, "The Moneychangers of the Temple: FDR, American Civil Religion, and the New Deal," *Presidential Studies Quarterly* 26, no. 3 (Summer 1996): 686.

19. Details about Bill Cox's life appear in Ken Davidson's sleeve notes to *Billy Cox: "The Dixie Songbird,"* Kanawha LP K305, 1967.

20. See Chapter Four of Barry Mazor, *Meeting Jimmie Rodgers: How America's Original Roots Music Hero Changed the Pop Sounds of a Century* (Oxford: Oxford University Press, 2009), for a discussion of Rodgers's influence and the scores of imitators he inspired (a phenomenon Mazor calls "yodelmania").

21. See Patrick Huber, *Linthead Stomp: The Creation of Country Music in the Piedmont South* (Chapel Hill: University of North Carolina Press, 2008).

22. "Roosters and Eagles," *Morgan Messenger,* October 24, 2012, 2.

23. Mike Seeger, conversation with the author, Lexington, VA, December 17, 2006. Seeger explained to me that in concert, the Ramblers made the parallel between Bill Cox and Woody Guthrie explicit in their stage commentary.

24. Arthur M. Schlesinger, *The Age of Roosevelt, Volume II, 1933–1935: The Coming of the New Deal* (Boston: Houghton Mifflin, 2003), 168.

25. Jerry Bruce Thomas, *An Appalachian New Deal: West Virginia in the Great Depression* (Lexington: University Press of Kentucky, 1998), 92.

26. Although he ran for governor of Tennessee in 1948 (as a Republican), Acuff generally avoided political content in his musical career.

27. Interestingly, George Davis, author of "Death of the Blue Eagle," later wrote a song about the United Mine Workers' welfare plan called "Miner's Dream Come True" (1955), the melody of which derives from Acuff's "Old Age Pension Check."

28. Roy Acuff, interview with Dorothy Horstman, Nashville, TN, September 8, 1973, reprinted in Dorothy Horstman, *Sing Your Heart Out, Country Boy* (Nashville: Country Music Foundation Press, 1975), 251.

29. Kevin S. Fontenot, *Our Senator Huey Long: Country Music and Louisiana's Kingfish* (unpublished typescript, n.d.) (author's collection).

30. Benjamin Filene, *Romancing the Folk: Public Memory and American Roots Music* (Chapel Hill: University of North Carolina Press, 2000), 142–43.

31. Guido van Rijn, *Roosevelt's Blues: African-American Blues and Gospel Songs on FDR* (Jackson: University Press of Mississippi, 1997).

# CHAPTER TWO

# Senator
# Glen H. Taylor

*Radio's*
*Utopian*
*Singing*
*Cowboy*

PETER LA CHAPELLE

THE ONE surviving newsreel clip of Glen Taylor's first day in the U.S. Senate suggested his national political career would be anything but stodgy. The newsreel, which is only partially augmented with sound, opens to darkness and then a caption: "Universal Newsreel: Congress Convenes." The year is 1945, and the viewer is bombarded with a succession of silent flickering images: an establishing shot of the Capitol building, and a succession of shots of Harry Truman and legislators and their wives hobnobbing and talking to the press. The camera then cuts to dark interior shots of new legislators being sworn in. All seems fixed in tradition and according to plan.

The mood then changes as the newsreel—still lacking narration— cuts to a bright outdoor scene. Four figures, a well-attired Taylor, his wife, and two young sons, cross the Capitol steps. They sit above a group of reporters, and Glen Taylor pulls out his banjo. The Taylors are dressed up: Glen in a tie, black fedora, and gray overcoat, his wife, Dora, in a feathered black hat and dress coat, and the boys in black hooded coats. Suddenly, *actual sound,* singing and banjo plucking, fills the air as the Taylors and their older son, Arod, break into their own version of "Home on the Range":

Oh give us a home
Near the Capitol dome
With a yard for little children to play

The parody continued with pleas for a humble abode with a couple of rooms for a family. Glen then leaned into the mic and said with an ever-so-slight Western drawl, "We realize these are serious times. However, I brought the banjo along for my own amusement," then sarcastically adds, "I do think it would be a good idea to put up a barracks here in Washington so new Senators would have some place to live."[1]

Taylor's singing stunt on the day he was sworn into the Senate might seem tame today in a world dominated by the norms of reality television, when a president tweets venom at pop stars and nary a brow is raised when two senators have themselves filmed for a survival TV series on a deserted island.[2] But in 1945, an era when even being the spouse of a movie actor was controversial for a politician, Taylor's stunt was downright earth-shaking. Here was an actor, a Western camp tent vaudevillian, and radio singing cowboy, baring it all on his first day on the job by singing—yes, singing—about his family's inability to find a place to stay amid the housing shortages that dogged many cities in the waning months of World War II. Senators were not supposed to act in this fashion.

As might be expected, the press had a field day with Taylor's theatrics, describing him as a "colorful" singing cowboy who was determined to fight any urge to yodel in the Senate chambers.[3] Perhaps most brutal was the *New York Times:* "A singing cowboy sang his swan song on the Capitol steps today and then (almost reluctantly, it seemed) went inside to take and took his oath as Senator Glen H. Taylor of Idaho." By describing the stunt as a final performance, the *Times* suggested in one fell swoop that he had doomed his political career.[4]

Such assertions were, of course, premature. Taylor proved an important figure on the left flank of the postwar New Deal coalition in Congress. He pushed for civil rights in the South long before most of his cohort and ran unsuccessfully in 1948 for the vice presidency with Henry Wallace on a third-party ticket. Taylor not only achieved high office but attained a level of visibility on par with such well-known liberal or populist country musician–politicians as amateur fiddlers Al Gore Sr., Robert C. Byrd, and Tom Watson (at least in his younger racially egalitarian days), as well as Alabama governor "Big Jim" Folsom, a Congress of Industrial Organizations–backed candidate and non-musician who nevertheless seldom ventured out without his Strawberry Pickers string band.[5] Known foremost in his home state as a radio cowboy and hillbilly singer, the liberal Taylor—like the conservative Texas flour salesman, hillbilly promoter, and songwriter Senator W. Lee "Pappy" O'Daniel and Louisiana recording star Governor Jimmie Davis—blazed a trail for balancing celebrity and a political candidacy decades before conservative politicians George Murphy, Ronald Reagan, Sonny Bono, Arnold Schwarzenegger, and Donald Trump made careers out of a start in the entertainment business.

Taylor's political ascent suggests that country music's appeal as a political tool went beyond the usual pack of established performers and conservative Southerners who often dominate accounts, that country music did not have to fit particular conceptions of ruralness and authenticity to be successful on the campaign trail, and that there were important regional variations of country music politics that far outside the South. Taylor, of course, never commanded the initial star power possessed by more conservative performer politicians such as Jimmie Davis (known for "You Are My Sunshine") and O'Daniel, the former liberal populist and onetime Roosevelt supporter highlighted in Gregory Reish's essay in this book. Taylor nevertheless skillfully used his more regionally focused cowboy and country music image to carve out a relatively successful and impactful career.

Taylor's political and music career, whether he was cognizant of the connection or not, closely parallels the way another young idealistic radical, Tom Watson, had used fiddling—in his case such songs as "Mississippi Sawyer" and "Buffalo Gals"—to drum up a crowd in his 1882 race for Georgia's House, before launching a national career as a racially tolerant, economically radical, third-party Populist candidate for the vice presidency. Watson, of course, made a marked and decidedly nasty turn away from such liberalism when he embraced white supremacy at the turn of the century, a course that Taylor would never take.[6] Not only did Taylor help prove that the connections between economic populism, liberal social and racial attitudes, and country music could be maintained in the twentieth century, but his example also foreshadowed such successful liberal country music races as Jim Folsom's 1947 anti–poll tax and pro-labor gubernatorial run.

Taylor's repertoire also suggests that there was no single path for success as a performer-politician. His music was not the tradition-bound public domain material that appealed to Watson, Gore, and Byrd voters but was largely composed of covers of well-established numbers from hillbilly child singing acts and from singing cowboy performers, along with Western-themed songs from the radio crooner tradition mixed with some additional influences from jazz, Tin Pan Alley, and polka. Instead, Taylor's music was what Richard A. Peterson has deemed "soft shell," a pop-oriented, crossover-focused variety distinguished from the grittier "hard-core" music of his more traditionalist minded contemporaries, a kind of music that might find ready appeal to the isolated farmers and miners of the Far West who relied on popular radio fare perhaps more than Southerners for entertainment and a sense of community.[7] Indeed, his musical choices themselves suggest there is an important political and strategic dimension to the hard core/soft shell debate that has been largely overlooked in the realm of country music electoral politics.

Taylor's interest in politics emerged in part because of a desire to eradicate the kind of poverty he grew up with. Taylor was born in Portland, Oregon, in 1904, the twelfth of thirteen children. His father was a left-leaning itinerant Disciples of Christ minister who had tried his hand at acting, law enforcement, and farming. The family was descended on one side from a group of Texans who had served in the Texas Rangers and from which the family asserts they received an inheritance of Southern folk music culture. Taylor's biographer, F. Ross Peterson, notes that the father's politics were "of the type that stressed the Golden Rule, brotherly love, and a modified Christian socialism."[8] By the time Glen Taylor was born, his father had already planted the family on a 160-acre farm near Kooskia, Idaho. Glen, however, was born on the road during one of his father's ministry trips to Oregon. With so many mouths to feed and because only ten acres of the Kooskia farmland was fit for crops, the Taylors often lived in poverty, forcing young Glen to help out by collecting firewood and herding sheep for neighbors. His family's poverty required him to end his schooling after the equivalent of a sixth-grade education.[9]

As a young man in the early 1920s, Taylor hit the road, performing in his brother Ferris's Taylor Players traveling vaudeville act. Taylor eventually joined another itinerant group where he met his longtime wife, Dora, in Great Falls, Montana, in 1928; together, they eventually formed their own traveling theater group. The pair combined their first names giving the company the moniker of the Glendora Players.[10] The troupe generally remained on the road for the next ten years, giving performances in the Northwest and central mountain West, often living on the verge of poverty. Competition with "talkie" motion pictures dampened profits, as did the Depression itself. We "ate jack rabbits more than once and sometimes we didn't eat at all," Taylor recalled in the 1960s.[11] In 1935, they had their first of three sons, Arod (the name an anagram of his mother's name), who eventually became the lead singer of their band and part of their performing group.[12]

By then the Depression had made it difficult for the acting troupe to make ends meet. Glen noticed that a rival theater troupe was raking in cash by offering a free "hillbilly music" dance after their plays and by performing hillbilly music for free on the local radio station to advertise their shows. Taylor hired his own band of well-rehearsed swing musicians, but when that did not work out, he chatted with his rival about why they were more successful. The rival conceded that rural audiences craved more heartfelt, folksy, old-time and hillbilly offerings by less polished musicians and with "corn enough to spare." Taylor then fired the swing musicians and took to learning banjo, while Dora worked on piano. Glen's brother Paul, who performed in Glen's troupe, learned the slide trombone, and Paul's wife, Gladys, took saxophone lessons.[13]

Paul Taylor purposefully wielded the trombone up front and in an ostentatious manner to emphasize his dramatic slides, and with a wider array of instruments, they could easily handle the era's pop songs.[14] Eventually, the troupe took up the name of the Glendora Ranch Gang, playing radio stations for free by day to drum up publicity while performing as a theater troupe and dance band combo at nightly paid performances.[15] In his autobiography, Glen recalled the audiences' desire for rural music in the mountain Northwest: "Out in the beat-up halls in those little farming communities and cowtowns, they loved us . . . Nobody ever missed the seven swing musicians and Paul never missed a chance to get in an arm's-length slide on that shiny brass trombone. As they say in show biz, 'We killed them dead.'"[16] Although Glen later joked about the band's inexperience and the naïveté of his audiences, the only known recordings of the band suggest that over time the Glendora Ranch Gang became better musicians and that they spent considerable time crafting their musical choices for an audience that demanded a sophisticated mix of pop, hillbilly, and jazz tunes suited for the dance floor. Realizing their limits as musicians, they hired a professional guitarist and accordionist to round out their ensemble. Dora and Glen appear to have served as vocalists during the early days, especially when addressing audiences on the radio, but their first son, Arod, would eventually come to serve as the band's lead vocalist when he reached the age of three.[17]

Even before this turn toward music, Taylor had begun to contemplate a political career. His autobiography retells how witnessing Idaho governor C. Ben Ross at a campaign rally led him to believe that he, as a practiced stage performer, had what it took to make it in politics.[18] Taylor, like Woody Guthrie and other agrarian radicals of the time, was particularly sickened by reports that growers and grain elevator operators were allowing produce and crops to rot in an effort to drive up prices while American citizens were starving.[19] But what seems to have motivated him the most was his chance encounter in the late 1920s with razor magnate King Camp Gillette's utopian writings when he was visiting a relative who had a sizable book collection.

Taylor described this introduction to Gillette's politics as almost something of a religious conversion experience: "I reached over and picked a book at random. That was the most fateful action of my life. The rest of my life and the lives of untold numbers of other people would be affected, altered, and made to flow in different channels because of that seemingly simple act . . . No scholar receiving a rare and priceless volume had ever been more appreciative than I."[20] Gillette, the inventor and original promoter of the famous Gillette razor, was a bit of a contradiction: a wildly successful capitalist who enthusiastically prophesized the coming of a new socialist-like economic order. But his vision was not exactly conventional socialism. Instead, he imagined a highly technological world where all members of society would be stockholders in a World Corporation that would assure more efficiency and fairness in production, less workplace drudgery, and the elimination of poverty.[21] Influenced by the fever of scientific discovery generated by the inventions of Nikola Tesla and Thomas Alva Edison and the utopias imagined by Henry George and Edward Bellamy, Gillette's planned-economy corporatism had a futuristic edge.

Gillette's primary goal was to restructure society toward a model of "production for use" where products would be efficiently created as they were needed by workers motivated by advancement in the corporation and sense of prestige and personal achievement rather than a wasteful focus on personal acquisition and profit, which dictated demand, supply, and price in chaotic ways. The details of how such drastic changes in society would gradually and voluntarily come into being were hazy at best and never entirely spelled out in three separate volumes Gillette wrote or co-wrote to explain his vision, but generally speaking, Gillette proposed that if enough believers bought stock, the World Corporation would be powerful enough to buy out competing firms and eventually structure the entire international economy around a single corporate entity. Gradually, this World Corporation would replace national governments, whose artifices would fall away like a husk, as a new peaceful, productive economic order sprouted forth.[22]

Utopian it was, but Gillette's ideal society also had a technological component. Gillette imagined thousands of giant, circular, glass dome–covered skyscrapers that housed 2,500 people each, all centered in a single Metropolis into which all of the North America population would transplanted. Gillette selected Niagara Falls, New York, the site at which Tesla helped develop a commercially viable hydroelectric facility, because it promised tremendous amounts of energy production. These skyscraper apartments and other buildings, which resembled cogs from an aerial standpoint, were to be laid out in intricate hexagonal patterns that appear more like a complicated blueprint for Kabbalah study than a traditional urban planning design and would be supplied by a central kitchen structure and electric line that would transport food "in a few minutes in sealed containers."[23]

One can easily imagine how eliminating hunger and building science-fiction metropolises might appeal to a poor young farm boy such as Taylor. Inspired by this vision, he committed to run for office and sought a place to settle his family and better his electoral chances. In 1938, soon after forming the Glendora Ranch Gang band, the Taylors choose Pocatello in southern Idaho. The Taylors were somewhat familiar with the area because they had stayed there with their theater troupe for short period in the late 1920s.[24] However, Taylor also realized that it would serve as a strategically savvy base from which to possibly eventually run for office. Situated some 70 miles north of the Utah border, Pocatello had strong railroad unions that could translate into potential liberal votes. Biographer F. Ross Peterson argues that the town also made sense in terms of his electoral prospects: as a northern Idahoan situated in the southern part of the state, Taylor figured he could carry the liberal mining and lumber-oriented northern half of the state, while also picking up farming votes in the more conservative, Mormon-dominated South.[25]

Meanwhile, Taylor was busy establishing himself as a public persona in the area through his music. Accustomed to using stops at radio stations to advertise their shows, the Glendora Ranch Gang convinced Henry Fletcher, owner of the local KSEI radio station, to let them try out a daily half-hour musical program for two weeks. After a positive response from the listeners, Fletcher made their program a permanent part of the lineup. The *Glendora Ranch Gang* program remained on the air in Pocatello for four years, with time off for campaigning and excursions with their theater and dance band troupe.[26] Arod Taylor does not recall his mother and father being remunerated for their program, but the family did use the program to advertise paid-admission dances and theatrical productions that were usually held in the evenings.[27]

Like many hillbilly bands, the Glendora Ranch Gang invited their audiences into the small KSEI studio to watch the performers broadcast. Onlookers would file into the station, a small house on the north edge of town, and find a place to sit or stand in the gallery. Directly ahead was a window that opened into the studio. "We would always fill up the gallery," Arod remembered. "People would come with their kids to watch us play." The band also opened their show with a theme song that appealed to rustic good life: "We like mountain music, ooh, we like mountain music, played by Glendora Ranch Gang band."[28]

The *Glendora Ranch Gang* show featured a mix of musical genres, connecting traditional and commercial country songs with other popular genres, in effect carving out a niche for the band as a cross-genre "soft shell" Western and hillbilly ensemble. Although it does not appear that any live KSEI broadcasts were recorded, a set of home recordings made by the family and their band on at least two separate occasions, the first most likely in 1939 and the second in 1941, gives some indication of the kinds of music the group regularly played. Although "authentic" Carter Family ballads and Acuff-type instrumentals are absent, Taylor's recordings on these Sears & Roebuck "Silvertone" brand home recording discs connect with prominent traditions within the hillbilly genre during the 1930s and early 1940s: the child radio star phenomenon and the singing cowboy and crooner traditions.[29]

Arod, who was three in the earliest set of recordings and five in the later recordings, lives up to his father's autobiographical admission that the young boy was really star of the band. He appears on every single one of the band's vocal recordings and is a soloist or dominant vocal presence on seven of the twelve other numbers.[30] The Glendora Ranch Gang was in good company in placing a cute kid at the center of their act. Hillbilly music's leading family, the adult-dominated Carter Family, had by this point also taken to putting the daughters, Anita, Helen, Jeanette, and June, on the air, but acts entirely dominated by children, such as father-son duo Asher and Little Jimmy Sizemore, as well as Western singer George Gobel, were also finding success on top national radio programs such as WSM's *Grand Ole Opry* and the WLS's *National Barn Dance*.[31] Arod's act with the Glendora Ranch Gang had much in common with the Sizemores. At the beginning of many Silvertone tracks and in between numbers, Arod played emcee, much like Little Jimmy, by introducing songs and vocalists, verifying the date and place of the recordings, and discussing his qualifications for stage or studio. Combining confidence with childlike charm, Arod's act was similar to Little Jimmy's radio exchanges with his father, which often featured the smaller Sizemore serving as an expert or authority on some aspect of the duo's music.[32]

The Silvertone recordings also reveal heavy influences from the singing cowboy subgenre and its connections with the movies, jazz and pop orchestration, and Western swing. We can especially see the latter influence in the song "When It's Springtime in the Rockies," a 1929 Tin Pan Alley piece that became the springboard for a Gene Autry film, and in the 1923 waltz "The West, a Nest and You," composed by jazz band leader and songwriter Billy

Hill.[33] By recording and promoting such songs, the Taylors were tapping into national obsessions with such singing cowboys as Autry, Roy Rogers, and Tex Ritter, who in 1930s had become a force on radio, in Saturday matinee films aimed at children, and in the recording industry.[34]

The biggest single performer influence on the Taylor family, however, was radio and film star Bing Crosby. Five songs recorded or made famous by the crooner appear in the recordings. The Glendora Ranch Gang recordings include an instrumental version of "An Apple for the Teacher," a pop love song which Crosby recorded with Connie Boswell, as well as Arod singing "Let Me Call You Sweetheart," Bing's 1934 hit. Another Crosby standard "Little Sir Echo," based on a 1917 Tin Pan Alley number aimed at children, appeared in Silvertone recordings with Arod singing lead vocals and his father Glen responding with "hello" as the song follows a call-and-response structure. Although in hindsight it seems odd that Crosby would influence a Western band such as the Glendora Ranch Gang, his popular and respectful covers of several cowboy songs in the 1930s gave credence to the claims of Western and hillbilly performers that their music formed a legitimate musical genre.[35]

Drawing on the band's cowboy songs and image, Glen Taylor made a concerted effort to dress in Western wear to appeal to live audiences and voters, joking that he "was togged out like Tom Mix."[36] At various times, he wore a bulky white Boss of the Plains–style Stetson or later a trimmer Cattleman. Photographs from the era show him also wearing Western-style "smile pocket" shirts and suits and jeans-style dungarees.[37] The band and Dora and Arod wore similar wear in publicity photos from the time.[38]

On the campaign trail, the Taylors' radio broadcasts and live appearances featuring music from the hillbilly, pop, Western, crooning traditions proved an indispensable tool in launching a career for a national legislative seat. Like many candidates without family connections or political pedigree, Taylor ran and lost many times. He ran for U.S. Congress in 1938 and for the Senate in 1940 and 1942, losing all three times but increasing the percentage of the vote he obtained in part because of his popularity as a cowboy and hillbilly performer. His missteps and triumphs in these early campaigns allowed him to slowly refine his public appeal, resulting finally in his election to the Senate in 1944. Music and his day job in broadcasting were an important launching pad for these campaigns.

Although he made inroads with the public through his efforts, Taylor could not count on the support of the political establishment and the news media. As a political outsider lacking deep ties to the traditional parties and local political machines, he had a prickly relationship at best with the press, which was often politically enmeshed with community elites. The fact that he also represented a left-wing faction of the Democrats in a state dominated by Republican-leaning newspaper editors and publishers did not make the situation any better. "There are eleven daily papers" in Idaho, Taylor recalled in his autobiography, "and they were all against me but one and it was neutral."[39] His hillbilly music pursuits, however, allowed him to overcome the natural advantages other elite-supported candidates might have had because it gave him an alternative way of reaching voters. Taylor's strategy of speaking out to fans on the radio and actually meeting them at performances in Mormon recreation centers and Grange halls played the same role in many ways that direct mailing campaigns, YouTube appeals, and Twitter feeds have in allowing more recent candidates to reach voters without relying on the support of the mainstream media. Music became a means of shortcutting the traditional alliances that a politician would have to secure with local editors and reporters and their sponsors, which often included wealthy merchants and the statewide power company, to get elected.

During his first run for office, a congressional seat in 1938, Taylor regularly announced his political rallies on his program on KSEI. He also briefly used the Glendora Ranch Gang's radio broadcasts to push his own political agenda by making short sermons during his broadcasts.[40] When KSEI station manager, Henry Fletcher, warned Glen that Federal Communications Commission rules prevented him from directly inserting politics into his radio program, Taylor suggested instead that the band broadcast supposedly neutral reminders about voting dates and educational statements about how to vote. Understanding Taylor's drift, Fletcher had no objection, and Arod proved instrumental in these so-called educational efforts, capitalizing on his child star appeal. "From then on, at end of each day's broadcast, while all the gang were playing and singing our theme song," Glen Taylor wrote in his autobiography, "Cal the announcer would lower the volume on the music and Arod, who was not yet three, would chime in with a public service exhortation, 'Be sure to vote right.'"[41]

The implication of these statements was that "voting right" meant voting the cute little singing cowboy's father into office.

Taylor also brought his Glendora Ranch Gang on the road in an effort to capitalize on the band's growing radio audience. "There had never been a campaign like this before, noisy street rallies with a cowboy band entertaining from atop an old Ford car, a candidate for Congress dressed like Tom Mix," Taylor recalled in his autobiography. "Heretofore, campaigns had been a terrific bore, dull uninteresting and stereotyped. For the first time a lot of people were *enjoying* a political campaign."[42] Despite car-top performances, Taylor lost in a crowded primary, finishing fourth in a field of eight.

Taylor threw his hat in again in 1940 after the death of longtime Idaho politician William E. Borah left a Senate seat up for grabs. Because it was a statewide race and Taylor could not afford lodging for his band, he left the additional musicians in Pocatello and traveled instead with Arod and Dora, who formed a hillbilly trio. In a typical appearance, Arod would sing several songs on top of their car through the PA system, and then Glen and Dora would join in. Finally, Glen would take the mic and talk about what he would do as a senator.[43] At the Idaho Democratic Convention that year, he also played up his cowboy image, wearing "a small red silk handkerchief around his neck," a blue suit "with red thread woven in," and high-heeled, Spanish-style boots "that tapered down to a spiked point no bigger than a silver dollar."[44] Although trio appearances were the norm during the final months of the campaign, evidence suggests that Taylor was actually campaigning earlier with his full entourage and, perhaps, to even greater fanfare. An advertisement about an April performance of the Glendora Ranch Gang in Soda Springs, Idaho, is instructive: "Free Entertainment by the Glendora Ranch Gang . . . featuring AROD, Age 4, America's Youngest Cowboy Singer and Yodeler." It also included a discussion of how "Glen H. Taylor . . . Candidate for U.S. Senate will speak briefly on the subject of 'Plenty for Everybody,'" promised a performance of a play titled *Castaways of Plenty,* and offered a dance featuring "Modern and Old Time Music by a Real Cowboy Band."[45] Although Taylor's bid was a long shot, he snuck past two strong competitors in the primary election but was soundly defeated—by some 14,000 votes—in the general election that year.[46]

In 1942, Taylor threw his hat in again for Idaho's second U.S. Senate seat. By then, the Taylors had a second son, and Glen had left KSEI to work at a war plant in San Francisco, believing it was his patriotic duty to support the war effort in any way he could. He ended up campaigning alone because Dora was busy with the new baby. With no band or family members to back him musically, Taylor relied instead on the western image he had cultivated as part of his musical pursuits. That June, he bought a saddle and a "blue rinse dapple gray Arabian" horse in Coeur d'Alene and then took part in a marathon 200-mile equestrian ride to Grangeville, stopping along the way at voters' homes and outdoor rallies. He had originally intended to traverse the whole state in a 500-mile ride. Taylor added an element of patriotism to this publicity-generating stunt by starting with participating in the Coeur d'Alene Fourth of July parade and pledging that the marathon trek was part of his effort to save gasoline for the war effort. "As you may imagine, the tongue-in-cheek story of a cowboy candidate so patriotic as to undertake a grueling five-hundred mile ride to save gasoline was printed even to the far corners of the land," he wrote in his autobiography. He also made use of his Western garb as an advertisement in itself: "Across the front back of my maroon shirt, Dora had sewn white letters, three inches high, which spelled TAYLOR, and under that, in two inch letters, SENATE."[47]

Along the way, Taylor mailed reports of his progress to the press and wire services. These press releases and postcards ended up getting just enough regional and national press to bolster him in the primary.[48] In these updates, Taylor stressed his image as a man of the people to win the votes of farmers and rural communities by relaying stories about such subjects as how his hand was gruesomely lacerated while opening a barbwire gate or how he spent a day baling hay. Taylor also handed out "Saddle Bag Campaign Cards" in the 1942 run that capitalized on his singing cowboy image by picturing him with Stetson and banjo.[49]

Although his adventures were successful in drumming up enough media attention to see him narrowly succeed in the Democratic primary, Taylor had also begun to come under attack for his associations with Gillette's utopianism. Despite these grandiose goals, Taylor's own political statements focused on more practical and mundane articulations of Gillette's vision, namely, finding a way to reopen factories closed by the Depression, coordinating the war effort, reducing unemployment, and better distributing the fruits of labor.[50] There was no talk of futuristic skyscrapers delivering automatic meals. Instead, he fretted publicly that farmers were being paid to let crops rot while Americans starved.[51] In an interview with the *Pocatello Tribune*, he also argued it was a patriotic duty to centralize some aspects of industry along Gillette's lines in order to win the war: "Many of our production experts are saying our war effort will not reach maximum efficiency unless it is coordinated into one production effort," and added, "I agree with them but the people, not Wall street, must own it."[52]

Even if watered down, Taylor's enthusiasm for Gillette did not go unpunished. In the 1940 campaign, he was Red-baited by the press and opponents who generally made little distinction between Taylor's call for gradual changes and the authoritarian command economies of Stalin and Hitler.[53] Worse, in the final weeks of his 1942 campaign for Senate, a group of southwestern Idaho merchants began circulating a letter, widely reprinted in the press, arguing that Taylor "had a scheme to wipe out all private business. He does not believe in the profit system. His philosophy of government is based on a book written by King C. Gillette entitled 'The People's Corporation.'"[54] Such assertions put Taylor on the defensive. He had to argue that his promises were not "communistic" but simply sought to make Allied war production more efficient.[55]

Attacks on his ideological influences also became an occasion for critics to dredge up criticisms that a cowboy singer and a comedic stage performer could not be serious about or fit for office. Perhaps most devastating, his own local newspaper, the *Pocatello Tribune*, lobbied against him, arguing it was "it was not fitting that the senator from Idaho should pick a banjo and sing cowboy songs as an argument for his fitness as a national legislator."[56]

Faced with attacks on his vocation and accusations that he was a closet totalitarian, Taylor lost his 1942 bid for the Senate, but he significantly improved on his 1940 run, losing by fewer than 5,000 votes. It was not until 1944 that he finally succeeded in obtaining a Senate seat after teaming up with a new campaign manager and retooling his look. This time he toned down his campaign style by eliminating the music stops and putting away his Western wear. Instead, he donned a conservative business suit and made an effort to reach out to both employees and employers. He also reduced the Gillette rhetoric and talked instead about creating an economy that mimicked the Farm Union and Grange "cooperatives" already famil-iar to many Idaho farmers.[57] Although it represented his arrival as a new and improved campaigner, Taylor's win in 1944 cannot be completely di-vorced from his growing reputation as a hillbilly performer and marathon equestrian. Success that year would not have been possible if he had not already established an image based on music, horse riding, and populist-utopian volleys at the rich and powerful. Once established in the public eye as a cowboy performer politician, he was a known quantity who could them demonstrate his better graces with a new outfit and speaking style.

In the 1944 race, Taylor narrowly beat out his primary opponent, a conservative Democrat who was critical of Franklin Delano Roosevelt's liberal New Deal reforms, but Taylor continued to face accusations that he was a socialistic "pink" or a "commie." Perhaps just as damaging were the continued accusations that his performing career marked him as lack-ing seriousness, qualifications, and temperament to serve in such an im-portant position. The *Idaho Falls Post-Register*'s endorsement of Taylor's Republican opponent in the general election was particularly brutal: "Glen Taylor comes before the people with a background principally of stage and radio entertaining, an honorable and essential business but hardly the type of experience and training that qualifies a man to represent the great state of Idaho in the United States Senate."[58]

Despite such attacks, Taylor narrowly won the election, buoyed in part by late-breaking and perhaps opportunistic endorsements from Democratic politicians who had come to admire Taylor's style. His win made headlines in newspapers around the nation with a wire story in which he claimed to have beat out Southern conservative Democrats such as W. Lee "Pappy" O'Daniel and Governor Jimmy Davis as "the first of the cowboy singers" to go into politics. "I was the first to start, and the last to get elected," he said.[59]

Once in office, Taylor reverted somewhat to form, occasionally drag-ging out the Western wear, his banjo, and his horse, but those occasions were rarer and usually connected with a specific political project. The 1945 "Home on the Range" stunt on the Capitol steps was certainly one piece of evidence that he might bring hillbilly music back more fully into his political pursuits. So too was his 1946 "Paul Revere Ride for Peace," which combined a cross-country equestrian marathon with stops that included solo performances of country songs on banjo and guitar. Beginning his horse ride in Seal Beach, California, Taylor hoped to travel all the way to the East Coast to protest Truman's foreign policy efforts that he argued were dividing the world into American orbit and Soviet orbit and foolishly pitting the two superpowers against each other.[60] Claiming to have been influenced by Gandhi's fasts and marches, Taylor was particularly angered by the proposed Marshall Plan, which he argued rebuilt Western Europe in a one-sided, United States–dominated sort of way. Taylor argued that the Truman administration's hostile approach to the Soviet Union was also pushing potentially independent Eastern European nations further into Soviet orbit. Taylor sang covers of country songs and traditional favorites at his stops, including a self-penned composition "Cowboy Joe from Idaho," but his ride was ended in Texas when Truman called a special session of Congress to consider several foreign policy issues.[61]

For the most part, Taylor now made headlines by taking political stances: his support of civil rights for African Americans and of Jewish aspirations for a state in the British Mandate of Palestine, his belief that the FCC should increase the availability of licenses to small radio stations, and his hope to establish a Tennessee Valley Authority–style "Columbia Valley Authority" for operating dams and managing the Northwest's watershed system.[62] Perhaps most dramatic, he outflanked the new Republican leadership by being the first senator to call for the Senate not to seat arch-segregationist Theodore Gilmore Bilbo (D-Mississippi) in protest of his repeated calls during the 1944 campaign to disregard the civil and constitutional rights of African Americans. Taylor then joined with eleven Democrats and the new Republican majority to try to deny Bilbo that seat.[63]

Despite the leading role he played in several of these initiatives, critics continued to combine attacks on his loyalty with depictions of him as flighty, rootless, and temperamental. Noting Taylor's difficulty in getting Truman or the Democratic Party's support for leadership positions in the Senate despite the fact that he generally towed the party line, national columnist Holmes Alexander diagnosed him as "hammy humorist" and "lightweight thinker" who was "strangely shy" for an actor and "sensitive about his lack of education and previous unsuccess in the world."[64] A Texas paper suggested that Taylor, with his "cowboy pants, boots and sombrero," presented himself as "non-senatorial" on the peace ride. Furthermore, since Taylor seemed to be repeating on the ride what war-mongering "Russian diplomats" had said, he was either a witting dupe of the Soviets or a misadjusted, hysterical individual who need "some device to attract attention and make headlines."[65]

Such criticisms followed Taylor and became even more biting once he switched parties and ran as Henry Wallace's vice presidential running mate on the Progressive Party ticket in 1948. Already dissatisfied with Truman's foreign policy, Taylor viewed the campaign as a way of highlighting issues neglected by Democratic Party and to push for what he viewed as the more liberal or utopian legacy of the Roosevelt's New Deal. Democrats worried the move would split the liberal vote and allow Republican Thomas E. Dewey an opportunity to nix the reelection of Truman.

Accusations that Taylor was emotionally unstable and a Red continued from both sides of the aisle but with renewed ferocity from liberals and Democrats. Marquis Childs, the same columnist who once praised Taylor, now focused on his Western roots, painting him as a paranoid, agrarian-populist "actor with a large streak of ham" who advocated a version of Gillette-inspired economic system that loosely resembled the "corporative state of Italian Fascism." The national columnist went on to argue that the anti-capitalistic streak of this "frustrated, intensely ambitious headline seeking individual" was grounded in the Western American tradition of hating the railroads and making angry denunciations of "soulless corporations."[66]

The Wallace-Taylor campaign itself was a return to form for Taylor in many ways. Music played a large, unprecedented role for a presidential campaign, for one. Although presidential campaign songs extend as far back as "Follow Washington" and "Adams and Liberty," Wallace-Taylor ensured its rallies would be accompanied by music in a particularly enthusiastic and modern way. The campaign hired People's Songs, a group of left-wing folk singers that included Pete Seeger, Woody Guthrie, Alan Lomax, Agnes "Sis" Cunningham, and Josh White. As a sort of outside vendor composed of singers and musicians who had a particular passion for the Progressive Party message, People's Songs proved an enthusiastic ally, sending individual musicians out with Wallace, Taylor, and their representatives at speaking events on the trail and helping to organize a folk, blues, and pop extravaganza at the national convention in July. Its weakness perhaps lay in the fact that many in the People's Songs lineup had associated with civil rights and labor organizations that critics claimed were front organizations for the American Communist Party.

Although the press generally attacked the Progressives as being quixotic idealists or dupes misled by Communist interlopers, reporters generally praised the way organizers had brought music into the fold. "The opening session gave promise that this would be the most musical of all national conventions," wrote a *New York Times* political reporter, who added, "The singing was led by an inter-racial volunteer chorus with the delegates joining in on many of the folk songs."[67] National columnist Thomas L. Stokes similarly argued that, despite the party's dim electoral hopes, the Philadelphia convention "was the most spirited and spontaneous of the three national political conventions in this city this year."[68] Indeed, there was something profoundly revivalistic about the fervor with which music was used on the campaign. Sure, presidential contenders had had strong campaign songs and convinced significant figures in the music world to write and perform for them before, but recordings and news coverage of the July convention suggest that this was the first campaign, perhaps since the Populists, to weave musical performances and even sing-alongs into very fabric of the event rather than just using a brass band to highlight the appearance of dignitaries or an occasional vocal performance to provide a sort of mental break for reflection between impassioned speeches.[69] The Progressives' staging of the 1948 event then set the scene in many ways for the way the mainstream parties were able to use television and its combination of words, images, and music to introduce even more to campaign jingles and songs in 1952 and beyond.[70]

Historical accounts of the collaboration between the Progressive Party and People's Songs generally argue that Wallace's inner circle hired People's Songs and dealt directly with only two People's Songs individuals: folklorist Alan Lomax, who handled musical arrangements for the campaign, and Mario "Boots" Casetta, a People's Songs staffer who maintained an office in party headquarters.[71] People's Songs cofounder Pete Seeger recalled that there was little interaction between performers and the candidates because the Progressive Party handlers were afraid that the People's Songs musicians were potentially too close to Communist Party members and that close connections with the songsters might besmirch the campaign.[72] Taylor's autobiography and biographies of Wallace are silent about the music issue, while Taylor's son Arod remembers meeting Seeger and Paul Robeson but not spending an especially large amount of time with the performers.[73]

Nevertheless, there seems to be some evidence that Taylor may have played a more instrumental role in working with music on the campaign or may have been instrumental in the decision to hire People's Songs in the first place. Taylor seemed to have at least some prior connection with the group well before he had even considered such a run. Photographs of Taylor singing with People's Songs' cofounder Pete Seeger, for instance, appear among a collection of images shot by a *Life* magazine photojournalist who covered the Congress of Industrial Organizations' Political Action Committee school in July 1946.[74] Arod Taylor said he has always suspected that his father may have played a central role in the decision to hire People's Songs.[75] Furthermore, it would seem odd that Taylor, who had significant stage and musical background and who had worked carefully with Idaho Democrats to put more life into their conventions, would have been completely removed from decisions about the hiring process of musical groups along the trail.[76]

At individual campaign stops, Taylor regularly sang and appears to have worked very closely with the People's Songs musicians that the campaign assigned him. He took the stage with Michael Loring at stops in Idaho and with Pete Seeger at rallies in Kansas and Iowa. At a stop in Iowa, he not only appeared with Seeger but also was photographed taking the stage himself to sing a few songs with his wife, Dora, and sons.[77] The *Modesto Bee* even noted that Taylor, Dora, and Arod "demonstrated their idea of the bipartisan foreign policy" by singing "different popular songs all at the same time."[78]

At the convention itself, the Taylors played a substantial role by performing a song after his acceptance speech before 30,000 at Shibe Park.[79] The four performed "When You Were Sweet Sixteen," a Tin Pan Alley composition published in 1898 by Irish American songwriter James Thornton.[80] A lighthearted love song, the number was given new life the year before when Perry Como turned it into a hit.[81] Glen Taylor sang lead vocal, with Arod, Dora, and their second son, P. J., harmonizing along on choruses.[82] Although some commentators applauded the effort, the performance also elicited hackles from the press, who viewed it as amateurish and portrayed it as yet another example of the Taylors' egotism and lack of decorum. Despite having earlier applauded the People's Songs performances in his newspaper column, Norman Thomas, a longtime Socialist presidential candidate and anti-Communist critic of the Progressives, argued that Taylor had enlisted his kin in an "excruciating barber-shop family quartet which he inflicted on millions of Americans listening on the radio." Thomas connected the attempt at drumming up emotion before such a large outdoor crowd with the rehearsed mass psychology of a Nazi or Soviet rally.[83]

The party, however, did not go far, finishing fourth in a crowded field of mainstream parties and plausible new contenders. Truman won the race, outpolling Republican Thomas E. Dewey despite challenges from the Progressives on the left and the Dixiecrats on the right. The Wallace-Taylor ticket polled only 1.1 million votes, mostly from the coasts and industrial centers, less than 3 percent of the vote nationwide. The Wallace vote was about 20,000 votes less than that garnered by Strom Thurmond, the pro-segregation Dixiecrat candidate who managed to earn 39 electoral votes because his support was concentrated in less populated Southern states. Nevertheless, the Progressives could have tipped the election to Dewey had they scored slightly better in Ohio, California, and Illinois.[84]

After the election, Taylor finished his term as a senator and even achieved some level of reconciliation with Truman. Nevertheless, his decision to run on the third-party ticket and the accusations that he was a nonserious musician and a pink continued to dog him. He caucused with the Democrats but was still treated as a traitor by many. Facing hostility from the leaders of the Idaho Democratic Party, he ran for reelection in 1950, but this time he hired a "Western country music" band, the Idaho Ramblers, to do the performances. The Ramblers featured a steel guitar player who seemed to inaugurate a full turn toward the national Western swing craze among hillbilly performers.[85] Taylor lost in the primary, a bitter and close election in which he asserted, with some evidence, that votes had been tampered with.[86] After two additional unsuccessful attempts to crack the Democratic primary for the Senate, Taylor finally retired from politics and moved to northern California, where he opened a successful business that sold Taylor Toppers, a special toupee that he had designed in part to hide his own baldness on the campaign trail.[87]

Ultimately, Taylor's topsy-turvy political and musical career has some lessons to teach historians and observers of country music and those studying liberal and left-wing politics. First, perhaps too much emphasis has been placed on country music as a Southern phenomenon if a band as far west as Idaho could develop the listenership needed to help catapult a musician to a senatorial seat. Although there were certainly elements of Southern culture that emerged within the Taylors' music—nods to Jimmie Rodgers in particular—it is clear that mountain Westerners were already developing a taste for a mix of music, a soft-shell amalgam that blended the sound and images of Westernness promoted by radio, Hollywood, and Tin Pan Alley with local manifestations of music and culture. Second, before the monopolization of the spectrum by the networks, rural radio proved an effective alternative means by which candidates who had been rejected by insular small-town and local establishments might reach voters. Finally, country music could prove, perhaps still does prove, an excellent medium by which a liberal or left-wing candidate could stress a connectedness with voters, but it could also be a double-edged sword: having a performing or broadcasting or cowboy background might help extend one's appeal while building up a political career, but it could prove a liability, especially for a liberal in favor of wide-ranging diplomatic endeavors with the Soviet Union, once one reached the national political stage. All performer-politicians face accusations of fickleness and artistic temperament to some degree, but it may just be that candidates with optimistic liberal or utopian political platforms are more susceptible to such attacks than are conservatives and others.

## NOTES

1. "Congress Convenes," Universal International News newsreel, January 4, 1945, as appears on Newsreels 1945, DVD37, a set of historic UIN newsreels compiled by Dr. Steven Schoenherr of the University of San Diego Department of History. It is not entirely clear why sound appears only on the Taylor segment of the newsreel or whether this newsreel was ever finalized and brought before a theater audience. It may just be a bit of abandoned "orphan" filmmaking.

2. Jeff Flake and Martin Heinrich, "Two Opposing Senators, a Deserted Island and an

Idea," *Washington Post*, October 21, 2014, https://www.washingtonpost.com/opinions/two-opposing-senators-a-deserted-island-and-an-idea/2014/10/21/127ef9e6-579 c-11e4-bd61-346aee66ba29_story.html?utm_term=.1c7d4e8e8709.

3. See, for instance, "95 Newcomers in Congress Are Colorful Crew," *Chicago Tribune*, January 4, 1945, 7; "Singing Solon Stands on Steps for Sympathy," *Pampa Daily News*, January 3, 1945, 1; "Singing Cowboy Not to Yodel as He Works at Job of Senator," *Mason City (IA) Globe-Gazette*, January 3, 1945, 4.

4. "Cowboy Sings Swan Song on Capitol Steps, Then (Reluctantly) Takes Oath of Office," *New York Times*, January 4, 1945, 36.

5. Carl Grafton and Anne Permaloff, *Big Mules and Branchheads: James E. Folsom and Political Power in Alabama* (Athens: University of Georgia Press, 1985), 31, 56–59.

6. "Curbstone Echoes Caught on the Wing," *Atlanta Constitution*, November 19, 1882, 1; C. Van Woodward, *Tom Watson: Agrarian Radical* (Oxford: Oxford University Press, 1963), 99–101, 107–11.

7. Richard A. Peterson, "The Dialectic of Hard-Core and Soft-Shell Country Music," *South Atlantic Quarterly* 94, no. 1 (1995): 273–300.

8. Frank Ross Peterson, *Prophet without Honor: Glen H. Taylor and the Fight for American Liberalism* (Lexington: University Press of Kentucky, 1974), 3.

9. Ibid., 3–4.

10. Glen Hearst Taylor, *The Way It Was with Me* (Secaucus, NJ: Lyle Stuart, 1979), 130.

11. Glen H. Taylor, letter to F. Ross Peterson, December 11, 1967, Glen Taylor Papers, MSS 252, series 2, subseries B, box 16, folder 1, Special Collections, Utah State University, Logan, Utah.

12. Taylor, *The Way It Was*, 130–42.

13. Ibid., 137–39.

14. Ibid., 129–37.

15. (Glen) Arod Taylor, phone interview by author, September 15, 2014, Millbrae, California. Glen Arod is Glen H. Taylor's first son. The Taylors have always called Arod by his middle name.

16. Taylor, *The Way It Was*, 138.

17. Arod Taylor, interview.

18. Taylor, *The Way It Was*, 147–51.

19. Arod Taylor, interview; ibid., 279.

20. Taylor, *The Way It Was*, 119–21.

21. Russell Adams, *King Gillette: The Man and His Wonderful Shaving Device* (Boston: Little, Brown, 1978), 134–37.

22. King Camp Gillette, *The People's Corporation* (New York: Boni and Liveright, 1924), 11–58.

23. King Camp Gillette, *The Human Drift* (Boston: New Era Publishing, 1894), 87–105; King Camp Gillette, *World Corporation* (Boston: New England News, 1910), 220–32; and Gillette, *People's Corporation*, 167–70. In many ways, Gillette's vision was a direct descendant of nineteenth-century French utopian philosopher François Marie

Charles Fourier's *phalanstères*, magnified on a mammoth scale. Fourier's phalanstères, named after the swift rehearsed protective phalanx maneuver of ancient Greek armies, were utopian communal compounds organized so that all may contribute, share their resources, and enjoy a decent standard of living. The French thinker imagined upward of fifteen hundred people living in a single extended structure that integrated rural and urban elements of life and production into an efficient, harmonious community. See Howard P. Segal, *Technological Utopianism in American Culture* (Chicago: University of Chicago Press, 1985), 67–69.

24. Taylor, *The Way It Was*, 110.

25. Arod Taylor, interview; Peterson, *Prophet without Honor*, 9.

26. Peterson, *Prophet without Honor*, 9.

27. Arod Taylor, interview.

28. Ibid.

29. Glendora Ranch Gang recordings, compact disc recorded from Silvertone disc, May 20, 1941. Twenty-six songs in all appear on the recordings, but several songs were recorded more than once in the set, sometimes in both instrumental and vocal form, giving us a total of twenty separate songs. "Sears: Complete Radio Departments" advertisement, *Milwaukee Sentinel*, June 15, 1941, section C, p. 8. Arod Taylor provided the author an audio CD copy of these discs.

30. Taylor, *The Way it Was*, 141–42.

31. See, for instance, Carter Family, *On Border Radio 1939*, audio CD, Arhoolie Records, 1995. On Gobel and the Sizemores, see Charles K. Wolfe, *Kentucky Country: Folk and Country Music of Kentucky* (Lexington: University Press of Kentucky, 1996), 60–61; W. K. Neil, "Asher and Little Jimmy Sizemore," *Encyclopedia of Country Music*, ed. Paul Kingsbury (Oxford: Oxford University Press, 1998), 486; and "Sizemore: Nashville Sound Is Upbeat," *Billboard*, July 15, 1967, 40, 51.

32. Glendora Ranch Gang recordings, especially track 15, "Little Buckaroo."

33. On "Springtime," see Ardis E. Parshall, "Mary Hale Woolsey: Always Springtime," *Keepapitchinin, the Mormon History Blog*, accessed October 15, 2014, http://www.keep apitchinin.org/2009/08/07/mary-hale-woolsey-always-springtime/. On Billy Hill, see Jack Burton, "The Honor Roll of Popular Songwriters: No. 64—Billy Hill," *Billboard*, June 10, 1950, 41. The lyricist Ted Lewis (nee Larry Yoell) was a jazz leader who specialized in performing ragtime and jazzed up Tin Pan Alley on vaudeville. See "Ted Lewis" in Scott Yanow, *Classic Jazz: Third Ear—The Essential Listening Companion* (San Francisco: Hal Leonard Corporation, 2001), 136.

34. Peter Stanfield, *Horse Opera: The Strange History of the 1930s Singing Cowboy* (Champaign: University of Illinois Press, 2002); Peter Stanfield, "Dixie Cowboys and Blue Yodels: The Strange History of the Singing Cowboy," in *Back in the Saddle Again: New Essays on the Western*, ed. Edward Buscombe and Roberta E. Pearson (London: British Film Institute, 1998).

35. Don Cusic, *The Cowboy in Country Music*, e-book (Jefferson, NC: McFarland, 2011), locations 1923–49; Gary Giddins, *Bing Crosby: A Pocketful of Dreams—The Early Years, 1903–1940* (New York: Little, Brown, 2009), chap. 17.

36. Taylor, *The Way It Was,* 159.

37. Numerous photos of Glen, Dora, and Arod in Western wear appeared in the Idaho and national press during the era. Peter Collier, "Remembering Glen Taylor," *Mother Jones Magazine,* April 1977, 42–48, includes a fairly comprehensive chronological collection of the Taylors pictured in Western wear at various time periods. Taylor's Western wear also seems to have increased in quality as he rose in office so that by his marathon equestrian "peace ride" in 1947 he was wearing a top-notch, tailored Western suit that looked like something famous country music tailors Nudie Cohen or Nathan Turk might have put together. See "Eastbound," photograph in photographic news collage, *Los Angeles Times,* October 27, 1947, 3

38. "Farewell Appearance: The Glendora Ranch Gang," advertisement, *Caribou County (IA) Sun,* December 19, 1940, 6.

39. Taylor, *The Way It Was,* 187.

40. Peterson, *Prophet without Honor,* 11.

41. Taylor, *The Way It Was,* 173.

42. Ibid., 171.

43. Arod Taylor, interview; Peterson, *Prophet without Honor,* 14; *Pocatello Tribune,* August 14, 1940.

44. Taylor, *The Way It Was,* 203.

45. "Free Entertainment" advertisement, *Soda Springs (IA) Sun,* April 25, 1940, 4.

46. "Glen Taylor, Cowboy Musician, Holds Slim Lead," *(Idaho Falls) Post-Register,* August 14, 1940, 1.

47. Taylor, *The Way It Was,* 229–33; Peterson, *Prophet without Honor,* 21–22.

48. Taylor, *The Way It Was,* 228–29; Peterson, *Prophet without Honor,* 19.

49. Taylor, *The Way It Was,* 233.

50. See, for instance, "Singing Cowboy Out to Corral Nomination," *Soda Springs Sun,* May 28, 1942, 1.

51. Arod Taylor, interview; Taylor, *The Way It Was,* 279.

52. "Taylor Jumps on Financiers," *Pocatello Tribune,* August 16, 1942, 1.

53. Peterson, *Prophet Without Honor,* 17.

54. "Idaho Merchants Rap Candidacy of Glen Taylor," *Post-Register,* October 29, 1942, 10.

55. "Singing Cowboy Out to Corral Nomination," 1.

56. *Pocatello Tribune,* August 16, 1942, as quoted in Peterson, *Prophet without Honor,* 20.

57. Taylor, *The Way It Was,* 204.

58. "'Bott' for Senator," *Post-Register,* October 22, 1944, 4.

59. "Cowboy Crooner Wins Seat in Senate," Associated Press story, *Fitchburg Sentinel,* November 9, 1944, 6.

60. "Idaho Senator Begins 'Paul Revere' Ride East," *Los Angeles Times,* October 27, 1947, 2.

61. "Senator Glen Taylor of Idaho Is Trying to Let America See How Soviets Must Feel," United Press International story, *Lubbock (TX) Evening Journal,* November 13, 1947, 16; "Senator Plans to Ride Horse across Continent," *Los Angeles Times,* October 21,

1947, 2; "Sen. Taylor Starts 'Paul Revere' Ride," United Press International story, *Daily Trojan* (University of Southern California), October 27, 1947, 1; "Horse Riding Senator Will Be Here Saturday," *El Paso Herald-Post*, October 30, 1947, 13.

62. On Taylor's pro–civil rights and Zionist record, see "Taylor Charged with Violating Segregation Law," *Albuquerque Journal*, May 3, 1948, 1; "Says Senators Ask Jews' Delegation," *New York Times*, May 23, 1945, 13; and W. H. Lawrence, "'Wallace or War' Keynotes Progressive Party Conclave," *New York Times*, July 24, 1948, 1. On radio, see "Puts FM in Field of Small Business," *New York Times*, December 14, 1945, 34. On the Columbia Valley Authority proposal, see "Cain Begins Slowdown Campaign against CVA," *(Idaho Falls) Post-Register*, April 24, 1949, 6.

63. Harold B. Hinton, "Bilbo Is Held Off," *New York Times*, January 4, 1947, 1.

64. Holmes Alexander, "What Will the Democrats Do about Glen Taylor?," *Los Angeles Times*, September 17, 1949, section A, 4.

65. "The Cowboy Crusader," editorial, *Odessa (TX) American*, November 26, 1947, 6.

66. Marquis Childs, "Taylor, Wallace's Running Mate, Is Actor with Streak of Innate Ham," *Janesville (WI) Daily Gazette*, August 20, 1948, 6.

67. Lawrence, "'Wallace or War,'" 1.

68. Thomas L. Stokes, "Washington Column," *(Hagerstown, MD) Daily Mail*, July 27, 1948, 8.

69. "Band Nine: Progressive Party Convention," *I Can Hear It Now—Vol. 2: Edward R. Murrow, Narrator*, phonograph, Columbia Records, 1949, ML 4261. Paradoxically, the Progressive Party Convention may have been the last time original songs were generated for the purpose of a campaign. I base my analysis in part on my reading of Robbie Lieberman, *My Song Is My Weapon: People's Songs, American Communism, and the Politics of Culture, 1930–50* (Urbana: University of Illinois Press, 1989), 126–39; Benjamin S. Schoening and Eric T. Kasper, *Don't Stop Thinking about the Music: The Politics of Songs and Musicians in Presidential Campaigns* (Lanham: Lexington Books, 2012); Stuart Schinler, "Campaign Music," in *Music in American Life: An Encyclopedia of Songs, Styles, Stars and Stories that Shaped Our Culture*, ed. Jacqueline Edmondson (Santa Barbara: ABC-CLIO, 2013), 177–78; Peter Argersinger, *The Limits of Agrarian Radicalism: Western Populism and American Politics* (Lawrence: University of Kansas Press, 1995), chap. 3; and Tom Waldman, *We All Want to Change the World: Rock and Politics from Elvis to Eminem* (Lanham: Taylor Trade, 2003).

70. See, for instance, Lieberman, *My Song*, 132–33, and Schoening and Kasper, *Don't Stop*, 122–23.

71. Richard Reuss with Joanne C. Reuss, *American Folk Music and Leftwing Politics, 1927–1957* (Lanham: Scarecrow Press, 2000), 198–203; Lieberman, *My Song*, 126–39; Ronald Cohen, *Rainbow Quest: The Folk Music Revival and American Society, 1940–1970* (Amherst: University of Massachusetts Press, 2002), 56–57.

72. Peter Seeger, phone interview, August 15, 2013, Beacon, New York.

73. Arod Taylor, interview.

74. Photograph, Sen. Glen Taylor (L) and Pete Seeger singing and playing at PAC

school, July 1946, Washington, DC, *Life* images, http://images.google.com/hosted /life/4c8bbd8a8d3ef5b4.html.

75. Arod Taylor, interview.

76. See, for instance, Taylor, *The Way It Was,* 203–5.

77. "Hear Senator Glen Taylor," advertisement, *Kansas City Star,* October 10, 1948, 56; "1,000 Hear Taylor Lash 'Dangerous Leaders,'" *Iowa City Press-Citizen,* October 14, 1948, 15.

78. "Taylor Will Speak Here Tomorrow at Luncheon," *Modesto (CA) Bee,* July 7, 1948, 8.

79. Curtiss D. MacDougall, *Gideon's Army* (New York: Marzani and Munsell, 1965), 529–31.

80. "James and Bonnie Thornton," in Frank Cullen, *Vaudeville Old and New: An Encyclopedia of Variety Performers in America,* vol. 1 (New York: Routledge, 2006), 1104.

81. See, for instance, "Retail Record Sales," *Billboard,* November 15, 1947, 27.

82. "Band Nine."

83. Norman Thomas, "Thomas Sees Third Party Platform as One of Trickery," *Oregonian,* July 26, 1948, 4.

84. Irwin Ross, *The Loneliest Campaign: The Truman Victory of 1948* (New York: New American Library, 1968), 246–47.

85. Arod Taylor, interview.

86. Peterson, *Prophet without Honor,* 169–71.

87. Taylor, *The Way It Was,* 407–9.

# CHAPTER THREE

# Weeping and Flamboyant Men

*Webb Pierce
and the
Campy
Theatrics
of Country
Music*

## STEPHANIE VANDER WEL

DECCA COUNTRY musician Webb Pierce was a highly successful 1950s recording artist of the Nashville country music industry. With the most number one country hits of that decade, he outshone many chart-hitting artists such as Eddy Arnold, Hank Williams, and Elvis Presley on Billboard's country music charts.[1] Yet chroniclers have largely ignored Pierce's market success and his musical contributions to honky tonk and rockabilly, both predominant styles of 1950s country music in which he recorded and helped to popularize. Historical narratives of honky-tonk music of the post–World War II period often focus on Williams's consummate ability to write and perform gripping songs that continue to serve as expressive templates of masculine failure and bravado for "hard" country styles. Within these histories, Williams's 1952 death appears to mark the end of the male honky-tonk era, leaving in its wake a country music aesthetic of polished arrangements of backup vocals and strings that have come to characterize the Nashville Sound. Scholars have often reported that it was not until Buck Owens's upbeat Bakersfield Sound or George Jones's Nashville-produced recordings that the honky-tonk poetics of masculine abjection came back into the commercial spotlight.[2] Well before Owens or Jones, however, Pierce had emerged as a skilled performer of honky-tonk ballads who attracted a sizable fan base. His tenor singing voice rendered dramatic and weeping tales of heartache to the wail of the electric steel guitar and later to the pedal steel guitar, reshaping the masculine pathos of loss and desire.

The question is, why have historians largely overlooked Pierce's musical mastery and market visibility? The answer is a complex one that must take into consideration the ways in which Pierce superseded the performative models of male honky-tonk music and provided a highly stylized and effeminate persona. Although in performance Pierce played the part of the weeping male figure who cried excessively over his emotional and romantic losses, offstage he made it a point to flaunt his commercial success and business savvy with flamboyant displays of material excess. He wore brightly colored suits designed by Nudie Cohn, drove a convertible car decorated with silver dollars and six-shooters, and charged tourists to view his exorbitantly expensive guitar-shaped swimming pool at his home residence in Nashville, despite the protests of his neighbors. His emphasis on personal grooming and fashion, characteristics often associated with the feminine, shaped his image into one of androgynous glamour, which stood in stark contrast to conventional representations of Cold War–era manhood and the country music industry's pursuits of middle-class respectability. Anxious about Pierce's flamboyance and effeminate image, country music trade presses continually attempted to mute his gaudiness by transforming him into a respectable, breadwinning family man who lived by the principles of self-control and good taste. Nevertheless, by the time of his death in 1991, the music industry remembered Pierce as a performer who "embodied all that was gaudy and glorious in country music."[3]

It just was not his eye for fashion, however, that set him apart from honky-tonk conventions. Pierce's stylized singing approach aestheticized the honky-tonk weeper. Since his vocal range was that of a tenor instead of a baritone (the voice type of Ernest Tubb and Williams), Pierce sang with ease and agility in a higher range. What is progressive about Pierce's image and vocal identity is that he broadened the expressive scope of honky-tonk music while helping to articulate different and, at times, contradictory ways of construing working-class identity. His emotive male body emphasized the ways in which working-class masculinity could be an ornate performance of gender bending that exceeded the established parameters of the country music industry generally and honky-tonk expression in particular. As such, this essay contributes to conversations about sexuality and country music by demonstrating the ways in which Pierce's performance embodied weeping males dressed in flamboyant fashions.

Since there has been little scholarship about Pierce's career, I pieced together his biography from Otto Kitsinger's retrospective and informative liner notes and Pierce's own publicity in several country music trade magazines.[4] The overall story that surfaced features many contradictory elements that have to do with the dueling dynamics of authenticity and commercialism, concepts that are often gendered as masculine and feminine, respectively.[5] Like in many biographies and publicity write-ups of country musicians, a repeating narrative in Pierce's story is the emphasis of his Southern musical roots. He is framed as a country boy from West Monroe, Louisiana, who had grown up on the family farm playing an inexpensive Sears Roebuck guitar. However, for Pierce, it took more than a foundation in Southern music making for him to make it in country music. As journalist Frank Harris stated in 1967, "Rarely has the world of show business seen a newcomer tackle the tremendous job of 'breaking the big time' with as much zest and determination as Webb displayed."[6]

Over the span of his career, Pierce's publicity stressed his commercial aspirations, often pointing out that Pierce's sheer perseverance, calculated connections with business leaders of the country music industry, and musical talent were the main factors that led to his illustrious career. As soon as he was discharged from military service following World War II, Pierce was determined to become a professional country performer, and he and his first wife, Betty Jane Lewis (whom he married in 1942), moved from their small hometown to the larger city of Shreveport in search of additional performance opportunities. While both Pierce and Lewis worked for Sears-Roebuck (with Pierce eventually becoming the buyer of men's clothes, already declaring his interest in fashion), the husband and wife team secured an early morning radio spot on KTBS as *Webb Pierce with Betty Jane, the Singing Sweetheart* in 1946.[7] Indeed, by 1949, each had their own individual recording contract with the independent label 4-Star Records. Pierce, who had a knack for discovering talented musicians, formed a band called the Southern Valley Boys with the singer Faron Young, pianist Floyd Cramer, steel guitarist Jimmy Day, and bassist Tillman Franks (who was also Pierce's manager during the Shreveport years).[8] With his skills as a performer and bandleader, Pierce and his ensemble (also referred to as the Louisiana Hayride Band) appeared on the rival KWKH's *Louisiana Hayride*—an up-and-coming barn dance program. Pierce even stopped appearing on KTBS to make it clear to the station's program director, Horace Logan, that he wanted to be regularly featured on the *Hayride*. Logan, who had a policy of not taking on musicians from competing radio stations, eventually hired Pierce in the latter part of 1949. By 1951, he had risen to be one of the *Hayride's* most prominent artists.[9]

Pierce's single-mindedness and ambition for a career in country music eventually drove his wife, Betty Jane, out of the marriage by 1950. Yet soon afterward, Pierce broke into the Nashville country scene when he signed with Decca Records in 1951, and he left the *Hayride* for the *Opry*, replacing Williams, who had been fired in 1952. Once in Nashville as an Opry guest and recording artist, Pierce quickly became visible as "the top Country singer of the day—and Decca's 'hottest' property," according to the trade magazine *Country Song Roundup*.[10] He recorded his first number one hit, "Wondering," (1951), a reworking of a Cajun folk tune.

Capitalizing on the song's success, Pierce established his performance persona as "The Wondering Boy" or "Wondering Webb." In the song, Pierce offers a youthful incarnation of masculinity, wondering or day-dreaming about the feminine and the possibilities of love and security without becoming moored to the masculine domestic breadwinner role or adopting a hypermasculine stance so as to rebel against such social conventions. Pierce's vocal delivery helps shape this pubescent identity of the "Wondering Boy." He immediately launches into a high range to begin the first four-bar phrase ("Wonderin', wonderin' who's kissing you"). After he holds onto the initial higher pitch (D4), he then descends via stepwise motion in a dotted rhythm followed by a triplet ("wonderin', wonderin'"), underlining the lightheartedness of his daydreaming. For the following four-bar phrase ("wonderin' wonderin' if you're wonderin' too"), he puts even more emphasis on the opening "wonderin'" lyric by reaching even higher in his range (E4). In effect, he sounds like a young, carefree man with his high-pitched voice dancing to the triple-meter pulse of the song. Moreover, apart from the bridge, where we learn of the male subject's desperation of praying for the return of his beloved, Pierce spends most of his time wondering about love with few concerns. As such, his "Wondering Boy" identity is not clearly tied to the topos of honky tonk—a style of music that addresses the complexities and paradoxes of adult love, sexuality, and alienation in a historical context marked by the social and cultural upheavals of the white Southern working class. Yet after his first hit song, Pierce recorded a string of successful numbers that not only took on the usual themes of honky tonk but also made those themes even more explicit. He paints an unambiguous picture of infidelity in "Back Street Affair" (1952) and dramatizes the lure of drinking in "There Stands the Glass" (1953), a song that radio stations banned until its popularity among listeners demanded it to be played, as reported by *Billboard*.[11]

Decca's Paul Cohen, realizing Pierce's efficacy as a performer and songwriter, gave him much autonomy in the recording studio. Not only did Pierce select his own song material, but he also chose which top Nashville session musicians would augment his band, the Wondering Boys (which regularly included Teddy Wilburn on rhythm guitar, Doyle Wilburn on rhythm guitar or string bass, Jay Kay on fiddle, Sonny Burnette on steel guitar, and Ike Inman on string bass). He decided the release dates of his recordings, often making numerous takes of the same song in search of that perfect sonic creation.[12] Pierce's outsized role in the recording studio—the large degree of control he had over the aesthetic directions, production decisions, and distribution timeline of his recordings—was extremely unusual for this era. Right when Nashville had arisen as a major production center of country music, Pierce appeared to be a musician who had his own artistic vision, picked out his song material, and helped produce his own recordings, qualities that often fall under the notions of male authenticity and creativity, not the feminine associated commercialism that Pierce came to embody and personify for many country music journalists and commentators.[13]

Pierce's hard work and musical talent met with unprecedented success. By 1955, he was the first artist to win *Billboard*'s coveted "Triple Crown Award" four distinct times with his recordings of "More and More" (1954), "In the Jailhouse Now" (1954), "I Don't Care" (1955), and "Love, Love, Love" (1955). Not only were these songs bestselling records, but they were also the most programmed on radio as well as the most played on jukeboxes. As *Billboard* stated in 1955, "No other artist in either country, rhythm and blues or pop classifications has won more than a single triple crown award since the special honors were inaugurated earlier this year."[14] Recognized by the both the popular music and the country music industries as the reigning star of the 1950s, Pierce's recording career eventually culminated in a total of 181 charted singles by 1976.[15]

In addition to being an effective performer and songwriter, Pierce had a shrewd ability to capitalize on business relationships and opportunities, often pushing the boundaries of "decent" business behavior. For example, he formed important and long-lasting professional and personal connections with prominent disc jockeys to encourage them to play his latest recording, helping to popularize his music. Specifically, he offered disc jockeys of far-reaching radio stations, such as Paul Kallinger of XERF in Del Rio, Texas, and Nelson King of WCKY in Cincinnati, various tokens of appreciation (such as wristwatches, expensive meals, and luxurious accommodations at Nashville's annual disc jockey conventions). These exchanges came before the payola scandal put an end to purchasing airtime through gifts or other forms of payment.

Pierce also was recognized as an industry leader soon after the country music business established itself in Nashville. As Richard Peterson and Diane Pecknold have individually demonstrated, WSM and the Grand Ole Opry in Nashville served as catalysts for the country music industry to centralize in Nashville. By the late 1940s, the industrial components of country music—the formal relationships between and among radio, touring, recording, song publishing, and songwriting—were firmly in place, enabling the country music industry to operate as a distinct identifiable field within the larger commercial forces of the popular music industry.[16] Within these developments, Pierce and Opry Artists service director Jim Denny established Cedarwood Publishing Company, which became one of Nashville's largest song publishers.[17] As a prominent recording artist,

Pierce convinced songwriters to give him equal ownership of their songs when he recorded them. He then encouraged the same songwriters to publish their material through Cedarwood, which would provide Pierce an additional cut of the royalties as the song publisher.[18] Yet it is important to keep in mind that despite his opportunistic business practices, Pierce helped a number of country songwriters, including Merle Kilgore and Mel Tillis, and discovered and promoted the talents of several important country musicians (including Young, Cramer, and the Wilburn Brothers) who helped shape the commercial and aesthetic directions of country music.

As the Nashville country music industry grew in prominence as a business and production center, publicists and journalists worked to promote the genre and artists as belonging to a respectable sphere of society. Industry personnel presented its participants as part of the middle class— the class stratum most associated with Tin Pan Alley—to compete against and strive for recognition from the Tin Pan Alley enterprise. Even in the 1950s, Hank Williams, with his marital problems, was presented as a devoted family man happily married to Audrey Shepard.[19] Pierce, however, defied all notions of middle-class decorum through his preoccupation with fashion and ostentatious glamour. He was a country star who had made it big, and he broadcast his economic and commercial success by means of flamboyant displays of wealth. Going against the routines that corporate America seemingly demanded of its gray suits and its blue-collar workforce during the Cold War era, Pierce embellished the visual markers of masculinity. He appeared in brightly colored suits embroidered with Western motifs (cactuses, wagon wheels, flowers, and lassos) or with music motifs (eighth notes, treble clefs, and 45 records), playing an essential role in presenting Southern blue-collar masculinity as a dazzling spectacle.

Although it was the beginning of an era when male honky-tonk singers (such as Williams) and rockabilly stars donned Cohn's spectacular designs (e.g., Elvis Presley's gold lamé outfit), Pierce became intricately linked to the fashion designer. Not only did Pierce wear Cohn's red, canary yellow, or turquoise suits, but he also purchased Cohn's custom-designed convertibles, transforming the automobile's symbolism of economic and geographic mobility into an over-the-top showpiece. Many working-class and rural Southerners had bought their first automobile during World War II with their defense earnings or soldier's pay. By the 1950s, stock car racing emerged as an emblem and expression of Southern working-class masculinity and virility.[20] But rather than buy an automobile geared for speed and racing, Pierce purchased a convertible built for show that turned working-class car culture into a glitzy exhibit. As publicized in *Country Song Roundup*, Pierce's 1962 Pontiac Bonneville has "13 guns mounted on it, and they are all real. The upholstery is all hand tool leather. There are a thousand silver dollars mounted inside, the floor boards are covered with *unborn* calf" (emphasis added).[21] Webb's Pontiac seemed to be in competition with Elvis's Cadillac (which was painted with a customized finish of crushed diamonds and fish scales) for the prize of most ornate. Like Elvis's Cadillac (which RCA sent on a national tour), Webb's publicity often showcased his car. For example, the cover for his 1962 LP, *Cross Country: Webb Pierce*, features the singer in a brightly colored turquoise suit decorated with gold lamé about to get into the convertible Pontiac. With the top down, the viewer is able to take in the entirety of Pierce's penchant for gaudy splendor.

"Ostentatious display is, particularly in American culture, often deeply gendered (as feminine) and racialized (as other, and darker—usually black and Latin)," as argued by Robynn Stilwell.[22] Pierce's performance costumes were not only extravagantly designed but also inspired by the dress of women. Designer Cohn stated that his creations were specifically patterned after "flashy looking women" and that "every man has an aspect of woman in his personality that longs to be expressed." The extensive floral embroideries along the sleeves of Cohn's suits for men, according to historian Peter La Chapelle, were "especially influenced by the dense statin-stitched embroidery present on the festive blouses and waistcoats, or *Keptáree*, that Ukrainian brides traditionally wore on their wedding days."[23] Pierce thus dressed in styles that embraced the feminine at a time when normative society more usually warned against the look and manner of "effeminates" and "pinks." Cold War–era politics prized social and political containment in support of normative gender roles as a means to protect the United States from what was believed to be the nefarious spread of Communism. With social and political leaders, namely, Senator Joseph McCarthy, linking homosexuality with Communism, much of American society grew fearful that overbearing and authoritarian women (a supposed phenomenon known as "momism") would effeminize their sons and churn out a generation of subversive gay men susceptible to the degenerative influences of Communism.[24]

Pierce combined his image of androgynous glamour with his "Wondering Boy" persona, offering an alternative image of country music masculinity sounded via a "hard" musical style. Although he addressed such topics as infidelity and focused on tales of defeatism and self-pity—common themes in honky tonk—Pierce did not present swaggering displays of masculine bravado.[25] The physical and symbolic site of the honky tonk itself has been interpreted as a man's world, one consisting of hard drinking and fighting, of "both camaraderie and violence."[26] Bill Malone identifies the activities of the honky tonk as comprising "ritualized expression of manhood," or as Pamela Fox writes, the honky tonk is "a masculinized 'home' for its patrons" who yearn nostalgically for the domestic and feminized ideals of the past.[27]

The music tied to the architectural, performative, and figurative site of the honky tonk was a response to the complexities of modernity, displacement, and the shifting roles of men and women during and after World War II. Honky-tonk performers often disclosed the anxieties of class and displacement largely through the metaphors of sexuality and domesticity. For instance, Al Dexter's "Honky-Tonk Blues" (1936), the first song to refer to the honky tonk as a distinct space, shapes the honky tonk into a hedonistic site of male sexual desire for a "honky-tonky baby girl." Ernest Tubb's music often encapsulates similar themes about the sexual lure and revelry of the juke joint in the song "I Ain't Going Honky-Tonkin' Anymore" (1941) and themes of masculine vulnerability in the hit "Walkin' the Floor over You" (1941). Here the male subject pines for the return of his beloved to their shared domestic life. While the protagonist remains home, the woman is the one who appears out in the world in her refusal to adhere to normative definitions of gender. Tubb's songs link the instabilities of romantic love to women's abandonment of the domestic sphere, a common narrative strategy in male honky tonk.[28] Hank Williams continues many of these sentiments in his music. He portrays the honky tonk as a site of masculine defeat in songs such as "Honky-Tonk Blues" and underscores the painful distinction of class contrasted with the ideological definitions of middle-class manhood in many of his honky-tonk ballads about unrequited love. As Richard Leppert and George Lipsitz have argued, Williams as a performer and songwriter "lamented the schisms between men and women, resisted the dominant oedipal narrative, and sought closer connections to women."[29]

Yet for some scholars, the discursive practices of honky tonk include self-conscious portraits of how white, Southern, working-class masculinity lies at the margins of modernity. With humorous or tragic sentiments, honky tonk, according to Barbara Ching, constitutes a burlesque of masculine abjection that articulates and makes fun of the subject position of the low other in American society.[30] In so doing, male performers of hard country "complicate or reject the 'natural,' 'uncultured' state that they supposedly reflect."[31] In this sense, honky tonk as a demonstrative "hard" country style intertwines the theatrical with the notions of the authentic. The lone honky-tonk male figure drowning his sorrows in the local juke joint, for example, "can at once function as a familiar circulating trope, prone to exaggeration, and as a 'realistic' representation of an identifiable bar culture embraced by this music's audience," according to Fox.[32]

Within the play of the theatrical with the authentic, Tubb and Williams (the main innovators of honky tonk) had established the style in the Nashville production center of country music. Tubb projected an image of sincerity, partly owing to his singing style, and embodiment of respectability as a well-established performer who knew firsthand the challenges of a hardscrabble life but overcame those obstacles with age and maturity. Williams, on the other hand, seemed to live a life that resembled the very tales of his songs about the cold and cheating hearts of women, masculine lonesomeness, and the sordid attractiveness of honky tonks.[33] Although the country music industry tried to market Williams as a content domestic breadwinner, his personal struggles with alcoholism and his turbulent marriage to Audrey Shepard were well known.

Unlike Williams, who "established a newly heightened mode of identification between performer and audience," Pierce continually made it clear that he was offering a rendition of the low other.[34] Yet he did not simply play the part of the down-and-out man who attempts to escape from his sorrows in the masculinized space of the working-class bar. Instead, he offered a stylized model of the weepy male that bordered on the effeminate and theatrical. Pierce, thus, was a "countrified spectacle," underlining the fact that his costumes and musical utterances were a "performance rather than a spontaneous expression of some pure emotion or state of being."[35]

Although artists such as Buck Owens clearly understood how to magnify country music's sad and lonely tropes in songs like "Act Naturally" (1963), Pierce, in the 1950s, had already intensified the sentiments of heartache and masculine vulnerability. With a high tenor singing voice, he exceeded the vocal traditions of Tubb and Williams and established a new standard of expression. His ornate singing style signaled emotional excess, and his visual showiness (symbolic of his material success) set him apart from the next generation of country artists, for example, George Jones and Merle Haggard, who looked more to Williams as their model, and conflated the biographical with the performative. Crucially, Pierce's songs of heartache did not extend to his personal life. His publicity, hiding the fact that he was married to Betty Jane before his career took off in Nashville, often presented him as an alluring bachelor until his (second) marriage, during which he continually showed off his success and fame. In other words, Pierce did not simply offer a burlesque performance of masculine abjection. His embodiment of showy fashion combined with this singing style pushed the gendered parameters of honky tonk to the effeminate, clearly defying the gender codes of 1950s country music.

Pierce's singing style was largely indebted to the crooning techniques that first became part of mainstream popular music in the late 1920s and early 1930s. The technology of microphone amplification encourages vocalists to croon their melodic lines and inflect their tones with subtle variations that include vocal slides and swoops, quiet sighs, hushed whispers, and understated exhalations. Popular singers such as Rudy Vallee, Gene Autry, and Bing Crosby emerged as national stars for the ways in which their crooning devices could convey emotional intimacy, vulnerability, and sincerity. As Allison McCracken has demonstrated, because of their widespread commercial success, these crooners did much to transform the image and the sound of white masculinity. Before Vallee, crooning had been associated with African-American and women performers, in particular the figure of the black mammy singing softly to her infant charges. Thus, when white men crooned about emotional matters of the heart, dominant society often heard this mode of vocal production as an aural example of gender and racial deviance, effeminacy, and even queerness.[36]

Throughout his career, Pierce situated himself within a context of 1930s crooning, stating how the cowboy crooner Gene Autry was a significant influence on his singing style and performance persona. Autry, who cultivated a singing cowboy image first on the Chicago radio station WLS and then in Republic's Hollywood films, adopted the crooning techniques of his contemporaries in popular music and projected an intimate singing voice that often crossed the heterosexual/homosexual divide. Although the cowboy is often envisioned as a heroic representation of masculinity who embodies the ideals of Manifest Destiny, American exceptionalism, and individualism, Autry's singing voice runs the risk of emasculating the Western figure.[37] In his lyrical songs of the open range, such as "Dear Old Western Skies" (1934), Autry includes a variety of crooning techniques. Through the use of portamento, he lingers over his vocal lines with elongated slides to and from sustained pitches, accentuates the ending of phrases with the use of a wide vibrato, and inflects his tone with timbral variations of vocal register.

Autry's singing style, however, contributes to his emotive persona on radio and in film as the singing cowboy who could freely express his emotions and desires. Nevertheless, as an effusive cowboy, he still has to defend his masculinity. When he starred in his first feature-length film, *Tumbling Tumbleweed* (1935), playing his radio and recording persona the singing cowboy Gene Autry, the ruffian characters accuse him of being a "lavender cowboy" for his intimate rendition of his sentimental hit "That Silver-Haired Daddy of Mine." He performs this number after learning of the murder of his father, making it clear that his immediate response is to mourn and express his feelings through song instead of declaring revenge or displaying a brawny masculinity. In film after film, Autry rescues his performance identity from that of the effeminate-sounding crooner by eventually proving that he could ward off wrongdoers and protect the underclass by playing the part of a heterosexual, valiant male hero-protagonist.[38]

Pierce, who, as was mentioned above, took Autry as his performative model, adopted many of the same qualities of the cowboy star. Like Autry, he wore stylized Western wear and developed a distinctly expressive singing voice. As he stated, "I used to try and sing like him and then I realized there's only one Gene Autry, I'd better develop my own style so then I started singing in the high register."[39] Unlike Autry, Pierce was not a baritone but a tenor. Yet in his higher range, Pierce developed a crooning mode of delivery and included vocal embellishments geared for the microphone. In other words, Pierce combined a high tessitura with vocal devices that engendered the sonic impression of intimacy, emotional vulnerability, and fragility.

Pierce also comes from a vocal tradition in country music where male singers have projected a range of registers and vocal techniques. Riley Puckett and Jimmie Rodgers include yodeling passages to their falsetto ranges in their commercial recordings for a hillbilly or old-time music market. Both were performers of vaudeville where the yodel was used in a variety of contexts: blackface minstrel songs, blues numbers, lullabies, and ethnic tunes. In his blues numbers and sentimental songs, Rodgers's yodels usually unfold in a limited range of sequential sixths in which he ascends to and descends from the sustained notes of a thin-sounding falsetto range, contrasting with his lower singing voice. Rodgers's yodels could signify a range of meaning—masculine swagger in his blues songs or a lone cry for the past in his nostalgic numbers.[40] The yodel is a technique that involves a glottal stop from the chest voice to the head voice, accentuating the break between registers. In contrast to Rodgers's languid-sounding yodels, country singers like Elton Britt could demonstrate an athletic Alpine yodel with a virtuosic display of moving back and forth over the break between registers and reaching and holding the high F5.

In his honky-tonk ballads, Pierce does not yodel or even feature elongated cries to his falsetto range. The closest vocal technique to a yodel that he employs is the vocal tear or hiccup, a device that involves highlighting the break between the chest and falsetto registers. In a slow song about heartache and desire, the singer's use of vocal tears literally sounds as if he were choking up with emotion as he croons his melodic lines.

What largely characterizes Pierce's singing voice is use of his upper tenor range. Many country artists have similar vocal ranges. Bill Monroe, the father of bluegrass, projects a high, clear tenor voice, singing harmony above the lead vocals and creating what has famously been referred to as that "high lonesome sound." Bluegrass singers have followed suit ever since, making the high tenor voice part of the norm of this country style. But Pierce develops his high singing manner within honky tonk, a style of music that has followed the conventions of popular music by favoring baritones over high-pitched male voices.

Lower-voiced male singers came to be the norm in 1930s popular music when clear divisions and hierarchies were being established along the lines of race, class, gender, and sexuality. When Rudy Vallee started his singing career as a crooner with a tenor voice, social commentators exploded with anxiety about his high effeminate whines. He did not sound like a proper man as he crooned largely to an audience of women about love and courtship. As McCracken argues, his intimate vocal aesthetic "blurred gender lines at a time when gender distinctions and behaviors were being newly emphasized, narrowed, and policed."[41] By the 1950s, when Pierce's songs hit the Billboard country charts, divisions along the lines of voice types and gender and sexuality were further cemented in the popular imagination. The pervasiveness of masculinist vocal norms in popular music and society at large resulted directly from the increasingly "federalized homophobia of World War II and the cold war."[42]

In contrast to Pierce, his predecessors in honky tonk, Dexter, Tubb, and Williams, were baritones. Although Dexter does include some crooning techniques of singing in a higher range with a light thin voice then dropping down into his lower tessitura, Tubb's singing voice is comparable in register to his speaking voice that helps infuse his narratives of heartache and masculine vulnerability with sincerity and realism.[43] Williams, on the other hand, includes a variety of vocal devices that highlight the distinct timbres of his lower and upper ranges, similar to Roy Acuff's vocal approach. Williams would often contrast his nasally strained higher register against the lower resonant timbres of his baritone voice.[44] In such songs as "Cold, Cold Heart," Williams reaches for the higher notes of the melody by tightening and raising his larynx and pushing his chest voice out through his nose, producing a singing voice that sounds as if it is about to break under vocal and emotional duress. Williams realizes sonically the emotional despondency of the displaced, working-class Southern man mourning the "loss of women as the embodiment of a mythologized 'home.'"[45] Although the honky tonk is a working-class bar—a predominantly masculine sphere—the music associated with this figurative and architectural space showcases emotional men crying over the ideals of some forgotten past and struggling with the anxieties of dislocation and alienation in industrialized urban centers. With Williams's vocal style of strain producing what sounds like raw emotion, his vocal mode and expressive narratives could be interpreted as belonging to the feminine, "the nonrational, the nonintellectual."[46] But in the same song, Williams can drop to the lower resonant-sounding range and swing the melody in a relaxed manner, offering a musical image of a confident man who easily melts the cold heart of his beloved. In his upbeat songs, like "Hey Good Lookin'" or "Honky-Tonkin'," Williams projects a vocal identity of masculine bravado as he plays the role of the carousing man luring women away from domestic settings for fleeting moments of sexual pleasure.[47] With his use of range, timbre, and register, Williams vocally provides a variety of emotions and subject positions, from the heartbroken male wailing in despair to a hypermasculine identity.

In his honky-tonk ballads, Pierce, on the other hand, continues and intensifies the vocal practices of emotional singing. He sonically enacts the weeping and wailing male subject who mourns over his heartaches and desperately longs for the feminine for emotional and domestic security—the linchpins of middle-class comfort. But he cultivates a different singing approach from that of Tubb or Williams. Although Williams sounds as if he has no need for a microphone, especially when he sings in his higher range, Pierce relies heavily on the microphone to amplify the vocal nuances of his upper register through ornamentation, shifts of timbre, and phrasing. Singing with a flexible larynx, Pierce's vocal ease and agility enables him to decorate his melodic lines with slides and mordents without belting his vocal line. Also, in contrast to Williams, who projects from the frontal area of the nasal chamber, Pierce, at different times, sings from the back of the throat or with an open throat for timbral inflections. He still produces a nasal vocality but one that does not sound excessively labored as he vocally decorates his melodic lines.

In this context, Pierce offers emotive and expressive techniques that would increase and lay bare the gender crossings of honky tonk. For his first Decca recording session, Pierce effectively demonstrates his displays of emotions in "If Crying Would Make You Care" (1951). The narrator, abandoned in love, pleads for his beloved to reciprocate his affections in the opening eponymous hook (the A phrase). His vocal line begins with a stark leap of a fourth, landing emphatically on the first scale degree to emphasize the word "crying," which he then embellishes vocally. He slides up a third to his higher range on the word "cry," projecting a clear tone on the long *y* sound by opening his throat while inflecting his tone with the use of a wide vibrato. He then drops a fourth on the second syllable ("ing"), sonically realizing the act of weeping. Supporting the melodic line, the harmonic movement from the tonic chord to the mediant harmony underlines his stylized tears by coloring the word "crying" with a minor inflection. He finishes the vocal line to explain that the point of his tears is to bring back his beloved, "If crying would make you care, I would cry a million tears or more." Pierce sounds as if he is already crying those million tears with each return of the A phrase (in this AABA song form). Thus, his singing paints a picture of a man weeping uncontrollably to win the heart of his beloved.

Pierce, however, is not alone in providing vocal embellishments in honky-tonk songs. Lefty Frizzell, Pierce's contemporary in honky tonk, also develops a more stylized manner of singing. Like Pierce, Frizzell inflects his phrases with vocal tears, melismas, sliding into notes and bending pitches. In songs like "If You've Got the Money, I've Got the Time" (1950), Frizzell croons his honky-tonk lyrics, offering a more polished and elaborate vocal approach for this hard style of country music. He also would sing from the back of the throat. However, unlike Pierce, he could mediate his crooning techniques by singing in the lower range of his baritone voice, the warm rich tones of the chest register. Like other baritone crooners, Frizzell remasculinizes his voice by using his lower range and sounding like a "proper" man. Bing Crosby also deploys the lower tones of his baritone range to mediate the crooner persona of effeminacy and queerness.[48]

Unlike Frizzell, though, Pierce croons about crying over his heartaches in the tenor range. As McCracken has noted, "Because gender roles were so strongly polarized in American cold war culture, and because homosexuality was still widely tied to gender presentation, any hint of femininity in men made them sexually suspect."[49] Also, in many of his songs, Pierce uses his upper register to enact the sounds of a weeping man. Frizzell may have sung about crying, but he does not necessarily use word painting to portray the very act of crying. Pierce weeps in his songs, similar to the way that Roy Orbison wails in his falsetto range "crying over you" in his song "Crying" (1961), offering an alternative mode of rock masculinity.[50]

Importantly, Pierce was not the only tenor to sing honky tonk in the 1950s. Hank Locklin, for example, had hit recordings, notably "Send Me the Pillow You Dream On" and "Please Help Me I'm Falling," which were not necessarily about loss but rather about being in love more generally. Locklin uses his tenor voice to express his devotion to his objects of desire, unlike Pierce who specializes in honky-tonk ballads that portray the tearful male protagonist, mourning the loss of the feminine in his failure to achieve domestic felicity. In "Crying over You" (1958), Pierce depicts a male subject who cries throughout the night over his broken heart. Exhausted from his excessive crying, the subject vows to stop weeping. Yet Pierce decorates vocally the word "crying" with a downward vocal slide of a third, once again affecting the sounds of sobbing in his melodic line, as if he is unable to hold back the tears. He strives but fails to keep his feelings under control. Although he attempts to present a virile image of manhood, one who plans on "painting the town," he falls victim to his despondency and alienation.

Pierce continually demonstrates that his emotions are the governing elements of his songs. For example, he wails dramatically the opening of his 1955 tune "Yes I Know Why (I Want to Cry)," in the highest part of his range, a cappella. Through the use of portamento and by singing behind the beat, Webb's expressive voice takes center stage to underline the male protagonist's emotional urgency and painful feelings of unrequited love. Moreover, Pierce's song bears some resemblance to Williams's "I'm So Lonesome I Could Cry" (1949). With both songs in triple meter, Pierce's phrase in his bridge "I'm so low, I could die" gestures melodically and lyrically to William's cadential line "I'm so lonesome, I could cry." The first part of each phrase (Pierce's "I'm so low" and Williams's "I'm so lone") includes similar melodic lines with each singer landing on the downbeat and holding onto the words "low" and "lone" in their upper registers, respectively. Pierce, however, surpasses the effusive utterances by singing the lyrics in a slightly higher range. Thus, he finishes the phase by declaring "I could die" at the melodic apex of F4 on the word "die" (a fifth higher than Williams's melodic climax on the syllable "lone"), outperforming Williams's vocal and lyrical sentiments. Whereas Williams could merely cry from his lonesomeness, Pierce's heightened lyricism makes it clear that he could die from his emotional lowness.

Pierce's dramatic vocal approach of slowly rendering his melodic lines with the use of slurs and slides in his upper tenor range effectively portrays tenderhearted or emotionally afflicted narratives. He, for instance, begins "Slowly"(1954) with a similar vocal and theatrical flair as in his crying honky-tonk ballads. However, he adds an additional component to the expressivity of the song by introducing the pedal steel guitar. On this song, Bud Isaacs plays a Bigsby double-neck pedal steel with two pedals, which allow him to provide a richer sonic texture of diatonic pitch bends.[51] "Experimenting with the melodic possibilities of the pedals," according to Timothy Miller, Isaacs aims "to imitate the sound of two fiddles playing harmony."[52] With the use of his first pedal, Isaacs begins "Slowly" in the middle range of the instrument, embellishing on the opening tonic harmony by gradually bending the tonic chord (in first inversion) into the subdominant and then back to the tonic. The pedal steel, then, leaps from the middle range to the higher register of the instrument on the dominant chord bending into and resolving to the tonic. Pierce attempts to match the high whine of the instrument by wailing a cappella an ascending stepwise three-note line on the word "slowly," in his upper range. As in his other weepers, Pierce's vocals are the main focus as he sings out of meter to elongate the word "slowly." His word painting continues as he renders a descending stepwise slide followed by a downward leap on the words, "I'm falling." Keeping the listener in suspense, Pierce eventually reveals that his precarious fall does not have to do with a broken heart this time. He croons that he is falling more in love with his beloved in the lower range of his voice, providing a warm, secure sound to his depiction of heterosexual desire. In what appears as a conventional romantic song, Pierce still does not act the part of a traditional man. The woman of the story is the one who takes an active role in winning over the love of the male narrator who "can't hide from my feelings no matter what I do." His focus on his emotions still governs the narrative of his songs.

Pierce's honky-tonk songs, however, were not the only cultural forms that featured emotional men during the decade. As Tom Lutz demonstrates, 1950s classic Hollywood melodramas, specifically the small subset known as "male weepies," presented plots in which male characters cried over the "pressures to strive to fulfill and at the same time reject the dominant male roles of the time."[53] Such films as *Giant* (1956) and *Home*

*from the Hill* (1959) responded to the masculine crisis of Cold War conformity by rebelling against the gendered and social confines of the era and
searching for a resolution that met or expanded upon gendered expectations. This process of gender (trans)formation often erupted in cathartic
tears. Male crying, thereby, could be a tool for social critique and political
change even as melodramatic narratives often encouraged its characters
and audience to weep for traditional gender roles.

I would argue that Pierce's tears were a response to the contradictions
of 1950s manhood. Like his counterparts in male weepies, Pierce sonically
realized the tears of his male protagonists to articulate the tensions between longing for perceived notions of traditional gender roles and want-
ing to reshape manhood into a model of identity that could break free
from Cold War–era definitions. Pierce, then, could weep over the loss of
the idealized past while still pushing for progressive models of masculinity. For example, his duets with the 1950s "Queen of Country Music," Kitty
Wells, illuminate the ways in which he could play a conventional masculine role while still sonically crossing gender divisions. Both Wells and
Pierce were Decca recording artists, climbing to the heights of their careers at the same time. As the country music industry noted, "Their voices
blend just beautifully."[54] Pierce's high tenor voice joins Wells's strained
alto in a similar register to illustrate that the contested terrain of romantic
love could cross gender boundaries. In their 1956 song "Can You Find It
in Your Heart?," Pierce plays the role of the carousing husband begging
to return to his domestic mate, enacted by Wells, who refuses to continue
a relationship riddled with deception. The song positions the sexualized
man—who desires but fails to win back the heart of his beloved—against
the monogamous women—a model of feminine respectability.

The song's arrangement, however, does not clearly distinguish between
the two vocal parts that represent these gendered subjects. The singers
exchange melodic phrases of the same range in an antiphonal setting, providing the effect of a shared sonic space. Wells, for instance, does not sing
a higher melody to separate her vocal line from that of Pierce. Also, Pierce
does not lower his vocal range to differentiate his singing role from that
of Wells. Instead, he matches Wells's vocal line note for note. Their performance is one of gender ambiguity. Apart from the difference in their
timbres—an agile tenor voice and a labored alto—there is little else to

distinguish Wells's vocal part from Pierce's. They contest and negotiate the terms of heterosexual love with the same melodic material and vocal ranges. Although he sings from the position of a carousing, heterosexual man, the vocal arrangement blurs his sonic identity with Wells's and gestures simultaneously to androgyny and the conflation of masculinity with femininity.

Pierce's high-pitched emotive voice combined with his flashy look and manner opened up new models of masculinity that bent gender norms and resulted in a campy sensibility. If camp is a form of "failed seriousness" that plays with the codes of sexuality and gender, then the incongruities arising from Pierce's enactments of weeping high-pitched males alongside those of conspicuous consumption serve as an example of country music's campy theatrics.[55] In other words, he played the part of the emotional heartbroken male while dressed like a Southern working-class dandy. As Susan Sontag had stated, "Camp is a vision of the world in terms of style—but a particular kind of style. It is the love of the exaggerated."[56] Pierce's image was based on the exaggerated and makes sense as a performance of Southern masculinity within country music when viewed through the lens of gay culture. Nadine Hubbs has demonstrated in her essay in this collection that the locus of homosexuality resided within the working class until the 1970s. In the 1950s, the gendered codes of the working class still shared much in common with those of gay culture. Pierce's singing voice and ostentatious image can still serve as reminders of the malleability and alternative forms of not only working-class masculinity but also Southern masculinity. Historians have illuminated the ways in which "the rural nature of the South, its class system, and segregation created a distinct gay and lesbian culture."[57] Within rural or small-town communities, individuals may have referred to lesbians and gay men as "old maids" or "sissies" in conversation, but few took public action against them. Gay culture was also a vibrant component of Southern urban areas, such as Atlanta and Richmond, as it was throughout the rest of the country. Tearooms and other public domains (for example, Atlanta's Piedmont Park or Richmond's men's rooms and bars) were known as important urban institutions for gay men despite the draconian lengths officials went to maintain sexual order and contain the burgeoning visibility of gay male culture in public, urban spaces.[58]

Pierce's playing with the hetero/homosexual paradigm and pushing against masculine conformity and restraint had much in common with the flamboyant performances of Liberace, who also had attracted a blue-collar and lower middle-class audience by the 1950s.[59] Unlike Liberace, Pierce was probably not a closeted gay man. Yet Pierce's emotional utterances combined with his glitzy costumes offered effeminate and stylized representations that had much to do with the established rituals of cross-dressing in Southern culture. For example, "womanless weddings," originating as Southern folk dramas, featured men dressed as brides and bridesmaids to lampoon a scared rite and to open up a cultural and theatrical space of gender and sexual fluidity similar to Pierce's performances.[60]

Pierce's stagy presentations did not preclude emotional identification, however. His audience could still understand the social purposes and take pleasure in his honky-tonk performances by becoming "engrossed by the situation and exaggeration simultaneously."[61] His singing voice, in particular, was instrumental in transporting listeners into the world of his musical tales of longing and loss, sentiments the members of his audience could relate to given their uneasiness about their changing circumstances. A female fan, for example, declared, "Webb has a voice that actually can make a body cry or laugh, depending on the mood Webb instills in the tune." Another female follower of Webb stated, "In all of my born days, I've never heard anyone sing as beautifully as Webb Pierce does."[62] The qualities of Pierce's singing voice—high range, crooned embellishments, sonic enactments of weeping—all contributed to his intensified vocal deliveries that so effectively reached the ears of his listening audience.

Because of Pierce's androgynous embodiment of fashion and effeminate singing voice, the country music industry attempted to sanitize his image by making him into a proper, heterosexual family man—the standard definition of Cold War–era masculinity and conformity. To do so, the country music trade press had to do more than simply peel away the layers of glitter: Pierce's very biography had to be altered. His publicity, for example, never mentioned that he had been divorced prior to his move to Nashville. Rather, he appeared as a young, attractive bachelor (younger than he actually was), whose appeal had to do with his heterosexuality. The article entitled "Wondering Webb," for example, declared it was surprising that Pierce at the age of 27 was still single. "Anyone would think by now he would be hitched for he's just as handsome, personable and versatile as a chap could be and you can well imagine all the girls that would find themselves available to the popular artist with black wavy hair and brown eyes."[63] In reality, Pierce was in his thirties and divorced when this publicity blurb was written.[64]

After Pierce had married (for the second time) and started a family, *Country Song Roundup* in 1956 took full advantage of advertising Pierce as a domesticated man: "Everyone knows Webb Pierce, the artist, but not many know Webb, the family man. On this page we proudly present exclusive photos of the nation's Number One Country Singer at home with his charming family. We hope this will better acquaint you with Webb— and also serve to introduce his charming wife Audrey and baby daughter Debbie." The article continued by emphasizing the centrality of domesticity to Pierce's astounding career: "With a wonderful family to inspire his every effort, it's no wonder that Webb Pierce has been so successful."[65] Locating the impetus of his success within the ideals of the nuclear family helped to mediate Pierce's flamboyant displays that questioned gender norms.

A 1955 *Country and Western Jamboree* article, however, appeared to struggle with how to frame Pierce: a known showman or a respectable, middle-class man. The accompanying photo captures the tensions between spectacle and restraint. Standing in front of his suburban home with his wife and daughter, Pierce seems to invite the reader into his home. Once inside, we see that Piece is a "family man" singing and playing his guitar to his "greatest admirers . . . his wife and daughter." In another photo, "Daughter Debbie" gives "daddy a bit hug!" Up against these idyllic images of domestic bliss, a photo captures Pierce in his dressing room preparing for a performance. Attired in one of Nudie Cohn's ornate designs, Pierce is surrounded by a number of other Nudie suits while he combs his jet-black hair back in his full-length mirror. The camera captures Pierce's reflection for us readers who are watching the transformation from breadwinning father figure to glitzy performer.[66]

Even in the late 1960s, the country music industry was hard at work, striving to shape Pierce into a dignified figure of country music. *Country Song Roundup* once again insisted that the country star was "an easy going soft spoken gentleman whose wife, children, home, and business reflect exactly what he is. There is no show for showiness. There is no snootiness for the sake of looking down on others. There is none of the 'nouveau riche' attitude for appearance."[67] Pierce's so-called good taste had much to do with this role as a breadwinning father, even though his penchant for extravagance was well known in country music circles. His publicity was meant to place him within the sanctity of the domestic, thereby disavowing his ostentatiousness.

Despite the efforts of the country music industry to mediate Pierce's flamboyant image, it did not work. In 1991, country music journalist Rich Kienzle asked the question of why Pierce, who was not nominated to the Country Music Hall of Fame until 1990, lost out to Tennessee Ernie Ford. Although Ford was an important artist, Kienzle wrote, "Webb's recording success far outdid Ford's." Kienzle points out that Pierce's business savvy set him apart from his contemporaries: "Pierce knew the Art of the Deal. He understood that music, even in the Nashville of the 50's, was a *business*" (emphasis in original). He wasn't necessarily one of those "good ol' boys whose business never extended beyond buying the next Cadillac... Pierce's plain-spokenness, business savvy and independence set him apart; he didn't cultivate the sweet image a Hall of Famer is supposed to project."[68] Kienzle's statements hold many contradictions. He gives the impression that Pierce's business tactics were far more sophisticated than the usual country musician. However, the country music industry, by late 1940s, was a well-established business with practitioners such as Ernest Tubb, Roy Acuff, and Fred Rose, to name a few, who definitely knew the "art of the deal." Moreover, independence and plainspokenness are qualities usually touted in biographies and historiographies of country musicians. Kienzle's explanations of why Pierce was not revered within the country music industry have to do with the concept of masculine authenticity. He did not mask his success with a persona steeped within the signs of down-home country credibility. As Kienzle alludes to, Pierce marketed an ostentatious image "with his guitar-shaped swimming pool and silver dollar-studded Pontiac . . . his rhinestone-encrusted Nudie suits and patent leather hair." Pierce's business savvy thus translated into showy displays of wealth and fashion that shaped his musical identity into an ornate staging of masculinity far from the country music industry's middle-class and heterosexual definitions of gender.

In general, Pierce's performative body was one of excess, spilling over the boundaries of 1950s containment and brushing against a camp aesthetic. The country music industry was embarrassed by Pierce's gaudiness and blatant artifice evidenced by the ways in which it tried to remake his image into one of "good" and moderate taste. With flamboyance, Pierce made it clear that masculinity could be an elaborate and demonstrative performance. In turn, the reasons that Pierce has been pushed to the sidelines of history have to do with how he challenged 1950s gendered and sexual norms. Aestheticizing the gendered codes of male honky tonk, his high-pitched singing voice and vocal embellishments effeminized the honky-tonk loner. He cried for the loss of traditional gender roles while broadening gendered expectations. Because he was such a prominent star of country music, he could encourage a new and progressive model of working-class masculinity that did not succumb to the acculturation of the middle class or to hypermasculine versions of working-class bravado. Rather, he reshaped working-class masculinity to be an identity associated with images of androgyny and glamour. He intensified the expressions of soft men, those "pinks" and "effeminates," during an era when gender and sexual divisions were clear and policed. As a result, restoring Pierce's forgotten legacy can serve to remind us of the ways in which country music conservatism can erase the nuances and significance of performance. With a closer look, we, too, can be dazzled by Pierce's turquoise and canary yellow suits and his high-pitched singing voice realizing the tears of social and progressive change.

## NOTES

1. Otto Kitsinger, liner notes to *Webb Pierce, The Wondering "Boy," 1951–1958*, Bear Family Records, 1990, n.p. Bob Battle, "Web Pierce . . . Comin' Back!" *Country Song Roundup,* April 1976, 9, stated that Pierce had 181 charted records and Arnold had 187.

2. Jocelyn Neal, *Country Music: A Cultural and Stylistic History* (New York: Oxford University Press, 2013), 157, states that when Hank Williams died, the era of honky-tonk music passed with him. Barbara Ching's *Wrong's What I Do Best: Hard Country Music and Contemporary Culture* (New York: Oxford University Press, 2001), 26–46, proceeds historically from Hank Williams to Buck Owens, Merle Haggard, and George Jones.

3. Edward Morris, "Webb Pierce Dead at 69," *Billboard,* March 9, 1991, 45.

4. Kitsinger, liner notes to *Webb Pierce.*

5. Diane Pecknold, *The Selling Sound: The Rise of the Country Music Industry* (Durham: Duke University Press, 2007), 32, notes that early country music fans did not always view commercialism and authenticity as mutually exclusive. But by the 1950s, as Richard Peterson, *Creating Country Music: Fabricating Authenticity* (Chicago: University of Chicago Press, 1997), 205–11, has demonstrated, the concept of authenticity became a governing principle that could explain country music's success in the 1950s, standing in stark contrast to the syncretic nature of Tin Pan Alley. For a discussion of how the concepts of male authenticity and female commercialism have worked in country music, see Travis Stimeling, "Taylor Swift's 'Pitch Problem' and the Place of Adolescent Girls in Country Music," in *Country Boys and Redneck Women: New Essays in Gender and Country Music*, ed. Diane Pecknold and Kristine M. McCusker (Jackson: University Press of Mississippi, 2016), 84–101.

6. Frank Harris, "Favorite of Two Decades," *Country Music Life*, January 1967, 33–34.

7. Kitsinger, liner notes to *Webb Pierce*.

8. "Web: Then and Now," *Country Song Roundup*, December 1953, 8.

9. Kitsinger, liner notes to *Webb Pierce*, reveals additional ways Pierce tried to secure a performance spot on the *Louisiana Hayride*, including forming Pacemakers Records and Ark-La-Tex publishing company with the show's program director, Horace Logan.

10. *Country Song Roundup*, February 1957, 21.

11. *Billboard*, February 13, 1954, 58.

12. Kitsinger, liner notes to *Webb Pierce*.

13. Travis Stimeling, "Narrative, Vocal Staging, and Masculinity in the 'Outlaw' Country Music of Waylon Jennings," *Popular Music* 32, no. 3 (October 2013): 343–58, discusses how Waylon Jennings and Willie Nelson challenged the business, recording, and distribution practices of 1970s Nashville music producers, establishing the outlaw movement, and invoked notions of masculine authenticity and creativity.

14. "Fourth Pierce Triple Crown," *Billboard*, November 12, 1955, 16.

15. Battle, "Webb Pierce ... Comin' Back!," 9.

16. Peterson, *Creating Country Music*, 14–25, and Pecknold, *The Selling Sound*, 42, provide a historical overview of the constituent elements of the country music industry.

17. Rich Kienzle, "Webb Pierce," *Journal of the American Academy for the Preservation of Old-Time Music* 1 no. 3 (June 1991): 16, also mentions that Pierce and Denny owned a number of radio stations and made several other joint investments.

18. Ibid., 16–17.

19. See, for example, Charlie Lamb, "A Girl Named Audrey," *Country and Western Jamboree*, September 1956, 10.

20. Pete Daniel, *Lost Revolutions: The South in the 1950s* (Chapel Hill: University of North Carolina Press for the Smithsonian National Museum of American History, Washington, DC), 94–96.

21. "Country Music's Pride and Joy," *Country Song Roundup*, August 1962, 18.

22. Robynn J. Stilwell, "Vocal Decorum: Voice, Body, and Knowledge in the Prodigious Singer, Brenda Lee," in *She's So Fine: Reflections of Whiteness, Femininity, Adolescence and Class in 1960s Music*, ed. Laurie Stras (Burlington: Ashgate, 2010), 67.

23. Peter La Chapelle, "All That Glitters: Country Music, Taste, and the Politics of the Rhinestone 'Nudie' Suit," *Dress* 28 (2001): 8.

24. Philip Wylie, *Generation of Vipers* (New York: Rinehart, 1942), 197.

25. Peterson, *Creating Country Music*, 168–72.

26. Pamela Fox, *Natural Acts: Gender, Race, and Rusticity in Country Music* (Ann Arbor: University of Michigan Press, 2008), 70.

27. Bill Malone, "Honky-Tonk: The Music of the Southern Working Class," in *Folk Music and Modern Sound*, ed. William Ferris and Mary L. Hart (Jackson: University Press of Mississippi, 1982), 122, and ibid., 70–72.

28. See Fox's *Natural Acts*, 78–79, for a discussion of the themes in male honky tonk.

29. Richard Leppert and George Lipsitz, "Age, the Body and Experience in the Music of Hank Williams," *Popular Music* 9, no. 3 (October 1990): 272.

30. Ching, *Wrong's What I Do Best*, 33.

31. Barbara Ching, "Acting Naturally: Cultural Distinction and Critiques of Pure Country," in *White Trash: Race and Class in America*, eds. Matt Wray and Annalee Newitz (New York: Routledge, 1997), 241.

32. Fox, *Natural Acts*, 72.

33. Ibid., 76–83.

34. Ibid., 83.

35. Ching, "Acting Naturally," 232.

36. Allison McCracken, *Real Men Don't Sing: Crooning in American Culture* (Durham: Duke University Press, 2015), 25–26.

37. For a more detailed discussion about Autry's crooning techniques and representations of masculinity, see Stephanie Vander Wel, "The Lavender Cowboy and 'the She Buckaroo': Gene Autry, Patsy Montana, and Depression-Era Gender Roles," *Musical Quarterly* 95, nos. 2/3 (Summer–Fall 2012): 207–51.

38. See Peter Stanfield, *Horse Opera: The Strange History of the 1930s Singing Cowboy* (Urbana: University of Illinois Press, 2002), 77–100, for a critical analysis of Autry in Western films.

39. Kitsinger, liner notes to *Webb Pierce*.

40. For more about the yodel, see Jocelyn Neal, *The Songs of Jimmie Rodgers: A Legacy in Country Music* (Bloomington: Indiana University Press, 2009), 19–25; Timothy Wise, "Lullabies, Laments, and Ragtime Cowboys: Yodeling at the Turn of the Twentieth Century," *American Music* 26, no. 1 (2008): 13–36; and "Jimmie Rodgers and the Semiosis of the Hillbilly Yodel" *Musical Quarterly* 93, no. 1 (2010): 6–44.

41. McCracken, *Real Men Don't Sing*, 14–16.

42. Ibid., 34.

43. Fox, *Natural Acts*, 78–79.

44. Leppert and Lipsitz, "Age, the Body and Experience in the Music of Hank Williams," 264, and David Brackett, *Interpreting Popular Music* (Cambridge: Cambridge University Press, 1995; repr. Berkeley: University of California Press, 2000), 91, separately discuss the ways in which Williams emphasized the timbral differences of his upper and lower registers.

45. Fox, *Natural Acts,* 64.

46. Ibid., 72.

47. Brackett, *Interpreting Popular Music,* 92.

48. For more details of how Bing Crosby remasculinized the crooner persona, see McCracken, *Real Men Don't Sing,* 264–310.

49. Ibid., 314.

50. See Peter Lehman, *Roy Orbison: The Invention of an Alternative Rock Masculinity* (Philadelphia: Temple University Press, 2003), for the ways in which Orbison's singing voice defies normative masculinity.

51. Timothy David Miller, "Instruments of Technology and Culture: Co-Constructing the Pedal Steel Guitar," PhD diss., University of North Carolina at Chapel Hill, 2013, 69–71.

52. Ibid., 69.

53. Tom Lutz, "Men's Tears and the Roles of Melodrama," in *Boys Don't Cry? Rethinking Narratives of Masculinity and Emotion in the U.S.,* ed. Milette Shamir and Jennifer Travis (New York: Columbia University Press, 2002), 186.

54. "Webb Pierce—Kitty Wells: Singing Together for the First Time on Records," *Folk and Country Songs,* July 1957, 8.

55. Chuck Kleinhans, "Taking Out the Trash: Camp and the Politics of Parody," in *The Politics and Poetics of Camp,* ed. Moe Meyer (London: Routledge, 1994), 186.

56. Susan Sontag, "Notes on Camp," in *A Susan Sontag Reader* (New York: Farrar, Straus, Giroux, 1982), 108.

57. Daniel, *Lost Revolutions,* 155.

58. John Howard, "Library, the Park, and the Pervert: Public Space and Homosexual Encounter in Post–World War II Atlanta," in *Carryon' On in the Lesbian and Gay South,* ed. John Howard (New York: New York University Press, 1997), 113, and Bob Swisher, "One Big Community," *Southern Exposure* 16 (Fall 1988): 29.

59. For more about Liberace's campy performances and appeal to blue-collar and low-middle-class audiences, see Margaret Thompson Drewal, "The Camp Trace in Corporate America: Liberace and the Rockettes at Radio City Music Hall," in Meyer, *The Politics and Poetics of Camp,* 149–81.

60. See Craig Thompson Friend, "The Womanless Wedding: Masculinity, Cross-Dressing, and Gender Inversions in the Modern South," in *Southern Masculinity: Perspectives on Manhood in the South since Reconstruction,* ed. Craig Thompson Friend (Athens: The University of Georgia Press, 2009), 239–265, for a detailed cultural analysis of womanless weddings.

61. Kleinhans, "Taking Out the Trash," 184.

62. "What the Fans Say about Webb Pierce," *Folk and Country Songs,* January 1957, 10.

63. "Wondering Webb," *Country Song Roundup,* June 1952, 8.

64. Pierce was born in August 1921, not August 1926. Kitsinger, liner notes to *Webb Pierce.*

65. *Country Song Roundup,* February 1956, 7. Pierce had married Audrey Grisham in November 1952. Kitsinger, liner notes to *Webb Pierce.*

66. Hannah Altbush, "America's Number One Hit Maker: Web Pierce," *Country and Western Jamboree,* May 1956, 8–9.

67. *Country Song Roundup,* Annual 1969, 28.

68. Kienzle, "Webb Pierce," 15.

# CHAPTER FOUR

# Stand Up to Your Man

*The Working-Class*
*Feminism of*
*Loretta Lynn*

## MARK ALLAN JACKSON

IN 1968, Tammy Wynette co-wrote and recorded "Stand by Your Man," which went on to reach the number one position on the country music charts and has since become an iconic song in a variety of contexts, appearing in films, television, and countless cover versions. Since its release, however, it has largely been interpreted as an unapologetic expression of woman as submissive helpmate.[1] Hillary Clinton derisively evoked this image in a 1992 interview with *60 Minutes* when she, along with her husband, defended him from allegations that he had engaged in an affair: "You know, I'm not sitting here—some little woman standing by my man like Tammy Wynette. I'm sitting here because I love him, and I respect him, and I honor what he's been through and what we've been through together."[2] Clinton clearly sets herself apart from an obedient and submissive spouse who automatically adheres to her husband's will and establishes that it is her own decision to support her beleaguered partner, thus marking herself a liberated woman and unlike the narrator (and co-writer) of "Stand by Your Man."

But long before this song gained its cult-like status and its reputation as an anti–women's liberation testimonial, Loretta Lynn recorded it and then prominently placed it on her 1969 album *Woman of the World/To Make a Man*, suggesting a kindred spirit both to Wynette and to the sentiments expressed in the song itself. Certainly, this supposed link in ideology fits with some elements of Lynn's public image, for she has long been marketed as a loyal wife, a devoted mother to her six children, a Christian, and a traditionalist. This portrait of Lynn follows in line with the gender expectations of the country music industry of an era when, according to scholar Rebecca Thomas, "a white woman who wanted to establish herself in the business kept her morals high, her skirts low, and her Christian virtue front and center. The flags for femininity—subordination, humility, and self-effacement—were non-negotiable."[3]

But Lynn has also taken many opportunities to speak out against conservative standards of male/female dynamics. In fact, feminist historian Glenna Matthews proclaims that in the late 1960s and early 1970s, Lynn functioned as a "public woman" who greatly expanded "the range of female experience receiving mainstream attention," even within "that bastion of cultural conservatism, country music," while also specifically setting the singer as a progressive voice in opposition to Tammy Wynette and the restrictive views expressed in "Stand by Your Man."[4] Matthews is not alone in framing this particular contrast. For in her first autobiography, which appeared at the height of her fame in the mid-1970s, Lynn responded to some views expressed in Wynette's iconic song and even specifically refuted the chorus's admonition to "give him two arms to cling to and something warm to come to when nights are cold and lonely": "There's plenty of songs about how women should stand by their men and give them plenty of loving when they walk through the door, and that's fine. But what about the man's responsibility?" But Lynn did not stop in positing this question. Instead, she forcefully answered it: "A man is supposed to give his wife a good time, too. Let him be tender with her once in a while, too. And it's even more important for two people to respect each other—you don't save a marriage just by putting on some sexy nightgown when your old man comes home from the factory. But maybe the old man could save the marriage by asking his wife, 'What do you think we should do about this situation?' No woman likes to be told, 'Here's the deal.'"[5] In these comments, Lynn calls for a true partnership, one where both the man and the woman comfort each other and also work together in creating an equitable relationship. Certainly, this push for a balanced responsibility for a marriage's survival does not represent an overtly revolutionary stance, although it does stand as a clear demand for gender equality.

In fact, if we survey Loretta Lynn's song lyrics, autobiographical writing, and interviews as a whole, we can find that this coal miner's daughter constantly stands up to her man (or men in general) on a number of issues and in various situations, revealing a rather progressive feministic belief system, even though she has explicitly stated that she found feminist icon Betty Friedan rather boorish in her expression of women's rights and that she is "not a big fan of Women's Liberation."[6] In making these comments, perhaps Lynn did not think that her drive for respect and equality rose to the riotous, anti-male stance of the Women's Movement as it was sometimes being represented in the mainstream press of the era. But no less an authority than Gloria Steinem has defined feminism as "the belief in the full social, economic, and political equality of women and men," a position that aligns with Lynn's own values as expressed throughout her public career.[7] Perhaps Lynn's concept of the feminine did not jibe with the suburban, middle-class, college-educated, bra-burning, hairy-legged, down-with-motherhood stereotypes of the women involved in this movement in the 1960s and 1970s, especially since many of Lynn's narrators and members of her audience were stay-at-home wives and mothers from the rural working class, just as Lynn herself had been. For whatever reason, Lynn has set herself aside from feminists, even as she often aligned herself with them through the comments she makes, the songs that she writes, and the stories that she tells.

Yet Lynn has set some limits to her expression of feminist values, for she has centered her discussion of gender equality primarily within the realm of family and home rather than the workplace or the legal system. But even though her songs are often drawn firmly within the domestic sphere, this move actually allows Lynn to personalize the feminist issues that she addresses while also setting each narrative as a subversive slice-of-life example of the situations faced by many women, especially those from the lower end of America's economic scale. This move is telling, for Lynn works mightily in her songs, in her autobiographies, in her interviews, and in her public appearances to present herself as an authentic working-class woman, as being a representative voice both from and for this group. For she was forever molded by her own working-class past as she suffered poverty and restriction as a child, as an adult, and as a mother. But even though in her stardom she can be viewed as having moved from this class designation, she always remains a woman facing the restrictions that come with her gender. These realities brand her work, informing her sympathies and offering a working-class woman's point of view. Thus, Lynn should be seen as both confessing and criticizing her own personal and private experiences as a working-class wife and mother even as she also reveals the underrepresented collective reality of many women from America's underclass who share her background.

In fact, Lynn's perspective actually offered its own brand of feminism and voiced a welcome rejection of the sentimental mother figure and long-suffering wife image that had often appeared in country songs in the past. For if we survey the history of country music up to the 1970s, we often find rambling men worrying and dominating their female partners, thus creating what scholar Barbara Sims condemns as an "imagery of suffer-ing" that projects martyrdom and masochism onto women as a whole.[8] But unlike many male country songwriters, Lynn decided to have many of her female narrators stand up and talk back to men, not only to those in their lives but also to those in the general public. Since she wrote many of the songs she recorded, Lynn often avoided the pitfalls suffered by other women country stars who sang male-authored songs that could project chauvinistic positions expressed through a female voice, which reinforced gender stereotypes. Instead, Lynn's ideology, expressed through her per-sonally crafted songs and her other autobiographical writing, is not con-trolled by these traditional representations of womanhood. In fact, Lynn and her narrators—although they may sometimes appear as comic in their presentation—often demand recognition, fairness, and respect. Loretta Lynn expressed this kind of feminist position in a number of her songs and other writings, especially those from the 1960s and 1970s, where she touched on new frontiers in the war of the sexes.

Early on, Lynn appreciated the power of the female perspective, espe-cially one that fought against notions of a male-centered worldview and female submission, and she attributes this drive, in part, to the example of Kitty Wells: "In the old days, country music was directed at the men—truck-driving songs, easy women, cheating songs. I remember how excited I got back in 1952, the first time I heard Kitty Wells sing 'It Wasn't God Who

Made Honky-Tonk Angels.' That was the women's answer to that Hank Thompson record called 'The Wild Side of Life.' See, Kitty was presenting the woman's point of view, which is different from the man's. And I always remembered that when I started writing songs."[9] Here, Lynn references one of the great song debates in country music. For Thompson's song (written by Arlie Carter and William Warren) details a husband longing for his wayward wife, who was lured by "the glamour of the gay nightlife" of the honky-tonk bars "where the wine and liquor flow."[10] Almost immediately, Wells recorded "It Wasn't God Who Made Honky-Tonk Angels," written by J. D. Miller, which firmly put the blame for the titular women on "married men [who] think they're still single," which "caused many a good girl to go wrong."[11] This song then became an anthem in its time, signaling a rather dramatic change in country music's presentation of women. As country music critic Dorothy A. Horstman notes of this song, "It hardly seems a radical notion today, but for a music and a culture in which the woman was either a jezebel or a long-suffering martyr, its impact was startling."[12] The appreciation for Wells's expression of a woman's view of the world to counter that of a man's has certainly shaped how Lynn has crafted many of her own songs, which has driven some of her lyrics into the political realm, even though she has flatly stated, "My music has no politics."[13]

Although Lynn may not think of her work as having a political agenda, it does expressly comment on the power dynamic between men and women, a push that comes in part through the personal reality of the singer's own life. Early on in her first autobiography, Lynn confesses, "Sometimes my husband tells me, 'I raised you the way I wanted you to be.' And it's true. I went from Daddy to Doo [the nickname of her husband], and there's always been a man telling me what to do." But of her father, Lynn often tells of a soft-spoken man who did not dictate to his wife.[14] However, she could be less flattering of other men, especially her spouse. For she admits that he was a drunk, a serial womanizer, and sometimes even physically abusive.[15] Even when reflecting on the whole of her life rather than just her marriage and after her most financially successful period in the early and mid-1970s, she found an overwhelming male presence: "Even today, men are telling me what to do. My husband, my lawyer, my accountant, my personal manager. In a sense, I still don't have complete control over myself. Maybe I never will."[16] But even as she admitted her own doubt about whether she would ever be rid of male authority, Loretta Lynn was making her most outstanding criticism of male domination, especially in relationships in general and marriage in particular.

In a vein rather similar to that in Wells's hit, Lynn points blame at a man for leading "an innocent country girl" astray in her song "Wings upon Your Horns," which she also used as the title of her 1970 album. The lyrics offer a tale of how a young woman falls in love. After her partner's "sweet talkin' ways ... turned a flame into a blaze" and his pledge of marriage, she engages in sex. But then he reneges on his promise, turning her into someone she "can't stand."[17] This kind of narrative, of a woman being sexually suspect due to a dishonest man, propels several of Lynn's earlier songs, including "When Lonely Hits Your Heart" (1965), which centers on a self-described "fallen girl." It also fits the larger honky-tonk narrative in song after song, where women are, as scholar Pamela Fox argues, often represented as "emblems of lost purity."[18] But unlike others of its kind, Lynn's song works to set the woman as a loving dupe and the man more as a demonic paramour, thus placing the blame squarely on him (and men like him). In addition, the title of "Wings upon Your Horns" can be read as graphically representing the deflowering act itself, frankly addressing the sexual act only suggested by the lyrics themselves.[19] The overall bold stance represented in this song reflected Lynn's own growing desire to honestly depict male/female relationships beyond what she was able to do ever before, especially those within the institution of marriage.

Lynn well knows the hardships that come with marriage, for she discusses them again and again in her public comments and writing. She never shies away from a frank expression of her own difficulties, even those of a sexual nature: "I never withheld sex from Doo. I thought wives was supposed to do it for their husbands and even though being a wife didn't come natural to me, I tried to be a good one."[20] But as already noted, she also admitted in her autobiographies that her husband fell well short in his obligations to her. Perhaps this personal knowledge spurred her suggestion in 1976 that marriage as a whole was not necessarily the best kind of relationship: "Maybe living together is a better idea than getting married when you're so young. It seems like some people don't start having fights until they get married. Marriage puts pressure on you sometimes, knowing it's a lifetime deal."[21] In this same era, the idea of marriage being an idyllic relationship or one that lasted forever was challenged by the growing reality of divorce.

Even as the post–World War II era saw marriage and birth rates soar, divorce also had its boom, resulting in part from women's newfound independence, relationships strained by long absence, and changes to the laws governing divorce. All these peaking trends dipped and then stabilized as the 1940s waned and the 1950s surged, resulting in creation of the stereotypical idea of the happy nuclear family. But as the 1960s turned into the 1970s, with the number of new marriages holding relatively steady, the divorce rate rose again. Just a few decades earlier, about 400,000 marriages a year came to an end in the United States, but in the 1970s, that number doubled and then tripled by the beginning of the 1980s, reaching its all-time high and establishing the narrative that half of all marriages will come to an end.[22] However, Lynn herself never divorced, perhaps driven by her own community's prejudice against it, for she was "taught that there wasn't no such thing as divorce among decent folks."[23] Still, she rejected the absoluteness of the institution of marriage in general, even though she stayed in a difficult one herself, which gave her insight into the potential ruin of this type of arrangement.

Certainly, country music recognized the reality of divorce early on. Perhaps tuning into the rise in divorces, in 1946, Merle Travis recorded "Divorce Me C.O.D.," a playful yet spiteful reflection on a failed relationship that the husband will only end through the mail. Later, at the beginning of the second postwar upturn in breakups, Wanda Jackson brought out "The Box It Came In" in 1965. Again, there is a joking quality to the song, even as it turns from sour to threatening in the final verse, where the box referenced changes from one that once held a wedding dress to an imagined coffin for the now-absent husband. But the most comic country divorce song that hit the charts has to be Jerry Reed's "She Got the Goldmine (I Got the Shaft)," which came out in 1982, just about the time when dissolutions of marriages in America showed the beginnings of a downward trend. But in contrast to the kind of humor in these examples, many of the country songs in this same era that discussed divorce carry a sorrowful tone throughout. In the same year that she released "Stand by Your Man," Wynette also had a hit with "D-I-V-O-R-C-E." Written by Bobby Braddock and Curly Putman, the lyrics lay out the misery a mother feels when she has to hide from her child the reality of the breakup of her marriage to a man she apparently still loves, although no reason for the divorce is noted. This song is pure lament for a family tragedy. In a similar sorrowful manner, Lynn herself commented on the harsh reality of divorce in "Mr. and Mrs. Used to Be," which was a duet with longtime singing partner Ernest Tubb. But this song was written by Billy Joe Deaton, not by Lynn.

When she finally offered her own self-penned perspective on the results of divorce in her 1973 hit "Rated X," Lynn speaks out on behalf of women who have gone through this experience. But Lynn's position in the lyrics stands in direct contrast with many other songs of the same era that touched on divorce. Instead of comically dismissing or lamenting the passing of the relationship, Lynn seriously addresses the perspective that men (and some women) sometimes take about the sexuality of divorced women, toward whom she generates a protective attitude. In Lynn's song, the breakup itself and the reasons behind it are not really addressed, except for the brief comment "things didn't seem to work out." Instead, she focuses on how men generally view divorced women. In the song, all formerly married women are warned that they are "gonna be talked about / Everybody knows that you've been loved once so they think you'll love again." However, Lynn really means "love" in the carnal rather than the romantic sense. These women become "some kind of goal every man might try to make," whether they are friends or strangers.[24] Thus, the male community's view of these women as a whole is predicated on the fact that they have had sex before, even if within marriage. Apparently, without their husbands, their sexual partnership is up for grabs, suggesting a kind of stereotypical desperation and supplication of these women. Lynn also dismissed this attitude in a note that accompanied the lyrics in her songbook *Honky-Tonk Girl*: "Once you have been married, if you got divorced or became widowed, every man takes it for granted that you're available, that you're easy. Maybe it's because they think that because we've been through so much, we're just ready for fun."[25] Although the men may have "minds eat up with sin," the still-married women come in for criticism in the song, too. For "the women all look at you like you're bad." But Lynn sets herself apart when she scolds, "I think it's wrong to judge every picture if a cheap camera makes a mistake."[26] Here, she makes those who have prejudged divorced women the guilty party, even transforming them into a faulty mechanism, and chastises all those who automatically see divorced women as easy sexual conquests or competition.

As noted, the issue itself mattered more in the 1970s than in other eras due to divorce rates being higher than ever before. The nation found itself with a growing number of people who had broken a traditional bond, and Americans had to find a way to incorporate this new reality into their beliefs about the nature of relationships, including the kinds of expectations that both men and women could have about marriage and whether or not it should come to an end. So it is not surprising that Lynn wanted to offer her own thoughts about a particular reality that she recognized concerning some people's thoughts about divorced women. In fact, during this time period, many women were confronting past gender roles and deciding that new kinds of power sharing and decision making were necessary for stronger, fairer relationships. They were also realizing that they had the power to control their own sexual images. Women were also considering new ways to control the biological results of marriage in particular and sex in general, and Lynn commented on this reality as well.

Lynn first took on this issue in song in 1971 but through words written by another writer, famed cartoonist and children's author Shel Silverstein. He had earlier come to some level of country music fame for having penned "A Boy Named Sue," which Johnny Cash recorded and charted in 1969. But Silverstein also created a number of other songs, some of which contain political/social commentary, such as "One's on the Way," which Lynn recorded. In this song, the exploits of wealthy and famous women are juxtaposed with the mundane realities of a stay-at-home wife and mother in Topeka, Kansas. While movie stars live the highlife in Paris and Las Vegas, this woman wrangles several squalling children, who will soon be joined by another babe, the one that is on the way. But near the end of the song, this mother also muses about "the girls in New York City" who "march for women's lib" and imagines that "the pill may change the world tomorrow."[27] But in Topeka, the narrator's household is a mess, awash with children, and without any help from her husband. Thus, the song presents a contrast between what a few independent, urban women can do, including engaging in political action and a call for control of their own bodies, but in small-town America, the average woman has to deal with the unmitigated results of human sexuality and its attendant burdens. Although somewhat hidden by the comic tone injected by the lyrics and Lynn's own performance of the song, a kind of lament lingers just below the surface, suggesting that the narrator would also like to have the opportunity to be more than a mother and a wife, to have more control of her life—and her body.

Perhaps the best example of Lynn's lyrical feminism is her 1975 hit "The Pill," which she co-wrote with T. D. Bayless, Lorne Allen, and Don McHan. In it, the narrator celebrates her new freedom from pregnancy, pointedly noting how her husband has always been carefree and unfaithful while she was tied down with "a couple [babies] in my arms" and "another's on the way," which echoes the situation in the Silverstein song.[28] This repetition ties into Lynn's underlying message, for she despises this kind of unequitable relationship, as she bluntly states in one of her autobiographies: "Well, shoot, I don't believe in double standards, where men can get away with things that women can't."[29] In the country music market, this song stands out as an unabashed and rather radical call for sexual liberation and biological control. Using a variety of chicken farm metaphors, the narrator comically points out the hypocrisy of her husband's rooster-like attitude, thus challenging the male sexual prerogative of the past and presenting an equitable sexual relationship wherein the female may also enjoy a variety of sexual liaisons without the social/economic restrictions that come with pregnancy, childbirth, and child care. In discussing the song as part of her argument about "social criticism" within "sarcastic humor" that "enables women to speak out in a non-violent, assertive way about adverse societal norms," critic Suzanne Bunkers emphasizes the underlying meaning beneath the comic image: "we laugh at her mockery of the 'henhouse' stereotype, but we take seriously her implicit message that women must control our reproductive capacity."[30] In fact, Lynn rejoices both in the song and in her own overall personal belief that the birth control pill will allow women greater control of their own lives: "I really believe in those words. It's all about how the man keeps the woman barefoot and pregnant over the years. I think it's great that women have a way of protecting themselves now, without worrying about the man."[31] Thus, Lynn means for the song to actually convey a specific political point in the ongoing debate about women's reproductive rights.

According to country music critic Joan Dew, through these two songs, Lynn became "the spokesperson for every woman who had gotten married too early, gotten pregnant too often, and felt trapped by the tedium and drudgery of her life."[32] Certainly, Lynn did touch on a hot-button issue with these songs, for a woman's ability to control her own biology had become much debated in this era due to the introduction and use of oral contraceptives in the United States. Although approved by the Food and Drug Administration in 1960, they were not available to all married women until 1965 and to all unmarried women until 1972, both these changes only brought about by controversial Supreme Court decisions. Many detractors predicted that sexual depravity would result, submitting that the nation would follow the path of Sodom and Gomorrah, while adherents celebrated women's newfound freedom from biological determinism.[33] But rather than see the subject in broad political terms, Loretta Lynn reacted to the issue from a personal perspective, even though she did not really use contraception much herself, of which her six children are proof. So even though she did not often avail herself of this product, she believed that it should be available to any woman who wanted to use it and concluded that her audience would want to know her honest position on this important public issue, despite any potential negative feedback: "I write about life . . . And boy, I got in all kinds of trouble [for recording 'The Pill']. But that's what people are interested in. They're not interested in fantasy stuff."[34]

Actually, for many years and in a variety of expressions other than just the songs "One's on the Way" and "The Pill," Lynn has ruminated on how her own pregnancies have been both a blessing and a burden. She made the subject of these songs stand as a personal testimonial when she announced in a 1975 interview in *People Magazine,* "If I'd had the pill back when I was havin' babies, I'd have taken 'em like popcorn. The pill is good for people. I wouldn't trade my kids for anyone's. But I wouldn't necessarily have had six and I sure would have spaced 'em better."[35] Here she simultaneously announces her love for the children she did have and presents the possibility that had she the opportunity, she might not have had some of them at all. This seeming contradiction reveals both the mother-centered public image of Lynn and the reality that she would have liked the choice of how and even if she were to take on this traditional role. Then, in her hit 1976 autobiography, Lynn again made the popcorn analogy but added, "I know what it's like to be pregnant and nervous and poor," thus directly tying the necessity of birth control to the economic realities of both having and raising children, especially for those on the lower rungs of America's economic ladder.[36]

But Lynn did not restrict her thoughts about birth control to her own experiences; she also realized that others had the same problems that she did. In her first autobiography, she bluntly stated, "I think a woman needs control over her own life, and the pill is what helps her do it."[37] But due to the controversial nature of the pill, some women—especially those who were poor or who lived in rural America—were not provided necessary information about the drug's effectiveness. However, Lynn felt that her song actually helped educate them on this issue. She told an interviewer for *Playgirl* magazine, "A doctor who travels around teaching sex education told me that 'The Pill' has reached more people out in the country and done more than all the government programs put together." She even revealed that many of her younger fans cheerfully demanded the song during her concerts, suggesting that they celebrated its message of female empowerment and self-determination.[38]

However, some radio stations also tried to keep Lynn's positive representation of birth control from reaching these listeners by banning this song, even as it found an audience, evidenced by its rise to the Top Ten of the country music charts. Lynn commented on this situation in one of her autobiographies: "When we released it, the people loved it. I mean the *women* loved it. But the men who run the radio stations were scared to death." She then explained how the views expressed in the song reflected a woman's reality while they also rejected a male-centric view of sexuality. She argues, "It's a challenge to the man's way of thinking. See, they'll play a song about making love in a field because that's sexy, from a man's point of view. But something that's really important to women, like birth control, they don't want no part of, leastways not on the air." Thus, she acknowledges the gap between some powerful men's views of birth control and that of the majority of women. In fact, the fear of this kind of negative reaction caused Lynn and her record company to hold on to the song for several years before she released it. This uncertainty was well founded, as noted, for many did condemn "The Pill," including politicians and preachers. But

Lynn's largely female audience rewarded her candor and her position on sexuality by making the song a hit, one big enough to force many stations to play it even in the face of this controversy.[39]

Her belief in "The Pill" and its message was not the only kind of public discussion of human sexuality that Lynn supported. In that same interview in *Playgirl* mentioned earlier, Lynn also praised sex education programs in public schools, noting how her last two daughters were never going to experience the ignorance of their bodies and reproductive system as she did as a young woman.[40] A year later she addressed this same topic in her first autobiography, noting again and again her own ignorance about her own body or the basics of human sexuality and its results. For example, in reflecting on her honeymoon, she admits, "My parents never told me nothing" about how sex actually works or about its results. In fact, she admits, "My Daddy used to tell me they got me by turning over a cabbage leaf—and I believed it." Then when describes the first time she had sex with her husband, the language used seems more akin to rape than lovemaking: "He finally more or less had to rip off my panties. The rest of it was kind of a blur. I guess I went into a fit and didn't know what he was doing. He didn't tell me nothing, so I just lay there." Even years after this first experience, she still had little understanding of sex, especially of her own pleasure, "having a climax and stuff." However, she took pains to make sure that her ignorance never became that of her own daughters: "Now I was different with my girls. I told them the facts straight off." In fact, she added, "I'm sure my little twins know more than I did when I got married. I think a mother should talk to her girls about it. But it was a different time back then."[41]

When Lynn produced a second autobiography in 2002, she took up the importance of sex education by again noting her own past ignorance and her desire that her daughters not follow her example. However, she also added that other women from more urban backgrounds during the era of her youth might have also needed direction concerning their own biological realities: "I don't think being from Butcher Holler had much to do with Mommy's reluctance to talk about such things. I fear that back in them days, that conversation was one a lot of girls in New York City or San Francisco didn't have with their mommies, either." In fact, Lynn's own reflection on what she did not know made her be such an advocate on this issue, as she notes, "knowing how *not knowing* feels made me want to explain as much as I could to my own children."[42]

Even more surprising, considering the typical view of the conservative nature of country music and its performers, Lynn also made some positive public comments on abortion: "I won't ever say anything against the abortion laws they made easier a few years ago. Personally, I think you should prevent unwanted pregnancy rather then get an abortion. I don't think I could have an abortion. It would be wrong for me. But I'm thinking of all the poor girls who get pregnant when they don't want to be, and how they should have a choice instead of leaving it up to some politician or doctor who don't have to raise the baby. I believe they should be able to have an abortion."[43] Once, Lynn even offered to help a young girl get an abortion, although the singer also urged the girl to have the baby and give it up for adoption or keep it herself. Lynn may not have been fully accepting of abortion, but she still felt that it could be an option and that it should definitely be a woman's own decision, a position that came with much potential for backlash in the era of the Supreme Court's *Roe v. Wade* decision and its attendant controversy.[44]

Taken together, all these comments show that Lynn has well contemplated her position on the biological rights of women—but she also felt that she was not alone in these views. In that same *People* interview mentioned earlier, Lynn suggests that her views expressed in "The Pill" and other of her songs were shared by her female fans: "The women buy the records and you'd better let 'em know you're just like they are"[45] Certainly, the rise in the use of birth control and the public discussion of other sexual issues during this era suggests she was correct, although her aggressive stance did put her in the role of an advocate of a position that was still controversial in America, especially in conservative circles. In fact, Lynn generally admits that her work is a kind of catharsis, a place where she can mediate on her own life: "I believe that me being able to write about things was my way of dealing with my problems. Just writing them down on a page made me feel better. And helped me understand what was happening in my life."[46] As a result, much of her songwriting stands as autobiographical, a kind of public revelation of her own difficulty in marriage, with her reproductive choices, and with the realities facing women as a whole in an era of change, especially those from the working class. Lynn had the desire to speak to women, and she felt the obligation to speak for them, too. Her female fans "could see I was Loretta Lynn, a mother and a wife and a daughter, who had feelings just like other women," and they "felt I had the answers to their problems because my life was just like theirs."[47]

Before, during, and after Loretta Lynn's tenure as America's number one country star, the musical tradition in which she expressed herself could be claimed to uphold certain conservative views of women. For example, Tammy Wynette took up the antifeminist anthem "Don't Liberate Me (Love Me)," penned by three men in the same era when Lynn was speaking out on women's issues in work that she had written herself. In this song, Wynette sings, "Today a group of women came to see me to convince me women don't have equal rights / And they left when I told them I feel equal to an angel while my man holds me at night."[48] However, country music has also always contained moments where subversive messages about the lived reality of an entire class have been broadcast back to themselves, making for the potential for change because the songs showed that a collective wrong existed rather than just an individual one. In particular, country music does contain many moments that push against conservative notions of a woman's place.[49] Thus, Lynn's songs, comments, and stances are not unique.

But she positions herself well above many of her contemporaries, such as Dolly Parton, in terms of her desire to overtly push for women's rights. In fact, Southern historian Margaret Ripley Wolfe explicitly pointed to Lynn as being a prime example of "Appalachia's feminine voices [who] have proved to be astute observers of the contemporary scene," emphasizing her work that "speak[s] openly to women's issues."[50] Unlike some other country songwriters or performers who might fear backlash from the industry or from fans, Lynn has never been comfortable adhering to any restrictive political line, especially when commenting on women's rights. In fact, many critics have noted Lynn's ability to link two cultural forces that are not always thought to be compatible: feminism and working-class country. For example, it has been argued that "Her brand of women's lib wore a blue collar," while Mary Bufwack and Robert Oermann, in their classic study *Finding Her Voice*, termed this link "her country-feminist point of view."[51]

Certainly, in her songs, Lynn pushes against notions of a male-centered relationship, one where cheating, drinking, abandonment, and sexual submission were the norms. But she does stop short of fully rejecting all traditional feminine roles. Due to her nuanced position on women's rights, some music critics and scholars who have commented on her work in the past merely see her as a moderate, one who has created songs that are "a neat and deliberate compromise between liberation and supplication" or that offer "unhappiness with the double standard, but never express feminist views."[52] But in her writing, Lynn never advocates for supplication or accepts a traditional sexual dynamic. Instead, she steadily demands equality and advocates for women's self-empowerment. The women in her songs may not ask for jobs at equal pay or demand that patriarchal laws be changed—they are often working-class housewives and mothers, not radical feminists. Yet they do explicitly condemn the restrictions of stereotypical gender roles. They may not offer a completely revolutionary revision of the male/female relationship, but they did insist that their labors and their sacrifices be duly noted and appreciated by their male counterparts. These women narrators also pushed for sexual self-determination. As a whole, they advocated for personhood, for equality. In effect, Lynn's songs and other public pronouncements did not accept the status quo of the typical gender configuration of the era.

Although she may downplay the notion that she is a feminist, Loretta Lynn most assuredly stands as a creative artist who demands gender equality, a woman who is more than willing to stand up to men and speak out on what she sees as the truth. In particular, Lynn's music proves a very realistic (self-)portrait of a working-class woman's life, giving voice to that experience and broadcasting it back to her audience, who were often women who shared her background and understood the issues embedded in the songs. Lynn expresses pride in who she is, even as she shared her sorrow about aspects of the life she was forced to live, especially due to a social structure that often placed a man above her and an economic system that restricted her options. But as she boldly stated at the end of her second autobiography, "Behind every great man is an even greater woman. Women think faster, move faster, ARE faster. And that is the dang truth."[53]

## NOTES

1. See Kenneth Morris, "Sometimes It's Hard to Be a Woman: Reinterpreting a Country Classic," *Popular Music and Society* 16, no. 1 (Spring 1992), for both an overview of the non-liberation interpretations of the song and the author's own alternative reading.

2. Hillary Clinton, *60 Minutes,* January 26, 1992.

3. Rebecca Thomas, "The Cow That's Ugly Has the Sweetest Milk," in *The Women of Country Music,* ed. Charles K. Wolfe and James E. Akenson (Lexington: University Press of Kentucky, 2003), 142.

4. Glenna Matthews, *The Rise of Public Woman: Woman's Power and Woman's Place in the United States, 1630–1970* (New York: Oxford University Press, 1992), 234.

5. Loretta Lynn with George Vecsey, *Loretta Lynn: Coal Miner's Daughter* (Chicago: Henry Regnery Company, 1976), 55.

6. Ibid., 156, 56.

7. Quoted in Celina Hex, "Fierce, Funny, Feminists: Gloria Steinem and Kathleen Hanna," *Feminist eZine,* para. 11, www.feministezine.com/feminist/funny/Fierce-Funny-Feminists.html.

8. See Charles Jaret, "Characteristics of Successful and Unsuccessful Country Music Songs," in *All that Glitters: Country Music in America,* ed. George H. Lewis (Bowling Green: Bowling Green University Popular Press, 1993), 174–85; Karen Saucier Lundy, "Women and Country Music," in *America's Musical Pulse: Popular Music in 20th Century Society,* ed. Kenneth J. Bindas (Westport: Praeger, 1992), 212–19; and Barbara B. Sims, "'She's Got to Be a Saint, Lord Knows I Ain't': Feminine Masochism in American Country Music," *Journal of Country Music* 5, no. 1 (1974): 24–30.

9. Lynn with Vecsey, *Loretta Lynn,* 118.

10. Hank Thompson, "The Wild Side of Life," Capitol Records, 1952, Side A.

11. Kitty Wells, "It Wasn't God Who Made Honky-Tonk Angels," in *Kitty Wells: The Queen of Country Music, 1949–1958,* Bear Family, 1993, Disc 1, Track 9.

12. Dorothy A. Horstman, "Loretta Lynn," in *Stars of Country Music: Uncle Dave Macon to Johnny Rodriquez,* ed. Bill C. Malone and Judith McCulloh (Urbana: University of Illinois Press, 1975), 313.

13. Lynn with Vecsey, *Loretta Lynn,* 173.

14. Ibid., x, 11.

15. Loretta Lynn with Patsi Bale Cox, *Still Woman Enough: A Memoir* (New York: Hyperion, 2002), xii–xiii.

16. Lynn with Vecsey, *Loretta Lynn,* 37.

17. Loretta Lynn, "Wings upon Your Horns," in *Wings upon Your Horns,* Decca, 1970, Side 1, Track 1.

18. Pamela Fox, *Natural Acts: Gender, Race, and Rusticity in Country Music* (Ann Arbor: University of Michigan Press, 2009), 92.

19. Lynn knew of this potential reading as her producer, Owen Bradley, told her as much as they were recording the song. See Lynn with Vecsey, *Loretta Lynn*, 119–20.

20. Lynn with Cox, *Still Woman Enough*, 33.

21. Lynn with Vecsey, *Loretta Lynn*, 52.

22. Betsey Stevenson and Justin Wolfers, "Marriage and Divorce: Changes and Their Driving Forces," *Journal of Economic Perspectives* 21, no. 2: 27–52. ; and U.S. Census Bureau, Statistical Abstract of the United States, 2011, 65. For an overview of the political and societal forces that resulted in changes to the laws and perceptions governing divorce in America, see J. Herbie DiFonzo, *Beneath the Fault Line: The Popular and Legal Culture of Divorce in Twentieth-Century America* (Charlottesville: University Press of Virginia Press, 1997).

23. Lynn with Cox, *Still Woman Enough*, xvi.

24. Loretta Lynn, "Rated X," in *Loretta Lynn: The Definitive Collection*, MCA Nashville, 2005, Track 14.

25. Loretta Lynn, *Honky Tonk Girl: My Life in Lyrics* (New York: Alfred A. Knopf, 2012), 98.

26. Lynn, "Rated X."

27. Loretta Lynn, "One's on the Way," in *Loretta Lynn: The Definitive Collection*, MCA Nashville, 2005, Track 13.

28. Loretta Lynn, "The Pill," in ibid., Track 15.

29. Lynn with Vecsey, *Loretta Lynn*, 55.

30. Suzanne L. Bunkers, "Why Are These Women Laughing? The Power and Politics of Women's Humor," *Studies in American Humor* 4, nos.1/2 (Spring/Summer 1985): 87.

31. Lynn with Vecsey, *Loretta Lynn*, 62.

32. Joan Dew, *Singers and Sweethearts: The Women of Country Music* (Garden City: Doubleday, 1977), 8.

33. For a useful and readable history of these issues, one that even reference's Lynn's song "The Pill," see Elaine Tyler May, *America and the Pill: A History of Promise, Peril, and Liberation* (New York: Basic Books, 2010).

34. Quoted in Jancee Dunn, "Loretta Lynn: Honky-Tonk Woman," *Rolling Stone*, May 27, 2004.

35. Quoted in Robert Windeler, "Loretta Lynn's 'Pill' Is Hard for Some Fans to Swallow," *People Magazine*, March 31, 1975, 24–25.

36. Lynn with Vecsey, *Loretta Lynn*, x.

37. Ibid., 62.

38. Quoted in Elliot Cahn, "Loretta Lynn: Country Western and Rebel Queen Sounds Off on Sex, Abortion, and Her One-Woman Crusade for the Pill," *Playgirl*, August 1975, 91.

39. Lynn with Vecsey, *Loretta Lynn*, x, 62.

40. Quoted in Cahn, "Loretta Lynn," 91.

41. Lynn with Vecsey, *Loretta Lynn*, 50–51.

42. Lynn with Cox, *Still Woman Enough*, 25–26.

43. Lynn with Vecsey, *Loretta Lynn*, 62.

44. Quoted in Cahn, "Loretta Lynn," 91.

45. Quoted in Windeler, "Loretta Lynn's 'Pill,'" 24–25.

46. Lynn, *Honky Tonk Girl*, 35.

47. Lynn with Vecsey, *Loretta Lynn*, 114.

48. Tammy Wynette, "Don't Liberate Me (Love Me)," in *We Sure Can Love Each Other*, Epic, 1971, Side 1, Track 5.

49. See Mary A. Bufwack and Robert K. Oermann, *Finding Her Own Voice: Women in Country Music, 1800–2000* (Nashville: Vanderbilt Press, 2003), for a wonderful history that details both the progressive and the conservative impulse in country music concerning women's roles.

50. Margaret Ripley Wolfe, "Waiting for the Millennium, Remember the Past: Appalachian Women in Time and Place," in *Women of the American South*, ed. Christie Anne Farham (New York: New York University Press, 1997), 168.

51. Bud Scoppa, liner notes, in *Loretta Lynn: The Definitive Collection*, MCA Nashville, 2005, 6, and Bufwack and Oermann, *Finding Her Own Voice*, 267.

52. Horstman, "Loretta Lynn," 318, and Ruth A. Banes, "Mythology in Music: The Ballad of Loretta Lynn, *Canadian Review of American Studies* 16, no. 3 (Fall 1985): 288.

53. Lynn with Cox, *Still Woman Enough*, 228.

# CHAPTER FIVE

# "I'm the Other One"

*O. B. McClinton*
*and the*
*Racial Politics*
*of Country Music*
*in the 1970s*

## CHARLES L. HUGHES

IN 1976, an African-American country musician named O. B. McClinton released the provocatively titled song "Black Speck." Over a loping beat, McClinton tells the story of a white country fan who is shocked at the race of the twangy singer on a Nashville nightclub stage. "That nigger sound like a redneck!," exclaims the fan, exiting the club before eventually returning with newfound admiration for the black singer. The plot twist that animates "Black Speck" relied on the listener's understanding of country music and blackness as assumed opposites, a familiar symbolism to 1970s audiences who had been conditioned to hear country music as the authentic expression of whiteness and the soundtrack for the racially reactionary New Right. Through this ironic tale, McClinton critiqued this broader ideology and offered his career as evidence of the tricky terrain that African-American country performers had to negotiate. After the song's release, McClinton remarked that he did the song for "blacks to know that I relate to being black" and that "if being black and proud would hinder me from succeeding, then I didn't want to succeed."[1]

"Black Speck" offers a fitting microcosm for the contradictions that

McClinton explored throughout his long career as both a performer and songwriter. As one of the few prominent African Americans in country music, McClinton used his musical work to reflect his attempt to carve out a position as a black man in a white-dominated sound and industry. Rather than deny this conundrum, he embraced it by forcing his audience to address the seeming disconnect between his sound and skin color. "Johnny Cash is the man in black," he slyly noted. "I am, too. But he can take his off."[2]

In one sense, McClinton's prominence, and the juxtaposition chronicled in "Black Speck," demonstrated a new opportunity for African-American country musicians in the wake of Charley Pride's breakthrough success. McClinton—along with such as Stoney Edwards and Linda Martell—was promoted as both a promising talent and a symbol of country's supposed racial progressivism. While Pride and others mostly eschewed racial statements or framed them in a vague rhetoric of color blindness, McClinton regularly drew attention to the contrast between his blackness and the cultural expectations surrounding country music. Several of his most notable songs—including "Black Speck"—made McClinton's race a central theme. Sonically, he incorporated R&B influences into what scholar Barbara Ching calls a "confrontational hard country sound" that troubled the tight linkage between country music and white traditionalism.[3] His interviews and press releases often spotlighted McClinton's place in the shifting terrain of country demographics. For example, even as country tightened its association with the Republican Party in the Nixon years, McClinton joined the 1972 campaign of Democratic presidential candidate Edmund Muskie. Charley Pride was far more prominent as an African-American country performer, but no one embraced that role with more enthusiasm or expertise than O. B. McClinton.

But McClinton's career ultimately demonstrated the limitations of country's embrace of black artists in this period.[4] He scored several minor hits and enjoyed long support from the Nashville recording industry, but he ultimately grew frustrated with his country career both creatively and commercially. McClinton lodged several significant criticisms of the musical expectations and professional limitations he faced because of his blackness, and he ended his career proud of his accomplishments but ambivalent about their ultimate impact. McClinton's failure to fully transcend the racial boundaries erected around country music and other genres in the 1960s and 1970s offered a disquieting counternarrative to country's stories of racial breakthrough and added a layer of ambivalence to seemingly hopeful material like "Black Speck." Like that song, McClinton's career ultimately reconfirms the racial othering and marginalization of even the most talented African-American country performer.

While only a minor star during his life, O. B. McClinton's name has become commonplace in popular and scholarly discussions of the long and rich history of African Americans in country music and—to a lesser extent—in appreciations of Southern soul, where he began his career.[5] McClinton is justifiably recognized as a pioneering black country artist and the more astute analyses use him to examine the difficult position faced by African-American country musicians in the wake of Charley Pride. Diane Pecknold, in particular, lists McClinton as an example of the paradox that made "country music resoundingly white without being expressly anti-black" in the days of civil rights, Black Power, and white backlash.[6] Still, his life and career deserve more extensive analysis as a rich illustration of the difficult racial and cultural terrain—both in terms of breakthrough and limitation—negotiated by African-American country singers in this crucial moment and throughout the genre's history.

Born in 1940 to a family of cotton farmers, McClinton was a product of the rural black experiences that produced so much popular music and political change in the twentieth-century United States. As a child, he chafed against the stifling conditions that limited the social and economic ambitions of black Mississippians, and McClinton later admitted that he "became what my father would call a 'troublemaker' in the daily routine of a farmer's life."[7] His father—Reverend George McClinton—may have expressed such concerns because he owned his own farm, later described by O. B. as "a big, 700-acre place, a most unusually sizable thing for a black man to own in Mississippi." This success made the McClinton family both more secure and more vulnerable than most of their neighbors, which surely heightened his parents' concern about the rebelliousness of their middle son.[8]

Despite these disagreements between father and son, McClinton's parents instilled in young Obie a deep and painful racial consciousness. They taught him that "being black in the Deep South in that time period was extremely rough," a lesson confirmed at age seven when his mother punished him after he tried to drink from a whites-only water fountain in a local store. Although McClinton resented the injustice, his mother's attempt to "frighten me into being a normal black citizen in a society that was lopsided" instilled in him a motivation to "prove that I was just as worthy of a drink of water out of that fountain as that white man who had just finished drinking."[9] As with many of his contemporaries, McClinton's early experiences with Jim Crow in what historian Nan Elizabeth Woodruff calls the "American Congo" fueled his desire to escape the economic and racial restrictions of his youth.[10]

Central to McClinton's expanding ambitions—and his burgeoning racial consciousness—was his love of music. An avid radio listener, McClinton used his family's battery-powered unit to dial in a variety of shows broadcasting from the twin music capitals of Memphis and Nashville. As part of the first generation of Southerners to enjoy full radio coverage, McClinton grew up in a sonic landscape that simultaneously challenged and reaffirmed the period's broader racial divisions. McClinton enjoyed "all kinds of music," from the country music on Nashville's *Grand Ole Opry* to R&B and blues from pioneering Nashville station WLAC to early rock and roll from Memphis's WHBQ. Like many of his contemporaries, McClinton absorbed these various sounds as part of a shared soundtrack that—on a musical level, at least—transcended skin color. "It's the artist himself who sets the mode of the song," McClinton told scholar Rob Bowman. "Johnny Cash can make a blues song a country song, and Muddy Waters can make a country song a blues."[11] McClinton observed these musical similarities from an early age, imitating various singers and writing his own genre-blending songs as he chopped cotton.

At the same time, McClinton also learned that a firm racial boundary separated the genres. "By the time I was old enough to realize that country singers were rednecks and that there *weren't* any black ones," he told journalist Barney Hoskyns, "I had developed a deep love for the music and my voice had developed a deep Southern twang. I got in a lot of fights because of it."[12] McClinton's love of country engendered racial suspicion and also shaped his professional desires. Although he still "daydreamed" about "singing on the Grand Ole Opry in Nashville, [with] the crowd giving this little black kid a standing ovation," McClinton also recognized that success in country music might be out of reach.[13] In other words, he recognized the persistence of what historian Karl Hagstrom Miller terms the "musical color line," a division erected by the recording industry in its earliest days that paralleled the rise of Jim Crow segregation by establishing "a firm correlation between racialized music and racialized bodies."[14] McClinton's parents also recognized this "musical color line" and apparently saw no greater likelihood of their son successfully transgressing it than they did with the strictures of social segregation. McClinton recalls "standing up in the cotton field singing [Elvis Presley's] 'Blue Suede Shoes' and [Tennessee Ernie Ford's] 'Sixteen Tons,'" which provoked his father to hit him with a stalk of cotton. "It was just that they didn't understand how a little kid from Senatobia, Mississippi, could aspire to sing on the Grand Ole Opry."[15]

At age 14, McClinton escaped Mississippi to spend a year with an older sister in Memphis.[16] This city had long been a destination for African Americans who saw it as a site of greater opportunity and freedom, and McClinton specifically hoped that there he could launch his musical career. He joined the Teen Town Singers, a local group organized by pioneering all-black radio station WDIA that offered a perfect opportunity for the young singer to demonstrate his vocal skill and versatility.[17] The highly competitive Singers performed a wide variety of music at local functions and charity events, showing off the skills of Memphis's black youth and becoming a training ground for a number of musicians who later became prominent in Memphis's R&B and soul explosion of the 1960s and 1970s.[18] Even within this talented group, McClinton stood out: he won a WDIA talent show with his version of Tennessee Ernie Ford's country hit "Sixteen Tons," a feat he replicated when he won his high school talent show with his version of local hero Elvis Presley's "Blue Suede Shoes."[19]

Presley's success, combined with the city's vibrant live-music scene and emergent record companies, meant that even young up-and-comers like McClinton could find work as a musician. As he attended Rust College from 1962 to 1966 on a choral scholarship, McClinton traveled between the campus in Holly Springs, Mississippi, and the clubs and recording studios in his adopted home. "I'd go to school all week," he recalled, "and then on weekends . . . I'd go to Memphis and hustle."[20] This "hustle" now included regular stops at record companies such as Stax, where McClinton shopped his compositions to the growing roster of artists who brought the Memphis soul sound to the world in the early 1960s. "I'd hang around Stax and when somebody'd come out that looked like they were important, I would run up to them and tell them about this great song I had."[21] McClinton's perseverance paid off when Stax star Otis Redding recorded McClinton's smoldering ballad "Keep Your Arms Around Me" on his second album.[22] But McClinton's greatest success in the 1960s came with a different Memphis soul label. He joined Goldwax Records in 1964, recording a few singles and writing several songs for local singer James Carr, whose first single was an intense McClinton ballad called "You've Got My Mind Messed Up." The song went to number seven on the R&B charts, establishing McClinton as an important soul songwriter and giving him a foothold in the music business.[23] Even as he moved into country music, his compositions remained on the soul charts into the mid-1970s.

His early soul hits presaged his later career in another way. Historian Brian Ward notes that McClinton's recordings were "very country," while Barney Hoskyns suggests that these early releases "anticipated his later forays into Merle Haggard–style country." Additionally, Goldwax head, Quinton Claunch, said that McClinton brought out the country influence in Goldwax's biggest artist. "[James Carr] was all for this country-style soul music . . . he tried anything we wanted to try and we just let him inject his feel."[24] At this point, though, McClinton's efforts remained entirely on amplifying the country influence in soul music as opposed to seeking country stardom itself, which still appeared to be nearly impossible for a black artist.

It became a little more possible in the late 1960s, while McClinton was serving in the military and stationed in Okinawa. "There was a guy who came back from leave and he brought an album of Charley Pride's," McClinton remembered. "I said, 'Boy, that's a country dude.'"[25] Releasing his debut album in 1967, Charley Pride became a major country star and a well-known symbol of the era's racial changes. McClinton recognized much of himself in another black artist (also from Mississippi) who had managed to crack the Nashville color line. "I never thought it would be possible that a black guy could enter the country music world," he remembered.[26] Inspired by Pride's success, McClinton wrote a set of country songs that he hoped would bring him success when he returned home in 1968.

But he did not go to Nashville to make it as a country artist, instead returning to Stax Records in Memphis.[27] In one respect, this move made no sense. Stax—under the leadership of new label head, Al Bell—had fully embraced both the politics and sounds of the Black Power Movement. In the late 1960s, Stax adopted the language and iconography of Black Power campaigns in its releases and ad campaigns. The company even allied itself with militant political organizations. But McClinton also knew that Bell was interested in diversifying Stax's catalog to include releases not associated with soul music or African Americans. Bell believed that such diversification would increase Stax's profitability and expand its reputation as a black-controlled musical powerhouse. Impressed by McClinton's demos, Bell signed the artist to a contract on Stax's subsidiary Enterprise Records. Beginning in 1971, O. B. McClinton became Stax's first country artist.[28]

The complex racial balance symbolized by McClinton reflected a larger and paradoxical moment for country music. On one hand, McClinton's signing to Stax embodied the possibilities of a post–Charley Pride transformation where a black singer could potentially find success in the genre. On the other hand, even after Pride's breakthrough, writers, politicians, and the musicians themselves continued to assert country as the sound of whiteness.[29] Soul music was often the specific sonic contrast for this supposed binary, while the Black Nationalist politics embraced by labels such as Stax was the explicit enemy of New Right politicians that celebrated country music as the sound of the "silent majority." So O. B. McClinton's attempt to make it in country music—on Stax Records, no less—simultaneously represented two seemingly irreconcilable cultural positions.

Stax's awareness of this duality led Al Bell to insist that McClinton record in Nashville, which he hoped would both ensure a high quality for McClinton's country records and legitimize him to the notoriously protective (and racially restrictive) Nashville establishment. They hired Jim Malloy, a white producer who—according to *Billboard* reporter Bill Williams—was brought in "to make sure the country authenticity is there" on McClinton's recordings.[30] They chose Monument Studios, a well-known site for hit country records, along with a group of top-notch Nashville studio players. McClinton had long performed country music and had made his name in Southern soul because of the country influence in his songs, but his record label still took great pains to make sure that nobody could doubt his stylistic authenticity.

This quest for legitimacy led to a painful moment that sullied McClinton's opinion of his debut album—ultimately titled *Country*—and foreshadowed later events. According to McClinton, Jim Malloy insisted that he alter his natural singing voice to avoid sounding too black. "He thought that the next black country singer had to be even countrier than Charley Pride," McClinton recalled. "In fact, he would come down out of the control room and say, 'You sound black on that word.' And I'd say, 'look at me, 'cause I am!'"[31] Malloy forced McClinton to push his voice into a higher and more nasal register, affecting a caricatured twang that felt wrong to McClinton in numerous ways. "I had been taught to sing from [the] diaphragm," McClinton remembered, harkening back to his training in the Teen Town Singers and in the college choir, and felt that this affected performance was "deceiving not only myself but . . . the public" through its weak attempt at racial disguise.[32]

Ironically enough, this forced vocal approach is most apparent on "Country Music That's My Thing," McClinton's self-penned assertion of independence in the face of racial essentialism. McClinton's voice sounds pinched and too high from the opening voiceover, where the singer describes how a friend accused him of being a race traitor: "You tellin' everybody you're a stone soul brother, yet you go to Nashville and sing." The friend demands that McClinton "explain" this paradox, and McClinton responds in a forceful chorus:

> You got a thing, I've got a thing
> All of God's children got a thing
> Country music, friend, that's my thing.[33]

McClinton goes on to describe a similar reaction from his "old lady"—who prefers the "sweet soul music" of James Brown to McClinton's "western boots" and "country songs"—and ultimately rejects both his friend and lover, telling them that they can find him in Nashville, where he will be busy with his country career.

Lyrically, "Country Music That's My Thing" fit in perfectly with a larger strategy—observable both with McClinton and Charley Pride—of artists presenting themselves as what Jeremy Colin Hill calls "a "country singer first . . . and a black man second."[34] This strategy allowed the singers to claim a position of color blindness that contrasted with the supposed racial separatism of Black Power and claimed common ground with the (white) country fans who rejected such nationalist assertions. It also, in Hill's words, "reinforc[ed] country music's whiteness" by implying that a black person who loved country music was an outsider in their race.[35] McClinton was unhappy at the final version of "Country Music That's My Thing," but its mixture of assertive lyrics and affected vocal make the record into a fitting debut for McClinton's ambivalent experience in country music.[36]

It is important to note that—despite McClinton's songwriting talent and wealth of songs—*Country* was made up primarily of cover versions, including a striking interpretation of Merle Haggard's backlash anthem "Okie from Muskogee." McClinton's take on Haggard's smash hit "exaggerated every aspect of the song," as Barbara Ching notes, including the "thickest hick accent possible," which may have been demanded by Jim Malloy.[37] Across the album, the exaggerated vocals and prevalence of novelty songs made McClinton appear to Rob Bowman as "self-effacing to the point of minstrelsy."[38] Angela Hammond also recognizes minstrelsy— and what she calls "self-deprecation"—in the way that McClinton's humor "reduc[es] any perceived threat and plac[es] him in his proper place of subservience to the mostly white audience."[39] Jim Malloy insisted on this broadly comic approach, too, which further angered McClinton. He called the album "just as phony a $3 bill" and railed against the lack of respect shown to him by his white Nashville producer, "I sat down with Jim Malloy and he'd pick the songs and he did all the production. He told me how to phrase. He did everything. I was just like a zombie."[40] This lack of artistic autonomy—combined with Malloy's racial insult—convinced McClinton that he needed to guide his own productions in the future.

McClinton's race was literally obscured on the album cover, which pictured the singer with his back to the camera. "The casual shopper would not notice that he was black," Rob Bowman points out, while also admitting that "Stax did include a color portrait shot of O. B. on the back."[41] This decision was not uncommon—Charley Pride's first albums were issued without a portrait of the singer, and it was only after Pride's first hits that his race was revealed to the country audience. Additionally, the album's evocative title, *Country*, was designed both to assert his legitimacy as a country performer and also perhaps to unconsciously disguise the racial identity of its artist; the singer was billed as "Country Charley Pride" on his earliest singles.[42]

Despite initial attempts to hide his race, McClinton's race figured prominently in coverage and promotion of his debut album.[43] In a remarkable December 1971 press release, Stax's publicity office noted that McClinton—who "is Black and sings country & western music"—represented a chance to tear down racial boundaries in both music and American society. "Country music for Blacks, like soul music for whites," the uncredited writer argues, "had always had a 'do not sing' sign on it," so McClinton "knew that the 'race problem' of his singing country & western was inevitable." Facing resistance from both black audiences (who called him "not truly black") and the white-dominated country industry (which had convinced black artists that it was "out of their place" to perform the music), McClinton condemns the implicit and explicit "musical color line" that could impair his music and limit his freedom: "I'm not ashamed to tell either Black or white that I love country music."[44]

The music press followed Stax's lead, presenting McClinton as a figure of racial breakthrough. "He really knows country," said reporter Claude Hall, "I'm really glad to see country music becoming integrated."[45] But the lofty optimism could not mask a more troubling subtext that suggested the tenacity of the musical segregation McClinton hoped to defy. In one item, *Billboard*'s Bill Williams noted that "O. B. McClinton, the great black country artist with Stax, made his first appearance at the 'Opry.' He didn't sing; merely stood in the wings as a spectator."[46] Released in early 1972, *Country* made little impact on the charts, as did the three singles issued from the recording.

McClinton's national notoriety increased when he joined the Edmund Muskie presidential campaign in 1972. Running for the Democratic nomination to challenge incumbent Richard Nixon, Muskie enlisted McClinton—along with black football player Rosey Grier and white folksinger Steve Goodman—to join him on the "Sunshine Express," a whistle-stop train tour throughout the contested state of Florida. San Francisco's black newspaper the *Sun Reporter* described the choice of McClinton as "an unprecedented move involving an unknown performer," and the singer warmed up the crowds at each stop before Muskie made his remarks; his songs included versions of Merle Haggard and Charley Pride.[47] McClinton also entertained the campaign staff as the train traveled between destinations, a situation that provoked a withering description from *Rolling Stone's* Hunter S. Thompson: "O. B. McClinton, 'the Black Irishman of Country Music,' was trying to lure people into the lounge car for a 'singalong thing.' It took awhile, but they finally collected a crowd. Then one of Muskie's college-type staffers took charge. He told the Black Irishman what to play, cued the other staff people, then launched into about nineteen straight choruses of Big Ed's newest campaign song . . . I left at that point."[48]

The racial tokenism observed by Hunter S. Thompson reflected a larger dynamic at play in Muskie's choice of the largely unknown O. B. McClinton. As a black country singer, he could theoretically unite two crucial and divided constituencies. First was African Americans, who were pivotal to Democratic Party success in Southern states in the aftermath of the Civil Rights Movement. At the same time, though, Muskie could reasonably surmise that McClinton's country songs might appeal to some of the white voters who abandoned the party in favor of such Republicans as Nixon, whose race-based "Southern strategy" was crucial to his 1968 win, and might also bring in breakaway Democrats like George Wallace, the segregationist Alabama governor then running his third insurgent presidential campaign. As one reporter noted, Muskie's route was purposely mapped onto Wallace's strongest sources of support during his 1968 presidential campaign. Muskie claimed that the integration of the entertainers "helps us to recognize the mistakes we have made in the past in dealing with each other, young and old, black and white."[49] Muskie railed against Wallace's divisive politics even as he courted them with his refusal to support forced busing, his use of "law and order" rhetoric, and his inclusion of a country singer on the "Sunshine Express."[50]

Wallace had many supporters among country artists and fans, as did Richard Nixon and other conservative leaders. So although numerous black soul singers campaigned for Democrats, McClinton's decision to ally with this party was a riskier proposition. The combination of his sound and skin color not only increased his attractiveness to Democrats like Muskie, trying to thread the increasingly narrow needle of Southern politics, but also left him outside the country mainstream that he appealed to in "Country Music That's My Thing" and that was so crucial to his success.

So McClinton's involvement in the 1972 election was a noteworthy (if limited) moment of divergence from the genre's primary political narrative. As the only prominent black country singer (and one of the only country singers of any race) to join with the Democrats, McClinton reflected his larger pursuit of artistic independence and personal autonomy.[51]

McClinton's second album for Stax/Enterprise reflected that new demand. The singer insisted on producing the album himself, returning to Monument Studios to lead the same group of Nashville studio musicians. He hoped that this new album—*Obie from Senatobie*—would more accurately reflect his creative vision. Most obvious and meaningful was the change in his voice. Relaxed and in a lower register, his vocals on the second album reflected the twangy sweetness that made him such an effective country singer but that had been missing on his debut album.

Ironically, given McClinton's concerns about the lack of original material on his first album, there is only one self-penned song on *Obie from Senatobie*. That song, the title track, is a fascinating parody of Merle Haggard's backlash anthem "Okie from Muskogee" that followed his cover of the song on his debut and further demonstrates McClinton's ability to simultaneously subvert and affirm country's dominant racial narratives. Framed as a story from McClinton's time in the Air Force, "Obie from Senatobie" finds the singer celebrating the "Mississippi town" where he came from. His fellow servicemen mock and dismiss McClinton's home, telling him to "hide his face" rather than admit that he came from such an unimportant spot. Instead, McClinton exclaims in an anthemic (and Haggard-esque) chorus: "You can just call me Obie from Senatobie." Since "my mama gave birth to me [there]," that means it is "the most important place in the world to me." Statements of rural or small-town pride in the face of derision from elitist city folk is one of the most common tropes in country music, and McClinton asserts his ownership of that tradition. But he goes further, and in a stranger direction, by including what Barbara Ching correctly calls "derogatory stereotypes about southern blacks." Most obvious is his claim that—in his hometown—"we still eat watermelon down at the courthouse," a clear homage to Haggard's patriotic line "we still wave Old Glory down at the courthouse." Ching suggests that by replacing Haggard's lyric, McClinton engages in a process that can be "easily interpreted as irony" or that he "lampooned" and "burlesqued" racism in the unexpected context of a reactionary country anthem.[52] Ching underestimates the possibility that McClinton's lyrics were (at least in part) a conscious attempt to appeal to the backlash audience through an easy racial stereotype, but she is correct to note the multiple readings possible in McClinton's sole original contribution to his second album.

The rest of *Obie from Senatobie* consisted of covers, including another Merle Haggard song (a brooding version of "Today I Started Loving You Again") and several contemporary soul hits, including Wilson Pickett's "Don't Let the Green Grass Fool You" and William Bell's "My Whole World Is Falling Down." McClinton applies a country vocal and arrangement to the original soul versions, resulting in a much more effective blend than the campy performances demanded by his first producer. McClinton understood the hybridity at work in his performances. "'Don't Let the Green Grass Fool You' had been recorded by Wilson Pickett, and that's very, very black," McClinton noted. "But I knew the first time I heard the song [that] the title itself was country."[53] McClinton's instincts proved correct: "Don't Let the Green Grass Fool You" and "My Whole World Is Falling Down" each became Top 40 hits on the country charts, McClinton's biggest hits as a performer.

In one respect, it is fitting that McClinton's biggest success on the country charts came with two soul covers. After all, McClinton had started in soul music and possessed a great affinity for the genres' musical overlaps. More broadly, many country music stars—black, white, or otherwise—covered popular soul songs during this period, with such artists as Barbara Mandrell and Johnny Paycheck having major hits with their versions of material that began with black audiences. Nonetheless, it seems significant that McClinton's biggest hit came not with a self-penned country song or stylistic hybrid but with countrified versions of contemporary soul hits. Perhaps the association between blackness and soul music was so strong that even an African-American country singer could not overcome its tenacious hold on the musical marketplace. McClinton further embraced this possibility by releasing covers of the Temptations' "I Wish It Would Rain" (which made it to number sixty-two on the country charts) and William Bell's "You Don't Miss Your Water" (which did not chart) from *Obie from Senatobie*. The album itself—which a *Billboard* writer said "will dispel any doubts about him being country"—also failed to chart.[54]

The predominance of soul covers may also have stemmed from his record label. Stax hoped that McClinton would offer a breakthrough into a
previously untapped market, but the label proved unable to successfully
promote a country artist. It was not for lack of trying. In 1973 and 1974,
even as the label collapsed, Stax continued signing country acts, allied
with independent producers and labels in Nashville, and sent McClinton
to appear at the Grand Ole Opry and the prominent Fan Fair convention.[55] Despite their best efforts, neither McClinton nor any of those on
the Stax country roster achieved substantial success.

Stax's failure in the country market reflected its lack of contacts in
country radio or promotions, but some at Stax felt that their struggle was
racial.[56] "We were out of our place," Stax executive Larry Shaw remembered, "We were threatened in Nashville at the country conventions."[57]
Shaw suggests that Stax's status as a powerful, politicized, black-controlled
company rendered them an outlier in the country community, and
McClinton agreed. He later claimed that "if it hadn't been for Stax, I might
never have been in country music . . . If you check over all these years,
there has only been one black artist signed for a major label and nobody
knew he was black when he signed."[58]

That artist, Charley Pride, remained an ambivalent figure for McClinton
during this period. Although his success had theoretically destroyed the
racial barriers in country music, McClinton and others found that Pride's
success did not create a path for others to follow: "I've traveled a harder
road coming behind Charley Pride than Hank Williams, Jr. did coming
behind his daddy. Many people looked on Charley Pride as an accident."[59]
McClinton was not alone in this frustration; in fact, some of the most
vehement comments came from black soul artists who wished to cross
over into country. Soul artist Jerry "Swamp Dogg" Williams, who loved
the genre and even scored a number one country hit when honky-tonker
Johnny Paycheck recorded his song "She's All I Got," said that "they always
let *one* [succeed] . . . They let a black guy in to sing some country, and the
motherfucker went all the way to the top. And they're like, 'We're not let-
ting any more of these cocksuckers in.'"[60] Sometimes physical boundaries
accompanied the figurative ones. Just as McClinton's first appearance at
the Opry was as a bystander rather than a performer, soul singer Millie
Jackson recalled that "I was supposed to appear on the . . . Opry [but my]

record company said, 'She's an R&B act. You can't promote her country.' So nothing happened."[61]

McClinton even wrote a song called "I'm the Other One" that joked about the widespread confusion he faced when performing in country venues.[62] McClinton remembered an incident where a fan kept requesting songs by Charley Pride, and his refusal to perform them led the fan to accuse McClinton of being "prejudiced."[63] Not only did McClinton have to prove his country bona fides, but he also had to differentiate himself from a more famous black counterpart.[64]

One key difference between McClinton and Charley Pride is that the former's songs openly talked about race and region. One of the most striking and problematic examples of this came at the very end of his Stax tenure, with "Dixie (She Was a Mama to Me)" in 1974. In this swelling ballad, McClinton begins by exclaiming:

> Mister, I just heard you talking about Dixie
> And I don't like the things you said
> If you can't say something good about Dixie
> Then you just better keep it in your head.

This startling affirmation of Old South nostalgia leads to McClinton defending the honor of his mother, a woman named Dixie, who struggled to raise him after his father abandoned them. This sentimental story of maternal love and struggle doubles as an extended metaphor that puns on the name's other meaning to assert the South's value and independence. "I'm the only son of Dixie," he proclaims, "I'll take my stand and fight and die for Dixie / Get outta here before Dixie's son comes down on you."

As with "Obie from Senatobie," McClinton's tribute to the South could be seen as a kind of reappropriation. He puts African Americans back at the center of Southern historical traditions and even subverts the oft-used image of a fallen woman as a symbol for the defeated South in the aftermath of the Civil War by making her African American.[65] But also as with "Obie from Senatobie," this song can be considered a capitulation to a language and ideology that was built on the historical refusal of black equality. As with other McClinton compositions, it is tempting to both overread its racially progressive possibilities and underestimate its place within a broader set of neo-Confederate paeans from this period.

Artists like Alabama, Hank Williams Jr., and Charlie Daniels offered musical tributes to "the South rising again" and accompanied these songs with the use of the Confederate flag. Neither reading is necessarily incorrect, but their simultaneity in "Dixie (She Was a Mama to Me)" demonstrates McClinton's ability and willingness to confront these complicated tropes.

"Dixie (She Was a Mama to Me)" was included on McClinton's final Stax album; he was released from his contract in 1975. Despite his frustration with some of the label's decisions, McClinton looked back fondly on his tenure at the black-owned company: "Al Bell did a really great thing. He did something that many executives won't do—let a new artist go into the studio and have control." They had failed to make him the next Charley Pride, but Stax signed McClinton as a country artist and allowed him a degree of artistic independence that enabled him to produce striking recordings such as "Obie from Senatobie" and "Dixie (She Was a Mama to Me)." This oversight was particularly important for McClinton because, as he noted, "I never got a chance to have that control again."[66]

For the next several years, working with a series of Nashville's best producers, McClinton repeatedly witnessed just how quickly that "control" could be taken away. A hot commodity in the aftermath of his Stax release, he first worked with powerful Mercury Records producer Jerry Kennedy. "I was as happy as a mule in heaven with his wings on," McClinton remembered, but his experience with Kennedy quickly turned sour. As with Jim Malloy in his first sessions for Enterprise, McClinton chafed against the producer's "very dominant" approach in the studio. "He didn't want me to open my mouth," McClinton remembered, and Kennedy's domineering approach and the racial undertones of this encounter left McClinton embittered: "Jerry cut three records on me. And needless to say, none of the three even bubbled under the Billboard charts."[67]

McClinton faced a similar dynamic with Buddy Killen, who had produced hits with both country and soul artists.[68] Although the two men shared a mutual respect and even friendship, the same lack of control that McClinton had previously experienced once again emerged in his sessions with Killen. In 1979, *Billboard* reporter Kip Kirby described a session with the two men. Kirby presents McClinton as a childlike figure who needed Killen's guidance and discipline to complete a successful session. She describes McClinton "hopping around" the studio while the session players waited for "more definite instructions" from Killen. Annoyed with McClinton, Killen yells "Doggone it, O. B., we're gonna have to teach you that meter isn't something you read on the back porch." When Killen ends the session before McClinton can add his vocals, the singer turns from "high spirits" to being "obviously upset." He pleads with Killen to let him finish, and Killen relents. "It's hard for me to say no to my artist," Killen told Kirby. Restarting the recording, Killen warns McClinton that "you better sing this real good or you're gonna have to go back to those cotton fields, right?" Kirby describes McClinton as "delighted" by the opportunity to continue the recording, and he "follows Killen's instructions" to complete the track.[69]

This astonishing article demonstrates that McClinton's autonomy and even dignity faced constant challenge in Nashville studios. Killen's supposedly "good-natured" jokes with the singer infantilize him (claiming erroneously that he did not know anything about meter, pitch, or other musical basics that he had mastered as a teenager and were essential to his professional life), and he also makes a crude reference to McClinton's roots as a black cotton farmer in Mississippi. Beyond Killen's outrageous comments, reporter Kirby presents this session in a thoroughly paternalistic fashion, with McClinton throwing a childish tantrum and Killen saving the day as the patient father figure. The equal collaboration between two professionals disappears, replaced by a condescending and demeaning portrait. Although this profile is a particularly egregious example of the racial disparities faced by black artists, it reflects the same troublesome dynamics that underscored the careers of African-American country performers, even in a setting that seemingly confirmed the value of musical integration.

This disrespect clearly stayed with McClinton, who addressed it in subsequent comments to Rob Bowman: "It's really weird to musicians in Nashville all the time, and they can't believe that I write a song 100 percent melody and lyric and don't play an instrument. I hear a melody and I start humming this melody in my mind and then I will write lyrics to go with this melody and everything is in meter." Buddy Killen's claim that McClinton did not know the difference between musical meter and a gas meter is noteworthy given this observation, and McClinton bemoaned that Nashville musicians often failed to recognize that his abilities were as legitimate as their more formalized approach: "I can get down with a good session guitar player who knows the [Nashville] number system and sing this melody . . . They'll play one chord, and if that's not right they'll say, 'What about this?' But I know when they play the right chord—it feels right."[70] Contrary to the presentation of McClinton as an untrained (and unprofessional) artist in the *Billboard* article, the singer himself stressed musical abilities that were defined and delimited by racial perceptions.

McClinton noticed this dynamic again in sessions for Epic Records, where he produced his final hits in 1979, including the novelty song "Soap," which gave him his biggest hit since the Stax days but was also his final Epic release. "You'll have to ask them why there was no more. It sure seemed like everything was going good, real good," McClinton bemoaned in his autobiography, and he believed race to be a factor in Epic's decision.[71] He also noted, "It's rough enough for a good singer to make it in country music with all the competition. Add to the roughness being black, and you can start dealing with square roots and multiples."[72]

With no backing from a major label, McClinton recorded for a series of independents in the 1980s, scoring a few minor hits (with such evocative names as "Not Exactly Free" and "Honky-Tonk Tan") and maintaining an active performing career. "They weren't the huge stadium crowds," he said, "but I was having fun and so were they." Despite his comfortable new role, McClinton remained hopeful that he would score another recording contract: "I had written some new songs that I was sure were going to get me back onto the charts with a major label that would let me do it *my* way."[73] Unfortunately, in 1986, McClinton discovered that he had terminal cancer. As McClinton's condition worsened, Buddy Killen and Ralph Emery organized a star-studded benefit for his family at the Stockyards, a popular Nashville restaurant that Killen owned.

In his autobiography, McClinton described this event as a sign of progress. "[My wife] Jo Ann and I were given a table right in front of the stage. Can you imagine that? Two people who used to have to sneak in the back of theatres and clubs and restaurants and bus stations when we were growing up in the South, now sitting as honored guests in the best seats in the house," he remembered, "I realized then just how far the black man—and the white man—had come over the last years." He recalled the difference between the "little Mississippi black child who in his innocence had 'mistakenly' taken a drink of water out of the 'white' water fountain and was beaten by his mother for doing it," and the adult who was "being honored, and cried for, by those stars and that Southern audience that was 99% white."[74]

McClinton made a similar argument in a speech to the assemblage of friends and coworkers at the end of the benefit. He plugged his TV albums by joking that "I am an Equal Opportunity Performer—you can see me in color on your black-and-white set." He recalled his mother's fears for her son as a child in Mississippi because "she always said I spoke my mind too freely." He thanked the crowd not only for their support in his illness but also for affirming his importance as a black man in country music. He closed by singing a recent composition called "The Only One," which— unlike the Charley Pride–referencing "I'm the Other One"—asserted his own role in transcending musical expectations and racial limitations. "Well, I've always been country / But, Lord, my skin is black," he sang, "And everywhere I've been / Somebody would notice that." Accused of being the "only one" of his kind who liked country, McClinton embraced this uniqueness and claimed the title. The song elides history, of course; McClinton was not the only black country singer and certainly not the only black country fan. But just as he had done with "Country Music That's My Thing," McClinton here centralized his race in examining the unique (and somewhat marginal) position that he retained in the country world despite his success and the love of his white contemporaries.[75] "I walked up to that stage, and there were all these redneck-looking dudes throwing their arms around me," he told Gerry Wood in one of his final interviews.[76]

Those interviews also revealed that—despite McClinton's happiness and pride at the Stockyards—he felt a deeper discontent about the way that his blackness had limited his country career.[77] "What's been so frustrating to me all these years is that I've had so many messages to get across," he told Wood, listing his "rough time" in breaking the "barriers" of radio airplay and record label support: "A CBS or RCA has never taken O. B. McClinton under their wings. And I was the type that would never hang around and mope and go in and make them mad by threatening people. When they overlooked me, I just quietly went on." McClinton's refusal to protest was not based on any faith in record companies or willingness to toe the line but in a belief that such assertions could only lead to further trouble. "I was never one to jump up and say 'Well, they won't play my record because I'm black,'" he claimed, "If that was their reason for doing it, they know it and I don't have to say anything about it for it to dwell in their heads."[78]

At the end of the conversation, he recalled his song "Back Road into Town," a soul hit for Stax artist the Staple Singers that describes the struggles of a rural black man—from an area similar to McClinton's hometown—to provide for his family in the context of poverty and white supremacy. Even though McClinton had achieved fame and financial stability, he reminded Wood of the song's ultimate lesson: "[At the] end of this song . . . [the man] died, and he never made it into town."[79]

When cancer claimed McClinton's life in 1987, he was buried near his parents' farm after a funeral in Senatobia. Another memorial took place in Nashville, and McClinton was honored by the Tennessee General Assembly, the Country Music Foundation's Walkway of Stars, and the state of Mississippi, which unveiled O. B. McClinton Road in the town of Gravel Springs.[80] McClinton has also been posthumously feted as a key figure in the history of African Americans in country music. He is featured on the 1998 compilation *From Where I Stand: The Black Experience in Country Music,* on a display at the Stax Museum of American Soul Music in Memphis, and on a plaque as part of the Mississippi Country Music Heritage Trail. Also, as mentioned earlier, his name is commonplace in works that consider race and popular music in the United States. Despite these realities, McClinton remains an underappreciated figure, often presented as a secondary participant in both country and soul stories. He is far less prominent or popular than African-American country stars like Charley Pride or Darius Rucker. Most significant, perhaps, almost all his recordings—including his classic albums for Stax—are out of print.

Still, the tangled pathways of O. B. McClinton's career offer a fascinating glimpse into the complex racial and cultural politics of country music in the 1960s and 1970s. In one respect, he represents the possibilities of a country moment defined by interracial musical crossover and the breakthrough success of Charley Pride. McClinton's work challenged the restrictions of country's supposed whiteness and pushed against racialized expectations in his music and his career choices. In other work, he demonstrates the limitations of those crossovers, belying any easy story of personal breakthrough or country music inclusion. As Stephen King and Renee Foster discuss elsewhere in this collection, this tension continues to define the experience of contemporary black country performers. Despite McClinton's repeated attempts (in both song and professional association) to demonstrate his country legitimacy and despite the support he received throughout his career, he also faced resistance rooted in the juxtaposition of his sound and his skin color. Although he looked back on his life as an example of larger racial progress, he also remained convinced that the racial barrier he most specifically hoped to transgress remained firmly entrenched. To McClinton, this seeming contradiction was a painful reality of the tight and tenacious relationship between country music and white identity.

"You can take a black guy to Nashville from right out of the cotton fields with bib overalls," he told Gerry Wood in 1986, "and they will call him r&b. You can take a white guy in a pin-stripe suit who's never seen a cotton field, take him to Nashville ... and they will call him country."[81] The career of O. B. McClinton—"the Chocolate Cowboy," "the black speck," "Obie from Senatobie," "the other one," "the only one"—demands a greater understanding of the deep complexity that exists just below that tenacious fiction.

## NOTES

1. Barney Hoskyns, *Say It One Time for the Broken Hearted: The Country Side of Southern Soul* (London: Bloomsbury Paperbacks, 1998), 174. I previously addressed "Black Speck," and I suggested that the song could also be about Charley Pride. See Charles L. Hughes, *Country Soul: Making Music and Making Race in the American South* (Chapel Hill: University of North Carolina Press, 2015), 137.

2. Gerry Wood, "Nashville Scene," *Billboard*, November 15, 1986, 34.

3. Barbara Ching, "Read between the Lines: Alice Randall and the Integration of Country Music," in *Hidden in the Mix: The African American Presence in Country Music*, ed. Diane Pecknold (Durham: Duke University Press, 2013), 272.

4. Elsewhere in this collection, Stephen King and Renee Foster explore the continuing tension surrounding country's relationship to African-American artists in their essay "'Leave Country Music to White Folk'?: Narratives from Contemporary African-American Country Artists on Race and Music."

5. Beyond sources mentioned elsewhere, see Richard Carlin, *Country Music: A Biographical Dictionary*, 2nd ed. (New York: Routledge, 2013), 256; Simon Frith, *Facing*

*the Music: A Pantheon Guide to Popular Culture* (New York: Pantheon Books, 1989), 58; Peter Guralnick, *Sweet Soul Music: Rhythm and Blues and the Southern Dream of Freedom* (Boston: Back Bay Books, 1986), 286; Nadine Hubbs, *Rednecks, Queers, and Country Music* (Berkeley: University of California Press, 2014), 70; Michael Kosser, *How Nashville Became Music City U.S.A.: 50 Years of Music Row* (Milwaukee: Hal Leonard, 2006), 111; and Bill C. Malone, *Country Music U.S.A.: Second Revised Edition* (Austin: University of Texas Press, 2002), 315–16.

6. Diane Pecknold, *The Selling Sound: The Rise of the Country Music Industry* (Durham: Duke University Press, 2007), 226.

7. O. B. McClinton and Gerry Wood, *Hard Way to Go: The O. B. McClinton Autobiography* (Key West: Gerry Wood, 1991), 5.

8. McClinton made these remarks in a 1973 interview for *Music City News* with LaWayne Satterfield. Interview is quoted in Irwin Stambler and Grelun Landon, *Country Music: The Encyclopedia*, rev. and updated 3rd ed. (New York: St. Martin's Press, 1997), 296.

9. Ibid., 5, 8.

10. In using the term, Woodruff quotes activist William Pickens. See Nan Elizabeth Woodruff, *American Congo: The African American Freedom Struggle in the Delta* (Cambridge: Harvard University Press, 2003).

11. Rob Bowman, "O. B. McClinton: Country Music, That's My Thing," *Journal of Country Music* 14, no. 2 (1991): 27. McClinton reiterated this sentiment in a discussion with music critic Barney Hoskyns, saying that the "only difference between [country and R&B] is the back-up instruments." Hoskyns, *Say It One Time*, 173.

12. Ibid.

13. McClinton and Wood, *Hard Way to Go*, 10.

14. See Karl Hagstrom Miller, *Segregating Sound: Inventing Folk and Pop Music in the Age of Jim Crow* (Durham: Duke University Press, 2010), 3–7.

15. Bowman, "O. B. McClinton," 23.

16. McClinton and Wood, *Hard Way to Go*, 11–12.

17. For more on WDIA, see Louis Cantor, *Wheelin' on Beale: How WDIA-Memphis Became the Nation's First All-Black Radio Station and Created the Sound that Changed America* (New York: Pharos Books, 1992).

18. See Hughes, *Country Soul*, 55.

19. Memphis rockabilly artist Carl Perkins wrote "Blue Suede Shoes" and scored a number one hit with it before Presley released his cover version. But McClinton specifically referenced Presley when discussing his performance. Bowman, "O. B. McClinton," 24.

20. McClinton and Wood, *Hard Way to Go*, 41.

21. Bowman, "O. B. McClinton," 24.

22. Quote from McClinton and Wood, *Hard Way to Go*, 44. In the autobiography, McClinton tells a curious story about his Stax experience. He recalls meeting with label head, Jim Stewart, in which Stewart offered him only $100 for a composition. "That just absolutely made me furious. It was a put-down, and I knew I could not make it through

school next year on a hundred dollars." In the context of the book, this appears to be McClinton's first encounter with Stax, even though—when talking to Rob Bowman—McClinton related the story as a positive encounter and story of personal perseverance. It is difficult to determine why this contradiction exists.

23. Rob Bowman goes so far as to say that McClinton's work "launched" the Goldwax label. Bowman, "O. B. McClinton," 25.

24. Hoskyns, *Say It One Time*, 87.

25. Bowman, "O. B. McClinton," 26.

26. McClinton and Wood, *Hard Way to Go*, 94. It is worth noting that McClinton's version of his discovery of Charley Pride is different in his autobiography. In this telling, he discovered a Pride album in the base's PX store.

27. He also recorded some country songs at Fame Studios in Muscle Shoals, where he had placed several soul hits. McClinton knew that while Muscle Shoals was "really hot as a rhythm and blues recording center," he could count on the versatility of Fame's celebrated studio musicians to cut successful country tracks. Ibid., 56.

28. Barney Hoskyns deftly notes that, although Stax might seem like an odd place to record McClinton's country work, Stax had recently found success with Isaac Hayes's soulful version of Glen Campbell's country hit "By The Time I Get To Phoenix." Hoskyns, *Say It One Time*, 174.

29. Beyond thinly veiled assertions by politicians like Richard Nixon and George Wallace, direct references infused nearly all aspects of country discourse during this period. This ranged from Merle Haggard's song "I'm A White Boy," recorded by Haggard and two other artists in the early 1970s, to journalist John Grissim's 1970 book *Country Music: White Men's Blues*.

30. Bill Williams, "Stax Now Represents All Forms of Music," *Billboard*, June 3, 1972, M-2.

31. Bowman, "O. B. McClinton," 27.

32. McClinton and Wood, *Hard Way to Go*, 106.

33. It is additionally noteworthy that this chorus is a direct reference to the slave spiritual "I've Got Shoes," which offers an additional level of subtext.

34. Jeremy Colin Hill, *Out of the Barn and Into a Home: Country Music's Cultural Journey from Rustic to Suburban, 1943–1974* (PhD diss., George Washington University, 2011), 162–63; for Pride, see Hughes, *Country Soul*, 136–37.

35. Hill, *Out of the Barn and Into a Home*, 163.

36. For more on "Country Music That's My Thing," see Barbara Ching, *Wrong's What I Do Best: Hard Country Music and Contemporary Culture* (New York: Oxford University Press, 2001), 43.

37. Ibid., 43. Ching does not mention Malloy's insistence on a different vocal approach in her discussion of McClinton's first album.

38. Bowman, "O. B. McClinton," 27.

39. Angela Hammond, *Color Me Country: Commercial Country Music and Whiteness* (PhD diss., University of Kentucky, 2011), 156–57.

40. Bowman, O.B. McClinton, 27.

41. Ibid.

42. Many country albums recorded by black soul singers were titled with some varia-tion of "country," a clear attempt to legitimize the albums in the minds of listeners who would not associate country music with African-American performers.

43. Stax/Enterprise advertisements, *Billboard,* June 3, 1972, M-8, 40.

44. "O. B. McClinton, the 'Black Country Irishman,'" Stax Records press release, author unknown, December 1971, in author's possession.

45. Claude Hall, "Vox Jox," *Billboard,* April 8, 1972, 21.

46. Bill Williams, "Nashville Scene," *Billboard,* September 2, 1972, 43.

47. Author unknown, "Senator Muskie Tags O. B. McClinton for Tour," *San Francisco Sun Reporter,* March 3, 1972, 34; McClinton songs from Clay Eals, *Steve Goodman: Facing the Music* (Toronto: ECW Press, 2006), 273.

48. Hunter S. Thompson, "The Banshee Screams in Florida," *Rolling Stone,* April 4, 1972, 163–64; reprinted in Hunter S. Thompson, *Fear and Loathing at "Rolling Stone": The Essential Writing of Hunter S. Thompson* (New York: Simon and Schuster, 2011). It should be noted that McClinton's "black Irishman" nickname was widely used during this period, including by Stax Records, which—as discussed earlier—even issued a press release by that name.

49. James M. Naughton, "Muskie Urges Floridians to Reject Wallace, *New York Times,* February 19, 1972, 16; Muskie quote from Eals, *Steve Goodman,* 272.

50. Naughton, "Muskie Urges Floridians to Reject Wallace," 16.

51. It is noteworthy that McClinton does not mention his trip with Muskie in his autobiography, nor is it discussed in the lengthy Bowman profile.

52. Ching has written about "Obie from Senatobie" in multiple places, and while her argument has shifted slightly in her more recent work on the song, her fundamental point remains the same. See Barbara Ching, "Read between the Lines," 269, and Ching, *Wrong's What I Do Best,* 43–44.

53. Bowman, "O. B. McClinton," 27.

54. Author unknown, "Billboard's Top Album Picks," *Billboard,* May 26, 1973, 52.

55. Author unknown, "Stax Country Group in Expansion Surge," *Billboard,* May 12, 1973, 27; Author unknown, "Over 150 Top Acts Entertain Fan Fair Fans," *Billboard,* June 23, 1973, 31; Author unknown, "Butler Spearheads Stax Strategy," *Billboard,* 2/9/1974, 50; Author unknown, "Stax Expanding Enterprise, Signs Country Artists," *Billboard,* May 25, 1974, 40.

56. Bill Friskics-Warren points out that Stax "didn't know the first thing about plug-ging records to country radio." See David Cantwell and Bill Friskics-Warren, *Heartaches by the Number: Country Music's 500 Greatest Singles* (Nashville: Vanderbilt University /Country Music Hall of Fame Press, 2003), 188.

57. Shaw is quoted in Rob Bowman, *Soulsville U.S.A.: The Story of Stax Records* (New York: Schirmer, 1997), 226.

58. Bowman, "O. B. McClinton," 28.

59. Wood, "Nashville Scene," November 15, 1986, 135.

60. Jerry Williams, telephone interview by author, June 14, 2007.

61. Quoted in Dave Hoekstra, "Soul Queen Known for Less-Than-Regal Throne," *Chicago Sun-Times,* July 14, 2006.

62. Reporter Eve Zibart suggested that this song was to be the centerpiece of "a concept album" that would discuss his feelings about being one of the only black country performers. See Eve Zibart, "Pop Notes," *Washington Post,* August 12, 1978, B7.

63. Wood, "Nashville Scene," November 15, 1986, 34.

64. Matthew Daniel Sutton deftly notes that Charley Pride rarely mentioned other black country singers—including McClinton—and left them out of his autobiography, despite repeatedly mentioning many white country heroes and contemporaries. Sutton links this to Pride's broader desire to express "no interest in . . . further integrating the ranks of country musicians." See Matthew Daniel Sutton, *Storyville: Discourses in Southern Musicians' Autobiographies* (PhD diss., College of William and Mary, 2011).

65. It also recalls the long tradition of musical tributes to mothers that—as Allison McCracken discusses—traced to the "mammy" songs of blackface minstrelsy and became central to the development of American pop music. See Allison McCracken, *Real Men Don't Sing: Crooning in American Culture* (Durham: Duke University Press, 2015).

66. Bowman, "O. B. McClinton," 29.

67. McClinton and Wood, *Hard Way to Go,* 110.

68. Killen, originally from Muscle Shoals, found particular success with an artist named Joe Tex, who scored a series of hits in the 1960s and 1970s with Killen producing. (Killen had even recorded a McClinton song—"Who Gave Birth to the Funk?"—on one of Tex's late-1970s albums.) See McClinton and Wood, *Hard Way to Go,* 140.

69. Kip Kirby, "Killen: He Thrives on the Challenge of Creating a Hit," *Billboard,* April 28, 1979, 56.

70. Bowman, "O. B. McClinton," 25.

71. McClinton and Wood, *Hard Way to Go,* 112.

72. Wood, "Nashville Scene," November 15, 1986, 34.

73. McClinton and Wood, *Hard Way to Go,* 115.

74. Ibid., 125, 128. McClinton also mentions a conversation with his mother earlier that day, in which his mother expressed skepticism at "how many real friends" McClinton actually possessed in the country music community.

75. Ibid., 137–38.

76. Ibid., 141. This interview, and several others with Wood, are included at the end of McClinton's autobiography.

77. See Gerry Wood, "Nashville Scene," *Billboard,* November 15, 1986, 34–35; Wood, "Nashville Scene," *Billboard,* October 10, reprinted in McClinton and Wood, *Hard Way to Go,* 167–69.

78. Ibid., 144–45.

79. Ibid., 144.

80. This road became internationally known as the site of Othar Turner's Family

Picnic, a gathering of Delta blues musicians and fans that takes place every summer. See Steve Cheseborough, *Blues Traveling: The Holy Sites of Delta Blues,* updated ed. (Jackson: University of Mississippi Press, 2009), 245. See also Author unknown, "Country Star Honored," *Tri-State Defender,* May 6, 1987, 1, and Author unknown, "Five to Join CMF's Walkway of Stars," *Billboard,* June 4, 1988, 35.

81.  Wood, "Nashville Scene," *Billboard,* November 15, 1986, 135.

# CHAPTER SIX

# "I'm a Radical for Real"

*An Oral History
of Country Music's
Original Outlaw,
Steve Young*

TED OLSON

SINGER-SONGWRITER STEVE Young has played a significant role in the evolution of country music, having been a pioneer of both the country rock and outlaw country movements and having inspired numerous contemporary Americana musicians. The country music establishment, however, has not adequately acknowledged Young for his contributions, although the musical footpaths he blazed became superhighways that provided other performers with established routes to stardom and success. The reasons for Young's relative obscurity are many, not least of which were his political radicalism and artistic nonconformity. In this oral history, Young tells his own tale of struggling against injustice, alienation, commercialism, and neglect. While long overlooked in his home country, Young is widely admired overseas among music aficionados uninfluenced by long-standing cultural biases within American society. To those listening beyond the din of America's mass media, Young is not a marginal figure but a major recording artist whose music is at the same time highly individualistic and universal.

For decades now, Young has been thought of chiefly as a good song-writer. As early as the mid-1960s, Young's songcraft attracted the attention of other musicians, and by the mid-1970s, many country, folk, and rock musicians were including Young's songs in their repertoires. Examples include Waylon Jennings's memorable 1973 version of Young's "Lonesome, On'ry and Mean," Hank Williams Jr.'s 1977 cover of Young's "Montgomery in the Rain," and the Eagles' 1980 hit rendition of the singer-songwriter's best-known composition, "Seven Bridges Road" (the Eagles essentially reworked a 1973 version of that song by Ian Matthews). In 1984, music critic John Morthland asserted that "Young was one of the best writers of the mid-seventies Nashville renaissance . . . Young is a master at evoking a specific time and place."[1] Young's best songs match poetically resonant yet direct lyrics to haunting hymn-like or bluesy melodies. Music manager Charlie Hunter assessed Young's songwriting as follows: "What is astonishing about Steve Young is his absolute honesty. You can trust him not to lie. He's not interested in easy answers. He's driven, twisted, tortured to find what the truth of a situation is, be it the truth of a relationship, the truth of his heritage as a Southerner or as an American."[2]

Many musicians, fans, and critics associated with country music and related genres consider Young to have long been a master performer. Lucinda Williams once remarked, "When I first saw Steve Young I was spellbound. As a writer, Steve is in a league with Dylan and Hank Williams. And he sings like an angel."[3] Waylon Jennings expressed his enthusiasm for Young's singing by declaring that "Young is the second greatest country music singer—to George Jones, of course. He has no earthly idea how great he is."[4] In *The Rolling Stone Record Guide* (1979), journalist Chet Flippo asserted that Young is "a fine, overlooked, underrated country performer."[5] In 1991, Townes Van Zandt praised the totality of Young's talent: "For that voice, that guitar, and those songs to come together in one person is a wonder."[6] Several of Young's albums are considered as having been historically important. According to critic John Lomax III, "Young's first LP, *Rock Salt & Nails* [1969], along with albums by Gram Parsons, Gene Clark & Doug Dillard, were the first examples of the scintillating blend of country, folk, and rock which later came to be termed 'progressive country.'"[7] Young's second album, *Seven Bridges Road* (1972), featuring several of his most influential songs, has been reissued multiple times over the years, while his fourth album, *Renegade Picker* (1976), has been cited as a highlight of country music's "outlaw movement."

But scholars of mainstream country music have for the most part completely ignored Young. For example, country music historian Bill C. Malone has to date granted Young just one sentence—in the first edition (1979) of Malone's book *Southern Music/American Music;* yet Malone misidentified Young's birthplace.[8] By not investigating Young's life or music, country music scholars have overlooked a compelling story and have inadvertently marginalized Young's position in the country music canon.

In an attempt to situate Young more centrally in that canon, I interviewed the musician on two occasions: March 29, 1992, and May 22, 2015. Transcribed from these interviews (both of which were conducted at Young's house in Nashville), the narrative of Young's life in music— presented in his own words but edited for continuity—reveals that he found mythic significance and survival through music. In addition to providing a vivid depiction of mid-twentieth-century social life within the Southern Appalachian foothills and the Deep South, Young's oral history offers keen insight into the evolution of contemporary American music. One revelation from this oral history is the degree to which Young embraced a progressive ideology. Alienated from conservative Southern society and compelled to leave the South, Young pursued a career that ironically brought him back to his native region.

When, during the 1992 interview, Young said, "I'm a radical for real," he was referring to his music as much as to his political and social attitudes. Using the word "radical" spontaneously, unself-consciously, and unapologetically, he believed that music was an expression of truth uncompromised by the expediencies of convention, power, and money. Young, who died March 17, 2016, was a radical seeker, and his oral history chronicled a talented artist pursuing freedom—emotional, spiritual, artistic, political— wherever that quest took him. This is his story, and these are his songs.

> I was born down in Dixie,
> I grew up in the South,
> Listening to good music
> And that's what I'm all about.
> **"Renegade Picker"**

I was born July 12, 1942, near Newnan, Georgia—in a house, not a hospital. The doctor was apparently not very helpful, so my grandmother on my mother's side of the family, Cora Phillips Horsley, took charge of things. Living among the back dirt roads and the farms of northwest Georgia, my parents didn't know much about their ancestry, and they didn't seem to be very interested in it. My mother, Frances Owen Williams Young, was of Welsh descent; my father, Kemp Kirby Young, was half Native American. What they had in common was they were both very poor. My family was very uprooted and troubled, was in its behavior more like a black family than a white family. We're talking about being poor and struggling, and having a long history of that.

My father was quite an unusual character, perhaps partly because he was half Cherokee. His mother, my grandmother Minnie Smith Young, remembered that her Cherokee ancestors were affiliated with the Bird Clan. My mother's relatives looked down on my father's side of the family. Yet it wasn't said that my father and his kinfolk were inferior because they were part Indian; it was said that they were lazy, didn't want to work, weren't trustworthy, that sort of thing.

My father's father died when my father was only 13. Grandfather Young (I don't remember his first name) was a misfit like many others on that side of the family; he didn't own any land like my other grandparents. I've seen photographs of him; they say he was a good guy. One day he was walking across this bridge in Carrollton, Georgia, and the sheriff's nephew, who was drunk and driving, hit him and killed him, and the story goes, the sheriff's nephew never had to pay any price for it. Strings were pulled, and no punishment was handed down. Now I don't know if that was because my grandfather was part Indian. The Youngs were caught in between cultures—they were no longer connected to their Cherokee roots, and they didn't exactly fit in the white world either. So they would have had a hard time working or holding a regular job.

My parents were basically traditional, my father trying to be the breadwinner, my mother staying in the home. My father had worked hard as a young man, farming with a plow and a mule, but he didn't like it. Not a person who really wanted to work, he'd hold a job awhile (usually an odd job in Newnan and Carrollton, like driving a cab or doing carpentry work), then he'd get disgusted and either quit or get fired. My father didn't really want to settle down; he wanted to wander, and so he wandered in and out of my life. He was a drifter, and yet he was a married man—that's what frustrated him. My father could be very charming. People liked him. He was also a kind of con man, in that he was always talking about inventing things. Sometimes he would get people to invest in these inventions, though I don't think that any of them ever materialized.

My mother had a wild sense of humor and lifestyle. She could be very outgoing and even aggressive, hardly what one would have expected from a southern white woman. In fact, she was very popular among black people, who liked her sense of humor because it was outrageous and daring. I have one sibling, my brother, Kim Young, who is six years younger than me. He has quite an Indian look to him (some of the Youngs do and some don't). Kim also grew to love music. He's a great singer, even to this day.

The only grandfather I ever knew was not a blood relative: Grandfather Horsley. Grandfather Young died in that accident, and my mother's father, Owen Williams, died as my mother was being born. Both Grandfather and Grandmother Williams (she later became Grandmother Horsley) contracted some fever that was going around and killing a great many people. They both fell deeply into a comatose state; he died from the fever, but she survived. To give you an idea of the stories Grandmother Horsley used to tell (and some of these have a mystical touch): she said that while she was in this comatose state, she had a dream where she saw her husband, Owen, standing across a field. She was happy to see him. She went to meet him; they were going to be reunited. And when she started to walk toward him, the earth started to open, to part, and the distance between them became too great, and he said, "Well, I'll come back and get you later." Then she woke up and he was dead, and she was still alive.

Grandmother Williams, my mother's mother, got remarried to this man named Horsley, who also lived out in the country. Before I was born, Grandmother and Grandfather Horsley had been farmers in the area between Carrollton and Newnan. They had owned fifty acres of land that I imagine were difficult to work. They lived in places with wood heat and no insulation and no toilets, the classic old southern poor white deal. Grandfather Horsley's family had once owned a mill, but they had lost it. So Grandfather Horsley had to survive by farming, but sometimes he and my grandmother would have a hard time making the crops pay off. And if they did get any money, he would blow it somehow—he'd go on a spree or get drunk. I guess he finally thought the way out of all that was to get a job at the steel plant. That's how my grandparents wound up in Gadsden, Alabama. Grandfather Horsley eventually had an accident, and the steel company cheated him out of a fair settlement. He got a raw deal. I grew up hearing stories from both of them about the good old days in the country, but by the time I was born, they had given that up and sold it for life in the small towns, for steady work at the steel mills. As it turned out, it really wasn't such a great new life. They probably knew a lot more peace and satisfaction out in the country than they ever did in town.

Gadsden was the nearest thing I had to a hometown. When I wasn't actually living there, I was visiting my grandparents there. After my father left for good, my mother struggled to survive. We lived for a time near Carrollton, in a log cabin on the edge of the woods. This was a hard place to live. Soon I went to live with my grandparents, who in effect became more like parents to me. So I grew up listening to all their stories—I got an older view of things perhaps.

What strikes you in hearing these stories about the old days is that people were so full of life, were more in touch with the earth. These stories tell us that life then was more involved with the elements and the earth and that there was more use of the imagination. Rather than watch television, people passed the time playing music in front of the fireplace or on the porch. I know that these stories are based on truth. Many of the things that my grandmother would describe in her stories I actually saw when I was a child. I saw things that most people today cannot recollect: I saw people plowing with mules; I saw people washing clothes in black pots with long sticks. These things may seem like part of another world to many people today, but they really happened.

By the time I knew him, Grandfather Horsley was selling fruits and vegetables at fruit stands. I would often go to Atlanta with him in his big truck, to buy fruits and produce from the farmers at the farmer's market there. That was not a very far distance by today's standards, but to me it was a big journey. Along the way, we would stop off at little restaurants where the early Elvis records would be on the jukebox. The farmer's market was a fascinating world: big stacks of watermelons, cantaloupes, and bushel baskets of purple-hulled peas. It was also a heavy, grim world. Sometimes the farmers would go there and sell all their stuff and leave, but sometimes they would just watch it rot, then get disgusted and blow their money getting drunk.

Later, I found out that Grandfather Horsley was also a bootlegger. His fruit stands were legitimate fruit stands, but they also sold liquor. This was illegal, because many of these towns and counties were dry. When I was a kid helping my grandfather out at his fruit stands, the law would sometimes stop by. They seemed to harass him unfairly, because he had gotten in trouble for bootlegging once before—back in the country in Georgia (the government had broken down his still and locked up his bank account). So I grew up hearing all these stories about the "evil government." Not that the government wasn't "evil" in some ways, but the story was more complex than it was presented to me.

Of course, one could look back and criticize these people. One could say that they knew nothing of all the stuff that people are talking about today: dysfunctional families, alcoholism, compulsive behavior. But nobody back then knew much about such things or talked much about them. They had no idea. They just did the best they could in trying to survive, and it was a tough life. My reaction to all this was to be stoic. I was encouraged to be that way—especially by Grandmother Horsley, who was the center of things in my family. To be stoic was to be an adult and to be tough. I was expected to take the pain and just go on, like a boxer would.

> Oh, Father, you have made many rivers,
> And I've followed them from the mountains to the sea.
> Now, would you make me one that flows beyond the sun,
> Would you make a ship and sail it there for me?
>
> **"Many Rivers"**

The music of the churches I attended as a kid was a great thrill for me. I've come to realize that, even today, church music is still a heavy influence on me—not only the music itself, but the attitudes behind it. The profound issues of life and death—most other musicians won't touch them, but they are very important to me. I've often experimented with such issues in my music; I've written songs about death, for instance. Native Americans certainly dealt with death, and they had some beautiful death songs. I'm very critical of organized religion, particularly of Western religion, and I personally want no part of it. Yet I have to give those old church-going country people credit for facing these issues in their own way. There was a down and pessimistic side to them, of course, but the people in those days talked freely about death and dealt with it and sang about it. Today what frustrates me is that death is brushed under the rug—people no longer want to deal with it.

The church I attended most often as a child was in Georgia, in that no-man's-land between Newnan and Carrollton. Although I hadn't really grown up in that part of Georgia, I had heard all the stories about it, about the Georgia countryside and the backwoods and the old Horsley farm-place and mill, and so on. I had also heard all about Cross Plains Baptist Church. Even when I lived in Gadsden, we'd often make the hundred-mile journey to visit our Georgia relatives, and while there we'd attend Sunday services at Cross Plains. It was always a thrill for me to go back there. There was a beautiful, shallow creek running by the church—Snake Creek, where people were baptized. When we would visit Cross Plains, I discovered that I could speak eloquently about God and religion. People were amazed with what I had to say. I soon realized that I had a certain power and that adults were surprised to hear a kid speaking in these ways.

But as a child I quickly saw that religion was not for me. I quickly realized that, from my point of view (and I came to have a radical view about it), religion was a very manipulative and fearful thing. I came to really resent it, having to hear all these threats: being told that God was coming any day when I least expected Him, being warned that the moon would turn to blood and the world would end, being reminded that there was no way to really please this guy—religion seemed to be an awfully dark thing.

My rejection of the religion of my kinfolks, I think, had to do with issues that my relatives never would have discussed in a thousand years. It had to do with my attraction to Native American ways and beliefs. It also had to do with my growing interest in things of the East, such as Buddhism. Of course, I wouldn't have been allowed to talk about Eastern religions or about such beliefs as reincarnation—that would have been considered "satanic." People there and then didn't even know what the word "reincarnation" meant, and if they did, I surely would have heard from them, "You wouldn't dare talk about such a thing."

My father's reaction to all this pain was interesting: spiritually he was an atheist—I think partly in bitter reaction to life or the world or the universe, and partly because of his father's death. He must have thought: "If this God would take my father so unfairly, then He didn't exist—just to hell with it all." I suspect that's how his atheism started to form. It took a lot of courage for him to feel that way. Apparently, he would egg on arguments if anyone approached him about religion: he would just tell them that "in this household we're all atheists." Like a Native American, he loved nature very much. He was also fascinated by science and technology; he was excited by the cosmos and by the idea of space exploration. After he left my mother, he moved to St. Louis with his second family and became a successful small businessman in the refrigeration business.

My mother would only come to religion in times of desperation; she was not very religious. Grandmother Horsley was religious—extremely so. She was very much into gospel singing and preachers and all that, and when I was younger, she would make me go to church with her. Grandmother Horsley was very much a part of this crazy Baptist cult—they were not at all official Baptists.

These people would make up their own doctrines. It was not like their preachers were trained in theology at some Baptist college. They were just called to preach by God, and all of a sudden, these preachers knew all the secrets of the universe and the only God. I remember this one preacher in Gadsden named McGuinness, who was a big hero to my grandmother. The deacons would sit in the front row of the church and the spirit of God would get into McGuinness and he would slap these deacons as he was preaching—it was some kind of repressed anger, I guess, but it was amusing to watch. The people that these preachers served were often called "footwashing Baptists," for that was something that they would do. My grandmother really believed in "footwashing," and she would debate with others about how footwashing was better than speaking in tongues and snake handling. One touching story that my grandmother used to tell was about this local kid who was mentally retarded; he had been to church and had seen the footwashing service, and so he gathered up all his animals and got them in a circle and washed their feet, too.

Grandmother Horsley was involved with all this in Gadsden, where she attended a number of these little churches with other poor white people. Everything would be going wonderfully in a church, then there would be some kind of fight, and part of the congregation would split off and form another church. I'd sing with the congregations of my grandmother's various churches, and as I recall, they were pretty good singers. We sang all the standards: "Farther Along," "I'll Fly Away," "Life Is Like a

Mountain Railroad," and "Amazing Grace." I never liked "Amazing Grace" as a kid, though I like it now. I did like the song that goes: "My home is not this world, I'm just passing through." And I've always liked "Wayfaring Stranger." That one was, and still is, just about my favorite; I love its haunting quality—it is both unusual and striking. There were a lot of great songs at church, and all these powerful images. There were important issues being dealt with in these songs, such as human suffering and a longing for release from that suffering.

At Cross Plains Baptist Church, most of these songs were sung a cappella, but they sometimes used a piano. They were down on guitars, though. In certain churches in Gadsden, guitars were allowed, and sometimes a guitar player would stop by and play rhythm to these songs—that was always a thrill for me.

> Ah, the guitar she's my old friend,
> She knows just where I've been,
> She understands how I feel,
> She knows the blues is real.
> **"Ragtime Blue Guitar"**

My earliest memory as a small child was telling people that I would be a musician, that I would write songs. I used to make up these long songs, and I would play them on my toy plastic ukulele. These songs would often go on for more than 30 minutes. People would gather around me to listen, and finally they would say, "Look, enough's enough." I loved music so much as a child that toward my teenage years I would tell people, "This is what I'm going to do—I'm going to be a musician." They would all put down my idea and say, "You can't do that. You need to be a fireman or something dependable." My mother particularly didn't want me to play music for a living. Perhaps my close resemblance to my father (I guess I had some of his mannerisms) frightened her into thinking that I'd follow in his footsteps.

My father told me, one of the last times I saw him, that when I was a small child I would make up stories. I would apparently talk about going on imaginary trips to Africa, or wherever it might be. He remembered that I would draw him into my stories, telling him about all the animals I would see on my trips. He was amazed that I had this ability. Since he himself enjoyed and valued music, my father supported me in my dream of being a musician. He was from a different mold than my mother. He was a far more flowing individual, and for sure that had to do with his being part Native American. When I was a teenager, I reconnected with my father. I played some guitar for him, and he was quite impressed—he was blown away.

By the time I was ten, I was writing down poems and lyrics. I wanted to set them to music and perform them. I saw a guitar advertised on the back of a comic book; it was the prize for selling a certain number of seeds. I got excited and sent away for some seeds. Soon I had sold enough to win the guitar; but when I opened the package, it wasn't a real guitar at all. It was this pasteboard thing—it didn't even have frets. I was very disappointed. You see, ever since I was a little child, the guitar was more than an instrument to me; it was like some sort of astral fantasy of another world.

Although I couldn't get a real instrument for a long time, I finally persuaded Grandfather Horsley to trade for this old Sears Silvertone f-hole guitar we saw one day in Collinsville, Alabama. He arranged a trade and got it for me. I hadn't anticipated how hard it would be to play the guitar. I thought I would just get a guitar and play, but I soon discovered how tough it was. This guitar had a good sound, but it had a warped neck, and the action was so high that my fingers would hurt playing a chord on it.

I learned an incredible amount on that guitar the first year I played it. People were amazed how quickly I picked it up, once my fingers got tough enough. Eventually, I decided that that guitar was holding me back, so I purchased a Gibson thin-body, non-cutaway, sunburst electric guitar. It cost me $125, a lot of money at the time. I probably bought the guitar using my mother's credit, after finally convincing her that I was sincere enough to spring for it. I couldn't afford an amp, but this guitar had a fairly decent sound without amplification.

A guitar teacher in Gadsden was one reason I learned so quickly. He had been to Nashville but had failed to get any foothold there. He returned to Gadsden and opened a guitar instruction studio in a small house. This man took a special interest in me, as if he sensed that, with some instruction, I could do something. I didn't study much with him, and I don't even remember his name, but he got me going in the right direction.

I've got another song about the South,
You know, it's white and it's black.
There ain't no banjo on my knee,
But that song is on my back.
### "Long Way to Hollywood"

I've always had a profound respect for blacks. I can honestly say that I identify more with black people than with white people. As a small child I became good friends with a number of blacks while helping Grandfather Horsley with his fruit stands, which were often located in or near the black parts of town. At Atlanta's farmer's market, I met many of the blacks who were there to buy things. They all called me "captain," even though I was only a kid. Around this time, I met Bell Brooken, an old black man with a big gold tooth who was my good buddy—he would just hang out at the fruit stand and talk. I also met two black teenagers named Raymond and Waymond. When I was about four or five, I wanted to go to the movies with Raymond and Waymond—these guys were my heroes. But they said, "We can't go to the movies together, because you're white and we're not." I know this will sound silly, but this was my honest response: "We can solve that. I can put on some black shoe polish." Things like that would endear me to them, because they could see that I was just a little kid who was perfectly sincere.

Grandmother Horsley's comments about blacks were no different from any standard white racist line. Yet her actions indicated something very different. I remember she would go visit several black friends, and she seemed comfortable having them as friends. I suspect that she felt more at home around blacks because she had a strong dislike for the rich white world. All my other relatives felt the same way—that the rich folks were out to get them. On a gut level, they all realized, even if they didn't outwardly admit it, that they had a lot more in common with blacks than with wealthy whites.

Other than church music, just about the only live music that I remember hearing back then was by street singers, usually black people playing for donations. I never knew their names. Occasionally, I'd see white guys singing on the streets, and sometimes they were blind; often they were playing gospel songs like "I'll Fly Away." All these street singers fascinated me. Then, authorities in Gadsden passed an ordinance to get rid of these guys. Years later, I wrote a song, "Ragtime Blue Guitar," to protest laws like this. I really don't remember whether the ordinance totally stopped the street singers. It might only have gotten them off the main street.

I distinctly remember traveling on a Greyhound Bus, from Gadsden to Georgia, with my grandmother. In the back of the bus was this old black man, who was singing while making rasping sounds with his loosely strung guitar. I was fascinated; I wanted to sit by this guy and listen to his blues. I remember staring at the strings and watching them vibrate. My grandmother was a little concerned, but she also thought it was funny that I would like this music. Yet at some level, she seemed to understand that it meant something to me. The blues influence has always been very important to me. At my RCA sessions during the mid-1970s, some musicians thought that my music was too bluesy for country. They didn't know I was so deeply influenced by that tradition.

By the time I was a teenager, I was aware of nonconformist views and very down on what I considered the bad aspects of white southern culture and the "good old boy" mentality. I knew that I wasn't a "good old boy," that I could never be one. I was really an outcast in the South—I didn't fit into it. Even though I look like a white man, I have had a hard time in the white man's world. I think my consciousness operates more like a Native American. Certainly, I'm very sympathetic toward Native Americans. The Native American is the most left-out person in America.

When I was in high school in Gadsden, my mother remarried, to this man named Dixon. We moved to Columbus, Georgia; then my stepfather's work took us to Beaumont, Texas. I finished high school there (the great albino bluesman, Johnny Winter, was in my class). I never really liked Beaumont. One year I made zeroes on all my tests because I wrote down comical answers, like the time when they asked me "Who discovered America?" and I answered "Dick Tracy." Did they really expect someone who was part Native American to answer "Christopher Columbus"? By then, I had concluded that school was ridiculously political—the whole educational system. In Beaumont, they told you how long your hair could be—it had to be very precise. I couldn't believe it. I thought that was wrong and that I had constitutional rights. I tried to get some of my fellow students to help me protest, but they thought I was crazy. So I began to make straight As in order to be included on the honor roll, thinking that would give me more power. Needless to say, that didn't give me much more power.

> There was sometimes people
> With a gun or a knife,
> But when they heard me sing
> I guess that saved my life.
> ### "Renegade Picker"

When I graduated from high school, I returned to Gadsden and stayed at Grandmother Horsley's place. I hung out in Gadsden and began to discover my own musical identity. I also worked in a hillbilly band at an Am-Vets hall in Talladega, Alabama, playing lead guitar. That was a real redneck place and very dangerous (many of the patrons carried guns). I used to get into clashes with these people, because I didn't really like them and they could sense it. They would talk with me and become irritated with what I would say. I was always getting into trouble, always an antagonist. This is not a very pleasant way to be, but I guess that's just part of my nature. One time, the leader of the hillbilly band had to step in to protect me from a group of rednecks. Yet all those people liked my playing—that's what saved me.

My stint with the hillbilly band was my first paying musical job (I made about $10 a night), and it also forced me to sing on stage. I didn't want to sing; all I wanted to do was play guitar, but the bandleader wanted me to sing "Kansas City." His voice couldn't cover the tune, and my voice could. And so I began to sing in public.

Grandmother Horsley and I began to have our differences. I'd come and go and come back and recuperate and leave again. I was living a Bohemian, drifting kind of life. I did a lot of drinking, and I discovered marijuana and speed, stuff like that. I spent more time in Montgomery and Birmingham, playing solo in clubs and bars. Soon people in both cities admired my ability to play guitar and sing. Then I would hit them with some of my political songs. If I was bold enough on a particular night, or drunk enough, I would reveal more of what I really thought. And sometimes I actually enjoyed putting salt on the wound. I would sing political songs of every description, including some I wrote making fun of George Wallace. I was crazy enough to do things like that when I was young. At a couple of concerts—one in Birmingham, the other in Montgomery—I held nothing back. I thought to myself, "I'm gonna go after this," and I did. I created quite a stir. In Montgomery, the junior Klansmen (the sons of the old established Klansmen—they didn't go around with a sign saying that, but everybody knew who they were) wanted to get me. They called me all the usual names: nigger-lover, communist, whatever. I had longish hair for that time and place, and I remember rednecks would point at me and say, "Look at that guy, he looks like Tarzan." Sometimes if I was especially angry and resentful, I'd egg them on by implying that I was a communist, which I really wasn't (though I still believe in some of the higher social-ist principles). But sometimes I would throw fat on the fire at the wrong moment. The junior Klansmen began to think of me as a dangerous folk-singing commie. I'd run into these people on the streets, and they'd make menacing, threatening remarks. I was attracting more and more attention, and the threats got worse. But I'd grown up around this stuff. I told the ju-nior Klansmen, "Listen, I understand this violence—I'll meet you with it, if I have to." They thought about that, and soon they came back to find me. This is the strange part of the story—in some ways I've lived a charmed life. The leader of the junior Klansmen, who had a reputation for being a terrorist and a bad dude, actually liked my music. He used to come and hear me sing, and at some level he admired my audacity. One would have expected him to meet with his buddies and tell them, "Get this guy!" Yet he told them to cool it, to leave me alone. He wasn't totally in control, though, so it remained a dangerous situation.

One time in Birmingham, I wrote a song protesting the local police de-partment, called "B.P.D. Blues." I don't really remember the song anymore, but it referred to Mountainbrook, the rich section of Birmingham. The song was based on an experience I had in Birmingham. I was perform-ing at this little club, and when the club closed, I gave a ride home to this black guy who worked there. I dropped him off somewhere in the proj-ects, then left. Before I got very far, a police car stopped me. The officer assumed that I was drunk—and knowing me, I probably had been drink-ing. But I passed the breath test; I definitely wasn't legally drunk. Still he arrested me, charged me with reckless driving, impounded my car, and put me in jail. I was in jail three days before I was allowed to make a phone call. When I finally got before the judge, I was so angry. I started to tell my story about what the police had done to me, about how they had abused my rights, but before I finished my story, the judge simply pounded his gavel and said "guilty." I had to pay a sizable fine. In protest, I wrote "B.P.D. Blues." I remember one part of the song:

> You can always get off the hook
> if your daddy's got a home in Mountainbrook
> the B.P.D. ain't no friends of mine.

The song also poked fun at Bear Bryant and Alabama football. One line in the song went something like this: "He got arrested for insulting Bear Bryant." Many white guys who heard this line thought it was amusing; not only did it not offend them but they even seemed to identify with it. After all, something like that could have happened in Alabama in the early 1960s—the police did have the power to arrest people like that.

Sometimes people don't know where you're coming from. I used to do a song about George Wallace. It was making fun of him, yet many people thought it was praising him. I remember when one guy realized in the middle of the song that I was satirizing Wallace; the man's mouth fell open, and he looked like he wanted to murder me.

I was a drunk then and would do some crazy things. I was young and reckless, didn't care what others thought about me. My need to sing protest songs grew out of my own personal anger, such as my resentment toward the "good old boys" for their mistreatment of blacks, Native Americans, and outcasts. My identification with politically helpless people was instinctive and personal, not aloof and abstract. In singing protest songs, I could self-righteously confront powerful people and take my anger out on them. It was all very emotional, but there was also sincere conviction on my part. I knew that some people were being mistreated, and I felt strongly that it was wrong. I also believed that it was right for me to stand up and say so.

> Ah, but I'm coming back, I will return,
> Oh, honey, now, wait for me.
> I'm bound to travel the USA
> 'Cross the desert unto the sea.
> **"Long Way to Hollywood"**

In 1963 I first left the South. Richard Lockmiller and Jim Connor sort of grabbed me by the collar and said, "Hey, get in the car, let's go to California."

Richard and Jim were both from Gadsden (Jim much later wrote "Grandma's Feather Bed," that John Denver hit), and they wanted to be folk stars. They admired me—my talent and my ability to play, even though I was a total wild man, drunk most of the time or getting that way. I was also a far-out liberal, getting into trouble in Alabama for my political views. But Richard and Jim put up with me, though they didn't agree with me at all.

Our trip across the country took us through the desert. When we hit the desert, you might say that my consciousness was flooded with profound images and feelings about Indians. The desert immediately felt like home to me. On the way west, we attended the wedding of Richard Farina and Mimi Baez. Apparently, Richard Lockmiller and Jim Connor had met Richard Farina and some of the Baez clan some months before in London. I don't know if my friends were officially invited to Richard and Mimi's wedding, but they decided to go. I was just along for the ride. The other people at the wedding didn't really expect us to show up, and they didn't want us to be there, especially Joan Baez, who, of course, was Mimi's sister. My only explanation as to why they looked at us in this way was that we were white southerners. In the 1960s, in my experience, a person, if he was a white southerner, was automatically looked down upon in "hip" circles outside of the South. Looking back on it now, I understand why the Baez clan might have felt this way: they had no idea I had risked my life by singing protest songs in Montgomery, while many other protest singers stayed in Greenwich Village where it was safe.

Once we got to California, Richard and Jim recorded three of my songs, and I played on some of their sessions. This was my introduction to the music business world. In 1963, California was a completely different world from Alabama. I found it hard to believe that Montgomery and Los Angeles were in the same country. I was both repelled and fascinated by L.A. It was a bizarre place, a place of great drama, of many worlds coexisting side by side—that's what fascinated me. And I was there in strange times, for drugs were everywhere. At first, it was all too much for me. L.A. started to feel quite unreal, very rootless. So, deciding that I needed to get back to my roots, to return home, I began a series of comings and goings, from L.A., back to the South, and again to L.A. Eventually, I realized that it was impossible for me to stay in the South.

When I returned to L.A. to stay, the city began to have a profound effect on me. Some said that L.A. was dangerous, but I never had any real trouble, and I didn't care if I did. To me, the ethnic diversity of L.A. was nurturing, much like the black culture had been nurturing to me while growing up in the South. If living in that city was dangerous, then so be it; in fact, maybe that had something to do with my fascination with it. I became part of L.A.'s folk scene, though I soon discovered that much of that so-called folk music was crummy and commercial. The other young musicians I met on the streets were much more competitive than I was—they were looking for success, often at any cost. I respected their talent, though I did not always respect the way they played the music business game. Of course, at the time I didn't realize how historic all this would be. In L.A. I was witnessing the first cross-breeding of country and folk with rock 'n' roll—even though I was just on the edge of it, again in my noncompetitive way. My conscious-ness, however it works and wherever I got it, is not competitive; it is not really looking to prove anything, it is just there. Anyway, we all did a lot of playing, picking, trying out ideas, experimenting. To survive, I'd do a few folk gigs around L.A. at such clubs as the Ash Grove and the Troubadour. Although I was still a drifter and a very lost beatnik, people liked to have me around, so they'd take care of me. I got to know all kinds of musicians, like Stephen Stills, Mama Cass, Tim Hardin, Van Dyke Parks, Chris Hillman, Gene Clark. And Gram Parsons—I particularly liked him. He was very warm and supportive of me; we had an unspoken bond, I think, because we were both from Georgia, because we both loved the music of the South, because we were both experimenting with music in this strange land of L.A. The drug issue, though, prevented me from hanging out much with Gram and many of these other musicians. I was a loner and was temporarily sober. I was involved with this Eastern religion that demanded I be sober and do meditation, and so I had suppressed my drug use and my drinking—I had been in trouble with it before. Also, I had married in L.A., and my wife was threatening to leave me if I didn't stop.

At one point, I left the music business—I couldn't make any money. I got a job as a mailman, but I turned out to be the worst mailman that L.A. ever knew; I would drink all night and then go to work. Then, in 1967, I got back into music by joining a group, Stone Country; we recorded an album for RCA—it was terrible. The members of Stone Country were always fighting about who should do what and what kind of music we should play. One element within Stone Country wanted to be the next big pop group, like the Association, but I was opposed to that. I would say, "Who needs that, I can't even relate to that." I guess I won the battle. After that album was released, some record producers apparently noticed my contribution—"Well, this record stinks, but we like this one guy." So I left Stone Country to record a solo album for A&M, and the group died.

> On a Greyhound bus I'm traveling this morning,
> I'm going to Shreveport and to New Orleans.
> You know rambling these highways and traveling these byways
> It's been making me lonesome, on'ry and mean.
> **"Lonesome, On'ry and Mean"**

In the early 1970s I owned a guitar store in northern California, in the Marin County community of San Anselmo. My wife named the store "Amazing Grace Music"; after about a year, I sold the store to a guy for thirty grand and went back to recording. In 1971, my son, Jubal, was born in a San Francisco hospital, and I soon realized that a child can change the way you look at things.

I wrote "Lonesome, On'ry and Mean" in 1972 and recorded it for my second album. Shortly afterward, Waylon Jennings recorded the song, and his version became one of the first "outlaw" country singles. Although I like Waylon's version of the song, I think that in many ways the "outlaw movement" in country music was a parody of itself. If these "outlaw" musicians are the ones who cashed in and are now part of the "good old boys," then I don't think they're true outlaws. Many of them are talented musicians and they've made some great music, there's no doubt about it. Yet, I'm disappointed with many of them. What do they really stand for? I've always been, in the true sense of the word, an outlaw. For a time during the 1970s, I believed that the other "outlaw" singers were radicals like me. I'm a radical for real. As it turned out, I was much more radical than they ever were, and I have not changed essentially—other than the fact that I quit drinking.

Those "outlaws" have always played a more commercial game than I have, that's for sure. Take Waylon Jennings. I think Waylon's voice is unique—I've loved it from the time I first heard it. He likewise admired me; in the 1970s he tried to help me be more successful with the country music establishment (I'll always appreciate Waylon for this). But I remember a funny story that says something, I'm not sure exactly what, about the "outlaws"—this is humorous to me, this is not a judgment. One time Waylon was going to be up for some Nashville country music award, and he asked Guy Clark and me whether or not he should accept it. I immediately said "No!"—and that was the wrong answer, that wasn't the answer Waylon was really looking for.

I have such a radical view of Nashville. Something happens when Nashville embraces music and processes it. My radical view is that whatever Nashville embraces, it's the kiss of death for creativity. Take Charlie Rich as one of many examples: the real Charlie Rich recorded in Memphis, and he was a great talent long before his Nashville success. Then, after some hits and a few awards in Nashville, Charlie at that award ceremony dared to question the choice of John Denver as "best country entertainer," or whatever, and from that moment on Charlie was relatively in exile; there weren't many more Charlie Rich hits after that. Believe me: that kind of power exists in Nashville.

I don't believe anything truly creative ever came out of Nashville. The original and great music of Sun Records came from Memphis. Merle Haggard, whom I don't agree with but who I think is a real artist and writer, came from California. Although the new Nashville musicians are technically very good, it soon becomes clear that something is missing in the way they play. Nashville music is so predictable; they tend to promote the same artists and songwriters, and they make use of the same studio musicians—all of which encourages a kind of assembly line production. When I first started recording, I always assumed that people wanted to hear something different—to hear some diversity, but I've learned that that's not necessarily the case. I've learned that people like the familiar, they like things from the same old well. That's comforting to them, I guess.

> Lord, I am a traveling man,
> And my Daddy, so was he,
> And every day when the sun goes down,
> Oh my Lord, I must be free.
> ### "Traveling Kind"

I've always admired the music of northern "folkies" like Pete Seeger, Bob Dylan, and Joan Baez; yet, I myself have never been accepted as a folksinger. About the closest I came to being accepted by the "folkie" hierarchy was my performance at the 1969 Newport Folk Festival. The problem has always been, I've never fit into any particular category—I'm a misfit. Perhaps things will change with time. Charlie Hunter, a manager of folk musicians, told me he thinks that fans now prefer folk music with a harder edge. What once scared people away from my music may now be the very thing that attracts them to it. Yuppies and young people who like the folk music of the South, Charlie said, have already accepted the music of Texas and Louisiana (both black and white), as well as the black music of the Deep South (the blues, especially) and perhaps the white music of Appalachia. The white music of the Deep South, though, has always been more menacing to these people, more frightening—northerners have tended to avoid it. Yet the folk music of white southerners is unique, reflecting the tensions of the region's history. As Charlie put it, I represent all of it: Texas as well as the Deep South—not to mention Appalachia, Nashville, and Los Angeles.

One thing I've gotten out of a life in music is travel around the world. It's uncanny the places I've been. I've discovered that it's easier for me to perform and sell my records overseas, perhaps because I'm more exotic there. Over the years, I've developed a strong following in Europe. Not that I'm a star there or anything like that, but I am more accepted there than in the United States. I've done tours for the State Department, performing in places like Palau, China, Mongolia, Egypt, and West Africa; I've met ambassadors and other political officials, some liberal, some conservative; sometimes there were conflicts, and sometimes there was mutual respect. My travels have deepened my appreciation for the music of other cultures; for example, Celtic music fascinates me—it's a very rich tradition. I find it interesting that contemporary Celtic musicians feel completely at ease blending the old with the new, using ancient instruments like the bagpipe alongside new instruments like the synthesizer. I also respect the fact that in their performances and on their records these musicians are not afraid to mix contemporary political protest songs with, say, mystical traditional ballads.

When it comes to recording, I agree with these Celtic musicians: the song should dictate the instrumentation. Although the acoustic guitar has always been my primary instrument (and I also play the Dobro and the banjo), I'm now very interested in synthesizers—all that electronic stuff. Certainly, one should go into the studio with an open mind, and one should have versatile musicians—the bigger array of paints you have to choose from, the better! That would be the ideal; in these times of limited finances, I think my next approach would be to go into the studio with a classic band—guitar, bass, and drums—then add intelligent combinations of instruments, both acoustic and electric. Above all else, I would try to avoid the assembly line production of Nashville, which casts virtually every song in the same mold.

Two of my albums, *Long Time Rider* and *Look Homeward, Angel,* were my attempts to move in a direction similar to these Celtic musicians. I think it's an exciting direction, though I've never found much agreement within the United States. I had to travel to France and Sweden to find the support and the people to make those albums. Once I played a concert in the United Kingdom with Scottish singer-songwriter Dick Gaughan, a proponent of progressive working-class values, and he seemed surprised by my music—by the fact that I wasn't like most American musicians. Europeans are aware that I'm different, and they accept and like that; I think they want the real thing, and I am the real thing.

> You know I've paid my dues, I've sung my blues,
> I've traveled lonely miles;
> I've loved and lost and paid the cost
> For the dreaming in my mind.

> **"Dreamer"**

People in the music business don't always act with a sense of fair play. Everybody leaps aggressively after opportunities, after stardom and money. I've never leapt after any of these things; I've just let them go by. My lack of a competitive drive has certainly been a problem for me in the sense of my making it in the music business, in terms of my being a star. Success really doesn't interest me all that much. I have a pure, naive view of my music.

I've always been an outsider, and I still am. I'm no fan of Nashville, that's no secret. It's a contradiction that I'm here. I still don't think much of Nashville, even though I've lived here now for many years. My heart is in L.A. I feel very comfortable living among Mexicans and being surrounded by their culture. It's amusing to me that Nashville is becoming more like California! The younger people are changing Nashville for the better. Nashville's culture is more tolerant and diverse now; I was ahead of my time.

Using the word "progressive" in relation to mainstream country music is meaningless because the country music industry has always reverted to commercialism. The industry always treats music like a commodity—like making and selling watches. In always catering to the market, the country music industry makes it difficult for the whole person to record. In the mid-1970s when I recorded in Nashville for RCA, my producer Roy Dea only understood one side of me, and I catered to that side. Roy liked me as a singer, but my voice had a lot of range, so it was hard for the band to accompany my songs the way I envisioned them; the recordings we made were not sufficiently "country" to receive much attention. While I myself don't try to define or limit country music, it at least should express a certain feeling, something that the yuppie-billies who never worked in the fields don't understand.

It's natural not to care about anything else when you're in the creative moment composing a song. Nashville songwriters tend to write by committee, and they want to get a pickup truck in there. But for me writing a song is the most difficult thing imaginable, because you absolutely have to tell the truth.

## NOTES

1. John Morthland, *The Best of Country Music* (Garden City: Doubleday, 1984), 421.

2. Quoted in liner notes to Steve Young's album *Solo/Live,* Watermelon Records, 1991.

3. Quoted in Kerry Dexter, "Legendary Songwriter Steve Young Readies First New Release in Six Years," *MTV News,* April 24, 2000, para. 3, http://www.mtv.com/news/821380/legendary-songwriter-steve-young-readies-first-new-release-in-six-years/.

4. Quoted in Brian T. Atkinson, *I'll Be Here in the Morning: The Songwriting Legacy of Townes Van Zandt* (College Station: Texas A&M University Press, 2011), 70.

5. Quoted in Dave Marsh with John Swenson, *The Rolling Stone Record Guide* (New York: Random House, 1979), 425.

6. Quoted in liner notes to Young, *Solo/Live.*

7. Quoted in liner notes to reissue of Steve Young's 1969 album, *Rock Salt & Nails,* Edsel Records, 1986.

8. Bill C. Malone, *Southern Music/American Music* (Lexington: University Press of Kentucky, 1979), 50.

# CHAPTER SEVEN

# "Them's My Kind of People"

*Cross-Marginal*
*Solidarity in*
*Country Music*
*of the*
*Long Seventies*

## NADINE HUBBS

In PREVIOUS work on country music, I have written of the many distortions in contemporary representations of the American working class, including not only the overwriting of working-class realities by middle-class narratives but the erasure of past working-class progressivism by presentist perspectives and prejudices. In this essay, I challenge and redress such misrepresentations with reference to a country music moment I am calling the "long seventies." My conception of country's long seventies encompasses music from Johnny Cash's 1968 chart-topping *At Folsom Prison* album through the late 1970s and certain releases of the early 1980s. The period interests me as one of social change and popular music generativity, among other things.

This was a time when commercial country music was a distinctly working-class culture form, largely white but with long-standing and formative African-American and Latino/a involvements as well.[1] In retrospect the period also appears as a turning point for realities and perceptions of the American working class. Since the late seventies, the working class, across all racial and ethnic categories, has suffered steady and substantial economic decline. And since the late sixties, following the social and cultural changes wrought by the Civil Rights and Counterculture Movements, both country music and the white working class have come to be seen as politically and socially conservative, as retrograde, and as bigoted—consequentially, given the cultural capitalization of social tolerance and the increased stigmatization of the bigot during this period.[2]

In what follows, I will cite seven long-seventies songs that, among their original country music audiences, modeled identifications within and across society's margins—between racial, sexual, and carceral minorities and poor and working-class folk of various stripes. In current mainstream perspective, however, such linkages are unexpected or even incomprehensible. Listeners today might wonder on what basis the songs' creators drew them. Indeed, when I play these songs for academic audiences, they are often taken aback on hearing queer, Mexican, or African-American (though not carceral or poor white) representation in country music. Many perceive bigotry from the first mention of the marginalized figure, even when they are admittedly unsure of the exact lyrics, the meaning of the song, or the particulars of its themes and vignette. These listeners often register discomfort and wariness about the very combination of topic and medium: racial, ethnic, and sexual minorities and country music do not mix. They brace themselves, expecting to hear something offensive, whether by dint of inadvertent ignorance or deliberate bigotry. Their responses are striking and suggestive of contemporary notions concerning who can take part in and be trusted with—in effect, who owns—discourse on subjects that fall into the latter-day, institutionalized realm of diversity.

That feeling is mutual. Just as the middle-class dislikes and distrusts the working class, the working class dislikes and distrusts the middle class, and these sentiments are vented in country music, particularly in the *antibourgeois* song genre. All of the long-seventies songs I cite below—six major-label tracks and one underground track—can (arguably) be heard as examples of this genre. They direct anger, resentment, and ridicule at middle-class social and cultural authority, styles of consumption and expression, and attitudes and judgments toward working-class or "country" people and lifeways (in American contexts, "country" rusticity is a frequent proxy for low social status).[3] Such antibourgeois expressions surface frequently in country music, from Hank Williams Sr. up to today. In my book *Rednecks, Queers, and Country Music,* I argued that listeners from the middle class and its "narrating class" sector of scholars, journalists, and public commentators have often since the seventies dismissed this angry expression as false consciousness or bad taste, but the sounds of white working-class protest in country must be properly understood as political.[4]

In my previous work, I engaged with country music to illuminate progressive histories of queer–working class affiliation and alliance. Now, I will cite several long-seventies country songs that conjure a more expansive alliance of white working-class people with members of multiple marginalized groups—African Americans, Mexican Americans, and the incarcerated, as well as queers.[5] I thus highlight a social-political theme that featured importantly in country music of the period. The theme of cross-marginal empathy, solidarity, and resistance was grounded in a notion with broad cultural currency at the time: that white poor and working folk shared marginalized and abject status, perspectives and understandings, and common cause with African Americans, Mexican Americans, queers, and the incarcerated.[6] Forty to fifty years on, however, cultural memory and cultural politics are such that, at the lyrics' first mention of minority identities, progressive country songs from the long seventies are frequently heard as bigoted. Present political challenges and social divisions underscore the need to revisit this past moment and prevailing notions of recent U.S. history. When heard with historical and class attunement, outside of misinterpretative frames, antibourgeois country music of the long seventies can attest to country music's progressivism in this pivotal period and give the lie to contemporary narratives that ahistorically conjure a perennially bigoted and reactionary white working class.

I have previously discussed, for example, how misinterpretation of anti-euphemistic discourse leads some listeners to hear David Allan Coe's sly queer-affirmative lyric in "Fuck Aneta Briant [*sic*]" as a homophobic statement.[7] Undoubtedly the song's messages can be confusing to listeners steeped in middle-class codes of euphemistic speech. Such listeners may stumble on Coe's vulgar humor or his language of "faggots," "goddamn homosex'als," and "yellow-bellied queers" in this paean to sexuality and domesticity in male prison culture, and they may thus misread its antihomophobic stance. These issues resonate from the opening stanza:

Fuck Aneta Briant! Who the hell is she,
Tellin' all them faggots that they can't be free?
Throw that bitch in prison! Maybe then she'll see
Just how much those goddamn homosex'als mean to me.[8]

In contrast to Coe and his gay epithets, the Miss America finalist, entertainer, citrus industry spokesperson, and three-time winner of *Good
Housekeeping* magazine's "Most Admired Woman in America" poll Anita
Bryant used only the institutionally sanctioned term "homosexual." In
this way, she upheld respectable middle-class norms as she led in 1977–
78 the most momentous antigay crusade in American history, denouncing "the homosexual lifestyle" and vilifying gays as a threat to children,
godliness, and the nation. Coe's lyric in this underground release mocks
middle-class language in the phrase "those goddamn homosex'als," but
otherwise it steers clear of euphemism. A crucial and constitutive rhetorical practice in middle-class worlds, euphemism is distrusted and despised
in working-class contexts, where it falls under headings of "pretty words,"
"happy talk," "blowing smoke," "kissing ass," and "bullshit."

Coe, a virtual poster child for sociologist Joseph T. Howell's "hard-
living" sector of the working class, took a position of queer affiliation and
affinity in "Fuck Aneta Briant."[9] Striking an autobiographical stance, the
singer-songwriter admitted to not only enjoying male attentions in prison
but to having inside knowledge and understanding of the queer. That is
not to say Coe spoke as a member of the social-sexual group he celebrated
and defended in this lyric. But in his bawdy humor, anti-euphemistic language, and antibourgeois animus, he did present himself as a queer admirer, affiliate, and fellow traveler.[10] Thus, with identificatory reference to
poor white, incarcerated, and queer people, and with irony, irreverence,
and wit, Coe in this long-seventies country track sounded a statement of
cross-marginal solidarity.

Having previously analyzed "Fuck Aneta Briant" as a working-class expression of queer acceptance, I will extend my analysis of the song here
in a framework of cross-marginal solidarity and resistance. I will also cite
six other long-seventies country songs that show intramarginal solidarity
across racial and ethnic boundaries. My discussion of these songs is far
from exhaustive. Rather, it is meant to be illustrative and suggestive of the

possibilities for further musical, historical, and sociopolitical investigation. Space limitations prevent me from pursuing such possibilities here, but I will do so in my current book project, *Country Mexicans: Sounding Mexican American Life, Love, and Belonging in Country Music.*

The feminist anthropologist Lila Abu-Lughod has exhorted scholars not to romanticize resistance as a sign of human freedom and resilience but, following Foucault, to use resistance as a "diagnostic of power," an indicator of power's particular workings in particular situations. "We could continue to look for and consider nontrivial all sorts of resistance," she writes, "but instead of taking these as signs of human freedom . . . use them strategically to tell us more about forms of power and how people are caught up in them."[11]

I do not much worry about writers romanticizing resistance in country music. Resistance in contemporary country, by contrast to other popular music forms, is seldom heard in terms of human freedom or resilience. Classic country is occasionally subject to such interpretation: Johnny Cash, Loretta Lynn, Willie Nelson, or Dolly Parton songs, for example, in retrospect at several decades' remove. But in mainstream commentary, contemporary country has been charged with intolerable resentment, bad taste, and phoniness. Middle-class, mostly white critics and commentators question, sometimes vehemently, the sincerity and authenticity of working-class stances and sentiments in contemporary country. Notably, they often hear working-class expression in country as fakery or pandering.[12]

I read middle-class whites' difficulty believing that the white working class might actually engage perspectives, values, and conditions different from their own as genuine and significant. It is an effect of the mutual alienation that James C. Scott has called "class apartheid"; of the blanketing dominance of bourgeois culture; of America's racialization of class; and of the professional middle class's self-referentiality amid increasing social, geographic, and economic segregation—the many racist and classist effects of which include blurring of the realness of white working-class existence (hence perceptions of fakery and pandering).[13] Accordingly, just to recognize country music in terms of working-class resistance is important. Still, heeding Abu-Lughod, we might further ask what country songs, and dominant-culture responses to them, can teach us about the operations of power on this site. So I will home in on some sounds of resistance in country songs of the post–civil rights era and some of the country music gestures that incur ridicule and dismissal. In this way, I will extend my previous argument that dominant-culture renderings of country's resistance as mere whining and phoniness contribute to an overwriting of white working-class politics and a rewriting of history.

Here and elsewhere I have discussed Coe's "Fuck Aneta Briant" as an expression of resistance that is mutually antihomophobic and antibourgeois. In this rhetorically complex defense of the queer, Coe presents himself not as a member of that social-sexual category stigmatized and besieged circa 1978 but as an insider nevertheless—a fellow traveler privy to intimate knowledge—and as an ally and true admirer, wisecracks and all.[14] One sign of this self-positioning is Coe's familiar use of gay pejoratives. To be sure, not every pejorative here signals camaraderie: the lyric suggests no cozying up to "Aneta Briant" when it tags her as "bitch" (or at any other point, for that matter). But Coe's "faggot" and "queer" are the objects of his narrator's appreciative, well-observed, and persuasive litany of prison queers' attributes ranging from tender to fierce. Still, who is this guy calling a faggot? Where does Coe get off using such words?

Well, he apparently gets off, in one sense of the phrase, precisely through the assistance of prison queers, who according to the song's narrator will "beat your meat" and "help you drain your hose." This sort of first-person testimony, in the song and at least one interview, is a partial answer to the question concerning Coe's assumption of authority in this realm. Notably, the unruffled reception of Coe's self-implicating lyrics by his notoriously hard-core audience suggests that the relatively progressive gender-based sexual systems of earlier twentieth-century working-class communities— where a male who took the "manly" role in sex with another male was deemed "normal," not queer—may persist in working-class worlds, even beyond the mid-twentieth century and outside prison walls.[15]

But more fundamentally, Coe's insider positioning has to do with cross-marginal identification. Coe did not (and does not) identify as queer but throughout his songwriting oeuvre and public self-representations has defiantly identified under other stigmatized labels, including those of redneck, ex-con, and (to quote a term of hate speech) "white trash." In "Fuck Aneta Briant," David Allan Coe assumed an inside perspective in his defense of the queer, invoking the words "queer" and "faggot" as if he had some insight on those positions. These were common usages in 1970s gay circles, where they resonated with complex layers of meaning, including both outwardly and self-directed irony. Coe's use of the terms in his lyric showed an assumption of insider familiarity. Whether this was justified is a fair question, but crucially, it is a question that calls for historicization and class awareness. His epithets mark out boundaries between Us and Them—but they are not the boundaries a contemporary dominant-culture reading might presume.

Coe's "faggot" and "queer" did not erect a barrier between a conservative, white working-class subject of country music and a feared and hated queer other. Rather, in this song, "faggot" and "queer" mock bourgeois euphemism and the horse it rode in on. And they assert the narrator's place among society's outcasts—as registered in the lyric via familiarity and cross-marginal solidarity linking the queer to the redneck and white trash, and to the outlaw and ex-con.[16] This constitution of the "Us," which is pivotal and defining vis-à-vis the song's moral and political message, is unrecognizable across historical and class divides—divides across which Coe's implicit sex-gender self-positioning as a prison "wolf" is likewise unintelligible.[17] But a similar political logic and affective structuring animate countless country songs from at least Hank Williams's midcentury moment on. Coe presents a species of the post-Hank country ethos that Steve Goodson identified as "hillbilly humanism," which holds that all people are equal before God and no one has the right to judge another.[18] I have identified here a particular embodiment of hillbilly humanism in Coe's cross-marginal identification, and it is one that featured in numerous other country songs of the period.

In "Fuck Aneta Briant," Coe's nonqueer narrator voiced his antibourgeois protest through antihomophobic protest, and vice versa. In "San Quentin" (number one, 1969) and other songs, Johnny Cash took up voices of the incarcerated to protest inequality, social injustice, and genteel hypocrisy (his protest music discography by that point also included *Bitter Tears: Ballads of the American Indian*, a 1964 LP honoring Native Americans and criticizing U.S. hypocrisy and injustice).[19] In "Colorado Kool-Aid" (number 50, 1978), the white singer Johnny Paycheck spun a comically grisly David and Goliath tale about the canny victory of the narrator's "little Mexican . . . buddy" over a towering bully in a bar fight. In the self-penned "Irma Jackson" (1972), Merle Haggard sang of a biracial couple whose true love is torn apart by senseless social prohibition; "But I'll love Irma Jackson till I die," Haggard's narrator vows above the twangy Telecaster of the Bakersfield sound. Haggard had previously sung a first-person narrative of love shattered by xenophobic and apparently racist "hate" in "Go Home" (1967), which presented a Mexican beloved named Maria and musical echoes of Mexican ballad.[20] In Stoney Edwards's "Poor Folks Stick Together" (number sixty-one, 1970), the narrator is stranded on a rainy highway. After being passed by a stream of fancy cars—"Cadillacs and Limousines one by one"—his hope finally dawns at the sight of a blue-collar icon: "Yonder comes a diesel / And them's my kind of people."

A superb honky-tonk vocalist in a countrypolitan era, Edwards was also a southern working-class African American in a format 1920s music industry executives had earmarked for southern working-class whites (that is, as "old-time" or "hillbilly" music, with southern working-class blacks relegated to "race" records, later known as "R&B"). In "Poor Folks Stick Together" he sang of finding compassion, trustworthiness, loyalty, and camaraderie not with the "half ... [that] has the gold" but, in apparent cross-racial antibourgeois solidarity, with long-distance truckers and other "poor" folks, "the kind that never let ya down."[21] One of Edwards's dozen-plus chart singles, "Blackbird (Hold Your Head High)" (number forty-one, 1975), asserted a message of racial pride in a bold anti-euphemistic gesture of its own. Although the phrase "just a couple o' country niggers" referred affectionately to the narrator's father and uncle and evoked the challenges they faced as touring string-band musicians, it caused the song to be banned by many country radio stations, the longtime guardians of bourgeois propriety in the country music world. Bob Dylan's use of the same epithet the same year in "Hurricane," his ballad about the wrongful conviction of the African-American boxer Rubin "Hurricane" Carter, caused no controversy when released to rock radio: it was heard as part of a political protest against racial injustice.

Having recognized cross-marginal identifications in long-seventies country and their divergence from present-day assumptions and alignments, we might ask where such identifications came from. We must recognize, first, that empathy and solidarity were fundamental bases of the cross-marginal identifications in each song just cited. Whether or not it squares with present notions of plausible or appropriate alliances, Coe, for example, appears to have positioned himself as a queer ally, sympathizer, and insider. Through his songs and image, Coe had established a public persona under the banners of ex-con, redneck, white trash, and outlaw, and in this period he and many others, both in and outside his social stratum, would have viewed his disrespectable, abject social status as analogous, adjacent, and at points even equivalent (for example, via "social deviant" classification) to that of the queer. In "Fuck Aneta Briant," he invoked his social marginality and intimate experience with prison queers to summon authority on the subject and to challenge the authority of the respectable, moralistic antigay activist named (by misspelling) in his title. Indeed, I would argue that Coe's self-positioning in "Fuck Aneta Briant" jibes with Cathy J. Cohen's vision of radical political coalition among marginal and anti-normative people, across boundaries of racialization, class, and homo/hetero identity, in her classic queer studies essay "Punks, Bulldaggers, and Welfare Queens"—though Coe's 1978 track clearly falls outside the particular queer activism moment Cohen addressed in 1997.[22]

In addition to empathy and solidarity, another basis for country artists and creators' forging of cross-marginal identifications was history. This includes a shared history of cultural and genetic othering hinted at by the prominent sexologist Havelock Ellis, writing at the turn of the twentieth century: "Even in Europe today a considerable lack of repugnance to homosexual practices may be found among the lower classes. In this matter, as folklore shows in so many other matters, the uncultured man of civilization is linked to the savage. In England, I am told, the soldier often has little or no objection to prostitute himself to the 'swell' who pays him, although for pleasure he prefers to go to women; and Hyde Park is spoken of as a center of male prostitution."[23] Ellis's expert discourse posited a connection between homosexuality and the working class and between both of these and the racially and culturally othered "savage." These ideas circulated for decades, not only through Ellis's influential, widely shared book *Sexual Inversion* (1896), volume two in his *Studies in the Psychology of Sex*. The belief in "linked" sexual, racial, and class pathology was authoritative, as he suggested, in the new science of folklore. It was also foundational in scientific eugenics, another field in which Ellis played a leading role.[24] Decades later, some country songs would push back against the same constellation of classed, racialized, criminalized, and sexual others, as we have seen—to protest not their grouping together but their shared stigma and devaluation.

In his ethnographic account of poor whites, race, and privilege, *The Color of Class*, Kirby Moss pointedly de-essentializes race. Whiteness in this book "is mined to one of its seldom considered representations—poor Whites—and largely defined through them." By examining poor whites' "experience within and on the margins of Whiteness," Moss, an African-American anthropologist and journalist, challenges other scholars' "normalized notions of Whiteness . . . as an 'unmarked category against which difference is constructed'" (here, Moss quotes George Lipsitz). In other words, Moss contests "an unmarked and unproblematized middle classness" (to borrow Stephanie Lawler's words in another context) that is enabled and assumed by prominent theoretical models of normalized, unmarked whiteness. At the same time, his nuanced treatment regards the label "poor whites" as a "discursive anomaly" insofar as it refers to "a group who, rather than identify or be identified with forms of poverty, identifies instead with forms of privilege because they see themselves in Whiteness and all of its promise."[25]

The complexities of race, class, privilege, and identification among low-income and low-status whites in the United States have inspired not only ethnography and social theory but a fascinating, if little-known, historiography. One example here is Grace Elizabeth Hale's *Making Whiteness: The Culture of Segregation in the South, 1890–1940*. Hale historicized the "invention of the color line" during the Civil War and the need for the southern white ownership class to win the alliance of poor whites. The owners' strategy was to emphasize their racial sameness with impoverished whites. At this pivotal moment and others (including twentieth-century episodes of interracial labor organizing), privileged, powerful whites encouraged poor, struggling whites to identify with racial sameness and to disregard socioeconomic difference—the poverty and low, exploited status that connected them to poor blacks.[26] The owners perceived the threat posed by cross-marginal solidarity between subjugated black and white southern laborers.

This history links to the scenario framed by Moss, in which contemporary poor whites identify with racial privilege over socioeconomic lack. His framing surely applies in very many instances, but it does not describe a perfect, stable, or uniform state. In truth, past white elites did not entirely succeed in securing poor whites' identificatory allegiance, and country music, although often viewed since the seventies as a monolith of reactionary politics, has given frequent voice to the ambivalence, resentment, and anger attending this fact. Its messages are often inaudible in the dominant culture, unheeded and misinterpreted by middle-class individuals constituted and privileged, hence incentivized, precisely by their difference from the working-class masses. Class distinctions, as Lawler observes, stand on not only middle-class taste but middle-class disgust for the working-class other. At the same time, "working-class disgust and contempt for the middle class," like that heard in antibourgeois country, "simply does not count: [the working class] lack the social authority to make their judgments stick."[27] So songs like "Fuck Aneta Briant," and more recently Gretchen Wilson's "Redneck Woman" (number one, 2004), Miranda Lambert's "Only Prettier" (number twelve, 2010), and many others, can rouse substantial enthusiasm and resistant sympathy in working-class audiences without gaining leverage or even recognition as political expression in the dominant culture.

If, however, we listen to country music with knowledge of and attention to social, linguistic, and musical style, we can hear the sounds of resistance to middle-class dominance and of identification *against* privileged positions of wealth and dominance, of bourgeois sexual respectability, and of white supremacy. In Cash, Coe, Edwards, Haggard, Paycheck, and elsewhere, long-seventies antibourgeois country music appears as a site of resistance where status quo social, political, and economic power is contested by producers and fans. But it is also a site where such power is reproduced today through the "symbolic violence" of dominant-culture misreadings of resistant country expression that erase the music's progressive threat and remake contemporary stereotypes of the white working class as America's "bigot class."[28]

This example illustrates how working-class people "become little more than personae in a bourgeois drama," in Lawler's words. "Their point in this imaginary is to be what the middle classes are not, could not possibly be, must defend against being, but on whom the projected fantasies of the middle class must come to rest."[29] Another illustration of this phenomenon is a cultural-historical setup I identified in *Rednecks, Queers, and Country Music*. For a hundred years—beginning with the invention of the homosexual by medicine, psychology, and sexology around 1870— the American working class, white and of color, was faulted for its primitive, immoral embrace of the queer. But then, after about 1970, following the women's, gay, and Civil Rights movements and social changes of the sixties, the U.S. working class was increasingly viewed as prime culprit in a new social problem: the primitive, immoral embrace of "homophobia" (the term arose in 1972). With this 180-degree reversal, the middle class that formerly owned heterosexual normalcy and queer aversion now owned queer acceptance, thus maintaining its purchase on respectability, moral value, and humanity.

The principle underlying such a reversal has been dissected in Bourdieusian social theory and, equally, in antibourgeois country songs like "Redneck Woman"—that is, whatever the middle class is or does is the right thing to be or do. As the British Bourdieusian scholar Elizabeth McDermott has put it, "The privilege of the dominant classes is that they possess social legitimation which is based on the power of the dominant to impose, by their very existence, a definition of what is valued and authorized which is nothing other than their own way of existing—they are at ease in the social world because they determine the legitimated way of existing in it—it is a self-affirming power."[30] Further, whatever the dominant class narrates about the past determines what is known as history. This authoritative history competes, however, with resistant histories, often inconceivable from a dominant standpoint—indeed, throughout this essay I have cited margins sources, both scholarly texts and country songs, that present accounts of past and present reality contradicting narrating-class versions.

A small but diverse body of scholarship, however, including some recent work, has recognized the past, present, and future potential of (what I am calling) cross-marginal alliances involving the American white working class. In his 1996 essay "Brown: The Politics of Working-Class Chicano Style," the cultural critic Curtis Márez writes of "intercultural" exchange and alignment between Chicano and white working-class sensibilities, constructing his argument throughout in relation to the long-seventies Mexican American country star Freddy Fender and his music. Márez analyzes the position of working-class whites as a group "barred" from the privilege of "abstract, disembodied, capitalized Whiteness" and focuses particularly on those who opt to "play out their racial identity along the borders," both making and unmaking whiteness-as-monolith. It is here that he locates possibilities for cross-marginal connection and exchange, through shared political and aesthetic engagements that are, once again, antibourgeois: "an opposition to uptight, upper-class restraint can . . . serve as the basis for the shared tastes of working-class whites and Chicanos."[31]

In *Lost Revolutions* (2000), historian Pete Daniel highlights multiple episodes of cross-marginal solidarity in the 1950s Jim Crow South. For example, Daniel writes of a Memphis professional wrestler who called himself Sputnik Monroe. He attracted large numbers of black fans and effectively integrated his arena audiences, defying Jim Crow laws. Although dismissed by many as white trash, Monroe is portrayed by Daniel as an example of the "musicians and athletes [who] often did more to undermine" southern segregation in the 1950s than politicians and officials did.[32] Focusing on the 1960s and 1970s, Amy Sonnie and James Tracy's *Hillbilly Nationalists, Urban Race Rebels, and Black Power* (2011) presents a history of, not white middle-class college students, but poor and working-class white radical activists, some of them migrants from the South, who joined with civil rights, Black Power, and Puerto Rican activists in Chicago and other cities to fight racism and inequality and who forged a feminism that addressed the needs and concerns of poor women.[33]

Márez, Daniel, and Sonnie and Tracy bring to light instances of cross-marginal solidarity and progressivism that challenge standard depictions of the American white working class as a perennial bigot class. Ibram X. Kendi's celebrated book *Stamped from the Beginning* (2016) can be read alongside these authors and, too, beside Hale's account of the invention of the color line by the southern owner class.[34] Kendi's book, subtitled *The Definitive History of Racist Ideas in America*, flips conventional wisdom by locating the historical origins of American racism not in racist ideas but in policies created by the powerful to perpetuate their own interests. Racist ideas, on Kendi's analysis, have been created afterward, to justify the racially unequal policies, and these ideas in turn have led to racial ignorance and hatred. Another key argument here is that antiracism and racism have advanced in recent times, concurrently. Leaving either/or debates in the dust, Kendi thus tracks the galloping, neck and neck histories of both racism and the effort to combat it.

We could further consider Kendi's insights—his materially focused, top-down analysis of the origins of racism and his recognition of the concurrent progression of both racism and antiracism—in the light of the staggering rise of American socioeconomic inequality since the late 1970s. Then, we might note that, despite intensive ongoing anti-racist efforts, U.S. racism has continued to advance during a period in which economic elites—the upper 20 percent and, astronomically, the 1 percent—increased their share of material power while others fell further, much further, behind.[35] I would also note that during these same decades in which material inequality soared to historic levels, the upper middle class (also known as the professional-managerial class, typified by postgraduate-educated professionals and bachelor's-degreed managers) grew from only 2–3 percent of the population after World War II to become some 20 percent of the population with enormous influence across American institutions and the media, where they make up the narrating class.[36]

Over thirty years ago in his magnum opus, *Distinction*, Bourdieu showed how taste, supposedly that most individual and subjective of attributes, is objective, class based, and central in the creation and justification of unequal classes. My research on U.S. country music and the working class suggests to me, however, that in our current neoliberal, hyperdigitized moment, taste and its function in producing identities and class hierarchies is frequently relocated in social politics; the same sense of aesthetic revulsion George Orwell portrayed in the statement "the lower classes smell" might be represented today in terms asserting that the working class's racial and sexual politics reek.[37] It may thus be time to reckon the extent to which social politics permeates or even supplants taste as a salient form of cultural capital. Writing in 1996 on country music and the white working class, the theologian and sociologist Tex Sample warned that the abjection of working-class taste "legitimates inequality."[38] Recent discourses about the U.S. working class and country music suggest that the abjection of white working-class political stances—whether real or imagined stances—legitimates inequality and, indeed, the abjection of white working-class people: today, to be labeled a bigot can mean that you deserve whatever you get.

Projecting contemporary political beliefs and alignments onto the past has consequences in the present. It creates both historiographic and real-life problems. The image of the perennial white working-class bigot, in combination with hyperwhitening representations of the working class, has contributed to the economic and social free fall of the multiracial U.S. working class since the late 1970s and has helped enormously to justify it. Antibourgeois country songs of the long seventies stand as an audible archive of past working-class progressivism and resistance and can still resist misreadings reducing their antihomophobic, anti-racist, coalitional, and counterhegemonic messages to regressive and reactionary meanings—if we listen. Failure and refusal to hear coalitional themes in long-seventies antibourgeois country demonstrates the power of confirmation bias (also known as *myside bias*), and it operates on the ruinous either/or logic according to which you're either with us or against us (where "us" equals the liberal-progressive middle class), tethered to the tautology whereby you're with us only if your social identity makes you one of us.

Accordingly, the post-1970s, post–Archie Bunker American cultural imaginary leaves little to no room for progressive social and political expression that is also white working-class expression. But then, the stereotypic perennial white working-class bigot is instrumental to the neoliberal tolerant bourgeois individual: the fixity of one secures the mobility of the other.[39] In the short run, this stereotype works to the benefit of the white middle class, shoring up its social, cultural, and moral authority and preserving its dominance in these realms. But in the longer run, it is devastating to all but that 1 percent of the global population who now own more wealth, and power, than the rest of us combined and for whom present conditions of runaway inequality have been working out very well.[40] In this moment, we cannot afford to ignore or diminish instances of progressive empathy and solidarity, wherever we find them. Far better to celebrate and emulate them and to extend the progressive coalitional ethos of "them's my kind of people" more widely across differences and boundaries.

## NOTES

1. Established circa 1923, early commercial country was a music of rural (more than southern) audiences, according to Richard A. Peterson and Paul DiMaggio; their

1968–72 survey revealed audiences as not distinctly rural or regional but composed mainly of midlife working- and lower-middle-class whites; see "From Region to Class, the Changing Locus of Country Music: A Test of the Massification Hypothesis," *Social Forces* 53, no. 3 (1975): 497–506. Scholars generally agree that the industry's "new country" and "young country" marketing campaigns, begun in the late eighties, worked to bring in more suburban and middle-class fans. Negative views of country still link it, however, to the white working class. A study by Omar Lizardo and Sara Skiles even shows this view having hardened in recent years; see "Musical Taste and Patterns of Symbolic Exclusion in the United States, 1993–2012: Generational Dynamics of Differentiation and Continuity," *Poetics* 53 (2015): 9–21. On African American country involvements, see especially Diane Pecknold, ed., *Hidden in the Mix: The African American Presence in Country Music* (Durham: Duke University Press, 2013). Far less is known about Mexican Americans in country music, but I hope to change that with my forthcoming book *Country Mexicans*.

2. I have made this argument at length in relation to perceptions of homophobia in the working class and in country music in "'Fuck Aneta Briant' and the Queer Politics of Being Political," in *Rednecks, Queers, and Country Music* (Berkeley: University of California Press, 2014), chap. 4.

3. See Barbara Ching, *Wrong's What I Do Best: Hard Country Music and Contemporary Culture* (New York: Oxford University Press, 2003), 17.

4. The term *narrating class* comes from Hubbs, *Rednecks, Queers, and Country Music*, 2 and elsewhere, and refers to the upper-middle-class sector of media professionals and expert commentators, including bloggers. Contrary to declarations of a digital democratization of the media, Jen Schradie shows that middle-class people are far more likely than working-class people to post public comments online—three times more likely in the case of college versus high-school graduates; see "The Digital Production Gap: The Digital Divide and Web 2.0 Collide," *Poetics* 39 (2011): 145–68. Hubbs, *Rednecks, Queers, and Country Music*, 12–15 and chaps. 1 and 2, builds an extensive case for associating country music with the working class, through its themes, audiences, and producers. This is not to say, however, that country represents only working-class positions or that all working-class people embrace it.

5. See Hubbs, *Rednecks, Queers, and Country Music*, chap. 4.

6. Disco was similarly a music of this period that brought together multiple marginal social groups—first, black and Latino gay men in New York City, and eventually, gay white men and queer and nonqueer women in and beyond the city. See Nadine Hubbs, "'I Will Survive': Musical Mappings of Queer Social Space in a Disco Anthem," *Popular Music* 26, no. 2 (2007): 231–44.

7. See Hubbs, *Rednecks, Queers, and Country Music*, 131–58.

8. David Allan Coe, "Fuck Aneta Briant" (side 1, track 5), on *Nothing Sacred*, D.A.C. Records, DAC-0002, 1978, LP. Lyrics transcribed by the author from the album track.

9. Joseph T. Howell, *Hard Living on Clay Street: Portraits of Blue-Collar Families* (Chapel Hill: University of North Carolina Press, 1973), 6 and elsewhere.

10. Likewise in public relations, such as Coe's (apparently) early 1980s interview with *Screw* magazine publisher Al Goldstein on Goldstein's long-running New York City local-access cable show, *Midnight Blue*, which I viewed at http://youtu.be/lo XmtX_cJLs.

11. Lila Abu-Lughod, "The Romance of Resistance: Tracing Transformations of Power through Bedouin Women," *American Ethnologist* 17, no. 1 (1990): 42.

12. See, for example, Bo Burnham's 2015 video of his country parody song, "Pandering," https://youtu.be/stVNdLmKGYw; David Hajdu, "The Famous Door: Blake Shelton's Cowardly Ass," *New Republic*, June 10, 2011; and the country music commentaries of Mark Judge and Wil Forbis examined in Hubbs, *Rednecks, Queers, and Country Music*, 39–42, 52–53, 61–63, and 99–100; see also Hubbs, chap. 2, "Sounding the Working-Class Subject," which is directed to fleshing out working-class culture for unfamiliar readers and others. On bourgeois insularity see Sean F. Reardon and Kendra Bischoff, "Growth in the Residential Segregation of Families by Income, 1970–2009," Russell Sage Foundation and Brown University, 2011, https://s4.ad.brown.edu /Projects/Diversity/Data/Report/report111111.pdf.

13. James C. Scott, *Domination and the Arts of Resistance: Hidden Transcripts* (New Haven: Yale University Press, 1990). Ethnographic research by Kirby Moss (among others) shows that Americans across classes associate low economic status with African Americans and Latino/as. This cultural script prevailed across identity categories such that even poor and working-class whites themselves often struggled to situate their existence, hence their own realness, as persons both economically disadvantaged and white; see Moss, *The Color of Class: Poor Whites and the Paradox of Privilege* (Philadelphia: University of Pennsylvania Press, 2003).

14. On the lyric's genuine queer appreciation, see Hubbs, *Rednecks, Queers, and Country Music*, 134–35, 153–55.

15. In his interview with Goldstein, Coe discussed his adolescent erotic formation while in juvenile detention as male focused and described his preference for small-breasted women as an ongoing effect of its influence. For further discussion of classed sex-gender systems in relation to Coe and "Fuck Aneta Briant," see Hubbs, *Rednecks, Queers, and Country Music*, 131–36, 152–58. On U.S. male gender-based sexual systems in twentieth-century prisons, see Regina G. Kunzel, *Criminal Intimacy: Prison and the Uneven History of Modern American Sexuality* (Chicago: University of Chicago Press, 2008). On the workings of such systems in early to mid-twentieth-century working-class life outside prison, see Esther Newton, *Mother Camp: Female Impersonators in America* (1972; repr., Chicago: University of Chicago Press, 1979), and especially George Chauncey, "Christian Brotherhood or Sexual Perversion? Homosexual Identity and the Construction of Sexual Boundaries in the World War I Era" (1985), in *Hidden from History: Reclaiming the Gay and Lesbian Past*, ed. Martin Bauml Duberman, Martha Vicinus, and George Chauncey Jr. (New York: New American Library, 1989), 294–317, and *Gay New York: Gender, Urban Culture, and the Makings of the Gay Male World, 1890–1940* (New York: Basic Books, 1994).

16. In songs, on stage, and in interviews, Coe has expressly self-identified under these labels.

17. My experience in playing Coe's song for contemporary academic audiences suggests that middle-class listeners are often unsure of the lyric's intended meaning. Goldstein in his early 1980s interview showed lack of understanding around the sexual subjectivity of a prison wolf whom Coe allegedly murdered when he tried to punk Coe. When Goldstein referred to the man as a homosexual, Coe stammered and struggled to respond: "I'm not sure he *was* a homosexual. . . . He wanted to fuck me in *my* ass. You know?" The singer attested that things might have worked out differently if the man had wanted Coe to fuck *him*. His explanation accords with Chauncey's account in *Gay New York* of a working-class sex-gender system, incommensurable with the homo/hetero binary, in which male-male encounters were defined by the gendered role each man took. Writing of earlier twentieth-century practices, Chauncey notes that "the line between the wolf and the normal man, like that between the culture of the prison and culture of the streets, was a fine one" (95) and that "being 'heterosexual'" was not a requirement of workingmen's "normal" status (97).

18. Steve Goodson, *Hillbilly Humanist: Hank Williams and the Southern White Working Class* (Tuscaloosa: University of Alabama Press, 1993); see also David Fillingim, *Redneck Liberation: Country Music as Theology* (Macon: Mercer University Press, 2003).

19. See Daniel Geary, "'The Way I Would Feel about San Quentin': Johnny Cash and the Politics of Country Music," *Dædalus: Journal of the American Academy of Arts & Sciences* 142, no. 4 (2013): 64–72. I note the years and highest positions of singles that appeared on the country charts to pursue a sense of the tracks' reception, circulation, and influence in a given moment.

20. A legendary songwriter whose many awards included Kennedy Center honors, Haggard sometimes called the little-known "Irma Jackson" his favorite among the hundreds of songs in his oeuvre; Tommy Collins, a fellow Bakersfield singer-songwriter, wrote "Go Home."

21. On this history see Karl Hagstrom Miller, *Segregating Sound: Inventing Folk and Pop Music in the Age of Jim Crow* (Durham: Duke University Press, 2010), 4–11, and see my discussion of it in *Rednecks, Queers, and Country Music*, chap. 2, in the subsection "The Middle-Class Origins of Country Music's Whiteness," 68–72.

22. Cathy J. Cohen, "Punks, Bulldaggers, and Welfare Queens: The Radical Potential of Queer Politics?," *GLQ: A Journal of Lesbian and Gay Studies* 3, no. 4 (1997): 437–65.

23. Havelock Ellis, *Studies in the Psychology of Sex*, vol. 2, *Sexual Inversion* [1896], 3rd ed. (Philadelphia: F. A. Davis, 1915), 21. See also 23, 24, and 212.

24. Siobhan B. Somerville identifies shared conceptual bases between turn-of-the-century sexology and eugenics and underscores Ellis's prominent involvement in both fields. I would note that Ellis's invocation of folklore here jibes with Miller's recent account, in *Segregating Sound*, of the founding of the American music industry, which links the industry's construction of segregated musical categories to folklore and its investment in racially distinct cultures. See Somerville, *Queering the Color Line: Race and the*

*Invention of Homosexuality in American Culture* (Durham: Duke University Press, 2000), 15–38.

25. Kirby Moss, *The Color of Class: Poor Whites and the Paradox of Privilege* (Philadelphia: University of Pennsylvania Press, 2003), 4, 2. Moss quotes and thus implicates Lipsitz in his critique of theories of undifferentiated whiteness. Curtis Márez lodges a similar critique against critical whiteness theorist Richard Dyer, who "whitewashes with too broad a brush, eliding the important class differences between particular forms of white racialization," in "Brown: The Politics of Working-Class Chicano Style," *Social Text* 14, no. 3 (1996): 119. I am grateful to Barry Shank for bringing Márez's essay to my attention. Stephanie Lawler, "Disgusted Subjects: The Making of Middle-Class Identities," *Sociological Review* 53, no. 3 (2005): 443 (emphasis added).

26. Grace Elizabeth Hale, *Making Whiteness: The Culture of Segregation in the South, 1890–1940* (New York: Vintage Books, 1998). In these matters Hale aligns, too, with a broader historiography, including, for example, Joel Williamson, *The Crucible of Race: Black/White Relations in the American South since Emancipation* (New York: Oxford University Press, 1984), and more recently, Nancy Isenberg, *White Trash: The 400-Year Untold History of Class in America* (New York: Viking, 2016).

27. Lawler, "Disgusted Subjects," 443.

28. I borrow the phrase *symbolic violence* from Pierre Bourdieu and Jean-Claude Passeron, *Reproduction in Education, Society, and Culture,* trans. Richard Nice (Newbury Park: Sage Publications, in association with *Theory, Culture & Society*, Department of Administrative and Social Studies, Teesside Polytechnic, [1977] 1990). The phrase *bigot class* comes from Hubbs, *Rednecks, Queers, and Country Music*, 4 and elsewhere.

29. Lawler, "Disgusted Subjects," 442.

30. Elizabeth McDermott, "Telling Lesbian Stories: Interviewing and the Class Dynamics of 'Talk,'" *Women's Studies International Forum* 27, no. 3 (2004): 184.

31. Márez, "Brown," 120.

32. Pete Daniel, *Lost Revolutions: The South in the 1950s* (Chapel Hill: University of North Carolina Press, 2000), 126.

33. Amy Sonnie and James Tracy, *Hillbilly Nationalists, Urban Race Rebels, and Black Power: Community Organizing in Radical Times* (Brooklyn: Melville House, 2011).

34. Ibram X. Kendi, *Stamped from the Beginning: The Definitive History of Racist Ideas in America* (New York: Nation, 2016).

35. See Emmanuel Saez for specific data on this upward redistribution of wealth, in "Striking It Richer: The Evolution of Top Incomes in the United States," June 30, 2016, update of an article that appeared in *Pathways* (Winter 2008): 6–7, http://eml.berkeley .edu//~saez/saez-UStopincomes-2015.pdf.

36. Barbara Ehrenreich and John Ehrenreich, "The Professional-Managerial Class" (pts. 1 and 2), *Radical America* 11, nos. 2 and 3 (March–April and May–June 1977): 7–31; 7–22. The 2–3 percent figure is my estimate, based on data in Alan Abramowitz and Ruy Teixeira, "The Decline of the White Working Class and the Rise of a Mass Upper-Middle Class," *Political Science Quarterly* 124, no. 3 (2009): 391–422.

37. Pierre Bourdieu, *Distinction: A Social Critique of the Judgement of Taste*, trans. Richard Nice (Cambridge: Harvard University Press, 1984). Orwell penned this much-quoted phrase as summary of dominant-culture knowledge he received as a child in early twentieth-century England. His sentence begins, "That was what we were taught." George Orwell, *The Road to Wigan Pier* (London: Secker & Warburg, 1958), 199.

38. Tex Sample, *White Soul: Country Music, the Church, and Working Americans* (Nashville: Abingdon Press, 1996), 76.

39. This mechanism is illumined in Beverley Skeggs, "Uneasy Alignments: Resourcing Respectable Subjectivity," *GLQ: A Journal of Lesbian and Gay Studies* 10, no. 2 (2004): 291–98.

40. Oxfam International, "Richest 1 Percent Will Own More than All the Rest by 2016," January 18, 2015, https://www.oxfamamerica.org/press/richest-1-will-own-more-than-all-the-rest-by-2016/. Since this announcement, Oxfam and others have published statistics showing still further concentration of wealth within the 1 percent.

# CHAPTER EIGHT

# Man against Machine

*Garth Brooks as*
*Player and*
*Provocateur*

## STEPHANIE SHONEKAN

GARTH BROOKS has sold more albums than any other solo artist in the world. He does not have the flamboyance of Elvis, the mystery of Prince, or the enigma of Michael Jackson. Even within the boundaries of country music superstardom, Brooks is not iconoclastic as is Willie Nelson, nor is he blustery like Toby Keith. He presents himself as an unassuming guy with an ordinary background. Writer Maury Dean describes him as "everyman . . . the boy next door."[1] Even his voice and instrumental ability have been described by some as unremarkable. But he is charismatic, and over the years, he has made music that somehow appeals to a wide range of people. This success has been the genius of Brooks. Some scholars have called this the "Garth Factor," that indescribable quality that has catapulted him beyond all the other country singers before, during, or after his debut.[2] Other critics and writers have bemoaned Brooks's ability to attract and retain such a wide audience. According to James Cobb, "contemporary critics regularly heap waves of abuse on Garth Brooks for his relentless pursuit of the mass market."[3] Indeed, because of the sheer size of his fan base, it may appear as if Brooks has been very strategic about establishing himself as a best seller who has acquired a giant share of the mass market. Whether this fact warrants the regular bouts of suspicion is questionable. If pop country is to embrace its evolved position as a sub-genre of American popular music, then certainly an artist's success in the market should be commended, not derided.

After nine studio albums and four compilation albums, Brooks went on a decade-long hiatus. He returned in 2014 with a new album, *Man against Machine,* and a tour that sold out very quickly. Although this release "didn't match his early Nineties sales domination, Brooks' comeback tour has been a blockbuster affair with multiple nights in every city grossing more than $1 million per show."[4] The mystery of how Garth Brooks has been able to return to the top of the country music charts remains a question about which critics continue to speculate. During his hiatus, other country artists—seasoned and new—have continued to release successful albums and embark on sold-out tours, so conventional wisdom may predict that Brooks would have difficulty finding space and reaching a wide audience once again. Conventional wisdom would be wrong.

In this chapter, I contend that Garth Brooks has been able to stay relevant and widely successful because he has carefully crafted a persona that has been based on two seemingly paradoxical aspects: First is his ability to be an authentic and consistent player, an artist who has perfected the ability to perform the role of storyteller and teacher with familiar didactic messages that are driven by a knowledge of biblical principles, a value that allows him to comfortably remain ensconced within the well-guarded borders of the country music establishment. Second is his unlikely role as a provocateur with progressive leanings; Brooks has pushed the envelope and challenged the conservative status quo on prevailing mindsets and paradigms that have defined country music culture for years. While Brooks's traditional persona has established him as a staple for the country music fan base, his willingness to push back, albeit risky for his relationship with his audience, opens up an avenue for gaining devotees outside the usual boundaries of country music. In a *New Yorker* article, Ian Crouch explains that "Brooks was both celebrated and maligned as the singer who introduced country music to a wide national, and then global, audience."[5] This overture and its outcome of reaching a wider audience that hitherto would have had limited access to country music represents the brilliance of Garth Brooks.

The song aesthetic of country music rests on the dramatic yet relatable stories that are written by artists or stables of writers in Nashville, Bakersfield, and elsewhere. It is these narratives that find a way to connect to the soul, spirit, and way of life of a demographic that cuts across both the white and rural and the white and middle-class populations. Citing George Jones and Garth Brooks, Richard Shusterman insists that "country's sung stories are often recognized by listeners as biographically linked to the singer."[6] Thus, it is mostly the songs that Garth Brooks chose to write and/or sing that will form the basis of my analysis. In any good country song, lyrics are narrative based, sending messages that are unambiguous and direct. This accessibility and honesty is the central tenet of what might be considered authentic country music songwriting, which has endured from American roots music to pop country.

Either by intent or by providential coincidence, Brooks has found himself beneficially positioned within and without the boundaries, and it is his career choices and his lyrics, with their nod or wink at a progressive message, that reveal the multifaceted nature of his consciousness. In "Standing Outside the Fire" on the *In Pieces* album, Brooks sings that life "is merely survived / if you're standing outside the fire."[7] This statement seems to be the mantra that has led Brooks through his career. He has chosen to dance with the flame and has taken risks that have sometimes burned him, such as his detour to an alter-ego Chris Gaines and his public divorce from longtime wife, Sandy Mahl, and subsequent marriage to fellow country music star Trisha Yearwood. In spite of these forays into what many traditional country fans may consider dangerous territory that could have adversely affected his career, the flames that have singed his wings have paradoxically allowed him to fly higher and longer than any other country artist. What separates Brooks from other country music artists is that he has also successfully flirted with progressive ideology, which certainly could have put him at odds with the undeniably conservative majority country music audience.

When Garth Brooks first moved to Nashville, Tennessee, from his hometown of Tulsa, Oklahoma, he was unsteady, timid, and unable to gain steady footing in the whirlwind, competitive Nashville environment where all country hopefuls go to try and make it. He did not last long, returning to Oklahoma the day after he arrived. When he returned to Nashville the following year, it was as if he had made a decision that this time he would be himself, choose the songs that he was most comfortable with, and forge a career for himself that did not shy away from shrewd business decisions and tricky subject matter. In his carefully crafted decision making, Brooks set himself on a path that was rife with both risk and compromise. On his *Fresh Horses* album, his song "The Change" presents what might be considered as his raison d'être: "what I do is so this world will know / that it will not change me."[8] This bold statement supplies the basis for his resolve as a songwriter and indicates a particular brand of sturdiness with the edgy stances he has taken, a steadfastness that implies that there is little chance that he will be moved by outside forces. He points not merely to the traditional boundaries but also to a wide "world," a space where he also feels comfortable. So while Brooks is an ordinary man "who gets lost in the crowd," as he sings in "When There's No One Around" on his *Sevens* album,[9] he is also willing to stand out in the country crowd by choosing to perform songs with content that sometimes leans left of country music's sociopolitical center.

The rest of this chapter will examine Brooks's ingenuity in this strategy by assessing how he has remained provocative every step of the way and on every studio album. Indeed, as Garth Brooks remains a consistent and effective "player" and "preacher" in country music, the most interesting way that he exemplifies himself as a superstar is as a provocateur, an edgier version of country music's everyman. Yet even in this role when he goes against the grain of the expected narrative, he is clever enough to do it skillfully. In particular, I am concerned with the ways in which this best-selling country music player has made careful forays into more dangerous progressive territory, while other artists who have tried to do the same have failed. For example, the Dixie Chicks were adversely affected by Natalie Maines's political statement criticizing President George W. Bush in 2002. The group has never achieved its previous success since the severe backlash from country radio and country fans. Also, when country artist Will Hoge performed his song "Ballad for Trayvon Martin," a tribute to the young African American who was killed by a man who utilized the "Stand Your Ground" Florida law, Hoge's song choice did not go well for him as he received some criticism from the country music establishment. Yet Brooks manages to walk that fine line that keeps him on the good, and lucrative, side of the fan base.

The focus here is on examining the layers of Brooks's profile as an ordinary man who has forged an extraordinary career by offering a challenge to what many see as a one-dimensional conservatism that is tightly associated with the country music industry. Jocelyn Neal refutes this common view of country music as "a monolithic whole, a musical genre that can be summarized with a quick stroke of a pen," and that these types of representations "are frequently invoked as a broad and homogenous manifestation of politically and religiously conservative, Southern whiteness, with its host of intrinsic associations."[10] Nevertheless, whether simple or complex, this is the scene and community within which Brooks operates successfully, veering away from the party line often and remaining accepted and acceptable within it.

When he has been asked about his influences, Brooks has often cited well-known provocateurs of different genres such as Americana's Bob Dylan and rock's Bruce Springsteen. As he toured with his 2014 album, he referenced more contemporary pop artists as more immediate influences. According to journalist Jerry Wofford, Brooks "talked about the tour for the first part of his press conference, saying he is influenced by musicians like Bruno Mars and Lady Gaga."[11] Both Mars and Gaga have exemplified the art of carving out a unique space within pop culture, the former with a fresh funk aesthetic and the latter with her choice of content and her out-of-the-box visual persona. Lady Gaga in particular has advocated for same-sex marriage and social justice issues that would be comfortable in liberal spaces. That Brooks cites her as a contemporary influence means that we should be willing to see him as someone who embraces not only her bright and blustery performance persona but also her gutsy embrace of progressive topics.

However, it is important to mention that Brooks also takes inspiration from country legend Hank Williams, who is considered country royalty. In many ways, Williams was the edgy bad boy of his time. He did in the late 1940s and early 1950s what Garth Brooks attempts to do in his own era. "Walking after Midnight" (*The Chase*) is Brooks's reference to Williams's song "I'm So Lonesome I Could Cry." Brooks's citing of Williams is at once both substantial and tangential, which old-school country fans would notice and appreciate: "I'm as lonesome as I can be" and "I stop to see a weeping willow / crying on his pillow." These lines are close to Williams's original lyric that references a lonesome "whippoorwill" which is too lonesome to fly. This allusion to the late great is a masterful nod to the entire fan base. As critic James Cobb explains, "when detractors dismiss Garth Brooks as the evil 'anti-Hank,' however, they fail to realize that, like Brooks, Williams and a number of the other 'pioneers' who are now enshrined in the Hall of Fame were also seen in their own days as threats to country music's identity and integrity."[12] Even though it makes sense to see Brooks in this light, he does not quite threaten country music's identity. He flirts with edginess while maintaining a secure stance.

Characterizations of country music vary from one writer or critic to another. As much as some argue for the complexity of country music's themes and characters, there is a general sense that the genre is really quite simple to understand. In fact, it is this simplicity, the down-to-earth nature of the music and the culture, that fans celebrate. Explaining this down-home essence of country music, Don Cusic writes that it "articulates the thoughts, feelings, lifestyles, concerns and topical issues of southern white working middle class in America."[13] David Fillingim corroborates this: "country music articulates assumptions that shape the worldview of the group that Hank Williams calls ... the common people."[14] Implied in these definitions is the idea of the roots of country music, buried in and sprouting from the rich folk and Americana music of the South.

Fully understanding the need to tap into these important roots, Garth Brooks remains a faithful player of the country folk values. On every album, he selects songs that are representative of this ethos, with themes falling in with the worldview to which Fillingim refers. However, I will posit that even as a mainstream country music player, Brooks exemplifies himself as unique, as he slightly or significantly reframes the usual themes in a way that makes him stand out as more progressive than the base. Because Brooks has straddled so delicately the conservative/progressive divide, it is important to explore his position in the center and then pivot to the ways in which he challenges the center on the basis of various topics, such as identity, region and occupation, gender and sexuality, race, politics, patriotism, and religion. If, as Michael Freeden observes, we are to consider the story of contemporary progressive thought as both "extensive and subtle" explorations by "individuals, groups, and institutions,"[15] then I contend that Brooks has ambidextrously been true to his roots but has also branched away extensively and subtly on all these topics.

A typical theme in country music is that of defining the identity of the country music fan. In "Alabama Clay" on *Garth Brooks,* the lyrics explicitly paint the identity of a person and a place. When Brooks sings that "his neck is red as Alabama clay,"[16] we know he is both celebrating and embracing the "redneck" identity that is so maligned by the mainstream but is regarded with much affection within the community. On the song "Face to Face," Brooks expands the concept of identity beyond the individual to the community. He sings,

> well now brother, wasn't it better dealin' with him (the bully) face to face
>
> ... ... ... ... ... ... ... ... ... ... ... ... ... ... ... ...
>
> Well little sister, wasn't it better, dealin' with him face to face.[17]

The reference here to a brother and a sister signals a pulling together of community that is both familial and communal. In other words, this song tells us that the community comes together as a family in the face of outside bullying. This kind of positive signaling to the community remains a consistent motif in Brooks's writing, most prominently in what many consider to be his signature song, "Friends in Low Places." According to scholar Elina Shatkin, this is "one of [Brooks's] best and most recognizable songs, it was a paean to low-class living."[18] A sense of who these people are as part of a tight-knit community emerges clearly in this song. The sing-along nature of the track also signifies a unity and solidarity among this group.

While Brooks's framing of the country music identity has always been comfortable and familiar, he made a marked controversial detour in 1999 by creating and personally embodying a new identity, one that was so far away from Brooks's typical persona that the artist has tried to erase all evidence that this alternative character ever existed. However, it is worth recounting his role as provocateur extraordinaire when he constituted his alter-ego Chris Gaines. Brooks's decision to step away from the formula that had brought him so much success into a persona that was so foreign (and as it turns out, threatening) to his loyal audience represents a move that was both brave and risky. Tossing aside his large cowboy hat, snug denims, large belt buckle, and wholesome toothy smile, Brooks as Gaines became moody, punky, brooding, and mysterious. Gaines was to be a mixture of R&B and rock and roll. This venture revealed what Heather MacLachlan referred to as "musical codeswitching."[19] The concept of "code switching" is a familiar one for groups that have to pivot from one identity to another. Dealing with how this phenomenon affects African Americans, Deric Greene and Felicia Walker explain that the practice of code switching involves "the alternation between different languages, two tonal registers, or a dialectical shift within the same language . . . [It allows for an] adapting to or negotiating various communication contexts [and is] used to convey social information for stylistic purpose."[20] This move is what Garth Brooks has done over the span of his career, adapting, dialectically shifting theme and focus, carefully calibrating his message, between his conservative country audience and his more progressive non-country fans. Brooks's Chris Gaines experiment represents this strategy.

When other artists have created alter egos for themselves, the departure has not been as distant or as divisive as the Brooks/Gaines journey. As Sasha Fierce, for instance, Beyoncé is still Beyoncé with a little more attitude. She is still an R&B-pop diva. Gaines compared with Brooks is a completely different character. Reflecting on this departure, Shatkin reveals that "the most successful country musician in recorded history, Troyal Garth Brooks, a balding, tubby everyman with a knack for wrapping simple truths in simpler songs, has shed 50 pounds, grown a soul patch, hired a team of slick music producers, and transformed himself into a pansexual pop star who resembles a tumescent harlequin."[21] Gender theorist Ayisigi Gonel defines "pansexuality" as "a sexual orientation that encompasses an attraction towards all." In fact, Gonel goes on to argue that the notion of pansexuality is an "anti-identity" that is both "progressive and transgressive," one that goes beyond bisexuality to a more open vista that allows the individual to explore any and all orientations.[22] Although one might argue that Shatkin's reference to Chris Gaines as pansexual is simply a projection based on stereotype and supposition, it is worth examining the visual aspect of Gaines's persona as prominently exposed in the centerfold of the liner notes of his only album. His spiky black hair falling over his eyes, his lower body tightly clad in black and white leggings, his legs crossed, and his hand resting on one hip offer an image that could be seen as both teasing and suggestive, perhaps even containing a condescending wink to traditional notions of identity, sexuality, and sexual orientation.

Beyond the visual, the fact that legendary R&B hitmaker Babyface helped to produce the album reveals the degree of sonic code switching that was required for the transformation. The product—one album, some music videos, and an entire backstory—was so far from the Nashville aesthetic and, as it turns out, the country music fan base that it fell flat. In other words, the project, which might be viewed as an experiment with progressive suggestions, flopped in the midst of a conservative country audience. As Shatkin notes, "For most country fans, it was alienating. Country is a genre that fetishizes 'sticking to your roots,' even if those 'roots' are a fantasy."[23] The Chris Gaines experiment was gutsy and brave; certainly, it was provocative to the point of almost derailing Brooks's entire career. However, as with everything else, Brooks found his way back to the center and miraculously reclaimed his position as a country music player with whom his audience could identify.

If, as many generations have argued, there is an "Us versus Them" mentality in American culture, Chris Gaines was an expedition from the "Us" to find a position with the "Them." Returning to his base, Brooks always establishes himself again in the country "Us." For instance, in answer to an imagined outsider's question about why the cowboy protagonist in the song "Night Riders" ropes or rides for short pay, the lyrics explain that those who are not in the inner circle would not understand because "they" have never spent time in the great outdoors and are, therefore, unable to appreciate what the base knows inherently.[24] The division between the "Us" and the "Them," the insiders and the outsiders, is clearly demarcated in this song. Even though this genre has made it to the popular music arena, the community is still very guarded, with folk who understand and identify with all aspects of the culture. Brooks has a keen understanding of this culture and embraces his own membership in these folk spaces by quickly reverting to it following the Chris Gaines diversion.

A related issue to identity in country music is geography, for many of the stories of country music are set in the West and the South. Here again, Brooks veers away from the center by questioning the staid notions of an established and static way of life in small-town/rural America, a message carried faithfully by most country music artists. For instance, "My Town" by Montgomery Gentry, "Home" by Dierks Bentley, and "Small Town USA" by Justin Moore romanticize these pastoral spaces as pristine and ideal but refrain from singing about the nagging social issues therein. In contrast, in "Nobody Gets Off in This Town" (*Garth Brooks*), Brooks offers a counter to the romantic view of the small town. Brooks tells us that there is little hope in staying and big motivation to leave: "Their cars and their dreams are all starting to rust."[25] This bleak and, for some, realistic picture of the traditional small town goes against the narrative told in the majority of country music songs.

Also, in "American Honky Tonk Bar Association" (*In Pieces*), there is a suggestion that winks at an expanded definition of the territory beyond the rural, the Southern, and the Western: "We're all one big family/ throughout the cities and the towns."[26] By expanding these boundaries, Brooks is also challenging the limitations of the territory, the identity, and, by extension, perhaps the associated age-old philosophies and ideologies, as well as the division between rural and urban. In his discussion of a "surprising electoral shift" in environmental ideologies in rural spaces, geographer Peter A. Walker cites a county that was and remains both Republican and conservative.[27] Cities and urban spaces are often framed as the opposite of conservative values. Thus, as Brooks widens his focus by embracing and valuing cities, he is nudging his audience to reassess their rural and conservative worldview.

As he did with the Chris Gaines experiment, Brooks finds a balance—going to the edge but never quite going over the ledge. In most of his other songs, he reinforces the notion of good, wholesome small towns. In the song "Dixie Chicken" on *The Chase* album, the story is set proudly in Memphis, Tennessee, "down in Dixie land."[28] It is in places like this that farming and working the land are found, and some of Brooks's songs celebrate this identity of the hardworking farmer. In "Somewhere Other than the Night" (*The Chase*), cowritten by Brooks, the farmer diligently works the field and encounters the hazards and hardships of the land. Even though the tired farmer says "damn this wasted land," there is still a reverence for the land, the work, and the small rural town. Brooks goes on to build the context for this individual, a space that is clearly juxtaposed against the urban spaces of city life:

> The city's just a prison without fences
> 
> . . . . . . . . . . . . . . . . . . . . . . . . . . . . . . . . . . . . . .
> 
> And at night he dreams of wide-open spaces.

In many songs, Brooks uplifts these American spaces that are rural, Southern or Western, the small towns and tight-knit communities. However, the fact that he made such a strong statement to the contrary in "Nobody Gets Off in This Town" and "American Honky Tonk Bar Association" leave a provocative opening in interpretation. These songs are the antithesis of the typical picture that is commonly painted of the small town.

The celebration of various occupations and pastimes is another important theme in country music. In particular, Brooks constantly goes back to the well-used tropes of the cowboy. Cultural critic Richard Shusterman explains that "by invoking the cowboy image of rebelliously rugged individualism while also recalling its reputed roots in the South, country music can project an image that is traditional, white, all-American."[29] Yet Brooks counters this rampant romanticism of the cowboy by introducing the subjects of death and suicide. The main character in "The Beaches of Cheyenne" (*Fresh Horses*) is a widow who is left behind when her husband, a bull rider, gets killed in action. Of course, this reference to a bull rider fits well within the borders of what a country music player would sing about; however, the idea that the widow then kills herself by jumping over a cliff is unusual as a regular theme:

> They say she just went crazy
> screamin' out his name
> she ran out into the ocean.[30]

These lines throw a shadow on the bright optimism and fervent pride that are attached to the idea and ideal of the cowboy. The death of the bull rider and the subsequent suicide of his widow are two blows to the typical narrative. The danger of the cowboy profession and the macabre consequences of the lifestyle are rarely mentioned. That Brooks tells this side of the story is a sign of his willingness to challenge the narrative.

Again, even as he ventures away from the core of the cowboy myth, Brooks maintains his audience by reiterating the usual narrative. "Cowboy Bill" on the *Garth Brooks* album tells the story of the titular figure, now an old man, who told tales that some doubted. When the town folks found him dead, "he was clutching a badge that said Texas Ranger / And an old yeller letter said, 'Texas is Proud.'"[31] Another song, "Wild Horses" (*No Fences*), tells of the rodeo that keeps pulling the protagonist back to obsessive behavior that prevents him from keeping his promises. As

Franke puts it, the cowboy continues to be "a central stereotype in country music."[32] More recently on the 2014 album *Man against Machine,* the song "Cowboys Forever" continues to celebrate the adventurous cowboy spirit of the West, as well as other blue-collar professions: cops, truck drivers, and soldiers. Each occupation highlighted in this song has been reiterated and reinforced by so many other country artists over the years, from honky tonk to pop country, reaffirming the playful and serious pastimes of country folk.[33]

But it remains the cowboy who dominates the imagination in country music, and Brooks knows this truth well. According to Bill Malone, the cowboy "will retain his appeal as long as Americans identify with the kind of freedom that he supposedly represents."[34] The story in "Much Too Young (to Feel This Damn Old)," a hit from his self-titled album, tells of an older cowboy and his discomfort with getting outdone by younger cowboys. The protagonist has lost his woman and his friends. All he has left is "a tape of Chris LeDoux, lonely women, and bad booze."[35] But even as he pays tribute to the free spirit of the cowboy, Brooks's thoughtful story in "Beaches of Cheyenne" offers some counter to the exuberance.

Continuing to challenge the traditional staple elements and bastions of country music, Brooks often pushes away from the standard constructions of gender, which he himself reinforces in many songs when he is acting as player. In his role of provocateur, he offers alternative, more progressive constructs of gender and revises gender roles that are considered normal in the country music community. Brooks's depiction of a male gender role in "The Night I Called the Old Man Out" (*In Pieces*) reflects a challenge to the traditional uncontested male relationship between a father and a son.[36] Typically, the respect between parent and child is a valuable aspect of family life. However, in this song, the protagonist calls his father out, as apparently his brothers had done in the past. The father takes him outside and punches him, and while the blood runs down his face, the tears also fall. While the traditional concept of masculinity is reinforced in this song, it is also contested as the protagonist lets his emotions flow visibly, an act that may not be readily acceptable in country culture. This song is reminiscent of Johnny Cash's "A Boy Named Sue" in which the main character seeks out a confrontation with his father, who named him Sue. Here, societal gender roles are foregrounded and questioned.

Returning to the Chris Gaines case is relevant here because the essence of that character did not quite fit the masculinity constructions in country culture, one that Brooks himself usually embodied. Curtis Ellison describes Brooks as cultivating and promoting "sincere masculinity" with an "image as a devoted family man." These, Ellison insists, "are essential ingredients of his unprecedented appeal in American popular culture."[37] As Gaines, Brooks offers another construction of masculinity that is shades away from his own, country-music-approved identity.

In addition, there are several instances of Brooks challenging extant women's roles and leaning toward more progressive notions of womanhood. In "Dixie Chicken" (*The Chase*), he overturns the good-girl image. The woman becomes the predator, preying on men, conquering them by using their money and moving on. Here the typical power dynamics are reversed, as they are in "She's Tired of Boys" on the *Man against Machine* album, which is a song about a woman who does the pursuing. In a genre and culture where men are hypermasculine and thus the power players, these songs appear as sharp departures.

Another way in which Brooks offers alternative framings of gender can be found in "That Ol' Wind" on the *Fresh Horses* album. Here a single mother is the main character, and the story is told of how she gives birth to a child out of wedlock, a result of a one-night stand. Again, this is not the typical story of womanhood in country culture. In a 2014 book, I argued that "white women of country culture have been portrayed as pure women, who mind the home, the children, and the husband. When women veer off this path, they are seen as deviants from the norm."[38] Although country music women artists, from Loretta Lynn to Miranda Lambert, have pushed the envelope on definitions of womanhood, men have seldom put forward that message. However, Brooks himself veers off the path by presenting women who have agency to step away from the normal expectations of womanhood.

Even more provocative is the interesting interpretation of intersectionality—gender and race—in Brooks's song "Rollin'" (*Fresh Horses*), in which a woman of mysterious ancestry is described by the protagonist. Her vernacular suggests a different sort of woman than the usual Southern belle or the typical angel-with-lace references (as is the case in "Cowboys and Angels" on the same album). This reimagined woman in "Rollin'" says, "Boy, I get the blues if the rhythm ain't got no soul."[39] This phrase, with its reference to R&B, the blues, and soul signifies strongly that the woman described could be African American. "Rodeo or Mexico" on the *Scarecrow* album is a song about a cowboy who goes to a rodeo in Mexico where he meets a Mexican woman with

> dark brown eyes
> with long black hair and
> English bad and broken.[40]

They spent the night together only to be woken up at the point of a knife and a deranged husband. The song ends with a question, "Does anybody know the Spanish word for wife?" In these two songs, Brooks adds to the alternative constructions of women by introducing characters who are neither white nor English speakers.

As is his typical strategy, however, Brooks retreats back from this provocative challenge of traditional, culturally constructed gender roles and returns time and again to the "norm." For instance, on "Learning to Live Again" (*The Chase*), a man rebounding from a broken heart goes on a blind date, appreciating the woman because she lets him open the door for her.[41] Again, in "Cowboys and Angels" (*Fresh Horses*), traditional gender values are highlighted in the lyrics, with men and masculinity being constructed as hard (leather), while women are softer (lace).[42] These traditional gender roles appear on every Brooks album, but departures such as "Rollin" and "Rodeo or Mexico" remind us that Brooks is different. Also, because the songs sprout from the nexus of gender and race, they point to a larger issue in country music culture that has to do with racial boundaries and romantic affiliates.

Along these lines, the question must be asked about why there are so few black musicians that have found success in the genre. Charlie Pride and Darius Rucker are the best examples of black artists who have made the successful crossover. The fact that there are so few others points to an important racial question. If nothing else, the dearth of black country stars in the genre's history points to a conservative association with racial issues. Stephen King and P. Renee Foster delve deeper into the history and evolution of black country music artists in this book, in the chapter titled

"'Leave Country Music to White Folk'?: Narratives from Contemporary African American Country Artists on Race and Music." Brooks represents a progressive slant by venturing right into the core of the race question as he does in "Thicker than Blood" (*Scarecrow*). It is a poignant song that asks why there is hatred and discrimination:

> And if blood is thicker than water
> then what are we fighting for
> We're all sons and daughters
> of something that means so much more.[43]

In fact, Brooks consistently introduces the theme of race, which is no surprise when considering that as part of the backstory for his alter ego, Chris Gaines, his character's best friend, Tommy, is actually black. It is worth mentioning that in the liner notes for the Chris Gaines album, Gaines thanks African-American R&B producer Kenny "Babyface" Edmonds and his wife, Tracy, with the words: "Both of you have treated me like an equal, when I know I'm not." It is an interesting choice of words, the highlighting of the complex and contested concept of equality so often discussed with reference to race in America. Even as himself, within the guarded parameters of the cowboy/rodeo myth, Brooks finds a way to bring up race on "Night Rider's Lament." On a cursory listen, it seems to be a regular country song story about a cowboy, an old man who looks back on his illustrious career and reminisces on the adventures. In one line, though, the cowboy looks over some old letters and ponders an envelope where he "tore off the stamp for black Jim." The adjective "black" is a surprise in this song and in this genre. There are few references in country music history where black people are explicitly included in a story. Even in music videos where an expansive view of the United States is suggested, such as Rodney Atkins's "It's America" and Brad Paisley's "American Saturday Night," there is no sign of American people who are "black."[44] In the music video of one of African-American Darius Rucker's first country hits, "Alright," there is only a momentary glimpse of a black couple among a sea of white faces. Thus, for Brooks to casually drop a reference to a "black Jim" in "Night Rider's Lament" is an indication of something different and something specific that falls outside the norm. There is no commentary beyond this adjective that qualifies Jim as a black man, but

it is enough to send a message: out there in the West, there are black cowboys too. This historical fact is rarely celebrated in country music.[45]

On *Man against Machine,* "People Loving People" tears away the shroud
that protects the country audience from engaging in contemporary discussions about race and other forms of discrimination that endure. This musical culture is still mostly white and conservative. It is, says Shusterman,
"a specifically white American ethnicity expressed in a distinctive ethnic
popular music."[46] "People Loving People" branches away from this stereotype, pointing out that people fear what they don't understand, including people of different "colors and the cultures."[47] According to Crouch
this song signifies that "country music's liberal conscience has returned
to the stage."[48] The simplicity of his persona and his ability to fit so well
into the traditional role does nothing to detract from his role as the radical revolutionary, one who pushes against the silence that seems so loud
to those listening. Jocelyn Neal characterizes the country music establishment's troubling relationship with race: "While the modern genre is free
from the most offensive redneck characteristics . . . , racial associations
remain firmly embedded in the minds of authors, listeners, and readers
alike. Further complicating the scene is a recent resurfacing of redneck references in contemporary commercial country."[49]

Throughout his career, Brooks has touched on familiar political hot
topics, the subjects that emerge during every election season. On his *In
Pieces* album, Brooks's song "American Honky Tonk Bar Association"
summarizes his secure membership in country music and extols all the
political tropes that are expected of a country music player. He bemoans
big government's interference with socialized support by highlighting
Uncle Sam's exploitation of taxpayers to support those on the welfare line.
The song goes on to encourage patriotism and nationalism. As expected,
"American Honky Tonk Bar Association" clearly underlies the political
views of the conservative Right, but it also suggests quietly that those who
are "down" need help.

Perhaps one of the most important aspects of Garth Brooks as player is
Garth Brooks as patriot, as a proud American for whom military service is
a primary way of indicating national pride. Artists from Merle Haggard to
Hank Williams Jr., Tim McGraw to Chely Wright, Toby Keith to Gretchen
Wilson have celebrated the service of Americans in the military. This

theme is a staple in this culture. Even the maligned Dixie Chicks embodied this unique brand of patriotism and pride in the military in several of their songs. Country music is an arena where patriotism is trumpeted loudly and enemies are clearly demarcated. This message is most visible in Toby Keith's "Courtesy of the Red, White and Blue," in which the singer pledges indelicately to kick the enemy in the ass.[50] This "big military" resolution sits well with country music's conservative base.

But Garth Brooks offers an alternative way of thinking about the military, enemies, and war. For example, "Belleau Wood" on the *Sevens* album is a beautiful story about forgiveness or about that moment when you view your enemy as simply another human being. It captures a rare moment during World War I when a song, "Silent Night," becomes the text for diplomacy. A German and an American sing it together "over the Belleau Wood that night"[51] during a Christmas truce, and the song concludes that, for a fleeting moment, there is no fear and there are no enemies. Brooks, keenly aware of the patriotism prerequisite in country music, deals more directly with its traditionally conceived significance in "All American Kid" (*Man against Machine*).[52] Nevertheless, here again, he offers a nuanced sensitivity. The song tells of a young person who goes to war and returns safely, but the song finishes by expressing hope that other people return, too. Within the lines of this song, there is a different kind of sentiment than what is found in Toby Keith's blustery "kick-'em-in-the-ass" attitude of "Courtesy of the Red, White and Blue." Instead, Brooks's "All American Kid" issues a compassionate hope for the safety of American soldiers. Similarly, his ballad "Ireland," on the *Fresh Horses* album, offers a careful and sensitive critique of the consequences of war. The lyrics raise the critical point that often in these wars, patriots do not really know what they are fighting or dying for.[53]

Implicit in these lyrics and in the general concept of patriotism is the value of a deep faith in God and country. As Cusic states, "religion—specifically Christianity—is deeply embedded in country music."[54] Exemplifying this aspect over the years, Brooks also has emerged as preacher extraordinaire. Each album, and most songs, have had threads of this part of the culture sewn through because he recognizes that country music is "the theological expression of the hillbilly or redneck."[55] Examples of this preoccupation with theology and faith can be found throughout Garth Brooks's career.

In "Face to Face" on *The Chase* album, the protagonist faces off against the devil, a rapist. The song is a biblical metaphor for what happens when one has to fight against the evil devices of the devil. Brooks's "man of faith" turns to prayer when challenged by evil. On "Unanswered Prayers" (*No Fences*), written by Brooks, the wisdom of understanding life's greatest blessings rests on the prayers of mortals that God chooses not to answer.[56] "The Cowboy Song" (*In Pieces*) portrays the unromantic life of real cowboys as they, at the end of a grueling day, sing songs, which include old church standards such as "Amazing Grace," "Bringing in the Sheaves," and "The Old Rugged Cross."[57] So Brooks has the spiritual aspect of country music culture covered widely and deeply.

But even in this sacred content, Brooks goes outside the understood borders of country music to contest some of the most sacredly held and narrowly interpreted American Christian values. His song "We Shall Be Free" (*The Chase*) is one track that goes against much of the perceived Southern Baptist playbook as it references global warming, homosexuality, race as an enduring issue, as well as what some may consider socialist leanings.[58] Brooks's "We Shall Be Free" reveals political views and an alternative to spirituality that swings most clearly to the left. Here he offers a potent theme that troubles the right-wing political stance of traditional country music culture, the focus on sexuality and sexual orientation, a hot topic in U.S. politics and one that has been used widely to raise fear and hostility so as to preserve the concept of traditional "family values." Brooks sings of a time "when we're free to love anyone we choose." This message clearly challenges the dogmatic opposition to same-sex relationships, to homosexuality, and extends even to constructions of gender identity. The fact that homophobia does not feature in country music as it does in some versions of hip-hop does not mean it does not play a central role in the culture. According to Maxine Grossman, "The absence of homophobia, in other words, stems not from acceptance or tolerance but from the erasure of homosexuality itself."[59] In effect, Brooks's message in "We Shall Be Free" rubs against the grain of the country music establishment, which is the most provocative message in the entire song, and perhaps in Brooks's entire career. As mentioned above, even the ambiguous, slightly androgynous appearance of Chris Gaines suggested a fluidly interpreted sexual orientation, a message that does not sit well with the country music establishment. When country singer Chely Wright stepped out of the closet in 2010, she experienced some significant but not unexpected backlash. In 2015, Wright responded to right-wing criticism of political correctness: "Something I've noticed on social media is that those who continually mock and complain that 'political correctness is rampant and ridiculous—yada yada yada' are most always straight, white, Christian males."[60] Brooks's message in "We Shall Be Free" resonates with the sentiments and frustrations expressed by Wright.

Heterosexual Garth Brooks, in his denim and large cowboy hat, makes a case for reserving judgment with regard to sexual orientation. *New Yorker* writer Ian Crouch explains how the song was inspired by racial tensions of the early 1990s: "That song, co-written with Stephanie Davis, according to Brooks, was inspired by the riots that year in Los Angeles, and it remains the most famous mention of gay rights in a country song. It was a hit, though not his biggest, and Brooks later noted that 'We Shall be Free' was the most controversial song that he'd ever released . . . which says a lot about the politics of country music."[61] The impact of this song, which has become an American music standard, if not a country music standard, is still strong. In a 2014 *Rolling Stone Magazine* retrospective, the song is referenced: "In spite of how far things have progressed in the 22 years since Brooks and Stephanie Davis wrote this (when there was no such thing as marriage equality in the U.S.), there's still a long way to go before the song's message is truly embraced. But for anyone other than Brooks, taking such a brave stand on record at that time could have been a country music career killer."[62] The question of how he reconciles these difficult topics to the conservative Christian view is answered in the very ingenuity of Brooks.

Even with what might be considered radical content, Brooks still references a faith that is recognizable to the country base. In other words, the only way to be free is through faith in God. "We Shall Be Free" may be considered Brooks's most significant and sustained detour outside the borders of country music, with a strong and broad message of social justice. It embraces activism as it deals with racism, classism, and homophobia, suggesting a rethinking of every other kind of inequality or social injustice. This kind of commentary is an extraordinary message in country music, even though Brooks sings that "this ain't comin' from no prophet / just an ordinary man." Yet this song, on the whole, pushes back against traditional notions of Southern religiosity, not to be confused with religion. He challenges the ways in which the Christian gospel has often been commandeered for dubious purposes, from the suggestive turning away from the pains of racism and other enduring oppressions to the explicit justifications for such injustices as slavery. Instead, in this song, Brooks sings with conviction: "When I close my eyes I see the way this world shall be / when we all walk hand in hand." This message resonates with the immortal words of Martin Luther King's "I Have a Dream" speech. "We Shall Be Free" deals clearly with poverty by imagining a world where,

> the last child cries for a crust of bread
> ... ... ... ... ... ... ... ... ... ... ... ... ... ... ... ...
> when there's shelter over the poorest head.

The song also celebrates and upholds the notion of free speech but, in the context of the entire song, does so in a way that seems just and opposed to the typical Southern sentiment that opposes political correctness: "When the last man dies for just words that he said." The reference to racism is pointed: "When the last thing we notice is the color of skin / and the first thing we look for is the beauty within." Perhaps Brad Paisley is inspired by this message in his 2014 experiment "Accidental Racist," on which he collaborates with LL Cool J.[63] Like Garth Brooks, Paisley attempts to erase color, which is perhaps ultimately not the best solution, because the standard of whiteness as rightness is powerful and prevalent such that erasure of skin color will inevitably set whiteness as the default. But the attempts of Brooks (and Paisley) are nonetheless worthy of note.

"We Shall Be Free" also takes on environmental justice, another provocative departure from the norm. He imagines a time "when the skies and the oceans are clean again," a reminder of Marvin Gaye's environmentally focused "Mercy Mercy Me." In addition, Brooks's song celebrates the values of American democracy by building a bridge between the polar opposites of liberal and conservative positions: "When this world's big enough for all different views / we shall be free."

As well, Brooks pushes the envelope by offering a brief but pointed critique of capitalism: "When money talks for the very last time." Judging from these lyrics and other songs Brooks has written or chosen to sing throughout his career, he seems to believe in a wider message than is usually expected in country music, one that focuses on love, inclusion, and mercy and challenges exclusion, supremacy, and rage. He ultimately emerges as a man who is neither sanctimonious nor judgmental.

The full impact of Garth Brooks as provocateur cannot be overemphasized or overlooked. Time after time, he has diverted from the scripted path for country music artists. The wide appeal of Garth Brooks is that he is believable as a conservative, progressive, preacher, and sinner. His complexity is pronounced as fans encounter him as a man who struggles with his own publicly broadcast demons; yet he always returns to the core of the country music community. He handily summarizes himself and his unique journey in "Against the Grain," which appears on the *Ropin'* album: "Nothing ventured, nothing gained / sometimes you've got to go against the grain."[64] Although it has been Brooks's edginess that has brought him an audience beyond the core country fans, he has managed to retain and satisfy his country audience because he always returns to the roots of the culture.

As player and provocateur, Brooks has built a career that is tangible, influential, and accessible to a wide range of fans of both conservative and liberal persuasions. He caters to the conservative traditional base and extends beyond that to a liberal fan base who can identify with some of his nontraditional, more progressive messages. His followers are fiercely loyal, which is why he was able to take so many years off and return at the top of the country music charts in 2014. After the thunder has stopped rolling and the friends in low places have all gone home, the ingenuity of Garth Brooks will continue to fly. Referencing the well-known song of another American music giant, Maury Dean aptly reminds us that Brooks "is a real nice guy—thoughtful and gentle. It would not be a good idea, though, to step on his *blue suede shoes*. Garth Brooks is America."[65]

## NOTES

1. Maury Dean, *Rock and Roll: Gold Rush* (New York: Algora Publishing, 2003), 517.

2. Patsi Cox, *The Garth Factor: The Career behind Country's Big Boom* (New York: Center Street, 2009).

3. James C. Cobb, "Rednecks, White Socks, and Pina Coladas? Country Music Ain't What It Used to Be . . . and It Really Never Was," *Southern Cultures* 5 (1999): 48.

4. "Garth Brooks Is Country's Top Earner in 2015," *Rolling Stone,* December 14, 2015, https://www.rollingstone.com/music/news/garth-brooks-is-countrys-top-earner -in-2015–20151214.

5. Ian Crouch, "Garth Brooks: Country Music's Square, Liberal Dad," *New Yorker,* November 13, 2014, https://www.newyorker.com/culture/culture-desk/garth-brooks -country-musics-square-liberal-dad.

6. Richard Shusterman, "Affect and Authenticity in Country Musicals," *Journal of Aesthetics and Art Criticism* 57, no. 2 (1999): 228.

7. Garth Brooks, "Standing Outside the Fire," *In Pieces,* Liberty Records, 1993.

8. Garth Brooks, "The Change," *Fresh Horses,* Liberty Records, 1995.

9. Garth Brooks, "When There's No One Around," *Sevens,* Capitol Nashville, 1997.

10. Jocelyn R. Neal, "Dancing around the Subject: Race in Country Fan Culture," *Musical Quarterly* 89, no. 4 (Winter 2006): 556.

11. Jerry Wofford, "Garth Brooks Launches Digital Music Service with Thousands of Artists Included," *Tulsa World,* September 5, 2014, http://www.tulsaworld.com/scene /music/garth-brooks-launches-digital-music-service-with-thousands-of-artists/article _0044129a-197d-536a-a9f9–2ff5fada95ee.html.

12. Cobb, "Rednecks," 49.

13. Don Cusic, *Discovering Country Music* (Santa Barbara: ABC-CLIO, 2008), 2.

14. David Fillingim, *Redneck Liberation: Country Music as Theology* (Macon: Mercer University Press, 2003), 6.

15. Michael Freeden, *Liberal Languages: Ideological Imaginations and Twentieth- Century Progressive Thought* (Princeton: Princeton University Press, 2009), 6.

16. Garth Brooks, "Alabama Clay," *Garth Brooks,* Capitol Nashville, 1989.

17. Garth Brooks, "Face to Face," *The Chase,* Liberty Records, 1992.

18. Elina Shatkin, "The Strange Case of Chris Gaines and Garth Brooks," *Journal of Popular Music* 25, no. 3 (2013): 394.

19. Heather MacLachlan, "The Greatest Rock Star Who Never Was: Garth Brooks, Chris Gaines, and Modern America," *American Music* 26, no. 2 (2008): 203.

20. Deric M. Greene and Felicia R. Walker, "Recommendations to Public Speaking Instructors for the Negotiation of Code-Switching Practices among Black English-Speaking African American Students," *Journal of Negro Education* 73, no. 4 (2004): 435.

21. Shatkin, "Strange Case," 389.

22. Ayisigi Hale Gonel, "Pansexual Identification in Online Communities: Employing a Collaborative Queer Method to Study Pansexuality," *Graduate Journal of Social Science* 10 (February 2013): 36, 40.

23. Shatkin, "Strange Case," 389.

24. Garth Brooks, "Night Riders Lament," *The Chase,* Liberty Records, 1992.

25. Garth Brooks, "Nobody Gets Off in This Town," *Garth Brooks,* Capitol Nashville, 1989.

26. Garth Brooks, "American Honky Tonk Bar Association," *In Pieces,* Liberty Records, 1993.

27.  Peter A. Walker, "Reconsidering 'Regional' Political Ecologies: Toward a Political Ecology of the Rural American West," *Progress in Human Geography* 27, no. 1 (2003): 14.

28.  Garth Brooks, "Dixie Chicken," *The Chase*, Liberty Records, 1992.

29.  Shusterman, "Affect and Authenticity in Country Musicals," 222.

30.  Garth Brooks, "The Beaches of Cheyenne," *Fresh Horses*, Liberty Records, 1995.

31.  Garth Brooks, "Cowboy Bill," *Garth Brooks*, Capitol Nashville, 1989.

32.  Astrid Franke, "The 'Broken Heart' and 'The Trouble with the Truth': Understanding Clichés in Country Music," *Poetics Today* 18, no. 3 (1997): 400.

33.  Garth Brooks, "Cowboys Forever," *Man against Machine*, RCA Nashville/Pearl Records, 2014.

34.  Bill C. Malone, *Singing Cowboys and Musical Mountaineers: Southern Culture and the Roots of Country Music* (Athens: University of Georgia Press, 2003), 115.

35.  Garth Brooks, "Much Too Young (to Feel This Damn Old)," *Garth Brooks*, Capitol Nashville, 1989.

36.  Garth Brooks, "The Night I Called the Old Man Out," *In Pieces*, Liberty Records, 1993.

37.  Curtis W. Ellison, *Country Music Culture: From Hard Times to Heaven* (Jackson: University Press of Mississippi, 1995), 264.

38.  Stephanie Shonekan, *Soul Country and the USA: Race and Identity in American Music Culture* (New York: Palgrave McMillan, 2014), 65.

39.  Garth Brooks, "Rollin'," *Fresh Horses*, Liberty Records, 1995.

40.  Garth Brooks, "Rodeo or Mexico," *Scarecrow*, Capitol Nashville, 2001.

41.  Garth Brooks, "Learning to Live Again," *The Chase*, Liberty Records, 1992.

42.  Garth Brooks, "Cowboys and Angels," *Fresh Horses*, Liberty Records, 1995.

43.  Garth Brooks, "Thicker Than Blood," *Scarecrow*, Capitol Nashville, 2001.

44.  Rodney Atkins, "It's America," *It's America*, Curb Records, 2009; Brad Paisley, "American Saturday Night," *American Saturday Night*, Arista Nashville, 2009.

45.  William Loren Katz, *The Black West: A Documentary and Pictorial History of the African American Role in the Westward Expansion of the United States* (New York: Harlem Moon/Broadway Books, 1971).

46.  Shusterman, "Affect and Authenticity in Country Musicals," 222.

47.  Garth Brooks, "People Loving People," *Man against Machine*, RCA Nashville, 2014.

48.  Crouch, "Garth Brooks."

49.  Neal, "Dancing around the Subject," 558.

50.  Toby Keith, "Courtesy of the Red, White and Blue," *Unleashed*, DreamWorks, 2002.

51.  Garth Brooks, "Belleau Wood," *Sevens*, Capitol Nashville, 1997.

52.  Garth Brooks, All American Kid," *Man against Machine*, RCA Nashville, 2014.

53.  Garth Brooks, "Ireland," *Fresh Horses*, Liberty Records, 1995.

54.  Cusic, *Discovering Country Music*, 165.

55.  Fillingim, *Redneck Liberation*, 6.

56. Garth Brooks, "Unanswered Prayers," *No Fences,* Capitol Nashville, 1990.

57. Garth Brooks, "The Cowboy Song," *In Pieces,* Liberty Records, 1993.

58. Garth Brooks, "We Shall be Free," *The Chase,* Liberty Records, 1992.

59. Maxine L. Grossman, "Jesus, Mama, and the Constraints on Salvific Love in Contemporary Country Music, *Journal of the American Academy of Religion* 70, no. 1 (March 2002): 92.

60. "Chely Wright, Country Singer, Blasts 'Straight, White, Christian Men' as Bullies," *Washington Post,* July 15, 2015, https://www.washingtontimes.com/news/2015/jul/15/chely-wright-country-singer-blasts-straight-white-/.

61. Crouch, "Garth Brooks."

62. "Man against Machine: Garth Brooks' 10 Most Defiant Lyrics," *Rolling Stone Magazine,* November 11, 2014, https://www.rollingstone.com/music/lists/garth-brooks-10- most-defiant-lyrics-20141111/the-fever-1995–20141111.

63. Brad Paisley, "Accidental Racist," *Wheelhouse,* Arista Nashville, 2013.

64. Garth Brooks, "Against the Grain," *Ropin' the Wind,* Liberty Records, 1991.

65. Dean, *Rock and Roll,* 517.

# CHAPTER NINE

# "Leave Country Music to White Folk"?

*Narratives from Contemporary*
*African-American Country Artists*
*on Race and Music*

## STEPHEN A. KING AND
## P. RENEE FOSTER

Some folks wear their hats way off to the side
With their pants down low and a gun tucked inside
Take a beer by the 40 and their chicken deep fried
I think we all know who we're talking about
The only dark I like is when I turn off the lights
The only hood I love is pointy and white
Can't trust you if I can't see your face at night
I think we all know who we're talking about

—Key and Peele

IN THESE edgy lyrics, the African-American comedy duo Keegan-Michael Key and Jordan Peele, creators of the popular sketch comedy show *Key & Peele*, explore the intersection of country music and racism through irony and hyperbole. In the skit in which this song appears, Key's character, apparently new to the neighborhood, invites Peele to his house and proceeds to entertain his guest by playing segments of three unnamed, and presumably, self-penned songs. With acoustic guitar in hand, Key sings the above lyrics, initially oblivious to the song's overt racism. At the end of the second verse, Peele—bewildered and incredulous—demands that Key stop his performance. Calling out the song's blatant racism, Peele objects strongly to the use of Klan symbolism. Key proclaims his innocence, surprised that Peele would associate a hood with the KKK. The hood, he concludes, is part of "traditional country music imagery, man, like a pick-up truck or sleeping under the stars, or your dog got killed or your wife left you." Attempting to make the case that his songs are not racist, Key plays the beginning of what turns out to be another, equally racially explosive song. Enraged, Peele exits the room in disgust. Unfazed, Key strums yet another song fragment until he realizes that the lyrics—indeed his whole repertoire—underscore long-held and malignant stereotypes of African Americans.[1]

These hyper-racist lyrics play into the popular imagination of country music as the "whitest, most segregated of all styles: the redneck soundtrack of the racist South."[2] Furthermore, Key's subject position—a black man playing country music—as well as his own obliviousness and forgetting, underscores the stereotype that country music is essentially hostile to African-American performers and audiences. Despite overwhelming historical evidence that African Americans played a significant role in defining and influencing the trajectory of country music, Jocelyn R. Neal observed that "within country music, black fans and artists are all too often regarded as the exception that proves the rule." At the same time, she acknowledges the perplexing racial paradox in country music. While any legitimate historical account of country music cannot escape the genre's multiculturality, the music is still considered by many today to be "white."[3]

This belief seemed to be the thinking of one disgruntled country music fan who tweeted country music star Darius Rucker in 2013 to "leave country music to white folk." In response, Rucker—who has successfully transitioned from his Hootie and the Blowfish rock persona to a highly successful country music star—fired back, asking whether it was "2013 or 1913." Rucker also promised that he would take his "Grand Ole Opry membership and leave your racism."[4] In subsequent interviews, Rucker discussed the racist tweet but also told stories about his personal experience as a recent crossover artist to country music. Ironically, although Rucker continues to receive hate mail from angry fans, he has remained a widely popular country music commodity. With "Don't Think I Don't

Think about It," Rucker scored the first number one hit by an African-American performer on the Hot Country Songs charts since Charley Pride's last number one hit in 1983.[5]

To facilitate understanding of the role of race in contemporary country music, a brief historical context is provided. We discuss early African-American influences in country music as well as how music developed a color line in the early twentieth century—demarcating white and black music—that segregated both artists and audiences. Moreover, while African-American musicians, including Charley Pride, played an important role in disrupting traditional understandings of country music and race, the music became publicly associated with the Ku Klux Klan and other white hate groups as well as Republican Party politics during the 1960s and 1970s.

Following this review, we analyze the narratives of contemporary African-American country artists—Darius Rucker, Rissi Palmer, Carl Ray, Cleve Francis, Frankie Staton, and Miko Marks, to name a few—and discuss collectively how they have experienced both racism and support from the industry and country music fans. These stories are not fully formed documents such as might be expected in an autobiography; rather, the narratives arrive in fragmented forms found in a variety of popular sources from the 1990s to the present. Stitched together, these stories coalesce around three major themes: racial discrimination, identity/identification, and perseverance/determination. In the end, African-American country artists not only provide compelling accounts of personal and institutional racism but also articulate arguments legitimatizing their involvement in country music. Indeed, in the last few years—particularly with the ascent of Darius Rucker as country music's new black superstar—the country music industry, including performers and fans, have become increasingly accepting of the black presence in a historically perceived "white" genre. The irony of this acceptance, of course, is the fact that African Americans have made their presence felt in country music since its inception during the early 1920s.

When novelist and country music songwriter Alice Randall learned she was the first African-American woman to write a number one country song—the 1994 "XXX's and OOO's: An American Girl"—she was excited but also bewildered because, as she argued, "African-Americans have had so much influence on country music—banjos, trading of solos, blues."[6] Country music scholarship clearly supports such a view.[7] In *My Country: The African Diaspora's Country Music Heritage,* Pamela E. Foster dismisses the popular notion that African Americans have had a minimal presence, and little influence, on the development of country music: "The reality is that black people have been involved in every stage of country music's development and in every facet. We are 19th century fiddlers and banjoists, we are shower singers and square dancers, record buyers and road managers, artist managers and musicians, lead singers and backup singers, writers and record label owners and executives, radio station executives and personnel."[8] To be sure, country music was never a white homogeneous music of the South.[9] While it is true that the music can trace its musical roots back centuries to English, Scottish, and Irish ballads (what we now think of as folk music), other musical influences also served as building blocks—vaudeville, Tin Pan Alley, minstrel, blues, and various strains of religious music.[10] From the beginning, white and black interaction was crucial. "Poor Anglo Americans and African Americans viewed each other with suspicion across the racial divide," writes country music historian Bill C. Malone, "but they exchanged songs and styles virtually from the time of their first encounters in the early colonial South."[11]

This racial cross-influence was evident in the music that would eventually become country music, "a commercial art form that coalesced only after rural American music met the technologies of radio and records in the 1920s."[12] Until the 1940s, however, the term "country music" was not in common parlance. Instead, the music was given other labels—"hillbilly," "old familiar music," "old-timey music," and "fiddle and banjo" music.[13] In his 2015 book, *Sounding the Color Line,* Erich Nunn argues that while this new commercialized popular music was "steeped in African American traditions and shared by whites and blacks," it quickly became "distilled into a form that came to be identifiably—indeed quintessentially—white in the public mind."[14] Nunn centers his critique on the "racialist" logic of folklorists such as John Lomax who believed music was intimately connected to race and biology; the popularity of Mississippi-born Jimmie Rodgers and his yodeling style that became publicly identified as white despite its African-American influences; and the record industry's policies that segregated music by race.[15]

The record industry's decision to market artists by race deserves additional attention. Prior to 1920, U.S. record companies marketed the music of most black singers to whites, a decision predicated on the assumption that African Americans did not have the buying power to be reliable consumers. But then in 1920, Mamie Smith and Her Jazz Hounds recorded several cuts, including the widely popular "Crazy Blues," for Okeh Records.[16] Smith's "Crazy Blues" was a commercial and critical smash, selling an extraordinary 75,000 copies in its first month.[17] To satisfy this unrepresented black consumer base, by 1922, Okeh Records and an increasing number of record companies had decided to catalogue music performed by black musicians as "race records." White performers such as Fiddlin' John Carson, who recorded one of the earliest country songs in 1923, were "hillbilly" artists. It should be noted that the various classification schemes were fluid and permeable: not all African-American artists were marketed in the race record category, and some white artists, such as the Allen Brothers, were listed as race record artists.[18]

The invention and marketing of hillbilly and race categories obscured the interracial dimension historically associated with the development and codification of American popular musical forms. The development of these musical markets also contradicted the lived experiences of Southern musicians and audiences who, according to historian Karl Hagstrom Miller, were exposed to a variety of musical genres from blues to classical music. "Music developed a color line," wrote Miller, "The blues were African American. Rural white southerners played what came to be called country music. And much of the rest of the music performed and heard in the region was left out."[19] Reflecting institutional and corporate decisions to codify country music as white, historically most country artists have been white, although black artists did appear, right from the very beginning—including DeFord Bailey, the first black artist to regularly perform at the Grand Ole Opry, from 1925 to 1941.

Not only was country music increasingly perceived as white music, but it was also developing a reputation as being racist. Perhaps the best example is country music's co-optation by the political right as well as white supremacist organizations during the 1960s and 1970s. Noting that country music had long held a presence in Southern politics prior to the 1960s, Thomas Ruys Smith describes in detail former Alabama governor George

Wallace's appropriation of country music during his 1968 and 1972 bids for the White House. Richard Nixon did the same during the 1972 presidential campaign.[20] The conservative and reactionary themes in many country songs (for example, traditional gender roles, religious fundamentalism, muscular patriotism) seemed to match the ideology of the conservative right and, to some degree, the extremist views of white supremacist movements. During the 1960s and early 1970s, a resurgent Ku Klux Klan continued its practice of appropriating country music (and other musical genres) to spread messages of hate and intolerance, a practice that began in the 1920s. Released on Reb-Time Records, Hateanny Records, and other underground record labels, Johnny Rebel (also known as Clifford Trahan), Son of Mississippi, White Rider, Odis Cochran and the Three Bigots, the Klansman and others pressed for continued legal (segregation) and extralegal (violence) tactics to quell advances by civil rights activism.[21]

Ironically, while Klan and other white supremacist groups were deploying country music to spread their message of bigotry and intolerance, a number of black artists crossed over to country during the 1960s and 1970s, many representing what is called "country soul." Like the intersection of the blues and country during the 1920s and 1930s, country soul is another example of country music's continued cross-pollination. Ray Charles's hugely successful 1962 *Modern Sounds in Country and Western Music* and the Arthur Alexander's 1962 hit, "You Better Move On" (later covered by the Rolling Stones), are early examples of how both genres would influence each other. Additional artists would follow or cross over to country, including Tina Turner, the Pointer Sisters, Al Green, Millie Jackson, Jerry "Swamp Dog" Williams Jr., and O. B. McClinton (whose work is considered by Charles Hughes in this collection). Years later, artists such as DJ Sinister (Tripp Lee) and Cowboy Troy (Troy Coleman) would push country into conversation with another "black genre": rap or what Troy has called "hick-hop," a topic covered in Tressie Cottom's chapter.

While the existence of country soul represents a more accurate historical picture of country's racial confluence, its reputation as a conservative, whites-only genre has not changed significantly since the 1970s. For example, consider the following newspaper, magazine, and weblog headlines— "Despite Lil Wayne and Kid Rock, Is Country Music Still Racist?" (2008), "Why Can't Country Music Deal with Race?" (2011), "How Country Music

Got More Racist" (2013)—for they illustrate that country continues to be (mis)understood as a racist music.[22]

In assailing country music's perceived racially exclusionary practices, critics point to the fact that in the music's ninety-plus-year history, very few African-American artists have achieved anything close to superstar status. Indeed, Charley Pride remains, perhaps with the exception of Darius Rucker, country music's only black superstar. Given the importance of Pride's story to contemporary efforts by black performers to position themselves in the country music industry, a brief overview is necessary. In 1963, after a stint in the military and failed attempts to enter Major League Baseball, Pride decided to pursue a career in music. On his initial visit to Nashville, Pride met his future manager, Jack Johnson, who ironically was looking for a black country music singer. At the end of 1965, Pride finally secured a record contract with RCA, and the record company released his first single, "Snakes Crawl at Night," without publicity photos because executives were concerned that his black face would alienate potential white consumers.[23] When Pride's third single, "Just Between You and Me" (1966), rocketed to the top of the country charts, eventually leading to his first Grammy Award, RCA finally came clean.[24] Rather than expressing outrage, Pride believed RCA's strategy was prudent, even protective: "Their strategy was to slip me into the tent and downplay my racial identity until the fans and the industry became accustomed enough to my music to accept me. I had no objection to that. I wanted to stand or fall on my music, not my skin color."[25]

The issue of race permeates Pride's revealing and unapologetic 1994 autobiography, *Pride: The Charley Pride Story*, and the singer devotes a brief chapter, "Confronting Race," to the issue. Pride confronts racist club managers and promoters and considers his first major U.S. tour to be a series of racial "tests"—"we played Houston—no problem. Okay, what about Charlotte?" For Pride, the "color issue was always there, hanging around with the unpleasant odor of an old wet dog lying on the doorstep. I had to find ways to deal with it." The singer's response to this racist odor was a mixture of indifference, tolerance, honesty, humor, and career-driven determination.[26] Pride's nonconfrontational approach no doubt played a role in his success. During his career, he charted thirty-six number one hits, earned thirty gold records, and was inducted into the Country Music

Hall of Fame in 2000.[27] According to historian Charles L. Hughes, the country music industry and its supporters viewed Pride's superstardom as "proof" that the country music was racially progressive, even color-blind: "As Pride ascended to stardom in the late 1960s, country's boosters in the industry and press heralded his success as proof of country listeners' racial tolerance and the Nashville industry's open-minded professionalism."[28] Pride's story also serves more contemporary needs, particularly among African-American country artists, as evidence that quiet perseverance will ultimately overcome industry and consumer intolerance. Almost without exception, media coverage of African-American country artists focuses on race—the role of African Americans in the development of country music, the rare black face in the largely white world of country music, the difficulty for black artists to succeed in country music, and the discrimination and exclusionary institutional practices. Unlike white artists, African Americans and other minorities will be asked questions about race. Looking at their narratives provides further insight.

In reflecting on her experience as a country artist, Rissi Palmer—who has since transitioned to a neo-soul and rhythm and blues artist—complained in a 2015 *Rolling Stone* interview that interviewers focused primarily on her racial identity while neglecting her art: "I never felt like we really got into my artistry, because the focus was always on the outward appearance."[29] Even in a two-minute segment about Mickey Guyton on Country Music Television's *Hot 20 Countdown* program, she was asked the proverbial question about race.[30] For his part, it is clear that Charley Pride is tired of answering questions about the dearth of black artists in country music. As he told one interviewer in 2006, "You should grab some people in the industry—see if you can get something out of them. They might just not want any more Charley Prides."[31]

Pride's quip reflects the first and dominant theme in our analysis—racial discrimination. While country artists such as Darius Rucker have received hate mail, the majority of stories focus on the role of the country music industry, specifically, Nashville, for permitting and perpetuating a climate of institutional racism. Industry decision makers—country music executives and radio programmers in particular—are often villainous characters in the stories. Cleve Francis has been one of more outspoken voices on the issue of race in country music. In the late 1980s, Francis—a cardiologist with a thriving practice—decided to, in the words of one journalist, "chase a career as a black, middle-age singer in the overwhelmingly white world of country music."[32] Francis signed with Playback Records in 1990 and released a single, "Love Light," in the same year. It drew positive critical attention and was a moderate hit for Francis. He was subsequently signed by Library Records in 1991, the "first prominent contract for a black country artist since Charley Pride."[33] Despite the early success, Francis's career faltered, and by 1995, he left Nashville and returned to his medical practice.

Francis, who experienced the ugliness of Jim Crow in his native Louisiana as well as racism at the Medical College of Virginia, speaks about the difficulties he encountered in Nashville during his abbreviated career. In his story, Francis attributed race as the reason or cause for his short-lived career: "I'll go to my grave believing that I had everything I needed to succeed. I wasn't a shoo-in, but I thought I would make it. But race was the elephant in the room. I was a black guy doing it at a time when black and white mattered . . . I just don't think they were ready for me."[34] For Francis, the industry's exclusory, racist practices made him feel like an outcast despite his musical abilities: "I've always felt I had the God-given talent to perform this music. But I was made to feel like I didn't belong in the music. On some level, I suspect it's no different than the feelings that blacks had when they were trying to integrate golf and tennis clubs. We are relegated to a token level. I have as much right to perform this music as anyone." In interviews, Francis is clear that he blames music executives and radio programmers, not the fans who "couldn't care less what color you are."[35] Indeed, as he remembered in a 2009 *Washington Post* interview, country music fans, in the U.S. and abroad, accepted him "hands-down" while on tour: "I never ran into one discriminatory situation the two–three years I was out there. Never."[36]

Although Francis notes his popularity on the road, he argues that America was racially polarized in the early to mid-1990s and that sensationalized media spectacles, the O. J. Simpson trial and Rodney King's horrific beating at the hands of white police officers, fueled the type of racial animism evident today in social movement campaigns such as "Black Lives Matter." This larger racial context impacted country music, Francis insists, and consequently had a negative impact on (white) radio programming decisions. The singer learned that some small radio stations threw his unopened press kit in the trash. Radio, he felt, abandoned him: "I think the problem was that there were radio people who just assumed my music was not viable, like they were dealing with a Martian, and the rest of the music was by Earthlings . . . So I believe my songs were almost treated like they didn't exist."[37]

A contemporary of Francis, songwriter and pianist Frankie Staton also experienced similar acts of discrimination. In the 1980s, she moved from her home in North Carolina to Nashville to pursue a career in country music. As one of the few African-American female artists in Nashville, she encountered an atmosphere of exclusion and suspicion. For example, a Music Row publisher accused her of lying about a song she tried to pitch to him; the executive did not believe she wrote it.[38] Similarly, Indiana country artist Kandy Lee's experience in Nashville was so poisonous that she decided to pursue independent labels rather than attempt to land a recording contract on Music Row. After receiving positive feedback on a demo she sent to Nashville, Lee hoped to secure a recording contract. Instead, her authenticity was challenged: "When I arrived for an appointment, they didn't believe it was me singing. How do you think I felt when they asked me if it was my voice on the tape?"[39] Apparently, both Staton and Lee should have been singing black music and not supposedly whites-only country music.

In separate interviews, Francis and Staton argued that while other musical genres have been "integrated," country music has been the glaring exception. "I love my country music. But I feel like the country music industry never asked us to come to the party," observed Staton, "I mean, what the hell is wrong here? Every type of music is integrated but country. They call it America's music, but it don't look like America."[40] While country music has exploited the success of Charley Pride as evidence of the industry's "color-blindness," Francis and Staton argue that Pride's success actually reflects the exclusionary nature of the business. In the late 1990s, Staton told a group of Nashville executives: "Well, there are some 32 million African-Americans in these vast United States. Thirty years have passed since you signed this brother [Charley Pride]. Do you truly, in your heart of hearts, think that this is the only black man in America who can sing country music? Because if you do, I can prove you wrong."[41] Staton proved her point when she spearheaded the successful Black Country Showcase in Nashville in February 1997 and established the Black Country Music Association (BCMA) the same year. Part of the group's mission statement bemoaned the lack of black involvement: "representation in country music is void of the contributions and participation of Blacks to the genre."[42] In one interview, Staton made it clear that she was not interested in involving just musicians but individuals who comprise the multifaceted nature of the industry: "Black people want to be involved at every level, from producers to booking agents to road managers to bus drivers."[43] The initial response was positive and affirming for Staton as she received hundreds of demos and press packs. Some African-American musicians and bands signed record contracts. The association achieved some early success but became less active in ensuing years, mirroring the difficulties of making it in country music.

In all, the narratives from a variety of country musicians—Cleve Francis, Frankie Staton, Carl Ray, Kandy Lee, Nisha Jackson,[44] and others—tell essentially the same story. In contrast, Darius Rucker's stories suggest that he has experienced very little in the way of institutional racism, although he noted in at least one interview that radio programmers were initially skeptical about the singer's chances in country music.[45] Rucker has experienced more personal—or fan-based—racism, although the incidents have been rare. As a member of Hootie and the Blowfish, Rucker received hate mail, especially after the band released "Drowning," a song critical of South Carolina's Confederate flag. This negative response did not cease when he crossed over to country music. Rucker intimates that much of this kind of commentary is directed at his perceived inauthenticity. Country music, some fans would argue, is a white genre: "Hate mail has been a part of my life. That's just the way it is. We still get it. People don't want me to be singing country music."[46] While performing onstage in Upstate New York, Rucker had to contend with some fans who used racial slurs to express their disapproval. For the most part, however, "people are coming to hear the show. No one is worried about what color I am."[47] The most public act of racism was the infamous 2011 tweet. Rucker responded: "I was absolutely shocked . . . That's something that I'm going to have to deal with the rest of my career, because I'm a black guy in country music and there are people who don't like that."[48]

Rucker has not been alone in receiving a less than enthusiastic response from some fans, although there is a range of how it has been expressed. For example, Miko Marks has encountered more covert racism or what she describes as "hints of racism." She provides a helpful illustration: "Say I'll be doing a show at a country club. And the oldest gentleman there was maybe 70 years old. He's standing there with his arms folded and he was just mad. He wasn't understanding what's going on. But after I finished singing Patsy Cline he's shaking his head in giving me a nod of approval. He came up and congratulated me for the wonderful job I had done."[49] Similarly, Trini Triggs remembered winning over an audience in Montgomery, Alabama after receiving less than a positive reception: "I was dressed all country—the hat, the whole deal, the way I dress all the time—and I could tell that people were just staring at me wondering why I was dressed like that. Upon getting onstage after [my] name was called out, you could hear people [groan]. Not halfway through the song, everybody was up to the stage saying, 'This guy is great.'"[50] To combat racism and racial stereotypes and prove their supposed authenticity as genuine country musicians, both Triggs and Marks had to persuade white audiences of their musicality and faithfulness to the country sound.

Other black artists have experienced what is arguably racism but attribute rejection as ultimately a business decision. Rissi Palmer, who eventually signed with 1720 Entertainment, remembered how the initial favorable reaction to her music turned sour when its executives learned her racial identity. Reminiscent of Charley Pride's "business savvy" reaction to RCA's decision in the mid-1960s to obfuscate his racial identity in promotional materials, Rissi felt that the decision was motivated by marketing concerns rather than purely one of race.[51] Despite all his success, Darius Rucker is even critical of Capitol records for signing him to a major record deal in 2008 because his band Hootie and the Blowfish were experiencing a career downturn. He intimates in an interview that his race should have been another factor in making a "wise" business decision: "If I was a record company president, and I was my brother, I wouldn't have given me a record deal . . . I would not have given a record deal to the black guy that was the lead singer in Hootie and the Blowfish."[52]

Indeed, music industry executives often reject claims of racism. Instead, their counternarratives remind the public that the music industry is, first and foremost, a business where decisions are made based on assessment of risk and return on investment. Profits must be made. It can be financially disastrous to invest millions in unproven artists, whether white or black. Bob Saporiti, at the time the senior vice president for Global Marketing at Nashville's Warner Brothers Records, argued there is no attempt to exclude African Americans from securing a record contract: "We look for quality and originality. I would love to have a black artist on our roster and an Asian artist, too ... The few that did [audition] didn't measure up to the standards we place on artists. We would love to have a black artist, but not for the sake of just having one. After all, this is a business."[53]

A second and related major theme is identity and identification. For many years, Charley Pride was the only visible black county artist and, thus, served as an important figure of inspiration and identification. For example, as a child, Carl Ray traveled with Pride and, subsequently, became more and more interested in country music.[54] Despite Pride's visibility and superstar status, the dearth of black country artists has denied African Americans an opportunity to envision their involvement, participation, and identification with the genre. For many African Americans, the black identity is publicly associated with certain musical forms, such as rap and soul, not country. For example, singer Rissi Palmer recalled that as a child, she found it difficult to identify with country music because there were few African-American artists: "When you're a child, you react to something that's familiar and looks like you. And there was nobody [in country music] who looked like me. Just being a kid, you don't see black country singers. So you don't think that's a possibility for you. You see black pop singers. You see black R&B singers. You see black rockers. So you say, 'If I'm black and I want to sing, then I probably have to sing R&B.'"[55] Interviewed in 2011, country artist Miko Marks found that other than Charley Pride, country music has lacked "solid [black] representation." Instead, according to Marks, "every time you put country music on—everybody is blonde, they're white; they're white males." It is difficult to identify with absence: "If you can't see yourself in that picture, how would you identify with that on any level? How can you build a relationship with it if there is nothing of you there? It's the same with golf and Tiger Woods."[56]

While acknowledging the problem of representation, Cleve Francis also blames African-American consumers for perpetuating the belief that blacks should not listen to country music because it is racist. According to Francis, "I think what some blacks unfortunately have done is to say, 'Here are these people who don't like us and this is the music they listen to, so the music must be racist music.' A lot of blacks who like country music have remained in the closet."[57] Rucker believes his success has allowed more and more African Americans to openly express their affection for country music.[58] In the end, black artists often occupy a liminal state between black audiences who reject their involvement in country music and whites who reject the black presence for entirely different reasons. As Cowboy Troy told a *Chicago Tribune* reporter, "Sometimes I do kind of feel I get the looks from people on all sides of the fence, black, white, Hispanic."[59]

Moreover, there is the public notion that country music is somehow incommensurate with the black experience, a notion that has been supported by influential individuals from the country music industry. For example, in a 2006 interview, Tammy Genovese, then head of the Country Music Association (CMA), argued that country music is alien to black culture and the black experience: "The black community's lifestyle is different from what we communicate in country music. We try to market to all types of people. But every culture has its own type of music, and that is something we can't change. Black people have their own types of music that they like to listen to, be that jazz, hip hop or whatever."[60] But contrary to such comments, artists such as Valierie Walker and Dwight Quick contend that country music was an intimate part of their rural American upbringing. Walker's parents raised her in an environment of breeding pigs and growing tobacco on a five-acre farm: "I never thought that county was just for whites, because all the blacks around here listen to it." Her family listened to the Grand Ole Opry. Quick was raised in North Carolina in a small town, where as a child he would attend church, fish for crawfish, and drink tea out of a Mason jar. To him, country music's stories were about the world he knew: "It was about my way of life. You're not going to hear no rapper talking about fishing, or drinking in a honky-tonk or eating rabbit—but that's all me."[61] Darius Rucker listened to country music as a child and his favorite television show was *Hee-Haw,* a viewing habit that drew the scorn of his siblings: "'Why are you listening to that white boy music?'"[62]

Similarly, singer Rhonda Towns, who performed songs by Wynonna Judd on *Star Search,* grew up listening to country music and believes its message has significant broad appeal: "I've always loved country music. Country music was played at my house, and I never felt like it belonged to anyone." She views country as "American music that [addresses] the lives of everyday people." While growing up in Anniston, Alabama, she was drawn to such female artists as Reba McIntyre and Tanya Tucker.[63] Staton effectively summed the obvious problem (stereotyping) with associating a musical genre with race: "Just because we're black doesn't mean all we listen to is rap, gospel, blues and jazz."[64]

Despite facing institutional and personal racism as well as lack of representation, black country artists repeatedly express the interconnected themes of determination and perseverance, the third and final theme. Both determination and perseverance are related to the importance of having musical allies—both black and white. For anyone to make it in the music industry, determination and perseverance are an absolute necessity. But for African Americans, determination and perseverance take on obvious larger social and historical meanings: individual and collective strivings to eliminate white privilege and the ideology of white supremacy through gaining access or eliminating the racial divide. In 2000, Rhonda Towns broke a color barrier in country music, not in Nashville but in Switzerland, where she performed at the annual International Country Music Festival. Despite her success as being the first black artist at this event, she has commented: "It's been hard. I was truly amazed by the way I was received in Europe. But Nashville is tough. I won't be denied, though."[65] Miko Marks vowed that she is going to "stick with it. I'm not gonna put this down." Noting the "embossed butterflies" on her acoustic guitar, she added, "These are butterflies, I'm gonna soar just as high as they do."[66]

Darius Rucker is an intriguing case study in perseverance and determination. Despite his star quality, he was willing to pay his dues by adhering to the traditional path followed by new country artists when starting out in the business; he went on a tour of radio stations to promote his first single: "When I went to Capital [Records], I said 'Look you guys, I want to go visit as many radio stations as I can.'"[67] The next rite of passage for country artists is to be the opening act on a well-established country star's tour. For Rucker, this was opening for Brad Paisley's 2011 "H2O Frozen

Over" tour: "I was the baby band. I played 30 minutes. But that's what I wanted to do . . . I wanted to experience building it from the bottom, you know, and trying to make it to the top. And that's how we did it."[68]

As a voice of defiance, Rucker told one interviewer, "If I ever let any racial stereotypes keep me from singing a type of music, I'd be bartending somewhere in Charleston [South Carolina] right now."[69] Despite still receiving hate mail, Rucker has made it clear that he will continue to pursue his country music ambitions because he refuses to quit country music. In a 2014 interview, Rucker flatly announced that "I never want to let anybody tell me what I can do. I always want to do what I want to do."[70] For many country artists, Charley Pride has not only served as an important ally but an important point of comparison. Rucker met Pride in 2012, and the two musicians have exchanged their personal stories about working in country music. Rucker is particularly interested in what life was like for Pride and the prejudice and discrimination the elder musician experienced during the 1960s and 1970s. As Rucker said, "No matter what happens to me as a black man in country music, I can handle it" because Pride confronted significantly more pronounced racism.[71] As Rucker explained in another interview, "I look at Charley Pride, who was one of the reasons I was able to do this. But I think, 'God, what must that guy have gone through to do what he did?'"[72]

As the elder statesman, Pride is certainly an ally and supporter for black artists. So are white artists. Fellow country music artists often serve as white allies via recording collaborations, as well as touring together. Big and Rich have recorded with Cowboy Troy, while Lady Antebellum was featured on Darius Rucker's hit "Wagon Wheel." Mickey Guyton and Darius Rucker have been featured as opening acts for Brad Paisley's tours. Verbal support is equally as important. Garth Brooks encouraged Carl Ray to keep writing despite the fact that "this music business is tough, especially for artists of color,"[73] and Big Kenny of Big and Rich publicly supported Rucker on a number of occasions: "We are dang lucky in this town that he showed up!"[74]

In conclusion, this chapter identified three major themes based on published interviews with black country artists dating from the 1990s to the present. The stories describe a country music industry that has both actively and covertly excluded African Americans from fully participating in what has become publicly defined, in the minds of many, as a white, racist musical genre. While the majority of African-American performers have identified institutional racism as a cause for the difficulty in becoming a successful country artist, others have experienced more personal, or fan-based, racism. Institutional and personal racism certainly explains the presence of the second rhetorical theme centered on identity and identification. Without a significant black presence in country music and the music's association with some of the more socially repressive elements of the dominant white culture, it has been difficult for African Americans to identify with the genre. At the same time, black artists grew up listening to country music, particularly those who grew in the rural South, and believe country music is their music, too. Despite the symbolic and material obstacles associated with establishing a career in country music, artists clearly expressed their determination to succeed. In all, through storytelling, black country artists position themselves as having a legitimate right to participate in country music. They refuse to leave country music to white folk.

The presence of white allies, including Brad Paisley, Big and Rich, and Lady Antebellum, as well as the remarkable success of Darius Rucker, suggests, on one level, a breakthrough for African-American country artists. Cleve Francis, who considers himself a link between Charley Pride and Rucker, attributes part of Rucker's success to what he calls "generational permission." In the 1990s, the country music industry was not ready for a black country singer. Now, he insists, "there's a new generation that's now allowing this to happen."[75] While this claim may be true, it is also true that Darius Rucker entered country music as an established brand as the lead singer of the hugely successful Hootie and the Blowfish. Someone who sells twenty million records will not be denied. As Carl Ray observed, "They're like any other businessmen. They want to market and assign people where they're going to get the biggest bang for their buck. What better way to use an artist like Darius, who already has a brand established? He was the perfect choice, and of course that takes nothing away from his talents."[76] As a result of his star power, Rucker—unlike Cleve Francis—has been accepted and embraced by the country music industry. Rucker has won Grammy and Country Music Association awards and has been nominated for Academy of Country Music and Country Music Television awards. He was inducted as a member of the Grand Ole Opry in 2012 and was a featured artist in the Opry's documentary concert film, *American Saturday Night: Live from the Grand Ole Opry,* which was released in December 2015. In another recent development, Mickey Guyton was nominated for the 2016 Academy of Country Music's New Female Vocalist of the Year award. These examples are evidence that the country music industry has embraced the black presence in ways that were certainly unheard of during Charley Pride's reign during the 1960s and 1970s and even during Cleve Francis's short-lived career in the 1990s.

Despite this success, Rucker and Guyton do not represent the transcendent breakthrough that will erase the public's perception of African-American country artists as anomalies, curiosities, or tokens. Perhaps that day will come when race is as invisible for black artists as it is for whites. Rissi Palmer once told a reporter that she dreams of a day when the discussion of her music will ignore race in favor of the music itself.[77] Charley Pride has taken it upon himself to promote a type of personal transcendence by stating that he is not an African American but an American who happens to play country music. While Pride's effort to remove himself from the realities of race is problematic, his post-racial identity suggests that transcendence, however envisioned and enacted, is a possibility.

## NOTES

1. Keegan-Michael Key and Jordan Peele, "Season Two, Episode Three: Country Music," *Comedy Central,* October 10, 2012.

2. Martin Hodgson, "The Hidden Faces of Country," *Guardian,* July 15, 2006, https://www.theguardian.com/music/2006/jul/16/popandrock3.

3. Jocelyn R. Neal, "Dancing around the Subject: Race in Country Music Fan Culture," *Musical Quarterly* 89, no. 4 (2006): 559.

4. Cavan Sieczkowski, "Darius Rucker Responds to Racist Tweet: 'Is This 2013 or 1913,'" *Huffington Post,* May 22, 2013, https://www.huffingtonpost.com/2013/05/22/darius-rucker-racist-tweet_n_3319629.html.

5. Mary Welch, "Darius Rucker Lets the 'Good Time' Roll [Interview]," *Biography,* May 24, 2016, https://www.biography.com/news/darius-rucker-biography-interview, January 14, 2018.

6. Quoted in Aaron Broder, "Country Music Songwriter," January 29, 2010, http://www.scholastic.com/browse/article.jsp?id=3753447.

7. Diane Pecknold, "Introduction: Country Music and Racial Formation," in *Hidden in the Mix: The African American Presence in Country Music,* ed. Diane Pecknold (Durham: Duke University Press, 2013), 1.

8. Pamela E. Foster, *My Country: The African Diaspora's Country Music Heritage* (Nashville: My Country, 1998), vi.

9. Nicholas Dawidoff, *In the Country of Country: A Journey to the Roots of American Music* (New York: Vintage, 1997), 10.

10. Bill C. Malone, "Turkey in the Straw: The Roots of Commercial Country Music," in *Will the Circle Be Unbroken: Country Music in America,* ed. Paul Kingsbury and Alanna Nash (New York: DK Publishing, 2006), 14–18; Cub Koda, "Old-Time Traditional Country," *All Music Guide to Country: The Experts' Guide to the Best Recordings in Country Music,* eds. Michael Erlewine, Vladimir Bogdanov, Chris Woodstra, and Stephen Thomas Erlewine (San Francisco: Miller Freeman, 1997), 549–51.

11. Bill C. Malone, *Don't Get above Your Raisin': Country Music and the Southern Working Class* (Urbana: University of Illinois Press, 2002), 14.

12. Ibid., 14.

13. Ibid., 16; Kurt Wolff, *Country Music: The Rough Guide* (London: Rough Guides, 2000), 1.

14. Erich Nunn, *Sounding the Color Line: Music and Race in the Southern Imagination* (Athens: University of Georgia Press, 2015), 45.

15. Ibid., 45–70.

16. Sandra R. Lieb, *Mother of the Blues: A Study of Ma Rainey* (Amherst: University of Massachusetts Press, 1981), 20.

17. Steven C. Tracy, "Introduction," in *Write Me a Few of Your Lines: A Blues Reader,* ed. Steven C. Tracy (Amherst: University of Massachusetts Press, 1999), 3.

18. Tony Russell, *Blacks, Whites and Blues* (London: Studio Vista, 1970), in Paul Oliver, Tony Russell, Robert M. W. Dixon, John Godrich, and Howard Rye, *Yonder Come the Blues: The Evolution of a Genre* (Cambridge: Cambridge University Press, 2001), 160–62.

19. Karl Hagstrom Miller, *Segregating Sound: Inventing Folk and Pop Music in the Age of Jim Crow* (Durham: Duke University Press, 2010), 2.

20. Thomas Ruys Smith, "'Bring Our Country Back': Country Music, Conservatives, and the Counter-Culture in 1968," *Studies in American Culture* 34, no. 1 (2011): 103–4, 121–23.

21. Beth A. Messner, Art Jipson, Paul J. Becker, and Bryan Byers, "The Hardest Hate: A Sociological Analysis of Country Hate Music," *Popular Music and Society* 30, no. 4 (2007): 516.

22. Charles Aaron, "Despite Lil Wayne and Kid Rock, Is Country Music Still Racist?" *Spin,* November 14, 2008, http://www.spin.com/2008/11/despite-lil-wayne -and-kid-rock-country-music-still-racist; L. Z. Granderson, "Why Can't Country Music Deal with Race?" CNN, November 8, 2011, http://www.cnn.com/2011/11/08/opinion /granderson-country-music-race/index.html; Noah Berlatsky, "How Country Music

Got More Racist," *Hooded Utilitarian,* May 25, 2013, http://www.hoodedutilitarian.com/2013/05/how-country-music-got-more-racist/.

23. Charley Pride with Jim Henderson, *Pride: The Charley Pride Story* (New York: Quill, 1994), 134, 143; David Vinopal, "Charley Pride Biography," *AllMusic,* n.d., https://www.allmusic.com/artist/charley-pride-mn0000165818/biography, May 30, 2015.

24. Anne Dingus, "Charley Pride," *Texas Monthly,* September 2000, 260.

25. Pride, *Pride,* 12.

26. Ibid., 151, 154–56.

27. Vinopal, "Charley Pride Biography."

28. Charles L. Hughes, *Country Soul: Making Music and Making Race in the American South* (Chapel Hill: University of North Carolina Press, 2015), 129–30.

29. Quoted in Jewly Hight, "Rissi Palmer on Soulful Comeback: 'It's Scary and Empowering,'" *Rolling Stone,* June 25, 2015, https://www.rollingstone.com/music/features/rissi-palmer-on-soulful-comeback-its-scary-and-empowering-20150625.

30. Country Music Television, "CMT Hot 20 Countdown," aired February 8, 2015.

31. Quoted in Hodgson, "The Hidden Faces."

32. J. Freedom du Lac, "Listen to the Doctor: Cleve Francis, Cardiologist and Country Singer," *Washington Post,* March 14, 2010, http://www.washingtonpost.com/wp-dyn/content/article/2010/03/05/AR2010030503116.html.

33. Johnny Loftus, "Cleve Francis Biography," *AllMusic,* https://www.allmusic.com/artist/cleve-francis-mn0000121490/biography, October 13, 2015.

34. Quoted in du Lac, "Listen to the Doctor."

35. Quoted in Nate Guidry, "Country Music's Blacklist," *Pittsburg Post-Gazette,* February 18, 2001, http://old.post-gazette.com/magazine/20010218country2.asp, November 15, 2015.

36. J. Freedom Du Lac, "Cleve Francis on Race, Country Music and the Chart-Topping Achievements of Darius Rucker," *Washington Post,* April 6, 2009, http://voices.washingtonpost.com/postrock/2009/04/cleve_francis_on_race_country.html.

37. Quoted in David Scheiber, "The Ballad of the Country Doctor," *St. Petersburg Times,* 23 April 23, 2000, http://www.sptimes.com/News/042300/Floridian/The_Ballad_of_the_Cou.shtml.

38. Quoted in David Scheiber, "Singing Out Proud," *St. Petersburg Times,* April 24, 2000, http://www.sptimes.com/News/042400/Floridian/Belting_It_Out.shtml.

39. Quoted in Guidry, "Country Music's Blacklist."

40. Quoted in Hodgson, "The Hidden Faces."

41. Quoted in David Scheiber, "African-American Country Music Backed by Lobby Group." *MTV News,* April 26, 2000, http://www.mtv.com/news/821452/african-american-country-music-backed-by-lobby-group/.

42. Black Country Music Association, n.d., http://blackcountrymusicassociation.blogspot.com/, December 4, 2015.

43. Quoted in Michael Perry, "Sharing the Stage: Blacks in Country Music," *World and I Magazine,* n.d., https://mhm8684.wordpress.com/, January 15, 2017.

44. John W. Rumble, "Black Artists in Country Music," *Encyclopedia of Country Music*, ed. Paul Kinsbury, Michael McCall, and John W. Rumble, 2nd ed. (Oxford: Oxford University Press, 2012), 37.

45. Quoted in "Country Music Star Talks Defying His Skeptics—Including Himself," *CBS This Morning*, April 2, 2014, https://www.cbsnews.com/news/country-music -star-darius-rucker-talks-defying-his-skeptics-including-himself/, January 14, 2018. .

46. "Darius Rucker Discusses Race and Country Music," interviewed by Lee Hawkins, WSJ Radio, September 15, 2014, http://www.wsj.com/video/darius-rucker -discusses-race-and-country-music/319B4C2D-69FC-434B-BE74-F39E8499D3C4 .html.

47. Quoted in "Country Music Star Talks Defying His Skeptics—Including Himself."

48. Quoted in Sieczkowski, "Darius Rucker Responds."

49. Lee Bailey, "Miko Marks the Spot: African American Singer Wants to Kick in Country Music's Door," VaTalent.com, n.d., http://www.vatalent.com/newsa .php?news_id=119, December 13, 2015.

50. Quoted in Phyllis Stark, "Trini Triggs Hopes to Break Barriers," *Billboard*, February 28, 1998, 40.

51. John Gerome, "Rissi Palmer Crosses Music Color Divide," *CBS News*, October 15, 2007, https://www.cbsnews.com/news/rissi-palmer-crosses-music-color-divide/.

52. Country Music Television, "Inside Fame: Darius Rucker," aired February 7, 2015.

53. Quoted in Guidry, "Country Music's Blacklist."

54. John Wenzel, "Interview: Darius Rucker and Blacks in Country Music," *The Know*, September 3, 2009, http://theknow.denverpost.com/2009/09/03/interview-darius -rucker-and-blacks-in-country-music/7051/7051/.

55. Edward Morris, "Rissi Palmer Finding Her Home in Country Music," *CMT News*, November 13, 2007, http://www.cmt.com/news/1574199/rissi-palmer-finding-her -home-in-country-music/.

56. Quoted in Dennis J. Freeman, "Black Country Music Singer Miko Marks Blazing a Trail," news4usonline.com, February 2, 2011, http://news4usonline.com/2011/02 /black-country-music-singer-miko-marks-blazing-a-trail/.

57. Quoted in Maria Odum, "A Physician Who Heals with Both Science and Art," *New York Times*, May 9, 1992, http://www.nytimes.com/1992/05/09/arts/a-physician -who-heals-with-both-science-and-art.html.

58. "Darius Rucker Discusses Race and Country Music," interview.

59. Quoted in Chrissie Dickinson, "Black Rapper Cowboy Troy Has Country in His Soul," *Chicago Tribune*, July 1, 2004, http://articles.chicagotribune.com/2004–07–01/fea tures/0407010097_1_cowboy-troy-country-music-cowboy-hat.

60. Quoted in Hodgson, "The Hidden Faces."

61. Ibid.

62. Quoted in "Country Music Star Talks Defying His Skeptics—Including Himself."

63. Quoted in Guidry, "Country Music's Blacklist."

64. Quoted in Hodgson, "The Hidden Faces."

65. Quoted in Guidry, "Country Music's Blacklist."

66. "Quoted in A. K. Shackleford, "Ga Ga: Miko Marks, the Next Big Country Singer," blindie.com, July 21, 2008, http://blindie.com/2008/07/21/ga-ga-miko-marks -the-next-big-country-singer/.

67. Country Music Television, "Inside Fame."

68. Ibid.

69. Ibid.

70. "Darius Rucker Discusses Race and Country Music," interview.

71. Ibid.

72. Quoted in Wenzel, "Interview: Darius Rucker."

73. Ibid.

74. Country Music Television, "Inside Fame."

75. Du Lac, "Cleve Francis on Race."

76. Quoted in Wenzel, "Interview: Darius Rucker."

77. "As Black Woman, Rissi Palmer Is Country Rarity," *Today*, October 15, 2007, https: //www.today.com/popculture/black-woman-rissi-palmer-country-rarity-wbna213 07946.

# CHAPTER TEN

# Reading Hick-Hop

*The Shotgun
Marriage of
Hip-Hop and
Country Music*

## TRESSIE MCMILLAN COTTOM

IN 2012, country act Florida Georgia Line released "Cruise." The song used a hip-hop cadence, structure, and imagery. The song and the band would later become identified with the 2010s trend of "bro country," which narrativized beer drinking, partying, and chasing girls. But it also sonically mimicked the braggadocio and rhythm of African-American popular music. This move is a departure from a genre said to "sound so white."[1] In essence, two genres of music that wrestle with and promulgate specific narratives of racial authenticity are, in fact, closely related. Certainly, it is not news that musical genres are racialized or that hip-hop and country music, in particular, play with legitimate expressions of racial identity. It is not news that country music has historically been bound up in other supposedly race-specific music, such as gospel and blues. However, at the time of Florida Georgia Line's huge hit, it was news that pop country could appeal to both hip-hop sensibilities and narratives about authentic white racial identity.[2] The two genres seemed diametrically opposed. Hip-hop music is characterized and often caricatured in popular culture as urban, black, and dangerous. Critics have derided themes of gang culture, violence, and misogyny in hip-hop music—often, deliberately ignoring hip-hop that does not fit that mold. In contrast, country music is characterized and occasionally caricatured as rural/suburban and white. Perhaps above all, popular culture constructs country music as safe. Critics may comment on country music's gender norms and narrow-mindedness, but almost no one thinks country music is dangerous. How then do we explain hick-hop—the merging of the most dangerous musical genre with popular music's safest musical genre?

This essay approaches that question from a cultural studies perspective. Stuart Hall argued that critical interrogations of culture as a political, epistemic, and economic system could decode how we live structural oppression in our everyday lives.[3] Popular culture matters—just as economic systems, political processes, and knowledge creation matters to popular culture. As a trained sociologist, I also take seriously how race, class, and gender pattern our social world through our experiences of it. Richard Peterson and Paul Di Maggio once used data on cultural tastes and country music to argue for musical styles as "indicators of emerging culture classes."[4] Culture classes refers to "groupings of individuals who share similar consumption patterns, yet do not distribute themselves neatly with respect to the traditional indicators of taste culture."[5] This essay considers the structural and organizational contexts of how these two forms of popular culture—hip-hop and country—were shaped and are consumed as indicators of culture classes to explore race, identity, and authenticity in the twenty-first century.

Born amid Reagan's urban apocalyptic landscape in exotic places such as Brooklyn and the Bronx, hip-hop music is a decidedly black, urban cultural product.[6] Unlike jazz, rock, and bebop before it, hip-hop maximized a unique moment in a disrupted corporate music industry to afford black artists control of the iconography of the latest iteration of race music. Country music may have once been the poor white man's attempt at singing the gospel and the blues, but it evolved as the symbolic culture of non-elite, working-class, rural whiteness. Its attendant values proudly defy middle-class cultural conformity and racialized urban imagery. Country fans unironically embrace faith, family, and country in a cynical pop culture world. Hip-hop fans may embrace the free market ethos of "money over bitches," but mainstream hip-hop is largely resistant to sentimental ruminations on hearth and home. How then do we understand the emergence of what the *Wall Street Journal* called "hick-hop," country music with hip-hop verses, hip-hop language, hip-hop posturing, and even occasionally actual hip-hop artists rapping in country songs?[7]

We are not just talking about an underground, marginal subgenre. For example, in 2013, a number one hit song by Florida Georgia Line was remixed with rapper Nelly, an effort lacking all irony that ended up in rotation on both country and pop radio. Also, Jason Aldean remixed his hit "Dirt Road Anthem," originally written by self-proclaimed country rapper Colt Ford and remixed with Southern rapper Ludacris. Earlier attempts at merging the two genres include Trace Adkins's "Honky Tonk Badonkadonk" and Dierks Bentley borrowing the hip-hop slang for crazy in "5-1-5-0" (itself borrowed from police codes). These songs are not the farce that was black country rapper Cowboy Troy. Instead, each effort represents a fairly seamless movement of hip-hop culture, language, and stylings into a musical form that defines itself in large part by how *not* black it is. How is it possible that country fans embrace Nelly and Ludacris popping up in hit country songs *and* fist-pump to Eric Church's melodramatic admonishment of the lost country white boy who thinks he is "too bad for a little square town" with his "hip-hop hat" and "pants on the ground"?[8] To be astonished by the hip-hop country crossover is to misunderstand the history of "race" music or the contemporary reality of poverty among rural whites. Not entirely unlike hip-hop, hick-hop is the cultural reflection of poor rural whites' resistance to the erasure of their material reality from cultural discourse.

Rising inequality and structural changes in the labor market that replaced good-paying skilled jobs with low-wage service work have hit poor whites hard.[9] At the same time, wealth has concentrated in urban centers while suburban sprawl has eaten away the landscape of rural America.[10] Literally, the "country" of which country music sings is diminishing rapidly. The American South is country music's spatial and symbolic ground zero, and the shifting demographic and economic realities reshaping poverty and mobility throughout the nation are particularly acute in this region.[11] This change explains, in part, the fault lines of acceptable hip-hop crossovers into country's musical backyard. Rendered largely invisible by ideological fetishes for pathologizing black urban poverty, country music remains a symbolic space for poor white culture to be centered. The adaption of black hip-hop culture speaks to the greater youth culture of popular music but also to the constraints of poor rural whites to contest their cultural representations even in country, the supposedly purest of all American white cultural products.

To understand why hip-hop is the means for this cultural crossover but not other genres, one must first understand that the neat marketing demographics that define corporate radio silos are not natural.[12] Culture is a messy entity that defies rigid boundaries and even outright ownership. There is a long history of interracial cultural making in every single genre of music, including that which would brand itself the most authentically American music genre: country music. In *Segregating Sound*, Karl Hagstrom Miller argues that the categories that we have inherited to think and talk about Southern music bear little relation to the ways that Southerners long played and heard music. I would add that these categories also ignore how Southerners actually lived.[13] Jim Crow was always better at policing public spaces and bureaucracies than it was at severing the intimate lives of Southern blacks and whites.[14] That reality is reflected in the sonic race-mixing that produced the genres we now take for granted as distinct and naturally occurring. That sonic refutation of distinct racialized spheres of social life can be heard in Lesley "Esley" Riddle's significant contribution to the famous Carter Family clan or spied in the black artists singing backup for a range of country stars. I point this out to refute the notion that country music is "white music." It is not, of course. Instead, it is an expression of ethnic, racial, and cultural miscegenation that marks all culture. But country music has been leveraged as a tool of whiteness, particularly as a powerful mechanism in the delineation of the cultural boundaries of rural, Southern, working-class whiteness.

Sociologically, we understand that rural Southern whites have experienced significant economic and social change over the past fifty years. Writer Chauncey DeVega argues that the "new white poor" comprise the formerly white working class and that they bear little resemblance to the toothless, uneducated "redneck" caricature used to erase this reality.[15] Travis Stimeling contextualizes these changes in his chapter in this volume, "Alternative Country Music and the American Midwest as Industrial Wasteland." Stimeling discusses how alt-country groups emerge as poverty transforms from an urban phenomenon to a white, suburban one. Similar changes have structured how culture forms like hip-hop and country music emerge from how people navigate macro processes such as poverty, (de)industrialization, and demography. Suffice it to say, census data show that while racial disparities among the impoverished persist, they have narrowed since the 1970s.[16] That shift is not because of greater mobility for minority groups but because of the expansion of white poverty. Today, 76 percent of whites will experience poverty by the time they reach sixty years of age. This reality is most acute for what some demographers call the "invisible poor": poor whites in suburban and rural rings throughout the country (especially the South and the Rust Belt).[17] More than 60 percent of the poor in outer urban rings that span the Appalachia and the industrial Rust Belt through the Midwest are white. The poor rural and suburban whites that make up the core country music audience are more likely to be born poor, live poor, and die poor today, regardless of educational achievement, than they were fifty years ago.[18] Rather than working hard all day in a union job and coming home to an ice-cold beer—a ritual memorialized in hundreds of country tunes—today's white poor are more likely to be working shifts at Wal-Mart or the Piggly Wiggly, if they are working at all.[19] This turn is a qualitative change in the day-to-day reality of non-elite whites, and they recognize this reality: just 46 percent of whites polled in a nationally representative survey think they "will have a good chance of improving their economic position based on the way things are in the United States."[20] That pessimism is a fairly accurate interpretation of the decline of upward social mobility for whites. Ideological fetishes that reward a hyperfocus on poverty as a black urban peculiarity often obscure that decline—a hard truth that often escapes both the political right and left. The reality of poor whites might be absent from our news, from our dominant narratives about poverty, and even from our academic research, but it is being played out in the country music soundtrack of their lives.

Our culture's relentless representation of poverty as a black underclass phenomenon obscures how hip-hop and country are embarking upon similar paths of cultural adaptation. If country music is the tool of a particular type of whiteness, then hip-hop can be understood as a tool for the delineation of a particular type of blackness. At its roots, hip-hop was the musical grandchild of the black Americans who made the great migration so great, and American music is the direct beneficiary of black migrants who, in their economic and social ambassadorships, were also cultural ambassadors. The men and women who traveled north and west to Chicago, New York, and California from Georgia, Mississippi, and the Carolinas carried with them the music, rhythms, instrumentation, and genius of black art, even as they toiled in the bowels of the industrial revolution for meager pay.

Cultural tools—here, music and musical styles—are a way for individuals and groups to define themselves, particularly in relation to how they would be defined by powerful hegemonic structures and sociological forces. Poor black people made the blues because social ills like segregation, black codes, and institutional violence gave them some blues to sing. Later, when the grandchildren and great grandchildren of those cultural ambassadors were living the disappointment of the northern dreams of their freedom-seeking foreparents, they started beating on tables and speeding up melodies to reflect the urgency of their social condition. They made hip-hop when political, social, and economic forces created the material reality that made it necessary to create hip-hop.

Because the peculiarity of whiteness demands it never be racialized in the ways that blacks are always racialized, it is easy to forget that white people are living among social, economic, and political processes similar to those that gave rise to hip-hop. Rising inequality in the United States is absolutely racialized, but it is by its nature a class construct from which whites are not exempt. The amorphous middle class has declined from 28.2 percent of the population in 1967 to 23.7 percent today.[21] This reduction has pushed ever more whites beyond the boundaries of middle-class respectability. The bifurcation of our social structure reinforces the ideology that rich white elites have little in common with their poor white brethren. Policing the boundaries between "white trash" culture and high culture becomes a way of solidifying the superiority of elite whites. The economic contrasts are being drawn ever more sharply and so, too, are the cultural contrasts. In popular culture, reality television either valorizes the white economic (if socially trashy) elite in the housewives of Orange

County or demoralizes the lives of Myrtle Beach trailer parks. Cultural critics and scholars alike have noted what writer Eric Deggans calls the proliferation of "hicksploitation" television and the demise of working-class settings like Archie Bunker's urban enclave on the 1970s *All in the Family*.[22] There is no middle in the popular culture depiction of whiteness because increasingly there is no achievable middle in the white economic class structure.

The resulting loss of upward mobility for poor whites influences their contemporary engagement with black cultural goods. Historically, when white folks wanted to enjoy black music without the danger of actually listening to black musicians, they simply put the black music in whiteface. The organizational logics—the prevailing organizational structure for an industry—made this particularly lucrative in the twentieth century.[23] Early on, that organizational logic favored large, paternalistic music companies. Operating in a sort of Wild West before copyright had deigned to catch up with new modes of producing and distributing cultural products, these music and entertainment companies were more Rockefeller robber baron than Rock-a-fella distribution deals. There was no negotiating with talent, for artists were hired, shaped, and packaged by music companies that had an unholy ownership over the performer, the music, and the product that was sold and played on radio.

These organizational logics do not materialize from thin air. They are produced by that cultural stew in which we are always being slowly roasted at temperatures just low enough to escape our awareness most of the time but hot enough to make us notice when change is afoot. Also, while culture is lived by us all, it is made for the young. Therein lies a special tension for hip-hop and country audiences. For when race music was capturing the hearts and, perhaps more important, the bodies and libidos, of white youth in the twentieth century, organizational logics responded to the dictates of a segregation by shaping black music into "rock and roll." Elvis's gyrations may have been dangerous, but thanks to anti-miscegenation laws, Ike Turner's would have literally been criminal and unnatural. The music that defines the culture of young people is intuitively understood by a society as an intergenerational hegemonic tool. It shapes how young people will acculturate into or, as sometimes happens, resist acculturation into existing hegemonic roles and structures.

Making black music over into whiteface was an organizational logic with a profit motive, but it did not operate independently of the social structure of hegemonic culture.[24] In fact, the two worked in tandem to exert control over the acceptable trajectories of white youth and the social dominance of whiteness over blackness. This dominance is reinforced by the malleable, phenotypic construct of whiteness, which is very much at the mercy of what was once called "miscegenation." The legal definition of blackness as anyone with "one drop" of black blood makes whiteness biologically fragile. Controlling white youth culture becomes a way to control the making of white babies by criminalizing black sexuality and especially criminalizing the intermingling of black and white sexual selves. If you have ever seen a young white woman "drop it like it's hot" when Jay-Z is played at a nightclub, you may see how hip-hop could be a problem for maintaining boundaries between black and white sexual selves.

Throughout most of U.S. history, an interlocking set of political, legal, social, and corporate norms empowered by white hegemonic racism colluded to strip black musicians of the means to own their art. In his book *Race, Rock, and Elvis,* author Michael T. Bertrand argues that Elvis did not steal black music as much as he borrowed heavily from all forms of music.[25] It remains that black music, as opposed to white roots music, was singularly translated to divorce the music from its black creators. Hip-hop, however, has steadfastly resisted being made over into whiteface. Sure, there has been Third Bass, the Beastie Boys, and the white hip-hop savior Eminem. However, unlike Elvis Presley (here a stand-in for the many, many white artists who borrowed black music to profit from its mass commodification for white youth), these acts were legitimized and produced by black artists—meaning that the audience could not access hip-hop without also getting a black face, a black pelvis, and all other aspects of blackness.

The power to effect that kind of legitimizing is a product of the times in which hip-hop was born. By the late twentieth century, the entertainment market was fragmenting. Radio was the primary point of distribution for music. Corporate entertainment companies, which are almost comically bad at predicting or shaping emergent technologies, did not see much room for growth in the music market. This reaction produced a laissez-faire attitude to building new markets and controlling the markets they already owned, pretty much lock, stock, and barrel. In the language of the culture, record companies got caught slipping. Because major labels were not much interested when new technologies emerged that rearranged the relationship between music maker and music distributor, they had not yet bothered to co-opt them. These boxes—the synthesizers, the drum machines, the turntables—seem quaint and low-fi now, but at the time, they represented no less than a revolution of the control over distribution of cultural product. You could make the music in your bedroom, duplicate it on tape decks, and distribute it at house parties and swap meets.

These black kids were making black culture, but they also were owning that culture's trajectory in ways not possible for their foreparents. This change is due in large part to the disruption of music models mentioned above, but it is also a function of the competitive nature of hip-hop. Historically, hip-hop MCs (or "emcees") earned their dominance publicly in "ciphers" or competitions among rappers, dancers, and deejays. A record company could not brand you the best. Only your peers— other black and minority participants in the culture—could make you the best. This guerrilla legitimization was a bottom-up process. By the time record labels caught on to the noise coming out of Brooklyn (or the Bronx, depending on your orientation), they were still thinking of it is as just race music 2.0 (or maybe 3.0). It would be years later before they understood what those badass black kids were really making: youth culture.

By then a crop of brash young black entrepreneurs owned much of their product and, as a result, much of their culture and some of its capital. Russell Simmons, Puff Daddy, Jay-Z, young music executives like Dame Dash, and others were then in a position to sell its youth culture to the major music labels. That ownership meant a type of legitimacy of the culture as black and of blacks as the gatekeepers of the culture. This control precluded a total whitewashing of hip-hop. For sure, major music labels eventually co-opted most independent black hip-hop makers, but they never got a chance to buy it wholesale, cut out the black middleman, repackage it, and sell it as authentically white.[26] In 1950, a white business executive like Jimmy Iovine would have stolen some beats from Dr. Dre and lyrics from Jay-Z and used them to make an Eminem. But in 1994, Iovine had to bring a white kid to Dr. Dre, who, in turn, made him Eminem.

When MTV, Fab Five Freddy, Kid Rock, MP3 sales, Billboard rankings, and corporate radio made it official—this hip-hop culture was *the* youth culture—it had to do so using black iconography—the only legitimate one available. Industry could not strip the blackness from the cultural product being sold without devaluing the product. The culture being shipped out from the powerful East and West Coast conglomerates to Middle America and rural America was then decidedly, irrefutably black. To be cool, to participate in the dominate youth culture as every American generation has sought to do for generations, white youth had to engage it through black language, black dress, and black sound. To be young, in many ways you had to effect blackness.

If those black kids were born listening to their parents' soul records, rural poor white youth were born listening to the country music that, although influenced by black musicians and performers, was always careful to make that influence invisible by the time the music entered the intimate spaces of homes and ears. But this new era was not their parents' time. These white youths do not have to wait for their youth culture to be distributed to them by the corporate radio stations or their parents' television choices. They can now listen to music in headphones. Their parents need never even hear it. Also, they do not wait for the music to come to them. They can go out and get it. The Internet, peer-to-peer sharing cultures, and hypersegmented cable television markets made youth culture a separate sphere from the adult sphere in ways it had not been in the early days of rock and roll. In the hip-hop era, white kids can partake in the youth culture without much parental or corporate control of how they access it or internalize it. With hip-hop lyrics, they are using the language and the posture of youth culture and grafting it onto the cultural tools of their particular space and place. But before this view descends into post-racial melting pot utopianism, let us be clear that when white kids do this transposing, they are divorcing hip-hop from blackness to make it more palatable, not entirely unlike white corporate radio did to rock and roll seventy years ago. That they are able to do it only within narrow purviews speaks to changes in structural authority over ever-declining white spaces, not to the declining significance of race.

Despite the narrowing of the purview, how white country audiences define authenticity determines which hip-hop–country pairings work.[27]

Hip-hop and country music construct authenticity similarly. That similarity provides a mechanism for white audiences to exert influence over black cultural adoption in white rural country music sonic landscapes. Nelly's verse on the Florida Georgia Line remix is notable not only for its presence but also for its seamlessness. Nelly's hip-hop career was always anchored by his authentic claims to midwestern southernness. From St. Louis, Nelly was not from one of hip-hop's East Coast dynasties. He could not draw on references to New York projects or use Harlem street slang to signal his legitimacy. Instead, Nelly did what Southern rappers like Outkast and Scarface have done: he redefined authenticity symbols from his specific cultural geography.[28] This music included a Southern cadence, introducing regional slang, and regular shout-outs to St. Louis cultural symbols. Nelly's hip-hop authenticity draws on his country authenticity. That Nelly's version of country is materially different from Florida Georgia Line's seems to matter less than that it exists.[29] The same is true of Atlanta rapper Ludacris's verse on Jason Aldean's remix of "Dirt Road Anthem." Nelly and Ludacris work while LL Cool J's verse on Brad Paisley's "Accidental Racist" does not. LL Cool J's verse does not fail just because he appears to be issuing a blanket forgiveness of racism on behalf of all black people. It falls flat, in part, because LL Cool J attempts to drag country iconography to the symbolic urban jungle of his native Queens, New York, from which he derives his hip-hop legitimacy. In contrast, Nelly and Ludacris linguistically slip into the rural white imaginary as familiars. The hoods from which they derive their authentic cred are suburban country. They are likely closer in actual and social distance to the poor suburban and rural hoods of white country fans than to those of elite whites. The crossover is made possible by the same U.S. spatial segregation that allowed Eminem access to black Detroit from 8 Mile or introduced Elvis to Arthur Crudup. Nelly's and Ludacris's visit to country music is paved by the historical spatial and cultural coexistence of non-elite whites and blacks. That is authentic history, authentically shared if not authentically owned by white country audiences. How country artists toe the line of authenticity while yielding to the popularity of hip-hop iconography exposes the limits of that power over the only musical genre that centers white poverty. However, when the dominant popular music is hip-hop music, the authority of country masses to contest what is authentically country gets extra complicated, real fast. Because the country audience is one of the most loyal, it can also be the most rabid. The sanctions issued for violating the complex code of authenticity and values that define country music can be some of the most artistically and economically severe meted out by any group.

For examples of the price of pop success and country sanctions, see Dolly Parton in the 1970s or the Dixie Chicks and Faith Hill in the first decade of the twenty-first century (and note the penalty appears highest and most often for women). The Dixie Chicks case is especially illuminating. While they were exiled not for crossing over but for violating country's political ethos, the swiftness of the country audience response is noteworthy. The pervasive belief is that big, bad, corporate country radio stations orchestrated the near immediate elimination of the Chicks from country music and popular culture. But Princeton researcher Gabriel Rossman's study of the Chicks controversy shows that the pressure to put this group out to permanent pasture was exerted by the country masses, that is, poor rural whites.[30] Top-down imposition of culture from elites has its limits. Although the poor white ex-urban and suburban country music audience may lack the material power to define themselves in the dominant ideology, they can and do shape what constitutes authentic country music. This constrained authority exposes how class defines the authority of whiteness differently. It also frames how poor whites have contested the ways in which hip-hop has been allowed to infiltrate country music.

To draw on popular culture memes is to necessarily draw on black culture because of the unique black legitimacy of hip-hop, and to draw on that black culture, country music has to engage blackness directly. Yet this pursuit of popular relevance risks violating deeply engrained racial beliefs of country's loyal but brutally responsive white, poor, rural fan base. This situation is particularly dangerous as many of those poor whites feel that they are being marginalized by economic elites, losing their social identity in an increasingly diverse America that does not necessarily default American to white and competing with ever more ethnic groups for a dwindling pool of good jobs and beneficial citizenship arrangements that have long been a social salve for their economic pain. Yet to not engage this black culture that is now youth culture, artists risk irrelevance as the youth contingent of their core white, poor, rural fan base listens to and adopts much of the hip-hop/youth culture. The top-selling examples of hick-hop, or this cultural fusion, exemplify the difficulty of that dance, while artistic approaches to navigating the tensions of cultural legitimacy speak to the fault lines running through race, class, gender, and culture.

Certainly, there is the wink-wink good times approach. This attitude is epitomized in Trace Adkin's "Honky Tonk Badonkadonk." The term "badonkadonk" is a black euphemism for a woman's ass. But it does not refer to just any ass. In the black cultural imagination, there has long existed a beauty ideal that has simultaneously internalized white beauty norms and resisted them through the valorization of "uniquely black" phonotypical traits.[31] As complicated as the notion may be, a rotund ass is one of those ideals.[32] Even as white norms have been internalized as a preference for light skin and straight or curly hair (as opposed to dark and nappy hair), a black woman's supposed "natural" dominance in the genetic market of rotund asses has resisted white adoption.[33] When Sir Mix-a-Lot wrote the official ode to rotund behinds in 1991, there was a reason that a stereotypically white valley girl voice, named Becky, opens the song with disgust for a "big ol' butt." As fat has become a class marker among whites, it has necessarily become a racialized class marker. A "big" anything has been conflated with "fat" in a way to make poor bodies non-normative.[34] Black bodies become trapped by this representation oddly irrespective of class, forming one of many other well-documented hegemonic distinctions that makes black inherently wrong by white standards in ways that money cannot buy you out of.[35] If you doubt me, ask Oprah. For all her money, she is still fat with a big ol' black booty, and it has caused her no small amount of existential crisis or marginalization.[36] It has been rumored that Joan Rivers once told Oprah "she must lose the weight!"[37] Oprah is one of the wealthiest women in the world. She could have bought Rivers a thousand times over. Being fat, however, opened Oprah up to a classed critique from someone many times her economic junior. This example shows the significant conflation of fat and inferior black bodies. A billion dollars cannot buy you out of it.

Some feminists and black womanists have long understood that beauty is not just about being aesthetically pleasing; beauty is a means of granting a certain type of legitimacy with attending access to material resources through, for example, marrying well.[38] When Adkins draws on the lexicon of black beauty ideals with badonkadonk, he must do so without lifting up black women as beauty ideals. It is a tricky maneuver. To pull it off, he couches the entire endeavor in humor. The woman Adkins is singing about has it "going on like Donkey Kong" and works her "moneymaker" to the chagrin of all the women present. The "poor ole boys" can't help but stare. Adkins is telling us that if a white boy—a Southern country white boy—cannot help but stare, then the woman in question must be white no matter the blackness of the language used to describe her. No self-respecting good ole boy would be caught dead looking at a black booty, certainly not while in the presence of white women. Thus, Adkins qualifies "badonkadonk" with "honky tonk," a quintessential country music setting. It refers to the small social gathering spaces that dot many white rural communities. Honky tonks exist in contrast to the country clubs of the white elite. Honky tonks play country and western, and maybe for a pretty girl, as Montgomery Gentry tell us in "Hell Yeah," they might play a little Bruce Springsteen. But Colt Ford warns in "Hip-Hop in a Honky Tonk" that a proprietor would be smart to keep the hip-hop off the jukebox because "rednecks" don't come to a honky tonk to hear no hip-hop.

The etymology of "badonkadonk" is inseparable from a black female beauty ideal. All such cultural ideals are a way of defining sexualized interest and attention. What we make sexually desirable in our culture also risks affording its power to its possessors. Women with a badonkadonk in a hip-hop song yield a certain power over men, albeit always constrained by dangerous heteronormative, misogynistic authority to define acceptable female sexuality. Still, black feminism is clear that any power can feel like a tool for liberation when your identities exist at the axis of multiple oppressions. A country musician could no more allow a symbol of black female power into a country song through an earnest appreciation of a badonkadonk than could a honky tonk in Colt Ford's world play Snoop Dogg. There's cultural appropriation, and then there's *cultural appropriation*. To blunt the blackness of the slang, Adkins must divorce the badonkadonk from black women. He does this feat by situating it within the honky tonk, where it is clear in country music that no blackness should be allowed to transverse. The humor is a signal that Adkins will be back in another tune with an appropriate ode to a blue-eyed girl he is allowed to sexualize earnestly sans humor. Employing the honky tonk as qualifier does not just place this hip-hop euphemism into a country music imagination but also situates it within a proper discourse of acceptable cultural exchange and sexual norms. Black lexicon and rhythms are acceptable within narrowly defined constructs that signal to listeners that white norms, including beauty, are still privileged.

Songs like Jason Aldean's "Dirt Road Anthem" take a different approach from that of Adkins. But for the guitar riffs and the slowed-down delivery, this is a hip-hop song through and through. It is brash and male—also, it big-ups Aldean's hometown. It has liquor, partying, and women, and it's riding the beat not entirely unlike LL Cool J's 1980s hip-hop love song, "I Need Love." There is no melody. Aldean does a country spoken word performance for most of the track. As in classic hip-hop odes to place, such as Jay-Z's "Empire State," Aldean draws on imagery and narratives of the down-home country towns that he loves. But unlike Jay-Z's ode to New York City, Aldean's is not a love song to a specific town. It is an allusion to a material reality: there really isn't a "country" anymore.[39] Family farms have given way to industrial farm giants like Monsanto. Watering holes have been enclosed by zoning laws and planned communities. Spray-painting the water tower can constitute a violation of the Patriot Act. You need expensive automotive computers to fix pickup trucks. People may be rural in that they do not live in cities, but they are increasingly suburban, not country. As white poverty has increased, so has the spatial concentration of poverty been impacted by the decline of rural America. Suburban poverty has grown faster than anywhere else in the country over the last decade, at a rate of 64 percent since 2000. A 2013 report from the Brookings Institution says that "job losses triggered by the Great Recession in industries like construction, manufacturing, and retail hit hardest in suburban communities and contributed to rising suburban unemployment and poverty."[40] This reality might explain why one rarely hears a country artist sing an ode to an actual rural town anymore. Instead, they harken back to the town of their childhood, which today is as likely to have a strip mall and a couple McDonald's as it is a drag strip and a Main Street. Or like Aldean, they romanticize a fictionalized Anytown, USA.

In this town of Aldean's, the boys live to fight, learn to love their women, and get in trouble on Friday nights. These are all old country music tropes. Only here, Aldean waxes poetic using the linguistic styling of hip-hop.

There are the sixteen bars (OK, eighteen or so), a musical bridge, and even space for a little call-and-response should the song be played live. And it has been played live. In fact, Aldean says the song started out as a tune strictly played at his live shows. He had no intention of recording it. However, his band noticed the extreme positive response from the audience every time they played it. Through the magic of cell phone videos and social networking, the song had become a record on its own as fans ripped, remixed, and reworked it as a single sans distribution. It could be argued that Aldean tripped into a hip-hop cipher and played catch-up by releasing the song on his album.

Aldean's "Dirt Road Anthem" is unique for its earnest deployment of hip-hop elements. He is not using it as comical capital for "cool points," as does Adkins or the tragicomedy that was Cowboy Troy. "Dirt Road Anthem" is also notable for who wrote it: Colt Ford. The same artist who wrote for himself the redneck anti–hip-hop manifesto, "Hip-Hop in a Honky Tonk," also wrote Aldean's quintessential country hip-hop song. Born in 1970, Colt Ford is two years younger than LL Cool J and would have been nine years old when Sugar Hill Gang's "Rappers Delight" brought rap to the mainstream and a teenager when Run-D.M.C. saved Aerosmith's career with their remake of "Walk This Way" in 1986. Ford likely understands the tensions between hip-hop and country and represents so perfectly its dueling duality in the music he produces because he, like his audience, embodies it.

The white poor and working class do not have a consistent narrative of racial identity in popular culture or policy. The closest we come to that kind of narrative is the one that emerges from the sociological and economic literature on class and mobility: poor whites, especially men, are being left behind in the new economy. The narrative only become more salient as the nation ramped up for the 2016 presidential election. Many attribute Donald Trump's popularity to poor whites who have been left behind. Poor and working-class whites, again, especially white men, are described as angry and racist. The tribal explanation for their anger goes something like this: unable to compete for fewer good jobs which increasingly require higher education, poor whites lash out at blacks and immigrants. In Trump, they may see a willing translator of their anger. It is an auspicious moment to think about how we can reconcile the popularity of black youth culture—hip-hop—among poor, working-class, and un-educated whites. One way to think about this moment is to consider an awakening of a visible racialized white identity through mainstream cultural symbols.

In many ways, poor white people are correct when they talk of losing their country. However, they are not losing it to blacks or immigrants. Neither are they really "losing," as that implies poor rural whites once owned this nation's promise in the material sense. The cultural divide between the white elite and the redneck white poor has existed in some form for generations. However, the hope of escaping one's redneck past is becoming less likely, while even the comfort of an actual country to ease that sense of loss is being gobbled up by suburbanization, by the collapse of middle-class work, and by rising income inequality. Poor whites are not losing their country but their "country": the symbolic hope of the utility of their whiteness to improve their material lives by rendering them visible and autonomous—and they are losing it to the white plutocracy. Sadly, rich whites do not have a banging soundtrack. Black folks do. When people like uber rich, uber white Gwyneth Paltrow is on national television dropping hot N.W.A. bars from memory, it is easy to see how poor white people can conflate the encroachment of black culture into their symbolic spaces with the dominance of the white economic elite over their material spaces.[41] They live a million social miles from both.

The success of hick-hop is grounded in mutually constituted authenticity of two genres that both value their respective authority to define that authenticity. While they cannot control the boundaries of popular culture, country fans can still erect limited boundaries of acceptable cultural remixing. The contestation of boundaries of that cultural remixing signal an awareness among poor whites of the structural limitations of whiteness as necessary *and* sufficient for social mobility. Most black Americans have been socialized to develop an awareness of the external constraints of blackness, eloquently described in W. E. B. DuBois's theory of double consciousness. The historical privileging of whiteness as a master identity has left poor whites with few such tools to navigate what that means in our new economic reality. Branding poverty with a black urban face simultaneously makes black poverty ubiquitous while erasing black lives, but it erases poor whites almost entirely.

Historically, participation in popular culture promised a type of upward social mobility into higher-status whiteness. It created a shared culture in which poor whites could assemble such cultural tools as language and dress to transverse mobility bridges out of backwoods United States of America and into middle-class, white United States of America. That bridge now seems to lead only to blackness, and god knows no one should ever want to end up there. The youth culture is developing a shared language, but the language is being shared and, in many ways, controlled by blackness (if ultimately for the economic benefit of corporate media). That this trend might actually represent similar cultural bridges to mobility really only antagonizes the diminishing utility of one's whiteness or, at least, the perceived diminishing utility. Sociology suggests it is still pretty good to be white in America, but it is quite true that it is not uniformly good to be white in America.

It is understandable how the benefits of whiteness can be hard to see for poor whites on which country music depends. It certainly must not feel true in their daily lives as they experience joblessness, poor health outcomes, shrinking social safety nets, and the near erasure of the poor and working class from television, movies, and pop culture, save but a trailer park minstrelsy or two. It could be that the shifting economic realities of poor whites is exposing an emerging group identity crisis. Living with that at your nine-to-five, or in your search for a nine-to-five, may be one issue. Dealing with this problem in the spaces where you should be able to exert some control—your personal spaces, your homes, over your children, in your honky tonks, and at your tailgate parties—could present a particular kind of crisis. White invisibility in national discussions of poverty may be a kind of privilege (one black Americans surely do not enjoy), but it is not without its perils. The erasure of the structural demise of social mobility for poor whites leaves them with few uncontested spaces, symbolic or material, to work through that group identity crisis. That it is hip-hop that provides them tools, albeit in limited and constrained ways, to explore that crisis is a function of hip-hop's domination of popular youth culture, spatial segregation of the haves from the rural have-nots, and shifting corporate logics. This structural change is reflected, as such things usually are, in the beautiful ugly culture people make as they try to construct their ideal selves under less than ideal conditions.

## NOTES

1. Geoff Mann, "Why Does Country Music Sound White? Race and the Voice of Nostalgia," *Ethnic and Racial Studies* 31, no. 1 (2008): 73–100.

2. Richard A. Peterson, *Creating Country Music: Fabricating Authenticity* (Chicago: University of Chicago Press, 2013).

3. Stuart Hall, "Encoding/decoding," *Media and Cultural Studies: Keyworks* (2001): 166–76.

4. Richard A. Peterson and Paul Di Maggio, "From Region to Class, the Changing Locus of Country Music: A Test of the Massification Hypothesis," *Social Forces* 53, no. 3 (1975): 497–506.

5. George H. Lewis, "Taste Cultures and Culture Classes in Mass Society: Shifting Patterns in American Popular Music," *International Review of the Aesthetics and Sociology of Music* (1977): 39–48.

6. Jeff Chang, *Can't Stop Won't Stop: A History of the Hip-Hop Generation* (London: Macmillan, 2007).

7. Hannah Karp, "The Unlikely Rise of Hick-Hop," *Wall Street Journal,* July 3, 2013.

8. Eric Church. "Homeboy," *Chief,* EMI Nashville, 2011, Track 6.

9. James N. Baron and Arne L. Kalleberg, "Good Jobs, Bad Jobs: The Rise of Polarized and Precarious Employment Systems in the United States, 1970s to 2000s," *Administrative Science Quarterly* 58, no. 1 (2013): 149–51; Sasha Abramsky, "The Other America," *Nation,* April 25, 2012, 11–12.

10. Elizabeth Kneebone and Alan Berube, *Confronting Suburban Poverty in America* (Washington: Brookings Institution Press, 2013).

11. Daniel T. Lichter, "Immigration and the New Racial Diversity in Rural America," *Rural Sociology* 77, no. 1 (2012): 3–35.

12. William G. Roy "'Race Records' and 'Hillbilly Music': Institutional Origins of Racial Categories in the American Commercial Recording Industry," *Poetics* 32, no. 3 (2004): 265–79.

13. Karl Hagstrom Miller, *Segregating Sound: Inventing Folk and Pop Music in the Age of Jim Crow* (Durham: Duke University Press, 2010), and Jane Elizabeth Dailey, Glenda Elizabeth Gilmore, and Bryant Simon, eds., *Jumpin Jim Crow: Southern Politics from the Civil War to Civil Rights* (Princeton: Princeton University Press, 2000).

14. This in no way minimizes the extreme, violent oppression of black Americans under Jim Crow. See Daily, Gilmore, and Simon, *Jumpin Jim Crow,* for a discussion of how the careful, brutal maintenance of Jim Crow laws reflects the challenges of their daily enforcement over time.

15. Chauncey DeVega, "The New White Poor Are Not Honey Boo Boo, They Sleep in Their Cars and Shop at Trader Joe's," *Alternet,* July 31, 2013, http://www.alternet.org /speakeasy/chaunceydevega/new-white-poor-are-not -honey-boo-boo-they-sleep-the ir-cars-and-shop-trader.

16. Carmen DeNavas-Walt and Bernadette D. Proctor, U.S. Census Bureau, Current

Population Reports, P60–252, Income and Poverty in the United States: 2014, U.S. Government Printing Office, Washington, 2015.

17. Ryan Cooper, "Galloping Economic Insecurity," *Washington Monthly,* July 28, 2013.

18. Daniel A. Sandoval, Mark R. Rank, and Thomas A. Hirschl, "The Increasing Risk of Poverty across the American Life Course," *Demography* 46, no. 4 (2009): 717–37; Ted Mouw and Arne L. Kalleberg, "Occupations and the Structure of Wage Inequality in the United States, 1980s to 2000s," *American Sociological Review* 75, no. 3 (2010): 402–31.

19. Chris Kromm, "Unions, the South and Justice at Smithfield," *Facing South,* June 6, 2006, https://www.facingsouth.org/2006/06/unions-the-south-and-justice-at-smithfield .html.

20. Trevor Tompson and Jennifer Benz, "The Public Mood: White Malaise but Optimism among Blacks, Hispanics," *The Associated Press-NORC Center for Public Affairs Research,* July 2013, http://www.apnorc.org/PDFs/Public%20Mood/AP-NORC _PublicMoodWhiteMalaiseButOptimismAmongBlacksandHispanics.pdf.

21. "The American Middle Class Is Losing Ground," *Pew Research Center,* December 9, 2015.

22. Eric Deggans, *On "Hicksploitation" and Other White Stereotypes Seen on TV,* podcast audio, NPR: Code Switch, MP3, 3:57, May 1, 2013, https://www.npr.org/sections/codeswitch/2013/05/10/178791792/on-hicksploitation-and-other-white-stereotypes-seen-on-tv.

23. Maureen Blyler, "Charting Race: The Success of Black Performers in the Mainstream Recording Market, 1940 to 1990," *Poetics* 30, no. 1 (2002): 87–110.

24. John S. Otto and Augustus M. Burns, "Black and White Cultural Interaction in the Early Twentieth Century South: Race and Hillbilly Music," *Phylon (1960–)* 35, no. 4 (1974): 407–17.

25. Michael T. Bertrand, *Race, Rock, and Elvis* (Champaign: University of Illinois Press, 2000).

26. Keith Negus, "The Music Business and Rap: Between the Street and the Executive Suite," *Cultural Studies* 13, no. 3 (1999): 488–508.

27. Richard A. Peterson, *Creating Country Music: Fabricating Authenticity* (Chicago: University of Chicago Press, 1997).

28. Kembrew McLeod, "Authenticity within Hip-Hop and Other Cultures Threatened with Assimilation," *Journal of Communication* 49, no. 4 (1999): 134–50.

29. Florida Georgia Line's very name is a practice in the same kind of explicit legitimacy claims to the U.S. South, country music's symbolic capital.

30. Gabriel Rossman, "Elites, Masses, and Media Blacklists: The Dixie Chicks Controversy," *Social Forces* 83, no. 1 (2004): 61–79.

31. Margaret L. Hunter, "'If You're Light You're Alright': Light Skin Color as Social Capital for Women of Color," *Gender & Society* 16, no. 2 (2002): 175–93.

32. Ladel Lewis, "White Thugs and Black Bodies: A Comparison of the Portrayal of African-American Women in Hip-Hop Videos," *Hilltop Review* 4, no. 1 (2011): 3.

33. Carol E. Henderson, "It's All in the Name: Hip Hop, Sexuality, and Black Women's Identity in *Breakin' In*: The Making of a Hip Hop Dancer," *Palimpsest: A Journal on Women, Gender, and the Black International* 2, no. 1 (2013): 47–58; Mireille Miller-Young, "Putting Hypersexuality to Work: Black Women and Illicit Eroticism in Pornography," *Sexualities* 13, no. 2 (2010): 219–35.

34. May Friedman, "Fat Is a Social Work Issue: Fat Bodies, Moral Regulation, and the History of Social Work," *Intersectionalities: A Global Journal of Social Work Analysis, Research, Polity, and Practice* 1 (2012): 53–69.

35. Abigail Saguy, "Why Fat Is a Feminist Issue," *Sex Roles* 66, nos. 9–10 (2012): 600–607.

36. Dominique Hines, "Anna Wintour Ordered Oprah Winfrey to Lose 20lb before Appearing on Vogue Cover," *Daily Mail*, May 19, 2009, http://www.dailymail.co.uk /tvshowbiz/article-1184436/Anna-Wintour-ordered-Oprah_Winfrey-lose-20lb-appearing -Vogue-cover.html.

37. joycollector, "Joan Rivers Tells Oprah Winfrey to Lose Weight," filmed January 1985, YouTube video, 02:05, May 26, 2011, http://www.youtube.com/watch?v=TAtj DjZa2eA.

38. Patricia Hill Collins, *Black Sexual Politics: African Americans, Gender, and the New Racism* (New York: Routledge, 2004); and Linda Martín Alcoff, *Visible Identities: Race, Gender, and the Self* (New York: Oxford University Press, 2006); Joane Nagel, *Race, Ethnicity, and Sexuality: Intimate Intersections, Forbidden Frontiers* (New York: Oxford University Press, 2003).

39. Jacqueline Edmondson, *Prairie Town: Redefining Rural Life in the Age of Globali zation* (Lanham: Rowman & Littlefield, 2003).

40. Elizabeth Kneebone and Alan Berube, *Confronting Suburban Poverty in America* (Washington: Brookings Institution Press, 2013).

41. Paltrow has demonstrated an affinity for both mainstream and unedited hip-hop lyrics in media interviews. In her acting life, Paltrow most frequently plays the iconic symbol of white femininity—pale, thin, blonde, and wealthy. In her nonacting career she is making a business of packaging that white femininity into a lifestyle brand. Her GOOP website, books, and tours feature white elite taste markers for public consumption. Seeing someone like Paltrow spit hot bars by groups like Niggas with Attitude (N.W.A.) juxtaposes her wealthy, white, female, elite, high cultural taste against what was once a black, poor, male low cultural product. Here, I am considering what that looks like not as a black cultural consumer but as a white working-class or poor consumer.

CHAPTER ELEVEN

# Alternative Country Music and the American Midwest as Industrial Wasteland

## TRAVIS D. STIMELING

ALTHOUGH COUNTRY music often invokes images of pastoral landscapes, idyllic family farms, and small-town life, the genre has been intimately linked to the industrial economies of the United States and Canada from its emergence as a popular commercial music in the 1920s. As several historians have demonstrated in their work on early country music, many of the genre's earliest stars were caught up in a large-scale migration from rural communities to newly formed industrial centers throughout the Piedmont South, and their music might very well be heard to reflect the thoroughly modern lives of these new industrial workers in both their embrace and critique of industrialization.[1] This trend continued throughout the twentieth century as thriving country music communities formed in such unlikely places as the steel mill towns around Wheeling, West Virginia; the automotive plants of Detroit, Michigan; World War II–era Los Angeles defense plants; and the factory towns of New England.[2] Many of the genre's most iconic songs—including the oft-recorded "Wreck of the Old 97" and "John Henry"; Bobby Bare's 1963 paean to migrant autoworkers, "Detroit City"; and country-pop group Alabama's 1985 working-class anthem "Forty-Hour Week (For a Livin')"—reflect the indelible impact of industrialized landscapes and industrial occupations on what journalist Nicholas Dawidoff has called "the country of country" and the people who compose, distribute, and consume country music.[3]

Country music's deep connections to the twentieth-century industrialization of the United States have been challenged since at least the 1980s when the trade policies of the Ronald Reagan administration, followed shortly thereafter by the North American Free Trade Agreement (NAFTA), radically transformed the nation's economic base and accelerated the deindustrialization of urban manufacturing centers throughout the country. In my consideration of deindustrialization, I adopt Barry Bluestone and Bennett Harrison's oft-cited definition: "a widespread, systematic disinvestment in the nation's basic productive capacity."[4] Ethnomusicologist Aaron Fox, for instance, has argued forcefully that the country music communities that he studied in central Texas and central Illinois resisted the nation's deindustrialization and the subsequent marginalization of the white working class in those regions.[5] Similarly, more recent studies of country music communities living in proximity to Appalachia's late-industrial mountaintop removal coal mines document the ways that Appalachian musicians have addressed the economic and cultural challenges emerging from radical mining techniques that require smaller workforces and incur dramatic environmental damage.[6] These studies notwithstanding, very little scholarship has examined the ways that country musicians and their audiences have addressed the deindustrialization of their communities and the broader issues surrounding late capitalism in the United States. Yet there is a growing literature on the effects of deindustrialization on rural and semirural communities throughout the country that demonstrates convincingly that residents suffer from chronic public health issues, a "brain drain" caused when talented people leave the community in search of employment elsewhere, poverty and unemployment, and lingering environmental issues.[7] Through their connections to—and denials of—deindustrialized rural and semirural communities, country music cultures can provide remarkable insights into the ways that the "hard-hit people" who inhabit such communities make sense of the economic, cultural, and environmental devastation of industrial capitalism.[8]

Although much writing on country music during the 1990s tends to focus on the songs that received widespread radio and television airplay (which largely avoided overt political discourse), the so-called alternative country movement that began to thrive during the early 1990s commented frequently on working-class issues and, as a consequence, provides a valuable entry point into understanding the effects of deindustrialization in small towns and rural areas of the United States. Alternative country music drew heavily on the roots of country music as well as the do-it-yourself ethos and sharp edges of the 1980s punk movement and, like punk, developed primarily in local music scenes scattered throughout the United States.[9] One important locus for this activity was the Interstate 55 corridor that stretches between Chicago and St. Louis, a hotbed of activity that gave birth to some of the alternative country movement's most influential early labels and bands.[10] Although the region is culturally and economically diverse, the I-55 corridor—as well as dozens of communities throughout Indiana, Illinois, and Missouri—bore much of the brunt of the late twentieth-century deindustrialization of the United States, often leaving idled factories, empty homes, and blighted infrastructure in its wake. Embraced by young people who encountered dismal employment opportunities and who witnessed the struggles that their families, friends, and neighbors faced in the wake of factory closures and industrial divestment, alternative country music proved to be a viable vehicle for some people to express their anxieties about the slow withering away of their communities. Geographer Tim Edensor observed that deindustrialized landscapes are often seen as "spaces of and for nothing," where "a range of deviant acts take place" and "people commonly identified as undesirable" live. He suggests that many people ignore the rich histories embedded in abandoned factories and warehouses, instead interpreting deindustrialized spaces as "wasteland[s that are] . . . devoid of positive social, material, [or] aesthetic qualities."[11] Describing alternative country music as "a music of forgotten places," geographer Robert Austin Russell has argued that the music organically created "a soundtrack to life in these places" that carved out "different spaces for . . . [the] experiences [of these people] to be told."[12] In his nuanced exegesis of Jay Farrar's songwriting with Uncle Tupelo and Son Volt, Russell reveals how dominant narratives of postindustrial fear have been challenged by musicians who embrace local industrial and cultural histories, leverage those histories to offer incisive critiques of corporations and policymakers, and construct places where others see threateningly empty deindustrialized spaces.[13]

Russell's observations can be extended by considering the musical contexts in which the rich, place-based lyrics of Uncle Tupelo cofounders, Jeff Tweedy and Jay Farrar, as sonic embodiments of the simultaneously empty and ghost-filled spaces of the postindustrial Midwest.[14] This musicalized aesthetic of deindustrialization is grounded in Farrar's and Tweedy's firsthand experiences of life in Belleville, Illinois, a middle Mississippi River Valley town that has witnessed the economic promise and environmental hardships of industrialization and the resulting ruins of deindustrialization. This essay is not the first to situate the musical creations of Tweedy and Farrar within the broader context of late capitalist alienation, nor is it the first to explore the ways in which Tweedy and Farrar have engaged with the local industrial and postindustrial histories of the St. Louis Metropolitan Area and the rural and semirural locations in its immediate vicinity, histories that prominently feature both country music culture and intraregional migration.[15] Instead, I seek to move beyond the general discussions of musical style found in the current literature on Tweedy and Farrar's music and toward a more musically grounded understanding of the ways that individual compositional, arranging, and production choices function discursively to express these place-based concerns.[16] Furthermore, this essay extends critical analysis of their music by suggesting that these issues not only formed the backdrop for the work of Tweedy and Farrar (as a group and individually) in the 1990s but also continue to shape their output to the present day.

Before discussing Tweedy's and Farrar's musical outputs, it will be necessary to offer a brief survey of Belleville's industrial and postindustrial history because, as the fans contributing to "the unofficial Uncle Tupelo archives" at factorybelt.net have demonstrated, their work is imbued with a profound sense of place, often through references to specific towns and communities in the region as well as local and regional history.[17] First settled in 1802 and established as the county seat of St. Clair County in 1814, Belleville, Illinois, has been at the forefront of American industrialization, serving first as a major center for flour milling, brewing, and coal mining in the nineteenth century and, by the first decades of the twentieth century, a center of manufacturing and heavy industry.[18] As a consequence of these activities, Belleville and surrounding St. Clair and Madison Counties had become, by the time of Farrar's and Tweedy's births in the late 1960s, an industrial dumping ground that bore the burdens of nearly three-quarters of a century of poor environmental decisions.[19] Belleville and other towns in the Metro East began to feel the effects of Rust Belt deindustrialization as early as the end of World War II, leaving thousands of unemployed blue-collar workers in its wake.[20] Efforts to revitalize the city of St. Louis as a center for tourism and high-tech industry during the postwar years further marginalized the region's working-class residents, whom urban historians Joseph Heathcott and Málre Agnes Murphy have described as "the collateral damage of the [city's] renewal war."[21] Furthermore, nearby East St. Louis, Illinois, became a national symbol of the deindustrialization crisis in the 1970s and 1980s as unemployment rates skyrocketed, residents left in search of better opportunities, and property values declined precipitously.[22] Such dramatic changes to the St. Louis area's economic and physical landscapes certainly led many residents to the dramatic conclusion that, as Steven High and David Lewis have suggested of the greater Midwest of the 1970s, "the higher standard of material wealth [generated by the rise of the middle-class during the postwar period] did not change the fact that industrial workers remained vulnerable to economic change."[23] Or as Jay Farrar recounted, Belleville simply "wasn't a happy place to be in the '80s."[24]

But Belleville and the St. Louis Metropolitan Area were not suffering in isolation. Rather, many midwestern cities witnessed significant declines in manufacturing jobs in the 1970s and early 1980s.[25] Scholars have documented the transition of numerous midwestern cities from thriving industrial centers that were dependent on a large force of (often unionized) labor to postindustrial places with boarded-up factories and chronically unemployed populations, including Flint, Michigan; Bloomington, Indiana; Decatur, Illinois; and Youngstown, Ohio.[26] Workplace communities that had been built around factories were fractured with each plant closing, which led to greater feelings of desperation and, as one criminological study suggests, a marked increase in homicide.[27] As a consequence of these transformations, High and Lewis note, "the Industrial Midwest of the United States . . . [was] re-envisioned as a no man's land between fading smokestack industries and the ascendant post-industrial economy."[28] Yet as Jefferson Cowie and Joseph Heathcott have so poignantly observed, these seemingly placeless towns continued to be home to hundreds of thousands of midwestern workers who demanded "respect for the despair and betrayal [they] felt . . . as their mines, factories, and mills were padlocked, abandoned, turned into artsy shopping spaces, or even dynamited."[29]

At the same time that towns and cities in the Midwest were losing their manufacturing bases, surrounding rural communities were also suffering from the family farm crisis of the 1980s, which also demanded that fewer laborers produce higher yields and, consequently, larger profits.[30] A 1986 essay in the *Nation* documented the impact of increasing pressure on family farmers during the height of midwestern deindustrialization: "The drop in farm income translates almost immediately into a drop in retail sales for local businesses. Predictably, businesses that sell mostly to farms are having the worst time, but all are hurting. Retail sales in Iowa's rural communities have slipped an average of 25 percent in the past decade. The decline in sales caused by reduced farm income has, in turn, set off a record number of business failures throughout the state . . . The closures sweep through a small town like a combine through a cornfield. As the local tax base erodes, schools are forced to consolidate, which destroys more jobs. This can be the deathblow for many small towns where the school is a major employer."[31] When coupled with land speculation that drove the prices of farmland to a bursting bubble, rural midwestern communities were fundamentally changed and, in the more than two decades since, have not yet recovered from the mass outmigration of rural people, as journalist Sarah Halasz Graham has demonstrated.[32]

By focusing attention on the ways that Farrar and Tweedy have musicalized the histories and landscapes of the deindustrializing American Midwest, it is possible to gain a deeper understanding of how their music grapples with the issues facing the residents of former manufacturing centers. A survey of the recorded output of Uncle Tupelo, as well as post-Tupelo bands Son Volt and Wilco, reveals two central stylistic tendencies that work to create a deindustrialized midwestern musical aesthetic: first, to represent the disjunctures of interior and exterior self, of rural and urban, and of rooted and rootless using stark juxtapositions of country and rock textures and timbres and, second, to represent the unvarnished, plainspoken, and realistic voices of white working-class midwesterners by avoiding reverberant vocal and instrumental sounds.[33] Although these

musical strategies may be heard in a wide range of alternative country recordings from the 1990s until the early 2000s, Farrar's and Tweedy's use of
these techniques amplifies, underscores, and complicates the first-person
narratives of the working-class white midwesterners who speak in their
songs and effectively depict the economic, environmental, and cultural
bleakness of the postindustrial Midwest.

Alternative country music's merger of country, punk, and rock textures
has been celebrated widely in the scholarly and popular literature on the
alternative country movement. Drawing upon punk's "do-it-yourself"
ethos and confrontational attitudes, alternative country music was a marginal music that thrived in the early days of Internet message boards and
that was distributed primarily by word of mouth and on a relatively small
scale.[34] By contrast, country music in the 1990s embraced the pyrotechnic
arena concerts of Garth Brooks and the pop dance moves of Shania Twain
and tightly managed radio playlists, much as commercial sprawl and big-
box retail stores homogenized the physical and economic landscapes of
the very towns that embraced mainstream country.[35] The juxtaposition
of country and punk/post-punk textures and timbres, like the "buy local"
campaigns that sprouted up in the wake of the big-box boom, placed alternative country music in stark contrast to hot country and offered hope
that country music had not been co-opted by corporate carpetbaggers.[36]
Cultural critic S. Renee Dechert has observed, for instance, that "alt.coun-
try's dialogue with traditional country and punk rock works in two ways
jointly, on a philosophical level and on a practical level. Philosophically,
alt.country adopted the punk DIY . . . attitude, a closer relative of traditional country's populism. In addition, the loud, aggressive sound of punk
revitalized and recontextualized traditional country themes."[37] Diane
Pecknold, too, has traced the Nashville country music industry's marginalization of alternative country artists, many of whom have tried to engage with the national music industry. Pecknold observes that alternative
country artists often performed poorly on "major labels or their subsidiar-
ies" in the 1980s "and were dropped after generating weak sales."[38] Like
the working-class people who were left behind as the nation's once strong
manufacturing base sought cheaper labor and higher profits, alternative
country musicians might be seen as a community that was left behind
by an increasingly global popular music industry that had little room for

boutique artists.[39] As such, one might very well hear significant portions of the alternative country movement as a politically and socially progressive response to increasing commercial control over country music and to the corporatization of U.S. culture more generally.

On the level of musical detail, however, this juxtaposition of country and punk styles functioned not only as a way to signify the marginal status of Uncle Tupelo, Son Volt, and Wilco but also as an important tool in their efforts to depict the complexities of life in a postindustrial town. Punk and country sounds are heard in dialogue within one another in a number of Uncle Tupelo's compositions dealing directly with the deindustrializing Midwest. The speaker in the band's 1992 single "Sauget Wind," for instance, discusses how the pollution emitted from the smokestacks of the Monsanto chemical plants in nearby Sauget, Illinois, have negatively affected his health.[40] During the song's two verses, Farrar strums a clean-sounding electric guitar using a combination of open-position chords and minor barre chords in a slow 6/8 time. Accompanied by light drums and a Hammond organ, the guitar texture creates a sparse, folk-inspired backdrop against which Farrar's non-reverberant baritone vocals can channel the speaker's matter-of-fact statements about the poor air quality and his declining health and that evokes the spare textures of such politically inspired folksingers as Woody Guthrie.[41] Yet the speaker's calm turns out to be little more than a façade that masks intense emotions when, at the conclusion of the first verse, the full band enters, expanding the frequency spectrum bi-directionally, dramatically increasing the recording's amplitude, and adding a jarring amount of noise to the mix through the sudden transformation of Farrar's guitar tone.[42] This interlude might be heard, therefore, to reveal the raw anger of the Belleville residents living almost directly downwind from Sauget's Monsanto emissions, who suffer the environmental and public health consequences of industrialization and are so bombarded with corporate misinformation that even "the weatherman . . . looks like a lie." After this emotional façade has cracked, the second verse's return to the textures, timbres, and volume of the first verse sounds like a dissociative coping mechanism.[43]

"Whiskey Bottle," from Uncle Tupelo's debut album *No Depression* (1990), offers further insights into the ways that this contrast of country and punk sounds works to highlight the psychological turmoil of the deindustrialized Midwest. The recording begins with a lengthy, thirty-seven-second introduction featuring a strummed acoustic guitar playing open chords and a distant, reverberant pedal steel guitar that invokes the sounds of Neil Young's melancholic 1972 album *Harvest*. As the title might suggest, "Whiskey Bottle" falls squarely in the vein of country drinking songs, as the first-person speaker in the song finds himself in an unfamiliar "three-hour-away town" in search of economic opportunity. Yet like the protagonists of Bobby Bare's "Detroit City," Merle Haggard's "The Sidewalks of Chicago," or Gram Parsons's "Hickory Wind," this speaker finds himself surrounded by "dirt and disgust" and desperately in search of "some air to breathe and something to believe." This sparse accompaniment continues until the beginning of the chorus, which finds the speaker in the depths of his despair and "a long way from happiness" and joined by heavily distorted electric guitars, electric bass guitar, and a full drum kit. In this chorus, the speaker rages in the moment, choosing to find salvation in drink instead of religion "just for now." Yet upon repeating the line "not forever, just for now" at the end of the chorus, the heavy rock backing drops out suddenly to reveal that the country-rock textures never left.[44] The jarring give-and-take between hollow country sounds and dense rock sounds might be heard to evoke a stoic white working-class masculinity that encourages men to find solace sitting alone in a dimly lit barroom fighting the demons that arise when they cannot find suitable employment and provide economic security for their families. The exterior self here is calm, if melancholy (and Farrar's flatly unemotional vocals reinforce that sense of calm), but the interior self is screaming in pain and frustration.

The straightforward, uncomplaining, yet plaintive discourse of the speakers in Farrar's songs is amplified in the recording and mixing techniques deployed in Uncle Tupelo's and Son Volt's recordings, as well as Farrar's solo recordings.[45] With notable exceptions, Farrar's vocal tracks are treated with minimal postproduction reverberation and are mixed toward the front of the proximal plane.[46] As a consequence, the speakers heard in these songs are not presented as romanticized or idealized figures whose voices come to us through a softening distance. Instead, these voices are intensely present and demand to be heard, much as the close-up portraiture of many Farm Security Administration photographers revealed the immediacy of the farmer's plight during the Great Depression of the 1930s.[47] The residents of Farrar's deindustrializing and postindustrial landscapes demand to be heard, but they do not shout. Rather, they speak purposefully and deliberately, and the choices that Farrar, Tweedy, and their collaborators made while producing and mixing their recordings simply highlight the intensity of the words.

Such stark depictions of the voices of neglected white working-class men can be found throughout Uncle Tupelo's, Son Volt's, and Jay Farrar's albums. In "No More Parades," which appeared on Son Volt's 1997 album *Straightaways,* the speaker meditates on the effects of global agribusiness to the rural communities of southern Illinois and southeastern Missouri. In this unnamed community, there are "no more parades" because the population that used to work the farms has instead "caught the bus" to the larger towns and cities where "think tank[s]" devise "schemes" that increase crop yields and profits while reducing labor inputs. Living in a place where the promise of the American Dream has "flicker[ed] out," the protagonist lives in an exploited industrial farmland where a "pesticide moon hangs" over a seemingly dystopian agrarian landscape. Set to a lilting acoustic accompaniment, Farrar's vocals in "No More Parades" are again located at the center of the stereo field and placed far forward in the mix. Little reverberation is added to his voice, and the equalization used on his baritone voice works to minimize its natural resonance. The speaker, as expressed through Farrar's voice, sounds unsentimental and unromantic in his outlook, despite the "tears flowing out of . . . [his] brain."

This practice can also be heard in Farrar's 2003 song "Cahokian," which uses the conceit of two large mounds located on either side of Interstate 55 in St. Louis's Metro East as a metaphor for the impending end of contemporary civilization.[48] The first of these mounds, the remnants of what many archaeologists believe to be the largest pre-Columbian city in North America, is located in Cahokia Mounds State Historic Site,[49] while the second is known locally as "Mount Trashmore," an immense landfill that has been growing almost directly across the highway from Cahokia Mounds for four decades.[50] Although the reasons for the Cahokians' disappearance has been widely debated in the scholarly literature, Farrar notes that "the new Mississippians" around St. Louis are bringing about their own certain demise by "building . . . mounds out of control, / Full of our finest throwaway things." Even as the consequences of rampant consumerism are about to bear down on the residents of the St. Louis Metropolitan Area, Farrar's voice betrays little concern. Rather, his vocal track—which is couched in the lush sounds of a small string ensemble and a rich-sounding acoustic guitar using a drop-D tuning (tuning the lowest string of the guitar down a whole step)—is calm, unemotional, and treated with only a slight touch of reverb. Placed far forward in the proximal plane of the mix, these acoustically dead vocals sonically replicate the powerlessness of the speaker in "Sauget Wind." Like the character in that song, the speaker in "Cahokian" has been stripped of his ability to effect change in his community as a consumption-based economy has replaced a production-based one, corporations have moved from devastated midwestern communities in search of more exploitable labor forces, and local residents are left with the residual waste and social problems of deindustrialization. Rather than complaining, though, these speakers—amplified by the mixes of the recordings in which they speak—can do little but bear calm witness to the seemingly inevitable entropy of their once-thriving communities.

Not everyone who lives within the songs of Uncle Tupelo, Son Volt, and Wilco has made peace with the postindustrial world. As the speaker in the 2009 Son Volt release "When the Wheels Don't Move" notes, the relocation of industry has left a community bereft of culture bearers who can guide the younger generation and pass along knowledge of the community's industrial heritage.[51] Embodying a stereotypical midwestern pragmatism, the speaker is equally critical of environmental rhetoric and agribusiness, preferring instead to embrace "God and nation" as the fuel that makes the United States run. The speaker's frustration is musicalized in the undulating harmonies that Farrar built around his voice: only two chords—D and A minor—rock ceaselessly back and forth on a distorted electric guitar as drummer Dave Bryson's groove becomes increasingly complex and the band gradually becomes louder. By the end of the song, neither the protagonist nor the music have gone anywhere, and the speaker is just as disempowered as before, even if his catharsis provided temporary respite from his anxiety. Farrar's vocals are again treated flatly and, when combined with the rather limited melodic range, might be heard not as a voice of someone who is resigned to taking jobs stocking the shelves at a big-box retail outlet but as a worker with a steely eyed resolve to fight his way back into the middle class by the work of his hands.

Still, other St. Louis–area workers who speak through the work of Uncle Tupelo, Son Volt, and Wilco have clearly decided to embrace the decline of midwestern industry and to celebrate in a sort of fin de siècle bacchanal. "Casino Queen," the second track on Wilco's 1995 debut album *A.M.*, finds the song's speaker spending a debauched night of gambling, drinking, and carousing with women at an East St. Louis riverboat casino of the same name.[52] Framed by what *Chicago Tribune* critic, NPR host, and Wilco biographer Greg Kot has described as a "finger-wagging, rooster-strutting riff," the song might be heard as a hypermasculine, Rolling Stones–style romp that does little more than celebrate familiar tropes of rock-and-roll excess.[53] Jeff Tweedy's raspy vocals, again located in the front and center of the mix and treated with minimal reverberation, reveal a speaker who is not simply celebrating but is rather out of control and in the midst of an alcohol- and gambling-fused bender. As is frequently the case in hypermasculine displays, "Casino Queen" might be also be heard to reveal a deeper crisis of masculinity emerging around the deindustrialization of the American Midwest during the 1970s and 1980s and the region's struggles to reinvent itself in the postindustrial economy of the 1990s.[54] Riverboat casinos have played a key, but often controversial, role in this transformation as cities such as St. Louis (which boasts five riverboat casinos in the St. Louis Metropolitan Area) and Chicago have hoped to attract tourism dollars that will offset the loss of heavy industry and manufacturing jobs.[55] Riverboat casinos are also a last resort for the speaker in Son Volt's "Methamphetamine" (2007), who observes that his only opportunities for financial stability come from "either watching these gauges for Monsanto / Or a bar-back job for the casino."[56] Heard through the lens of midwestern deindustrialization, "Casino Queen" is less about friends having a good time at a local casino than it is about risking one's "last token" on a last-ditch effort to transform one's economic lot, to assert one's masculinity in the face of an economic situation that does not permit men to construct their masculinity through work and deal with what historian Steven High and photographer David W. Lewis have characterized as deindustrialization's "displacement of industry and industrial workers to the cultural periphery."[57]

Jay Farrar, Jeff Tweedy, and their collaborators have deployed several important musical techniques to depict the concerns of people left behind by the deindustrialization of the American Midwest in general and the St. Louis Metropolitan Area in particular. As part of the larger St. Louis Metropolitan Area (and the Metro East, more specifically), the communities that are described in the work of Uncle Tupelo, Son Volt, and Wilco have become the hollow, polluted sacrifice zones of late capitalism. The work of these Belleville, Illinois, musicians, in its un-self-conscious embrace of punk and country styles and deliberate use of key production and recording techniques, skillfully embodies the tensions and anxieties felt by so many men and women who see no viable future for their communities and lack the financial means, the political clout, or the personal confidence to leave in search of opportunity elsewhere. In many ways, these sometimes-uncomfortable sounds echo the embrace of hip-hop by poor white youth in the same communities, as Tressie Cottom's essay in this volume details. Consequently, their music calls for a dramatic reinterpretation of these deindustrialized spaces, a reinterpretation that seeks to recapture their rich histories and to fill them with the voices of the people who called those factories, warehouses, and modest abodes home during the twentieth century.

Unlike the nuanced (or at least contrarian) characters found in much alternative country music, the characters in mainstream country are commonly flat and static, seldom commenting on the nature of their working conditions and always grateful for the opportunity to contribute to the economy. As ethnomusicologist Jeff Todd Titon remarked in "Music and the U.S. War on Poverty," "instead of eliminating a culture of poverty, modern technology . . . is impoverishing the culture."[58] Although he speaks of mountaintop removal coal mining in Appalachia, the same could be said of contemporary country radio, which reinforces the idea that "good Americans" work hard and retire peacefully to a life filled with grandchildren, all while a sizable population is not afforded the opportunity to work hard and, if they are lucky enough to retire, have limited access to grandchildren who live hundreds of miles away as a consequence of generations of brain drain. Alternative country music, therefore, presents opportunities for compassionate engagement with marginalized working people through a powerful affective medium. Yet for all of their efforts to change the discourses around working people and the spaces they inhabit, alternative country musicians appear to have had little appreciable

effect on mainstream discourses around the effects of midwestern deindustrialization and the systems that allowed for the rapid and systematic
deindustrialization in the first place. In a media landscape that privileges
mainstream country music, the voices of alternative country musicians
are marginal, much like the working people about which many alternative
country songs speak.

A previous version of this essay was presented at the 2013 meeting of the American
Musicological Society. The author would like to thank Matt Meacham for reading an
earlier draft and providing insights into the nuances that distinguish the communities of
this region from one another.

## NOTES

1. William F. Danaher and Vincent J. Roscigno, "Cultural Production, Media, and
Meaning: Hillbilly Music and the Southern Textile Mills," *Poetics* 32 (2004): 51–71;
Patrick Huber, *Linthead Stomp: The Creation of Country Music in the Piedmont South*
(Chapel Hill: University of North Carolina Press, 2008).

2. Consult, for example, Ivan M. Tribe, *Mountaineer Jamboree: Country Music in
West Virginia* (Lexington: University Press of Kentucky, 1984), 43–72; Craig Maki with
Keith Cady, *Detroit Country Music: Mountaineers, Cowboys, and Rockabillies*(Ann Arbor:
University of Michigan Press, 2013); Ivan M. Tribe and Jacob L. Bapst, *West Virginia's
Traditional Country Music* (Charleston: Arcadia Publishing, 2015), 25–46; Peter La
Chapelle, *Proud to Be an Okie: Cultural Politics, Country Music, and Migration to Southern
California* (Berkeley: University of California Press, 2007), 76–110; and Clifford R.
Murphy, *Yankee Twang: Country and Western Music in New England* (Urbana: University
of Illinois Press, 2014).

3. Nicholas Dawidoff, *In the Country of Country: People and Places in American Music*
(New York: Pantheon, 1997). For more on the relationship between country music
and industrial labor, consult Norm Cohen, *Long Steel Rail: The Railroad in American
Folksong* (Urbana: University of Illinois Press, 1981), and Archie Green, *Only a Miner:
Studies in Recorded Coal-Mining Songs* (Urbana: University of Illinois Press, 1972);
Huber, *Linthead Stomp*.

4. Barry Bluestone and Bennett Harrison, *The Deindustrialization of America:
Plant Closings, Community Abandonment, and the Dismantling of Basic Industry* (New
York: Basic Books, 1982), 6. For detailed discussions of the ways in which Midwestern
communities have negotiated these economic transitions, consult, among oth-
ers, Jon C. Teaford, *Cities of the Heartland: The Rise and Fall of the Industrial Midwest*
(Bloomington: Indiana University Press, 1993), 211–52; Steven High, *Industrial Sunset:
The Making of North America's Rust Belt, 1969-1984* (Toronto: University of Toronto

Press, 2003); Joseph Heathcott and Málre Agnes Murphy, "Corridors of Flight, Zones of Renewal: Industry, Planning, and Policy in the Making of Metropolitan St. Louis, 1940–1980," *Journal of Urban History* 31 (2005): 151–89; and Peter Cole, "A Tale of Two Towns: Globalization and Rural Deindustrialization in the U.S.," *WorkingUSA: The Journal of Labor and Society* 12 (December 2009): 539–62.

5. Aaron A. Fox, *Real County: Music and Language in Working-Class Culture* (Durham: Duke University Press, 2004), 74–106, 253–57.

6. Jennie Noakes, "'From the Top of the Mountain': Traditional Music and the Politics of Place in the Central Appalachian Coalfields" (PhD diss., University of Pennsylvania, 2008); Travis D. Stimeling, "Music, Place, and Identity in the Central Appalachian Mountaintop Removal Mining Debate," *American Music* 30, no. 1 (Spring 2012): 1–29.

7. David G. Whiteis, "Poverty, Policy, and Pathogenesis: Economic Justice and Public Health in the US," *Critical Public Health* 10, no. 2 (June 2000): 257–71; Patrick J. Carr and Maria J. Kefalas, *Hollowing Out the Middle: The Rural Brain Drain and What It Means for America* (Boston: Beacon Press, 2009). For a more focused discussion of these issues in southern Illinois, consult Sarah Halasz Graham, "The Gone Generation: The Rural Brain Drain and the Future of Southern Illinois's Small Towns," *Southern Illinoisan*, June 14, 2015, http://thesouthern.com/news/local/rural-brain-drain/the-gone-generation-the-rural-brain-drain-and-the-future/article_c616d149–94cd-56f8-b1bb-ed3dbbf77137.html.

8. The term "hard-hit people" originated with Alan Lomax, Woody Guthrie, and Pete Seeger's song collection *Hard Hitting Songs for Hard-Hit People* (New York: Oak Publications, 1967) and was also the title for West Virginia–born songwriter Hazel Dickens's 1981 solo debut album (Hazel Dickens and Bill C. Malone, *Working Girl Blues: The Life and Music of Hazel Dickens* [Urbana: University of Illinois Press, 2008], 22). See also Barbara Ching, *Wrong's What I Do Best: Hard Country Music and Contemporary Culture* (New York: Oxford University Press, 2003), 8–25, and Fox, *Real Country*, 20–45.

9. Steve S. Lee and Richard A. Peterson, "Internet-Based Virtual Music Scenes: The Case of P2 in Alt.Country Music," in *Music Scenes: Local, Translocal, and Virtual*, ed. Andy Bennett and Richard A. Peterson (Nashville: Vanderbilt University Press, 2004), 187–204; Nancy Park Riley, "Underground Not Underexposed: Bloodshot Records, Alt. Country, and the Chicago Live Music Scene" (PhD diss., University of Georgia, 2014), 63–66.

10. Riley, "Underground Not Underexposed," 70–104.

11. Tim Edensor, *Industrial Ruins: Space, Aesthetics and Materiality* (Oxford: Berg, 2005), 8–9.

12. Robert Austin Russell, "Looking for a Way Out: The Politics and Places of Alternative Country Music" (PhD diss., University of Iowa, 2009), 5.

13. Ibid., 100–101, 114–15, 121–22, 124, 126–30, 137–39. Edensor notes that musicians working "in some of the marginal realms of popular music," which alternative country music certainly is, occasionally draw on "the imagery and aesthetics of the contemporary

industrial ruin" (*Industrial Ruins*, 42). Here, I am using Chris Hedges and Joe Sacco's definition of a "sacrifice zone," which they describe as "those areas in the country that have been offered up for exploitation in the name of profit, progress, and technological advancement"; see Chris Hedges and Joe Sacco, *Days of Destruction, Days of Revolt* (New York: Nation Books, 2012), xi.

14. It should be noted that Russell does discuss musical aesthetics, although he limits his discussion to broad traits such as instrumentation and nonspecific musical references to country and folk style. See, for instance, "Looking for a Way Out," 129.

15. S. Renee Dechert, for example, has observed of Uncle Tupelo's "Graveyard Shift" (1990) that "a ... source of isolation stems from the exploitation of employees trapped in dead-end jobs that dehumanize and exploit"; see Dechert, "'Oh, What a Life a Mess Can Be,'" 81. See also Russell, "Looking for a Way Out," 114–15, 126–30; Stevie Simkin, "'The Burden Is Passed On': Son Volt, Tradition, and Authenticity," in *Old Roots, New Routes: The Cultural Politics of Alt.Country Music*, ed. Pamela Fox and Barbara Ching (Ann Arbor: University of Michigan Press, 2008), 192–93, 212–15; "Pops Farrar: 1930 to 2002," *No Depression*, October 31, 2002; and Chris King, "Bon Voyage, Pops Farrar," *Commonspace: Grassroots Civics and Culture in St. Louis*, October 2002.

16. Examples abound to illustrate this point, but Russell, "Looking for a Way Out," 129–30, typifies the superficial, style-based approach to musical analysis that has been deployed in much writing on Uncle Tupelo and alternative country music, more generally. This should not, however, be seen as a shortcoming of the work in question; rather, it is a matter of disciplinary inclinations and biases that privilege lyric over sustained musical analysis. More recently, Jason Kirby has offered a more nuanced exploration of Uncle Tupelo's musical output; see Jason Bianchi Kirby, "Antimodernism and Genre from Country-Rock to Alt.Country, 1968–98 (PhD diss., University of Virginia, 2016), 149–215.

17. factorybelt.com: The Unofficial Uncle Tupelo Archives, "References in the Songs," http://www.factorybelt.net/referecnes.htm, September 18, 2013. Russell suggests that alternative country music uses "places and place-imagery ... to create ... [a] sense of authenticity" ("Looking for a Way Out," 125; see also 126n264).

18. Matthew Heidenry, "Belleville, Illinois," *Gateway Heritage* 23, no. 1 (Summer 2002): 45.

19. Tweedy was born on August 25, 1967; Farrar on December 26, 1966; see Greg Kot, *Wilco: Learning How to Die* (New York: Broadway Books, 2004), 11; *Wikipedia*, "Jay Farrar," http://en.wikipedia.org/wiki/Jay_Farrar> October 17, 2013. See also Craig E. Colton, "Environmental Development in the East St. Louis Region, 1890–1970," *Environmental History Review* 14, nos. 1/2 (Spring-Summer 1990), 100, 104–5, 109 fig. 5.

20. Steven High points to "two great waves of plant closings [that] inundated the region [the Rust Belt] between 1969 and 1984, washing away millions of jobs," but Heathcott and Murphy observe that St. Louis city leaders were already concerned about plant closures as early as the mid-1950s (High, *Industrial Sunset*, 6; Heathcott and Murphy, "Corridors of Flight, Zones of Renewal," 176). Furthermore, Teaford

observes that "St. Louis's population dropped by almost fifty percent during the thirty years" between 1950 and 1980 (Teaford, *Cities of the Heartland*, 211).

21. Heathcott and Murphy, "Corridors of Flight, Zones of Renewal," 160, 166–80.

22. Teaford, *Cities of the Heartland*, 222.

23. Steven High and David W. Lewis, *Corporate Wasteland: The Landscape and Memory of Deindustrialization* (Ithaca: ILR Press/Cornell University Press, 2007), 3.

24. Quoted in Kot, *Wilco*, 12.

25. High, *Industrial Sunset*, 6.

26. Steven P. Dandaneau, *A Town Abandoned: Flint, Michigan, Confronts Deindustrialization* (Albany: State University of New York Press, 1996); Jefferson Cowie, *Capital Moves: RCA's Seventy-Year Quest for Cheap Labor* (Ithaca: Cornell University Press, 1999; paperback ed., New York: New Press, 2001); Steven K. Ashby and C. J. Hawking, *Staley: The Fight for a New American Labor Movement* (Urbana: University of Illinois Press, 2009); Sean Safford, *Why the Garden Club Couldn't Save Youngstown: The Transformation of the Rust Belt* (Cambridge: Harvard University Press, 2009); Chad Broughton, *Boom, Bust, Exodus: The Rust Belt, the Maquilas, and a Tale of Two Cities* (New York: Oxford University Press, 2015).

27. High, *Industrial Sunset*, 52; Rick A. Matthews, Michael O. Maume, and William J. Muller, "Deindustrialization, Economic Distress, and Homicide Rates in Midsized Rust Belt Cities," *Homicide Studies* 5, no. 2 (May 2001): 104.

28. High and Lewis, *Corporate Wasteland*, 8.

29. Jefferson Cowie and Joseph Heathcott, "Introduction: The Meanings of Deindustrialization," in *Beyond the Ruins: The Meanings of Deindustrialization*, ed. Jefferson Cowie and Joseph Heathcott (Ithaca: ILR Press/Cornell University Press, 2003), 1.

30. Cole, "A Tale of Two Towns"; J. L. Anderson, *Industrializing the Corn Belt: Agriculture, Technology, and Environment, 1945–1972* (DeKalb: Northern Illinois University Press, 2009).

31. Osha Davidson, "The Rise of the Rural Ghetto," *Nation*, June 14, 1986, 820.

32. John McCormick, "Lessons from the Farm," *Newsweek*, May 9, 1994, 50; Graham, "The Gone Generation."

33. This methodology extends my previous work on the Drive-By Truckers. See Travis D. Stimeling, "'Stay Out the Way of the Southern Thing': The Drive-By Truckers' Southern Gothic Soundscape," *Popular Music and Society* 36, no. 1 (2013): 19–29.

34. Kelly Birchfield and Barbara Ching, "Alt.County Chronology," in *Old Routes, New Routes: The Cultural Politics of Alt.Country Music* (Ann Arbor: University of Michigan Press, 2008), 233–39; Peter Doggett, *Are You Ready for the Country*, paperback ed. (New York: Penguin, 2001), 491–501; Lee and Peterson, "Internet-Based Virtual Music Scenes"; Diane Pecknold, "Selling Out or Buying In? Alt.Country's Cultural Politics of Commercialism," in *Old Routes, New Routes: The Cultural Politics of Alt.Country Music* (Ann Arbor: University of Michigan Press, 2008), 28–50; Riley, "Underground Not Underexposed," 27–69.

35. Bruce Feiler, *Dreaming Out Loud: Garth Brooks, Wynonna Judd, Wade Hayes, and the Changing Face of Nashville* (New York: Avon, 1998); Joli Jensen, "Taking Country

Music Seriously: Coverage of the 1990s Boom," in *Pop Music and the Press*, ed. Steve Jones (Philadelphia: Temple University Press, 2002), 183–201; Riley, "Underground Not Underexposed," 43–45; Stacy Mitchell, *Big-Box Swindle: The True Cost of Mega-Retailers and the Fight for America's Independent Businesses* (Boston: Beacon Press, 2006).

36. For more on punk's role in alternative country music, see Aaron Smithers, "Old Time Punk," in *Old Routes, New Routes: The Cultural Politics of Alt.Country Music* (Ann Arbor: University of Michigan Press, 2008), 175–91; Simkin, "'The Burden Is Passed On,'" 204–8.

37. Dechert, "'Oh, What a Life a Mess Can Be,'" 78.

38. Pecknold, "Selling Out or Buying In?," 31.

39. Strong evidence for this phenomenon is laid out in the documentary film *Before the Music Dies*, Roadwings Entertainment, 2006.

40. Russell, "'Looking for a Way Out,'" 128n268; "References in the Songs." "Sauget Wind" was originally issued on a Rockville Records seven-inch and was included on the 2003 reissue of the band's 1991 album, *Still Feel Gone*.

41. It is not much of a stretch to compare Farrar to Guthrie, especially in light of his work on the 2012 Guthrie tribute album *New Multitudes* (Rounder). Molinaro, among others, has cited Guthrie as a vital point of connection to the alternative country movement ("Urbane Cowboys").

42. Simkin traces such dramatic changes in timbre, tempo, and dynamic to "bands such as Husker Dü, the Pixies, and Throwing Muses [who] were building their songs around slow/fast structures and quiet/loud dynamics" (Simkin, "'The Burden Is Passed On,'" 204).

43. For a broader discussion of this tendency in Farrar's songwriting, consult Russell, "'Looking for a Way Out," 114–15.

44. "Graveyard Shift," from Uncle Tupelo's *No Depression*, serves as another example of the ways that mix can play a role in shaping this narrative, particularly in the use of a punchy electric bass sound and the sharp cutoffs heard at 0:29–0:37, 2:46–2:53, and 4:30-end. Kirby has suggested that these jarring shifts could be the product of the Minutemen's musical influence on Uncle Tupelo (Kirby, "Antimodernism and Genre from Country-Rock to Alt.Country," 167–75).

45. For an extended discussion of Farrar's attitudes and approaches to recording, consult Simkin, "'The Burden Is Passed On,'" 199–203. For a useful point of comparison in Wilco's recordings, consult Sheena Hyndman, "The O'Rourke Factor: Authorship, Authority, and Creative Collaboration in the Music of Wilco," *Musicological Explorations* 8 (2007): 7–31.

46. One notable example is "Whiskey Bottle" (Uncle Tupelo, *No Depression*, Rockville, 1990). For a broader perspective on the type of analysis being deployed here, consult, among many others, Leilo Camilleri, "Shaping Sounds, Shaping Spaces," *Popular Music* 29, no. 2 (2010): 199–212; Ruth Dockwray and Allan F. Moore, "Configuring the Sound-Box, 1965–1972," *Popular Music* 29, no. 2 (2010): 181–97; Jay Hodgson, "Outline for a Theory of Recording Practice with Reference to the Mix of Pink Floyd's 'Speak

to Me' (1973)," *Journal on the Art of Record Production (Academic)* 1, no. 1 (2007), http://www.artofrecordproduction.com/content/view/200/104/, December 15, 2007; Serge Lacasse, "'Listen to My Voice': The Evocative Power of Vocal Staging in Recorded Rock Music and Other Forms of Vocal Expression" (PhD diss., University of Liverpool, 2000); Allan F. Moore and Ruth Dockwray, "The Establishment of the Virtual Performance Space in Rock," *Twentieth-Century Music* 5, no. 2 (2008): 219–41; Travis D. Stimeling, "Narrative, Vocal Staging and Masculinity in the 'Outlaw' Country Music of Waylon Jennings," *Popular Music* 32, no. 3 (2013): 343–58.

47. John Molinaro has highlighted the use of Farm Security Administration–style photography in some alternative country publications; see John Molinaro, "Urbane Cowboys: Alt. Country in the 1990s," MA thesis, University of Virginia, 1998, http://xroads.virginia.edu/~ma98/molinaro/alt.country/jm-thesis, November 18, 2017.

48. Jay Farrar, *Terroir Blues*, Artemis Records, 2003.

49. "Cahokia Mounds—Learn—Interpretive Center," http://www.cahokiamounds.org/learn/interpretive-center, October 13, 2013.

50. KMOV-TV, "Hulking Milam Landfill Nearing End of Its 40-Year Lifespan," August 30, 2012.

51. Son Volt, *American Central Dust*, Rounder, 2009.

52. Wilco, "Casino Queen," *A.M.*, Reprise/WEA, 1995.

53. Kot, *Wilco*, 5, 92.

54. For additional discussion of hypermasculine façades in country and alternative country music, consult Stimeling, "'Stay Out the Way of the Southern Thing,'" and "Narrative, Vocal Staging and Masculinity in the 'Outlaw' Country Music of Waylon Jennings," *Popular Music* 32, no. 3 (2013): 343–58.

55. John C. Navin and Timothy S. Sullivan, "Do Riverboat Casinos Act as Competitors? A Look at the St. Louis Market," *Economic Development Quarterly* 21 (2007), 49; B. Grant Stitt, Mark Nichols, and David Giacopassi, "Does the Presence of Casinos Increase Crime? An Examination of Casino and Control Communities," *Crime & Delinquency* 49 (2003): 253–84.

56. Son Volt, *The Search*, Transmit Sound/Legacy, 2007.

57. High and Lewis, *Corporate Wasteland*, 25.

58. Jeff Todd Titon, "Music and the U.S. War on Poverty: Some Reflections," *Yearbook for Traditional Music* 45 (2013): 81.

# CHAPTER TWELVE

# The Politics
# of Covers

*Johnny Cash,*

*Rick Rubin,*

*and the*

American Recordings

## JONATHAN SILVERMAN

IN 1994, Cash released his first album with producer Rick Rubin, *American Recordings*. This particular work felt different from the singer's previous releases, even though many of the features of Cash's work on *American Recordings*—recovering old classics, re-imagining others' works—were a component of other efforts, including work done for his previous label, Mercury. The trouble was that these past albums, although dutifully released and promoted, could not find cultural resonance in the places where Cash had found it before. Part of that disconnect had to do with the way Mercury albums sounded; while the music was interesting, it did not register as being current or at least current enough so to be played on modern country stations. It did not sound old, at least old in the way that it might be on classic country. It did not sound like rock and roll or folk, so crossover possibilities were remote.

But even with a lukewarm response to his releases in the late 1980s and the early 1990s, Cash still had a prominent place in American culture for a few reasons. He had a daughter, Rosanne Cash, who was active in contemporary music circles; a former son-in-law, Nick Lowe, had introduced him to another cohort of musicians; and he had been part of the country music supergroup the Highwaymen, which put his name in the cultural conversation for a while. More important, he was simply an interesting and colorful musician whose work people still listened to, even if they tended to ignore his latest offerings. For these reasons, Rubin thought Cash was worth taking a chance on. Rubin was famous for producing rap, most notably LL Cool J, Public Enemy, and the Beastie Boys, but also had turned to producing rock, including the Red Hot Chili Peppers' now classic *Blood Sugar Sex Magik*. He was notably different from Cash's recent producers, including longtime collaborator Jack Clement, because his associations with genre were decidedly not country; although Clement worked with a wide variety of artists, he was largely a country producer. But Rubin was not beholden to previously held ideas about Cash's genres and was open to the type of experimentation displayed in Cash's famous prison albums in the 1960s. Those were produced by Bob Johnston, who also had a varied clientele, including Bob Dylan and Simon and Garfunkel.

*American Recordings* was bold in its simplicity, with Cash playing acoustic guitar with no accompaniment, recording his own songs, and covering others, chosen in consultation with Rubin. In settling on the acoustic form and in almost meta-acknowledgment of Cash's musical autobiography with its song contents, *American Recordings* was a statement of retro-progressiveness, an album that looked back to move forward. His next album, *Unchained*, largely recorded with Tom Petty and the Heartbreakers, was even more radical—it can be seen as greatly expanding country music possibilities, creating the new form of Americana, or abandoning genre altogether. In this album, Cash, Rubin, and Petty focus on song over genre, a rejection of country music as it was in the 1990s—a genre that embraced the new and a particular type of slickness. Four more albums followed, as a well as a boxed set of alternative takes. The American Recordings series relaunched Cash into mainstream consciousness. As a result, Cash appeared on *The Simpsons*, and his video for "Delia's Gone" appeared on *Beavis and Butthead*; he also won two Grammys related to the series, had his song "The Man Comes Around" appear as the opening song of *The Dawn of the Dead* reboot (and more recently in *Logan*), and covered the Nine Inch Nails' postmodern tearjerker "Hurt," whose accompanying video was interspliced with footage from various Cash documentaries (including the sublime *Johnny Cash: The Man, His World, His Music*). Cash's renewed relevance suggests that his work with Rubin had significant resonance within popular culture.

Some of that resonance was political, at least in Rubin's view. In promoting *Unchained*'s Grammy win, the producer employed Cash's famous "bird," the iconic photo in which Cash is giving the finger to the camera taken by Jim Marshall at the San Quentin concert. Rubin added the now infamous text, "American Recordings and Johnny Cash would like to acknowledge the Nashville music establishment and country radio for your support."[1] In a sense this was the most overt political stance Cash made during the *American Recordings* period. By taking aim at the institutions of country music and its metonym, Nashville, Rubin's missive was making the claim that the institutional system of genre-dictated music promotion was problematic, with the evidence that the Grammys had shown Cash's relevance.

But the real politics of the series are more significant than a marketing postcard. It is much more instructive to take the albums as a positive and progressive stance when it comes to playing music. While there are few elements of obvious political and progressive content in the series of albums, progressiveness in art can measured in ways other than authorial intent. I argue here that the work Cash and Rubin do with the series— particularly in the first two albums—has a political and progressive impact in three overlapping ways. The first concerns the fashion in which *American Recordings* treats songs and popular music as artistic achievements beyond the typical limits of genre, for Johnny Cash took songs from a variety of genres and reinterpreted them in his own way, showing us how universal songs can be despite their genre categories. The second concerns a system that valued genre adhesion for its marketing ease; the American Recordings series made a statement that genre did not matter as much as performance. As his longtime producer Jack Clement noted, Cash was his own genre, although when pressed, he called Cash "broadly folk."[2] But such a title was not helpful in getting his music recognized in the 1980s and 1990s, although he received more opportunities than most musicians to try; few major labels would have signed an artist in his midfifties as Mercury had in 1987. Therefore, this album of acoustic originals, commissioned songs, and covers was in its very existence a political statement. The third way concerns Cash's emergence as a relevant older musician in a musical landscape geared toward younger musicians, an important touchstone for artistic expression. Cash was still relevant as an older artist in this period; he sang on U2's "The Wanderer" in 1993, and that year Cash had appeared on *Late Show with David Letterman* twice—well before *American Recordings* came out.[3] What was different was the wholesale change in tactics and expression that Cash undertook in the series; it primarily built on his artistry and legend rather than his genre. Cash's mere recording with Rubin—the erstwhile rap producer—was bold. The impact beyond that move is even more uncertain but potentially bigger than the ones I described. What if Cash's move forced music executives and booking agents to reassess their focus on young artists? What if it made audiences take note of alternative ways of presenting music? What if a new genre, Americana, took shape, as Cash's son, John Carter Cash, claims as a result of Cash's efforts in the American Recordings series?[4]

I am no fan of rhetorical questions, and these above are decidedly so—proving impact through cause and effect is nearly impossible, and a number of factors complicate the task of showing the full influence of Cash's American Recordings series. Still, given the ways perception of Johnny Cash changed in the last ten years of his life—from a career in the 1980s and early 1990s circumscribed by the limits of his genre to one where his work was recognized by popular culture and the music industry—suggests that his work did have a significant impact. I primarily focus on the first two albums because the others are forged by their momentum after *American Recordings* and *Unchained* and also circumscribed by Cash's progressive illness in the 1990s and early the next decade before his death in 2003. The first two set the tone for the rest of series, even though arguably the cultural touchstone of the whole series is "Hurt," from *American Recordings IV*, released not long before Cash died. In this video, Cash displays the ravages of age in a way that is both personally powerful and societally meaningful.[5] But before "Hurt" and Cash's death, there were *American Recordings* and *Unchained,* and they changed Cash's life and arguably the lives of his audiences.

What makes the impact of Cash's new albums so compelling is that they are political in a way different from Cash's previous forays into politics and music in the 1960s and 1970s. In the 1960s, Cash had undertaken a highly political music agenda. The most outwardly political—and progressive—music statement was his Native American concept album, *Bitter Tears,* and the two prison albums, *At Folsom Prison* and *At San Quentin.* But one could argue that Cash's early Columbia album, *Hymns by Johnny Cash,* was political in a more personal way and that thematic such albums as *Ride This Train* and *Johnny Cash Sings Ballads of the True West* were folk albums made to address political and historical concerns about the nature of American history and culture. There is also an argument that his ABC television show, in its very existence in its period, is also political. Although he suffered some backlash from Southerners when he sang about Native American issues, his reputation for being a politically engaged member from the South, when the region's politics were often decried by the rest of the country, was intact.[6]

The prison albums, both of which charted in the top ten, and the television show helped put Cash in the mainstream spotlight, but once he got there, he struggled with the politics associated with his new status. Cash famously said he was a "dove with claws" when asked if he was hawk after a trip to Vietnam, a stupid metaphor (doves have claws) that Cash soon disavowed.[7] Even "Man in Black," the song in which Cash claimed the mantle of protest hero, was less a political call to action and more a personal protest primarily about economic inequality; it did not touch on subjects such as race and gender, although it did touch on class, itself often a controversial issue.[8] In the 1970s, he also stood behind President Richard M. Nixon but declined to play Guy Drake's "Welfare Cadilac" (*sic*) at the White House, announcing he was a born-again Christian on national television. But this political maneuvering did not work to keep his newfound audiences, the ones who gravitated to him after the successful *At Folsom Prison* and *At San Quentin* albums and a presence on national television with the funky, cheesy, and groundbreaking *Johnny Cash Show.* When it came down to it, Cash could not balance his appeals to a broader audience with his ties to his country audience, which expected a pro-war stance and other conservative orthodoxies.[9]

In this era, Cash moved to Nashville, became born again, and left his show and made a movie about Jesus called *Gospel Road.* But he did not exactly withdraw from the mainstream either. He made multiple television appearances, such as on *Columbo* as a murderous country singer. He also has spots on *Sesame Street* (featuring a notable duet with Oscar the Grouch) and *The Muppet Show.* His music career also thrived, for he had one last hit with "One Piece at a Time" in 1976, toured with fellow Americana grey-beards, The Highwaymen, and remained an active touring musician.

Still, Cash's popularity began to wane in the mid-1970s as a combination of changing styles in country music, his own personal religious conversion, and muddled political views cast him from mainstream popularity to country music staple. In the 1980s, Columbia/Sony dropped him after having recorded him since 1960; Mercury signed him soon after, but he felt abandoned by the company: "Before Rick Rubin came along ten years ago, I had declined to the bottom of the ladder on people of importance at Mercury/Polygram in Nashville. It didn't hurt me all that much because I expected it. I expected it when I saw that there was no interest in my recordings, and since there was no real purpose to having a recording career, that it would all fade away. I was kinda ready for it to happen."[10]

But was Cash's subsequent move to Rubin political itself? To be clear, I believe everything is political in the larger sense of the word. The word "political" comes from the Middle French *politique,* meaning "political, relating to the state or public affairs, of or relating to (especially benevolent and constitutional) government, (of an action or thing) judicious, expedient, sensible, useful, (of a person) prudent, sagacious."[11] The first half of the definition is in line with the most common and formal sense of the word, and the last part seems to suggest that politics is a form of personal expression and a positive one. As Clare Bambra, Debbie Fox, and Alex Scott-Samuel note, the "most prevalent definition within mainstream political discourse . . . places very restrictive boundaries around what politics is—the activities of governments, elites and state agencies—and therefore also restricts who is political and who can engage in politics (i.e., the members of governments, state agencies and other elite organizations)." They define a "much more encompassing view of politics: politics is everything; it is a term that can be used to describe any 'power-structured relationship."[12] Their definition comes from Kate Millett's simple but revolutionary idea of what politics is: "The term 'politics' shall refer to power-structured relationships, arrangements whereby one group of persons is controlled by another."[13]

While there are definitions of politics that put it squarely in the relationship to the political establishment, there are also political structures in any institution, including the music industry, Cash's chosen field. While Cash's political intentions have varied over time, music has long had political connections. One comes in the content of songs; something like "We Shall Overcome" or the Who's "Won't Get Fooled Again" or the Rolling Stones' "Street Fighting Man" have political content.[14] There are also the relationships between people in the music industry; in a broad definition of politics, relationships between band members, managers, and record companies, whether based on race, gender, class, content, finance, and so on, are all political because of the varied nature of power relationships.

There is also the issue of genre in music. Certainly, Cash is broadly defined as country, but he has a place in the genesis of rock and roll (and is a member of its Hall of Fame) and won a Grammy for folk music. To some degree, Cash has a paradoxical relationship to country music; he is both insider and outsider, enough to make his entrance into mainstream culture easier, especially in the prison album and Rubin eras. But his move to Nashville in the 1960s after giving Los Angeles a try actually seemed a reluctant concession to his place in country music. As Jennifer C. Lena and Richard A. Peterson note, "Musicians often do not want to be confined by genre boundaries, but . . . their freedom of expression is necessarily bounded by the expectations of other performers, audience members, critics, and the diverse others whose work is necessary to making, distributing, and consuming symbolic goods."[15] In addition, sociologists think of genres as "systems of orientations, expectations, and conventions that bind together an industry, performers, critics, and fans in making what they identify as a distinctive sort of music."[16] In those systems are political relationships and realties that range from what acts get signed and where their music will be played to the interpersonal relationships within those systems. As Peterson observes, country music involves a process where artists, record companies, and country radio continually reinforce a sound that is popular: "This institutionalized commercial music machine is inherently conservative, acting as a giant gyroscope that keeps country music on a fairly narrow track, since each new song and each new artist created in this way is a close copy of the one before."[17] For Cash, those binds were definitely from country music, and his songs primarily charted there his entire career, despite a desire to place Cash outside that genre. Accordingly, because of who he was, Cash's choice to record with Rubin was notable and unsettling for everyone in the system.[18] At the same time, it seemed to energize both of them, Rubin because he was working with an artist arguably with a type of legacy he had never worked with before, and Cash because of the opportunity to appeal to different audiences. The statement the pair was making with their partnership was simple and complex.[19] Before Rubin decided to record Cash in the 1990s, Cash seemed destined to go to Branson to join other country music and popular performers in the grind of twice-a-day shows, but a deal to perform there fell through.[20] Still, he was left to reside in what Warren Zanes called "the neglected, shabby pastures in which first-generation rock and rollers were left to graze."[21] Cash remained confined to the country music canon, a circuit performer who occasionally broke out into the mainstream but whose new work rarely mattered to cultural tastemakers.

But even after his pairing with Rubin, Cash took a lower political profile in his renewed career in the 1990s, which might have seemed surprising for someone who had a reputation for being political, based largely on his earlier work related to prisons and Native Americans. He might have been worried about his reception from what he saw as a conservative audience if he expressed liberalism; at the same time, he might have worried about his reception from a liberal audience if he outwardly expressed his Christianity. Both worries would have been grounded in experience; there is some evidence his conservative audience was put off by his folk music and social activism in the 1960s and early 1970s, and Cash himself believes that his open confession of his Christianity was responsible for his television show being canceled in 1971.[22]

During this period, Cash seemed to be in no mood to announce himself as a political force. Witness this 2003 interview with Lev Grossman in *Time* in which Cash seemed to—but not explicitly—express displeasure with current political events. At one point, Grossman and Cash had this exchange:

> LG: Do you watch the news?
> JC: Yeah, quite a bit.
> LG: Do you feel pessimistic about the way things are going?
> JC: I just wish we would ... I wish we would ... mmm. Not going to get into that, Lev.[23]

The interview implied—but did not express—disapproval, and at this point in his career, Cash seemed unwilling to go any further. You can sense this in the way Grossman frames the conversation, by emphasizing

Cash's verbal cues when answering a political question in a way that suggests a different answer. Cash benefits in this formation because it gives the reader the sense of Cash's political feelings, which allows Cash to have those feelings and yet not express them, which could alienate his long-standing country music audience. There are other ways of reading this moment: perhaps Cash did not like the way the question was phrased or he *liked* "the way things are going" and did not want his new *American Recordings* series fans to know. In any case, one gets the *sense* that Cash believes having a public political view was not in his interest.

There is no doubt this fear of political involvement was well founded, not only because of Cash but also as witnessed in the fallout of another Rubin client, the Dixie Chicks, who found themselves shunned after lead singer, Natalie Maines, expressed disapproval of Bush while she was thousands of miles away in England.[24] Yet to categorize Cash as fearful is to underestimate his savvy and boldness. Grossman is interviewing Cash because he matters in 2003, because he produced work that resonated with audiences, and while Cash was careful, his six-album set with Rubin was bold in its insistence that the performer and the song were or at least could be at the center of American pop expression.

In 1993, when Cash began recording *American Recordings,* he still had one primary audience, the aging demographic associated with classic country radio often played on AM stations in rural, unpopulated areas of the country. He toured regularly, although the size of his venues varied greatly, and he was a well-regarded figure outside these contexts. When Cash released *American Recordings,* the juxtaposition of the sixty-something Cash with the bearded bard of consumable rap and hard rock was striking, something that both men seemed conscious of. There were other symbols associated with the album—the stark cover with Cash in some sort of Western/cowboy overcoat, his hair blowing in the wind, with the two black-and-white elemental dogs on each side of him, and the immediately accessible font and lettering "C A S H," which suggested and then became a brand. There was the video for "Delia's Gone" with model Kate Moss, where Cash wields an old-timey pickup truck and some rope, produced with a nostalgic tone after shooting on a windy day.

These were the most obvious nods toward marketing *American Recordings,* a necessary part of getting anything listened to. But the symbolism did not stop with the marketing, and it is part of the claim that his new work is political. *American Recordings* makes its most significant progressive statement through Cash's acoustic guitar. Cash plays all the songs himself, with some small vocal help but with no accompanying instruments. Here, the acoustic guitar is an implicit rebuke of the highly produced Nashville sound popularly played on country music radio. But it also addresses classic country, which is adorned in its own ways, including some of Cash's own earlier efforts. For Cash's longtime producer, Jack Clement, favored more ornamental production, which worked in its own context.

But can Cash's work with Rubin be considered explicitly progressive? To be progressive means changing and engendering change. Progressivism has had two primary meanings as it relates to music. One is attached to the political meaning of progressivism, historically connected to the social and political movements of the early twentieth century, for example, efforts to ban immoral behaviors such as drinking and gambling and to encourage more democratic voting. The other is a much smaller *p:* the growth of progressive rock, the so-called prog rock of King Crimson and Yes.[25] Emily Robinson asks and answers her question about the connections between politics and art: "What makes social democratic politics and prog rock 'progressive'? The obvious answer is that they are both about improvement, about striving for advancement—whether that is measured in terms of social justice or musical experimentation." She adds, "But there is nothing exclusive here. Definitions of what constitutes 'progress' are clearly subjective. One person's great leap forward is another's worrying decline."[26]

Talented musicians want to move forward. Each song, each album is a chance to make another statement about art to the world. As Warren Zanes describes the process that Tom Petty goes through in his fine biography, *Petty*, the musician keeps drawing on a combination of his own life experiences, his artistic development, and industry context in producing new albums. Petty's career is exceptional in its scope and length, but his concerns about moving forward are not. As Robinson notes, "Part of the attractiveness of 'progressive' as either a political or cultural term is that it is anticipatory, with connotations of being 'ahead of your time.'"[27] Although the definition of progressivism here is small *p* when it comes to the political, it also reflects a realistic definition to attach to art making.

If politics in music are about the state of genre, progressivism in music means the consequences of moving forward. I think Cash is progressive in the way he thinks about genre and song and in the way he operates without thinking about age as a limiting factor.

Cash's use of the acoustic guitar announces to listeners that Cash is both confident and vulnerable, not afraid of relying on his own voice and guitar playing and yet subject to limitations in production that necessarily produces. There is something both very modern and very old about this form of recording. Careful to announce that at least some of the work had been done at Cash's house, Rubin relies on the modern conception of the guitar's symbolic place in popular music.[28] It reads as sincere, honest, authentic, real. Of course, those qualities are cultural constructions; we have decided the associations beyond the sound the guitar generates when someone plays it. Acoustic guitar is in the same category of vinyl records, which are now enjoying a renaissance. People play vinyl records out of the same impulse—because those recordings sound authentic, closer to the intent of the recorder. Yet even if you concede that vinyl has better sound quality, which is not fully agreed on by experts, the active physicality of playing a record mirrors the intensively physical nature of playing the acoustic guitar.[29]

But rather than merely nostalgic uses of technology, I would call both acoustic guitar and vinyl records a type of retro-progressiveness, a way of moving forward by looking back. Both enact a type of "care" that practitioners in the Brooklyn/Portland/Austin school of living practice in coffee shops, restaurants, and other service industries, notably parodied in *Portlandia*.[30] Retro-progressives want the physical to mean something in a digital age, and they want audiences to pay attention to this conception; retro-progressiveness is both personal and public. Rubin and Cash use this conception as a way of countering the intense production associated with popular music, showing in their perception how the basis of music is elemental. In an earlier work on Cash, I borrowed a term related to architecture from Mathew Frederick, "informed simplicity," the idea that simplicity does not simply mean simple but also that it can be a distillation of more complex ideas.[31] *American Recordings* is the epitome of informed simplicity; behind this acoustic album are Cash's 50 years of artistic choices and Rubin's 20 of production choices wrapped into 13 songs played with an acoustic guitar.

The album effectively re-creates Cash's artistic persona as a way of re-introducing him and contextualizing him in his own music and projecting him as an embodiment of music authenticity. The album is good; Cash's voice and guitar playing are excellent. It sounds like Cash, timeless and weird and occasionally haunting; there are quirks and revelations. The album also relies on his personal connections. Cash gained and lost a son-in-law, Nick Lowe, who had married his daughter, Carlene Carter. The Nick Lowe crowd included Elvis Costello, and Cash covered his "Big Light" for the 1987 *Johnny Cash Is Coming to Town* in an ornamental, country kind of way. But in 1994, Cash's "Beast in Me," originally by Lowe, does different work on *American Recordings*. Cash sings about the beast being caged "by frail and fragile bonds" and as one who "rants and rages at the stars." These lyrics certainly sound like our idea of Cash, playing on his prison associations and bad behavior. "Beast" is about everybody, of course. But Cash's take reads as autobiographical, especially in the light of his self-told history of sin and redemption. What is the political or even progressive nature of such a pseudo-confessional song? Not much, one would think. It is autobiography or rather "autobiography"—is the song really about Cash or rather a perceived "Johnny Cash" who Cash and Rubin use as a nod toward authenticity—not about either small or big *p* politics. Even covering an English songwriter who collaborated with a quirky roots/country singer, Dave Edmunds, in *Rockpile* and with traditional country rejecters John Hiatt and Ry Cooder in *Little Village*, the song is still not political, not really. Yet there is that guitar, the one that puts the voice over the sound, puts the man over the production, although Rubin's anti-production is still production. The mythos of the recording studio in the living room lives large in the shadows of this album in much the same way that the garage lies behind every tech startup myth.[32]

Still, much of the album is highly religious, which is well camouflaged. In "Down There by the Train," the Tom Waits cover, "Redemption," and "Why Me Lord?," Cash sings about religion without a catchy pun and with straight-up devotion. The mix of the "Cowboy's Prayer" and the traditional "Oh, Bury Me Not" is unusual and, as Robert Hilburn notes, touches on Cash's love of religious imagery outside the church. "Like a Soldier" is also about redemption, although it is deliberately ambiguous about who is the redeemer—the narrator's companion or God. Then there are the songs about unredeemable narrators. "Delia's Gone," which is technically Cash covering himself from the early 1960s version, is a revenge song, without the class consciousness associated with "Folsom Prison Blues" or "San Quentin." "Thirteen," about an unredeemable narrator, a song that Glenn Danzig commissioned for Cash, also fits Cash's care for the unredeemable he showed in his prison albums. The most outwardly political song of the bunch is "Drive On," about a Vietnam veteran coming to grips, many years later, with what he suffered in the war.

Two songs are noteworthy for their inclusion as live versions: "Tennessee Stud" and "The Man Who Couldn't Cry." Cash's performances on both are great. "Man" is a silly song about masculinity and criticism and the mean ways people treat one another and seems remotely autobiographical. "Tennessee Stud" tells the story of a man and a horse, the erstwhile Tennessee stud, and the man's adventures in finding a mate. In both songs, the audience is a problem, whooping and hollering every time sex or violence is intimated. It reduces Cash in the sense that he becomes the object for the audience's projection of what it means to be Johnny Cash in this case. That Rubin and Cash included these songs suggests desperation. Although it apes the prisoners' response in the two live prison albums, they do not carry the same perceived authenticity. Robert Christgau, one of the few critics who did not like the first two Cash-Rubin collaborations, is especially critical: "To applaud his live 'Tennessee Stud' without wincing at the Viper Room assholes cheering in all the wrong places is to kowtow to the company line that Rick Rubin has rescued a Nashville legend from Nashville." Christgau's critique is notable because he sees Cash as a country musician who shares his art with a particular audience, and he is skeptical about the Rubin project more generally: "One reason Johnny Cash is a great artist is that he knows his core fans, a subset of the ordinary folks who've always bought Nashville product doo-doo choruses and all . . . As I understand history, it's an American miracle that anyone can create good art for this audience. But these two records ain't it. Whether they convince anyone else depends on who believes the hype."[33]

Underlying this criticism is the question of whether the Cash-Rubin collaboration is authentic. As I wrote in an earlier work, the very concept of authenticity is problematic because it is immeasurable, prone to personal preference, and becomes hard to maintain if one should achieve it.[34]

David Sanjek finds that "debates about authenticity really come down to distinctions about repertoire" in that "It's almost as if each of us were programming a jukebox and endeavoring to prove our personal list superior to another's." He finds this phenomenon to be particularly acute "whenever the mainstream taste of the wider public descends into a pattern that the cognoscenti consider debased" as it results in "Dismissing the Top Ten out of hand and replacing it with cultish preferences [that] bear an unappetizing similarity to the educated classes barricading themselves against the barbarians at the gates."[35] Although Christgau does not explicitly invoke the term, he questions whether the marketing of the project outstrips its value.[36]

It is difficult to read intent into anything Cash and Rubin do. In one sense, they seem like true believers when it comes to the power of song; their choices seem borne of respect for both the music they choose and Cash's ability to make the music his own in terms of performance. They are both consummate music industry insiders, so they are aware of audience perception and reception. Inside the machine, they read as outsiders. But anyone who has navigated their two genres, country and rap, with any success has a deep knowledge of the music business. In other words, the political cannot be read by intent—*American Recordings* and *Unchained* have to be treated as slippery postmodern texts because the men who made them are consummate insiders/outsiders who understand markets and audiences *and* love music.

In that way, Christgau does raise the issue that would seem to discount the partnership; it is essentially a metaproject, commenting on itself and the careers of both Rubin and Cash. Yet if one can get beyond authorial intent (acknowledging that *American Recordings*' author is Rubin, Cash, and the songwriters) and think about the work the album does, you come to more interesting conclusions. In *American Recordings,* Cash and Rubin were in effect saying that the initial foray into music, the man and his guitar, was more important than the machinery that made Cash a star. Rather than building on that particular model in the remaining American Recordings albums, Cash and Rubin decided to go even further in the second album in the series, *Unchained.* Cash covered Beck, Soundgarden, and Tom Petty and used Petty and the Heartbreakers as his backup band (Petty's voice is especially noticeable on a number of tracks). To this listener, the standouts are "Rowboat," a cover of a Beck song; "Sea of Heartbreak," (cowritten by Paul Hampton and Hal David, himself one half of the David–Burt Bacharach pairing who wrote "Raindrops Keep Falling on My Head," among other classics); "I Never Picked Cotton," first covered by *Hee-Haw* helmer Roy Clark; and "Rusty Cage," by alternative music giant Soundgarden. There are again religious songs: "Spiritual," "Unchained," and "Meet Me in Heaven," and "Kneeling Drunkard's Plea." At the same time, he also covered the Carter Family, so his break with country music was not complete—nor was it meant to be. Indeed, the audacity of the approach was to equate *all genres,* to suggest that songs (or perhaps the performance of them) were larger than genre. This willingness to experiment, to eschew traditional genre boundaries, suggests a type of rebellion, moving forward against his past, a rejection of Nashville, which had rejected him first. I have not included much about the songs' lyrics from either of these albums in this essay simply because I think that the modes of production, which are original, and the choices of song, which are a form of curation, are more important politically than the lyrics of these songs.

Although I have focused thus far on *Unchained* and *American Recordings,* there are other significant political moments that come later in his career. Cash becomes ill before putting out *American III: Solitary Man* and never fully recovers, but that difficult reality does not stop him from recording interesting work. *American III* is a beautiful album, with a mix of carefully chosen songs both from Cash and those he covers, which include Tom Petty's "I Won't Back Down," which sounds more insistent than the original, U2's "One," Nick Cave's "The Mercy Seat," and the title track from Neil Diamond. The album is more confident than the first *American Recordings* album and does not hold itself to strict accounting to acoustic material; the producing touch is light but not absent. Cash's voice was clearly diminished from the full-throated efforts of *Unchained,* but in a way, the performance does not suffer; Cash is moving into a different phase of his career—mastery in the face of decline.

*American IV* mirrors *Unchained* in that the songs vary greatly in style. There are acoustic songs now backed with a band and, new to the series, three duets: one with indie music icon Fiona Apple in Paul Simon's "Bridge over Troubled Water" and another with Nick Cave in Hank Williams's "I'm So Lonesome I Could Cry." The musical choices vary so greatly in terms of period and presumed genre that it seems to cement the idea that songs transcend genre. There are two songs that offer political statements worth noting. The first comes from the title track, "The Man Comes Around," a song pretty openly about the apocalypse, from Revelations in the New Testament. Cash deflects the song's content in two ways. In the song itself, Cash's voice first comes from what sounds like a crackling old radio, indicating a type of metaconsciousness about the song that obscures its religious content. As I have written before, in several moments, including his liner notes, he explained that the song came to him in a dream about Queen Elizabeth, during which she called Cash a "whirlwind," which becomes "whirlwind in the thorn tree." I do not think Cash was only trying to deceive, but he did divert the reader from the song's religious content when he referred to Queen Elizabeth, not ordinarily a symbol of piety. Who knows what the *intention* of this obfuscation is—is it simply Cash being a little cagey about the religious material, a legitimate explanation, or something in between? The other significant moment comes from "Hurt," especially the video, which shows an aging Cash and June Carter Cash interspliced with shots of a decaying House of Cash Museum and clips from his music and acting career. Cash is probably the oldest performer to get this type of music video treatment, and if not the actual oldest, he more acutely displays his age in this video than anyone in memory, especially given the sharp contrast with his young, virile persona displayed in this video mix. In some ways, the most progressive part of the Rubin-Cash legacy is this notion that musicians can make meaningful music late in their career and show the ravages of time.

Still, there is no explicitly political agenda associated with these albums, and in terms of system critique, both Cash and Rubin are longtime members of the music industry. What they did, in fact, was use traditional marketing tools associated with young artists to break or rebreak Cash as an artist. Their visual shot at the country music establishment through the Bird ad muddles the work because it is industry standard to promote and play young artists associated with country music stations, not geared toward the work Cash has produced over time, work that often lacks the signifiers associated with country music.

Reading Cash through his life as liberal versus conservative or even political at all not only gives us indeterminacy but also confuses our sense of what politics even is. In other words, we are going to have to infer rather than determine the political intent of the American Recordings series or rather what type of political act it was to record with Rick Rubin. For this producer's goal was not to appeal to that limited audience; he wanted a younger one. But he also wanted to operate within Cash's context as a musician. So when the two hooked up, Rubin and Cash took an approach that both embodied the familiar elements of Cash's career and engaged with more modern music. But in choosing acoustic music, including songs, commissions, and covers from musicians other than country artists, Cash was making a statement about the nature of country music and the limitations of genre.

A case may be made for a progressive reading of Cash and Rubin nonetheless, and it requires a type of post-cynical look at the work because the first thing we have to think about is the collective savviness of the enterprise, which is off the charts (to deliberately use a pun). *American Recordings* is retro-progressive; *Unchained* is a more straightforwardly political statement about genre and expression, which culminated in Rubin's ad directed toward the "country music establishment." "Solitary Man" and "The Man Comes Around" show that age may actually enhance musical performance and cement the idea that genre is generated from production and reception rather than song construction.

You have to put yourself in the world after these albums and ask what has changed; in a way, that is the measure of progressivism. Cash reaffirmed the play in genre that others, such as Neil Young and Bob Dylan, have taken before, yet came from a recently obscured classic machine and the type of generic rebellion contextualized within a career commonly associated with such. Son John Carter Cash has the most optimistic view of the impact of the ad and the two albums, saying the "ad really shook Nashville up," calling it a "wake-up call" that signaled that "perhaps country music was broader and more expansive than the power brokers in Nashville had assumed." But any neutral listener would find it difficult to characterize either *American Recordings* or *Unchained* as country, and I suspect Rubin did not either. The whole point of Johnny Cash's impact is that he was a country person in a popular world; few of his signature songs that reached mainstream ears would really be classified as traditional country. His *voice* clearly signaled country, but his music varied wildly. But Carter

Cash actually gets to the real impact later in his appraisal: "It was after this ad appeared that the genre of Americana took root and became firmly established in our culture. This movement owes a great deal to my father's records on American Recordings."[37] This estimate seems correct, and in fact, the nonprofit Americana Music Association formed in 1999.[38] But because Americana was consolidated after Cash's albums with Rubin does not definitively make Cash Americana either. Genres are meant to provide marketing channels for the industry to its listeners, and perhaps the Americana genre was useful in helping Cash, alt-country stars like Uncle Tupelo, and other old-timers such as Bob Dylan, Merle Haggard, and Willie Nelson find new audiences, but it would be wrong to define Cash (or Dylan or Haggard or Nelson) that narrowly. Had Cash been in a position to actively appeal to Americana audiences to the exclusion of his more traditional ones, he might have found a more welcoming home for active political engagement. As Travis Stimeling notes in this volume, their audiences allowed such alternative country groups such as Uncle Tupelo, Son Volt, and Wilco to be overtly political, a position that mainstream country had largely avoided in the 1990s.[39]

To me, it goes back to song. In a world before Spotify, Napster, and iTunes, before separating songs from albums became easier, Cash's statement on the nature of genre opened up the field for any number of covers that appeared in the time after, notably the Austin band the Gourd's sublime cover of Snoop Doggy Dogg's "Gin and Juice" (and, perhaps less notable, Duran Duran's cover of Public Enemy's "911 Is a Joke").

In essence, Cash and Rubin moved—progressed—the case for artistic interpretation as a form of authenticity back into the cultural conversation. It is completely appropriate to argue the opposite, that Cash was a one-off, that the only thing that progressed was his career, and not very much. It places Cash within the active music industry at the age of 62; it flattens genre, it hints at the universality of reinvention; it changes the calculus of who records and why. In an arena when almost anything can be argued as adhering to a particular term in the right conditions, it is easy to conclude that Cash with Rubin was both political in its rejection of country music establishment and progressive in its rejection of genre.

## NOTES

1. American Recordings advertisement, *Billboard,* March 14, 1998.

2. Jack Clement, in discussion with the author, March 22, 2006.

3. "Late Show with David Letterman (A Guest Stars and Air Dates Guide)," *EP Guides,* December 17, 2015.

4. John Carter Cash, *House of Cash: The Legacies of My Father, Johnny Cash* (San Rafael: Insight Editions, 2011), 112.

5. One can definitely make a case for albums three and four being significant pieces of work, and I'll return briefly to four to talk about Cash and religion. But to some degree, their *difference* is muted compared with *American Recordings* and *Unchained.*

6. Christopher Wren, *Winners Got Scars Too: The Life of Johnny Cash* (New York: Dial, 1971), 184.

7. Jesse Walker also references this story in an obituary in *Counterpunch.* Cash called the remark stupid in Larry Linderman's *Penthouse* interview in August 1975: "Johnny Cash: The *Penthouse* Interview." In clip file, Frist Library and Archive at Country Music Hall of Fame and Museum, Nashville, TN.

8. Johnny Cash, "Man in Black," *Man in Black,* Columbia, 1971.

9. The amount of work on Cash and politics has burgeoned lately and includes Michael Stewart Foley's work on the Vietnam War, "A Politics of Empathy: Johnny Cash, the Vietnam War, and the 'Walking Contradiction' Myth Dismantled," *Popular Music and Society* 37, no. 3 (2014): 338–59, and Daniel Geary's work on the prison albums, "The Way I Would Feel about San Quentin": Johnny Cash and the Politics of Country, *Daedalus*142, no. 4 (Fall 2013): 64–72. Antonio D'Ambrosio's *Bitter Tears, a Heartbeat and a Guitar: Johnny Cash and the Making of Bitter Tears* (New York: Nation Books, 2011), is comprehensive, and Leigh H. Edwards's *Johnny Cash and the Paradox of American Identity* (Bloomington: Indiana University Press, 2009), the first scholarly book about Cash, covers Cash's politics within the context of Southern masculinity.

10. Sylvie Simmons, liner notes, *Unearthed,* by Johnny Cash (Nashville: Lost Highway Records, 2003), 7.

11. *Oxford English Dictionary,* 3rd ed., s.v. "politic."

12. Clare Bambra, Debbie Fox, and Alex Scott-Samuel, "Toward a Politics of Health," *Health Promotion International* 20, no. 2 (June 2005): 187–93.

13. Kate Millett, *Sexual Politics* (Garden City: Doubleday, 1970), 23.

14. David A. Graham, "The Surprising History of 'We Shall Overcome,'" *Atlantic,* May 5, 2015.

15. Jennifer C. Lena and Richard A. Peterson, "Classification as Culture: Types and Trajectories of Music Genres," *American Sociological Review* 73, no. 5 (October 2008): 698.

16. Jarl A. Ahlkvist, "What Makes Rock Music 'Prog'? Fan Evaluation and the Struggle to Define Progressive Rock," *Popular Music and Society* 34, no. 5 (December 2011): 643.

17. Richard A. Peterson, *Creating Country Music: Fabricating Authenticity* (Chicago: University of Chicago Press, 1997), 228–29. Diane Pecknold's *The Selling Sound: The*

*Rise of the Country Music Industry* (Durham: Duke University Press, 2007), explores the nature of commercialism and country music.

18. Robert Hilburn, *Johnny Cash: A Life* (New York: Back Bay Books, 2013), 539–55.

19. Cash and Rubin were suggesting that his voice and individual songs were more important than what Geoffrey Stokes's *Star-Making Machinery* (a reference to a Joni Mitchell quote) describes. Stokes compares the music process in the 1970s to Hollywood: "The record we hear on the radio or on our equipment is the end product of a long chain of events that shapes the nature of the music as surely as the commercial imperatives of the thirties' Hollywood dream factories changed their films—which in turn changed their audiences." Stokes addresses not only the popular authentic image of music's beginning but also its seedier side: "The rock chain may begin with a musician strumming his guitar in a tenement walk-up, but it includes a bewildering array of technology, armies of lawyers and accountants, and considerable wheeling and dealing in money and in drugs." Geoffrey Stokes, *Star-Making Machinery: The Odyssey of an Album* (Indianapolis: Bobbs-Merrill, 1976), 2–3.

20. Hilburn, *Johnny Cash*, 530–34.

21. Warren Zanes, *Petty: The Biography* (New York: Henry Holt, 2015), 173.

22. David Ragan, ed., *The Great Johnny Cash* (New York: Macfadden-Bartell, 1970), 21–22; Christopher Wren, *Winners Got Scars Too: The Life of Johnny Cash* (New York: Dial, 1971), 166–67; Johnny Cash with Patrick Carr, *Cash: The Autobiography* (San Francisco: Harper San Francisco, 1997), 274, 275.

23. Johnny Cash, interview with Lev Grossman, *Time*, September 23, 2003.

24. Greg Mitchell, "Ten Years Ago Today a Dixie Chick Dared to Hit Bush on War—and a Hate Campaign Began," *Nation*, March 10, 2013.

25. I'm not going to get into the weeds here about genre when it comes to prog rock, but here is one scholar's take: "By 1973 progressive rock—commonly referred to as 'prog'—was a widely recognized label for a style of rock music most notable for its incorporation of sensibilities, forms, and sounds from Western classical music." Ahlkvist, "What Makes Rock Music 'Prog'?," 640.

26. Emily Robinson, "Ahead of Their Time: From Progressive Rock to the Progressive Alliance," *Juncture* 22, no. 3 (2015): 220. Daniel T. Rodgers, in his wide-ranging discussion of historical characterizations of progressivism, notes that there are three components commonly associated with the movement: "To put rough but serviceable labels on those three languages of discontent, the first was the rhetoric of antimonopolism, the second was an emphasis on social bonds and the social nature of human beings, and the third was the language of social efficiency. These three did not add up to a coherent ideology we could call 'progressivism.'" Rodgers notes that the term is better thought of as action rather than thought: "To think of progressive social thought in this way is to emphasize the active, dynamic aspect of ideas. It is also to admit, finally, that progressivism as an ideology is nowhere to be found." Daniel T. Rodgers, "The Promise of American History: Progress and Prospects," *Reviews in American History* 10, no. 4 (December 1982): 123, 127. This historical notion connects well with what current political actors think of the term. According to John Halpin, senior adviser on the staff of the

Center for American Progress, "At its core progressivism is a non-ideological, pragmatic system of thought grounded in solving problems and maintaining strong values within society." Andrew Garib, "What Is Progressive? A Young Person Attempts to Define the Meaning of Progressivism Today," *Alternet*, July 25, 2005.

27. Robinson, "Ahead of Their Time," 223.

28. Russell Hall, "Producer Rick Rubin Talks about His Work with Johnny Cash," *Performing Songwriter Issue 79* (July/August 2004).

29. Mark Richardson, "Does Vinyl Really Sound Better?" *Pitchfork*, July 29, 2013.

30. See the "Is It Local?" episode from season 1.

31. Matthew Frederick, *101 Things I Learned in Architecture School* (Cambridge: MIT Press, 2007), 45.

32. Dan Heath and Chip Heath, "The Myth about Creation Myths," *Fast Company*, March 1, 2007.

33. Robert Christgau, "Virtue Unrewarded, *Village Voice*, June 14, 1994, n.p., https://www.robertchristgau.com/xg/rock/cash-94.php.

34. Jonathan Silverman, *Nine Choices: Johnny Cash and American Culture* (Amherst: University of Massachusetts Press, 2010).

35. David Sanjek, "All the Memories Money Can Buy," in *This Is Pop: In Search of the Elusive at Experience Music Project*, ed. Eric Weisbard (Cambridge: Harvard University Press, 2004), 171–72.

36. Jack Dickey, "How to Survive 13,000 Album Reviews," *Time*, February 24, 2015. This article discusses Robert Christgau's career and his musical ideas.

37. Carter Cash, *House of Cash*, 111–12.

38. Giovanni Russonello, "Why Is a Music Genre Called 'Americana' So Overwhelmingly White and Male?," *Atlantic*, August 1, 2013.

39. Stimeling's essay "Alternative Country Music and the American Midwest as Industrial Wasteland" appears in this volume.

# Contributors

**TRESSIE MCMILLAN COTTOM,** PhD, is an assistant professor of sociology at Virginia Commonwealth University and faculty associate with Harvard University's Berkman Klein Center for Internet & Society. She studies race, class, gender, and inequality across various kinds of institutions. Her research on technology and on race, class, and gender, as well as her work on higher education in the new economy, has been supported by the Microsoft Research Network's Social Media Collective, the Kresge Foundation, and the University of California at Davis's Center for Poverty Research. Her latest book, *Lower Ed: The Troubling Rise of For-Profit Colleges in the New Economy,* was published by the New Press in 2016. Her public scholarship on inequality, work, education, and culture has been published in the *New York Times, Washington Post, Slate,* the *Atlantic Monthly,* and *Dissent.*

**P. RENEE FOSTER** is faculty emeritus in the College of Business at Delta State University. Foster was a contributing writer to *Reggae, Rastafari, and the Rhetoric of Social Control* and the *Routledge History of Social Protest in Popular Music.* Foster also serves on the editorial review board of the *Small Business Institute Journal.*

**NADINE HUBBS** is a musicologist, historian, and theorist with interests in sexuality, gender, class, and race. Her writing on topics including Morrissey, Springsteen, 1970s disco, Radiohead, gay Americana composers, and postwar country music has appeared in the *Journal of the American Musicological Society, Genders, GLQ, Popular Music, Southern Cultures, Women and Music,* and other publications. She is the author of two award-winning books: *The Queer Composition of America's Sound* examines twentieth-century constructions of national and sexual identity by the Copland-Thomson gay composers' circle, and *Rednecks, Queers, and Country Music* investigates ongoing contests between middle- and working-class whites, the classing of gender, and the post-seventies "middle-classing of the queer" by listening to country music. Her forthcoming book is titled *Country Mexicans: Sounding Mexican American Life, Love, and Belonging in Country Music.* She is professor of women's studies and music and faculty affiliate in American culture at the University of Michigan, where she also directs the Lesbian-Gay-Queer Research Initiative.

**CHARLES L. HUGHES** is the director of the Memphis Center at Rhodes College. His acclaimed first book, *Country Soul: Making Race and Making Music in the American South,* was published by the University of North Carolina Press in 2015. He has published and spoken extensively on race, music, and the South. A native of Wisconsin, Hughes is also a musician and songwriter.

**MARK ALLAN JACKSON** specializes in political expression in American music. He has published essays, reviews, and commentaries in such journals as *American Music,* the *Journal of American History, Popular Music and Society,* and the *Journal of American Folklore.* Three of his edited compilations of American folksong recordings have appeared through the West Virginia University Press Sound Archive Series, including *Jail House Bound: John Lomax's First Southern Prison Recordings, 1933,* which won the 2012 Brenda McCallum Prize of the Archives and Libraries Section of the American Folklore Society. The University Press of Mississippi published his book *Prophet Singer: The Voice and Vision of Woody Guthrie* in 2007. Currently, he works in Middle Tennessee State University's English Department, where he teaches courses in American folklore and popular culture.

**STEPHEN A. KING** is professor and chairperson of the Communication Studies Department at Eastern Illinois University. King has published two books: *Reggae, Rastafari, and the Rhetoric of Social Control* and *I'm Feeling the Blues Right Now: Blues Tourism and the Mississippi Delta.* His work appears in the *Southern Communication Journal, Journal of American*

*Folklore, Popular Music and Society,* and the *Journal of Popular Culture* as well as edited books, including *The Resisting Muse: Popular Music and Social Protest, Routledge History of Social Protest in Popular Music* and *Social Controversy and Public Address in the 1960s and Early 1970s.* King serves on the editorial board for the *Rock Music Studies* journal.

**PETER LA CHAPELLE** is professor of history at Nevada State College, in Henderson, Nevada. La Chapelle is author of *Proud to Be an Okie: Cultural Politics, Country Music and Migration to Southern California* (University of California Press) and is in the process of finishing a second book, tentatively titled *Not Ready to Make Nice: A Political History of Country Music,* which examines the relationship between country music and political campaigns over the course of the twentieth century. La Chapelle lives in the Las Vegas area where he teaches U.S. western and cultural history and instructs undergraduates on how to use oral history to preserve the local past.

**TED OLSON** is the author of *Blue Ridge Folklife* and of two collections of poetry, *Breathing in Darkness* and *Revelations.* Music section editor and associate editor for the *Encyclopedia of Appalachia,* editor of *The Bristol Sessions: Writings about the Big Bang of Country Music* and *A Tennessee Folklore Sampler: Selected Readings from the Tennessee Folklore Society Bulletin, 1935–2009,* and book series editor for the University of Tennessee Press' Charles K. Wolfe Music Series, Olson has also edited collections of literary works by Sherwood Anderson, Sarah Orne Jewett, and James Still. A producer and liner notes writer for numerous documentary recordings of Appalachian music, Olson has received six Grammy Award nominations for his work as a music historian. He teaches at East Tennessee State University.

**GREGORY N. REISH** serves as director of the Center for Popular Music and Professor of Music History at Middle Tennessee State University. His previous appointments have been at Roosevelt University, Buffalo State College, the University of Hawaii at Hilo, and the University of Georgia. A musicologist with a broad range of interests, Reish has published and presented on topics extending from the Italian avant-garde to American old-time music of the 1920s and 1930s and has co-produced several releases for Spring Fed Records. As a singer and multi-instrumentalist specializing in traditional American styles, he has performed and conducted workshops across much of the United States and Japan. His current research focuses on old-time and bluegrass guitar styles, the evolution of the country string band, South Texas conjunto music, and *son jarocho* from the Mexican state of Veracruz.

**STEPHANIE SHONEKAN** is associate professor of ethnomusicology and black studies at the University of Missouri. Her dual heritage combining West Africa with the West Indies allows her to straddle the black world comfortably. She has published articles on afrobeat, Fela Kuti, and American and Nigerian hip-hop. Her books *The Life of Camilla Williams, African American Classical Singer and Opera Diva* (2011) and *Soul, Country, and the USA: Race and Identity in American Music Culture* (2015) explore the intersection where identity, history, culture, and music meet. In 2008, inspired by the music and revolution of Fela's mother and the Nigerian market women's revolution of the 1940s, Shonekan wrote and produced a short live action film titled *Lioness of Lisabi*. The film was awarded first prize at the Chicago International Children's Film Festival in 2010 and by the Girls Inc. Film Festival in March 2012.

**JONATHAN SILVERMAN** is associate professor of English and director of American Studies at the University of Massachusetts–Lowell. He is the author of *Nine Choices: Johnny Cash and American Culture* (University of Massachusetts Press, 2010), the coauthor of *The World Is a Text: Writing, Reading, and Thinking about Culture and Its Contexts,* and the coeditor of *Remaking the American College Campus: Essays* (McFarland, 2016). He has served as the Fulbright Roving Scholar in Norway (2007–8) and was a John H. Daniels fellow at the National Sporting Library (2013–14).

**TRAVIS D. STIMELING** is associate professor of musicology at West Virginia University, where he is also the director of the WVU Bluegrass and Old-Time Bands. His books include *Cosmic Cowboys and New Hicks: The Countercultural Sounds of Austin's Progressive Country Music Scene* (Oxford University Press, 2011), *The Country Music Reader* (Oxford University Press, 2014), and *Fifty Cents and a Box Top: The Creative Life of Nashville Session Musician Charlie McCoy* (with Charlie McCoy, West Virginia University Press, 2017).

**STEPHANIE VANDER WEL** is associate professor of historical musicology at the University at Buffalo (SUNY). Her research and teaching interests focus primarily on the singing voice, performance, and representations of gender, class, race, and region in country music specifically and popular music and American music more generally. She has presented papers at a wide variety of national and international conferences, and her research and reviews appear in *The Oxford Handbook of Country Music, Musical Quarterly,* the *Journal of the Society for American Music,* the *Journal of Southern History, Southern Spaces,* and the revised Grove Dictionary of American Music. Her book *The Singing Voices of Hillbilly Maidens and Cowboys' Sweethearts: Country Music and the Gendering of Class, 1930s–1950s* is in production with the University of Illinois Press.

# Index

www.ingramcontent.com/pod-product-compliance
Lightning Source LLC
Chambersburg PA
CBHW030642270326
41929CB00007B/166